THE MAFIA

THE MAFIA

The Complete Story

Al Cimino, Jo Durden Smith,
and M. A. Frasca

Picture credits

Getty Images: 18 (Hulton), 23 (Hulton), 26 (Bettmann), 35, 52 (Hulton), 62 (Hulton), 65, 83 (New York Daily News Archive), 88 (Hulton), 100 (Hulton), 102 (Bettmann), 138 (Popperfoto), 140, 146 (Hulton), 150, 156 (Mondadori), 168, 174, 182 (Bettmann), 196 (New York Daily News Archive), 216, 232 (Hulton), 238 (Bettmann), 247 (Bettmann), 256 (Hulton), 269 (Bettmann), 279 (New York Daily News Archive), 286 (Hulton), 310 (Alberto Pizzoli/ Sygma), 330 (Bettmann), 339 (Bettmann), 358 (Hulton), 362, 368 (Hulton), 381 (Franco Lannino-Michele Naccari/epa), 387 (Hulton), 441 (AFP)

Shutterstock: 130, 442

Topfoto: 31, 116 (Keystone Archives), 263, 405 (The Granger Collection)

ED Archives: 221

Press Association: 18 (AP), 420 (AP)

This edition published in 2019 by Arcturus Publishing Limited
26/27 Bickels Yard, 151–153 Bermondsey Street,
London SE1 3HA

Copyright © Arcturus Holdings Limited

AD005865UK

Printed in the UK

CONTENTS

INTRODUCTION

'You live by the gun and the knife and you die by the gun and the knife.'
MOB INFORMANT JOE VALACHI TO THE McCLELLAN COMMITTEE, 1963

The Mafia, or Cosa Nostra, first appeared in North America in the late nineteenth century, when gang members arriving from Italy, especially Sicily, settled in New York, Chicago and other urban centres, bringing their criminal ways with them. Loansharking, extortion, kidnapping, racketeering – they did it all and their reach grew quickly. It wasn't long before these gangs were clashing with each other and with existing Jewish and Irish mobs as the newcomers gained a firm foothold in the New World.

The 1920s brought Prohibition and with it an unexpected windfall for the mobs. There was money – lots of it – to be made from the illegal transportation and sale of liquor in the United States. America was dry and the mobs were eager to provide. Crime was bigger business than ever before and even the authorities were prepared to turn a blind eye in order to get their take. Criminals such as Jack 'Legs' Diamond and Al Capone seemed to call the shots, but it was Lucky Luciano who became the pre-eminent mob boss and who created the Commission, the ruling body that to this day oversees all mob activity and disputes, thereby reducing in-fighting. It was also Luciano who divided the New York Mafia into five families and was shrewd enough to work with the Jewish and Irish mobs, making crime more efficient and truly organized.

It took a while for law enforcement officials to move effectively against the Mafia, some apparently not even realizing – or not admitting publicly – that the organization existed. It wasn't until 1957, when police broke in on a high-level mob meeting taking place in Apalachin, New York, that the existence of the Mafia was unquestionably verified, with

further confirmation provided by mobster Joe Valachi in 1963 during his testimony to the US Senate Permanent Subcommittee on Investigations while on trial for murdering a fellow inmate in prison. His testimony was broadcast on radio and television, giving the American public their first real and often chilling view of this shadowy organization.

In 1970, the Racketeer Influenced and Corrupt Organizations (RICO) Act provided for extended criminal penalties for acts performed as part of an ongoing criminal enterprise, such as the Mafia. Significantly, it became possible to prosecute Mafia bosses who had ordered an offence, as well as those who had actually committed it.

Under RICO, any member of the mob – a popular name for the Mafia – could be sentenced to 20 years' imprisonment and fined $25,000 if they had committed any two of 27 federal and eight state crimes, which included murder, gambling, extortion, kidnapping, bribery, robbery, drug trafficking, counterfeiting, fraud, embezzlement, money laundering and arson. Convictions for these crimes served as evidence for a new crime – racketeering to benefit an illegal enterprise.

Individuals harmed by these criminal enterprises could collect triple damages and those charged under RICO laws could be placed under a restraining order to seize their assets to prevent their dispersal.

Since then a whole raft of other strong initiatives have been put in place to curb the power of the Mafia. Despite this, it remains a powerful force today, controlling organized crime operations in New York, Chicago and Montreal, in particular. But the success of the Mafia would not have been possible without the ruthless methods that the crime bosses employed. Albert 'Mad Hatter' Anastasia, Benjamin 'Bugsy' Siegel, 'Big Paul' Castellano – the list of Mafia victims seems endless. Included in this book are the most important Mafia killings – the executions of the rival bosses, the informers, the feuds, even some of the hitmen implicated in the assassination of President Kennedy. They're top of the lists of the 'made men', the associates and freelancers who paid the ultimate price.

These harsh new laws have put many of the old-style Mafia bosses away for good and have done much to impoverish the mob. However, there are always young mobsters waiting to fill the shoes of the older generation and there are always fresh rackets they can get into. As retired FBI agent David W. Breen says: 'They're like the Chinese army – you kill one and there are ten others to take his place.'

***

In Italy, significant inroads were made into the power of the Mafia by the Maxi-Trial of 1986, which saw hundreds of gangsters in the dock. More were tried in absentia and simply went underground. Mafia wars also thinned out the ranks.

Those imprisoned were held under restrictions outlined in Article 41-bis of the Prison Administration Act. They could be held in solitary confinement, refused the use of the telephone, banned from sending or receiving money and denied visits from family members. This meant that it was impossible for them to go on running a criminal organization from prison. However, with the Mafia shackled, its rivals flourished, leading to the rise of the Camorra in Naples, the 'Ndrangheta in Calabria and the Sacra Corona Unita in Puglia.

Among Italians and Italian-Americans there seems to be no shortage of young men who want to live 'the life'. This means that you have pockets full of money when others are worried about paying their bills. It gives you standing in society. These days, it also means flash cars, flash suits, bling, beautiful women and fine champagne.

On the other hand, you must have no scruples. You must be able to turn your hand to any form of crime, no matter what the consequences are for others. You must be willing to kill friend, foe – and innocent bystander – without a qualm and be prepared to torture others to death if that is what you are told to do.

Equally you must accept that your closest associates are likely to do that to you, too. Few Mafiosi have died in their beds of natural

causes. Those going into 'the life' must accept that they are going to die in a hail of bullets, or after prolonged torture at the hands of fellow mobsters, or at best will spend many years in jail. It is the price you pay. This book tells the stories of a number of characters who have accepted this pact with the devil.

PART ONE

THE ORIGINS OF THE MAFIA

For over 2,000 years, most of Sicily's rural population endured tyranny and suppression at the hands of feudal overlords and foreign conquerors. With no formal government to protect them, the people gathered together in what they called *cosche* (literally, the leaves of the artichoke) to protect themselves from rules imposed by the unwanted landowners. These small, local clans, made up of blood relatives and neighbours, created their own dialect to ensure a degree of secrecy and developed a culture based on a disregard for the law. It is said that these tight-knit alliances form the roots of the Mafia.

CHAPTER 1

THE DEATH OF DON CALOGERO VIZZINI

On 4 July 1954, one of the most powerful Mafia bosses in Sicily, Don Calogero Vizzini (known as Don Calò) died. His body was laid in state in a church in his home town of Villalba, where he had been mayor. Politicians from his party, the Christian Democrats, and high Roman Catholic churchmen came to pay their respects, along with the heads of other Mafia families, newspapermen and large numbers of people from the surrounding countryside. On the church door, according to the writer Norman Lewis, was a notice of his death, which read in part: 'Wise, dynamic, tireless, he was the benefactor of the workers on the land and in the sulphur mines. Constantly doing good, his reputation was widespread both in Italy and abroad.

'Great in the face of persecution, greater still in adversity … he receives from friends and foes alike the grandest of all tributes: he was a gentleman.'

The notice was not wrong. Though the illiterate ex-farmer, who rarely wore anything more elaborate than baggy trousers and a grimy shirt and could hardly speak anything but his native dialect, may not have been a gentleman in any familiar sense of the word, he had certainly had his share of 'persecution' and 'adversity'. He had spent 20 years in Mussolini's

Italy either in jail or on the run from Il Duce's emissary to Sicily, the 'Iron Prefect', Cesare Mori, and he did indeed have 'a reputation' that was 'widespread both in Italy and abroad'. More than anyone else, the slovenly Don Calò had been responsible for the fact that the American part of the invasion of Sicily had been successfully accomplished in a matter of days. Picked up by a special force, and made an honorary colonel in the US Army more or less on the spot, this down-at-heel mayor had ridden with the American spearhead and had become affectionately known as 'General Mafia'.

After the war, Don Calò became a power in the land for the Christian Democrats and at the time of his death was both rich and immensely powerful. It was therefore not surprising that his flower-decked bier should have been attended by a guard of honour, one of them his successor, Giuseppe Genco Russo. Few people noticed at the time, though, that a cord ran between Russo and his ex-chief's body, a cord down which flowed, by an article of Mafia faith, the ichor or essence of Don Calò's power, preserved into the next generation. If nothing else, the cord signalled the presence of something in the church much older than Christianity, almost as old as the mountainous landscape of Sicily itself.

Some six years later, a book was published which was to become Italy's first-ever international bestseller. It was called *The Leopard*, and the author was a Sicilian grandee: Giuseppe Tomasi, Prince of Lampedusa and Duke of Palma. It was centred on the figure of the prince's great-grandfather – here called Don Fabrizio – and set at the time of another 'liberation': Major General Guiseppe Garibaldi's arrival in Sicily in the early 1860s prior to the unification of Italy.

The plot of the 'novel', inasmuch as there is one, revolves around the prince's nephew, Tancredi, an ardent Garibaldist, who falls in love with a beautiful 17-year-old, Angelica Sedàra, whose father is mayor of the area surrounding the prince's summer palace. The mayor is another Don Calogero. He is slovenly, immensely rich and powerful and 'is understood to have been very busy at the time of the liberation'. It is implicit that he is a Mafioso – his 'greedy' and 'overbearing' father-in-law was found

dead, with 12 shotgun wounds in his back, two years after Don Calogero's marriage. But he also has, the prince finds out, very great influence in politics: he has rigged the local vote on the question of unification on behalf of his party, so that the result in the area is a unanimous 'yes'. Don Fabrizio, then, when he is invited to become a senator in a new all-Italian parliament, sees the face of the future and recommends Don Calogero Sedàra instead. The Mafia is on its way into politics at a national level as the book moves on.

The Leopard was made into a film by the aristocratic Italian director Luchino Visconti, with Burt Lancaster playing Don Fabrizio, and also starring Alain Delon and Claudia Cardinale as Tancredi and Angelica. It was set firmly in the nineteenth century. But is the book it was based on in part a portrait of the period immediately after the Second World War? And is Don Calogero Sedàra really Don Calò Vizzini? It is impossible to know. But the picture of the poverty and buried violence in the landscape that is portrayed in the book could be applied to virtually any time in the three or four hundred years before the beginning of the 1960s. Only the clothes, the carriages and the constant presence of the *lupara*, a type of sawn-off shotgun traditionally associated with the Mafia, prevent it from applying to any time in the past two thousand years.

A countryside well served, for example, 'as a swimming pool, drinking trough, prison, cemetery. It … concealed the carcases of beasts and animals until they were reduced to smooth anonymous skeletons.' Village women are seen 'by the flicker of oil lamps … [examining] their children's trachoma-inflamed eyelids. They were all of them dressed in mourning and quite a few had been the wives of those scarecrow corpses one stumbles over at the bends in the country tracks.' The poverty in the book is absolute; the riches of the Prince, expressed mostly in vast estates and decaying palaces, are guarded and run by men whose shotguns were 'not always innocuous'. The poverty and the violence in the book, the land, palaces, guards and politics – these could have come from virtually any time. And it was they who provided the mixture peculiar to the island that gave rise to the poisonous historical residue that is the Sicilian Mafia.

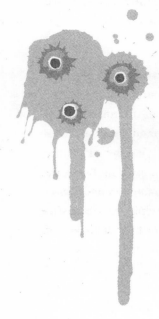

CHAPTER 2

HEARTLAND OF THE MAFIA

Sicily is not an ordinary island. For two thousand years before the discovery of America, it paid a steep price for being in the middle of the Mediterranean Sea, and therefore, roughly speaking, at the strategic centre of the known world. Situated between the Italian mainland and North Africa, Sicily was vulnerable to raiders from the north of Italy and invaders from Phoenicia, Greece, Carthage and a whole host of European countries. It was a prize to be captured and held, and so it was – by the Greeks, the Romans, the Byzantines, the Arabs, the Germans, the French and any other arrivistes. As for its social system, it was the Romans who set the pattern. They systematically deforested Sicily and turned it into a feudal colony whose job was to feed the mainland – and themselves – with wheat. Vast estates worked by slaves stretched all the way across the island; and although the wheat largely disappeared, the estates and the slavery didn't. Long after the world's attention had strayed elsewhere, Sicily remained feudal – peasants were only given the right to own land in the early nineteenth century. But vested interests and the legal chicanery of landlords ensured that very few did so until another century or more had passed.

Sicily was in a sense, and had always been, an island version of Russia, softened by citrus groves planted by the Arabs, but a Russia nonetheless. Until the beginning of the twentieth century, three-quarters of the island belonged to aristocratic landlords who shut themselves up in distant palaces or disported themselves in the Western European equivalents of Moscow and St Petersburg. There was no Renaissance or Reformation here, no Enlightenment, no merchants' guilds, city-republics or law-making princes – simply back-breaking toil, a festering resentment of the state, in whatever form it took, and, of course, crime.

CRIME IN SICILY

Crime in Sicily has always been identified one way or another with island patriotism, with resistance to the occupier. Writers in the eighteenth century described a secret sign language in Sicily which they said dated back to the time of the Greek tyrants. Crime was also made possible by the sheer difficulty involved in travel into the interior over mountainous terrain. Until the twentieth century, roads were almost non-existent. Officers of the law were meagre in number and dispersed, so banditry was for a long time a sound career option for young men who remained protected from the law if it arrived by clan and family loyalties. These loyalties, particularly those of close kin, overrode everything else. Not for nothing is the basic unit of the Mafia called 'the family'.

In a sense, however, crime was also built into the ancient feudal system. The absentee aristocracy needed managers for their estates, both to ensure and enforce the work of sharecropping peasants, and to protect the land, its buildings and its livestock not only from bandits, but also from the spread of liberal ideas. They needed strong-arm men

Overleaf: From the 18th century, banditry and racketeering have been a recognizable ingredient of Sicilian rural life

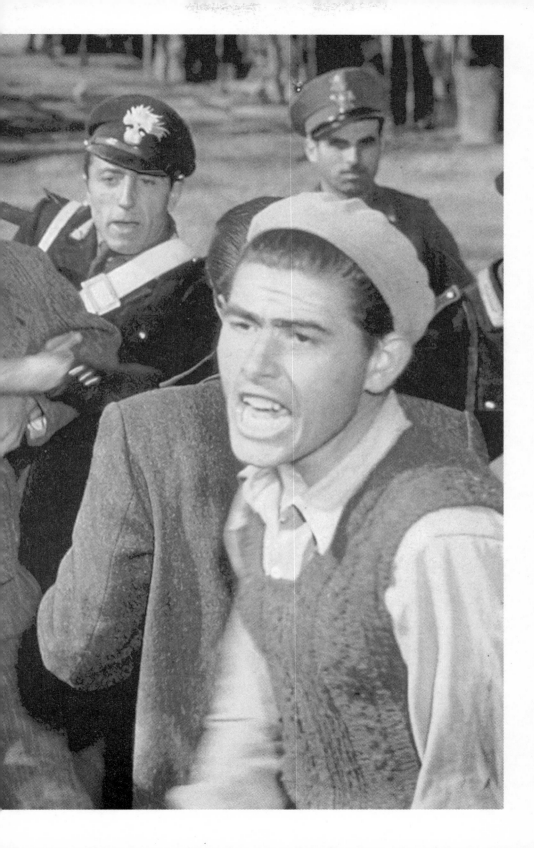

with local power and influence, men capable of wielding the *lupara* and with not too much respect for the law. The distinction between bandit, 'family' man and estate security, in other words, was often in the end slight. The managers and the men they hired exacted a price from both sides of the divide for imposing order: a percentage from the peasants for looking after their interests, and a percentage from the masters for continuing to insure theirs. Meanwhile, of course, they could also freelance as the very bandits they were supposed to be providing security against. The protection racket was from very early times a particular Sicilian speciality. There was immense pressure on landlords to hire bands of brigands as their personal *guardani*, and co-operation with the forces of law was virtually unknown.

One reason for the lack of co-operation was that though the state was totalitarian, the laws which upheld it in Sicily were a mess of conflicting statutes produced by successive invaders. Court cases were interminable and it was in everyone's interests – the peasants, the outlaws, the aristocracy and the officers of the court – that the law's delay should be short. Many judges, after all, had to buy their posts; clerks of the court were paid little or nothing. It was therefore expected that a 'man of influence' would soon come calling or else would take care of the matter himself. One eighteenth-century traveller recorded the existence in Sicily of a secret justice society more effective than the courts, one in which all members were sworn to obey its judgments.

Banditry, the protection racket, anti-liberal politics, bribery, secret justice societies, families: everything that created the Sicilian Mafia, then, was already in place well before the nineteenth century – everything, that is, except perhaps its name.

CHAPTER 3

THE MAFIA EMERGES

According to historian Denis Mack Smith, the word 'Mafia' first appeared in Sicily in 1863, when a dialect play was based on life in the island's main prison was performed in Palermo. The play was called *I Mafiosi della Vicaria* and it popularized a word already used by criminals and by landlords looking for strong-arms. Its origins are still unclear. There have been suggestions it derives from the Arabic *ma fia* or 'place of refuge', a description used after the Norman invasion by Arabs who were enslaved on their new conquerors' estates or from a combined Sicilian-Arab slang expression meaning 'protector against the powerful'. Others have suggested it comes from a secret acronym used by Sicilians when they rose up against the Normans, or from *mahjas*, the Arabic word for boasting. But whatever the word's origins, the people now identified by it had been at work long before it came into common usage.

Names of gangs such as the Beati Paoli and the Revengers were first recorded in the eighteenth century, as were the names of few bandits. Don Sferlazza, a seminarist and outlaw, was involved in a family vendetta but, as a priest, was immune from punishment. Kidnappings for ransom were frequent, according to the records, as were cattle rustling, food

smuggling and illegal control of water sources. There was even a popular religious cult of the criminal called the Decollati, in which prayers were offered to executed wrongdoers in shrines full of bones.

But the gangs only came out into the open collectively with the rebellion of 1848 against the island's Bourbon rulers, when they swept into Palermo from the countryside to join the fighting. They were joined by a gang led by a ferocious woman goat-herd called Testa Di Lana, who had a vendetta against the police. By the time order was restored, the Sicilian state had virtually collapsed, and gangs like the Little Shepherds and the Cut-throats were, according to Mack Smith, 'the one flourishing form of association in Sicily. The chief of police had to co-operate with some of them, so Scordato, the illiterate peasant boss of Bagheria, and Di Miceli of Monreale, were now employed as tax collectors and coastguards and became rich. Law enforcement in the hill town of Misilmeri was handed over to the famous bandit Chinnici, who found a common denominator between lucrative kidnapping and the suppression of liberalism.'

BEYOND THE UNIFICATION OF ITALY

Liberalism, though it was the enemy of their aristocratic sponsors, was in the end, however, to be the friend of the Mafiosi. When Garibaldi arrived in Sicily in April 1860 to start the unification of Italy, he found the gangs useful, if unreliable, allies. And when unification finally arrived, the Mafiosi – as they were later to do in Russia – found it all too easy to subvert the liberal institutions he founded. The first national election gave them a new tool: the manipulation and delivery of votes. Trial by jury guaranteed them virtual immunity, since few individuals were brave or rich enough to stand up to them publicly with a verdict of 'guilty'. Charities and credit institutions became grist to their mill, and even the new Bank of Sicily was not immune. The Mafiosi used it to channel funds to their political allies. An early director of the bank was first kidnapped and then murdered after irregularities were found.

Guiseppe Garibaldi recognized and utilized the influence of local Sicilian gangs in his efforts to pacify unrest in Messina and Palermo in 1860. His victories there and in nearby Naples were the first in his quest for the unification of Italy.

However, neither liberalism nor unification did anything to improve the ordinary peasant's lot. Nor were they useful to Sicily as a going economic concern. Taxes went up and so did food prices. The local silk and textile industries collapsed. Hostility against the mainland, the national government and its institutions grew – among churchmen, aristocrats, lawyers, peasants. Everyone, whenever necessary, now used the good offices of the Mafia, even though its stocks-in-trade were violence and fear. In the 1860s, the British consul in Palermo wrote: 'Secret societies are all-powerful. Camorre and maffie [sic], self-elected juntas, share the earnings of the workmen, keep up intercourse with outcasts and take malefactors under their wing and protection.'

A decade later, an Italian government report stated bluntly: 'Violence is the only prosperous industry in Sicily.'

EVERY SICILIAN FOR SICILY AND THE MAFIA

The degree to which even the church and the landowning aristocrats colluded with the Mafia at such an early date now seems extraordinary. Palaces were opened up to assassins, and the local Catholic Church hierarchy – which regarded the north and its government as godless – at best turned a very blind eye. At worst, in the words of a report written by a northern MP in the 1870s: 'There is a story about a former priest who became the crime leader in a town near Palermo and administered the last rites to some of his own victims. After a certain number of these stories the perfume of orange and lemon blossoms starts to smell of corpses.'

Seventy years later, the Mafia bandit Salvatore Giuliano would attend tea parties at the archbishop's palace in Palermo, even though he was at the time a prisoner in Ucciardone prison. Forty years after this, another archbishop declared that Tommaso Buscetta, the first and most important of the witnesses finally to give evidence against the

Mafia, was one of the three greatest enemies of Sicily. This was just two years after the word 'Mafia' had entered the Italian criminal code for the very first time, even though the organization had been denounced as relying on official protection by an Italian minister ofjJustice over a hundred years earlier. The response at that time was to become a litany from then on, both in Sicily and later in America: 'The Mafia is a fabrication: the invention of northern policemen.'

PART TWO

THE NINETEENTH CENTURY: EARLY HOODS AND STREET BRAWLERS

Mobs proliferated in the major cities of nineteenth-century America, but they generally acted independently and were constantly at war with each other. Organized crime was yet to come. Collusion between the gangs and political forces was marked, for politicians at all levels constantly used the brute force of the mobs to get ahead. The newspapers did the same, hiring gangs so they could muscle out the competition and expand their circulation.

Mobs such as the Five Points Gang and the Eastman Gang in New York City made life difficult for the average law-abiding citizen and honest cop alike. But there were other elements too. Black Hand (*Mano Nera*) extortion (used by Italian criminals preying exclusively on their fellow immigrants) was also rife in cities such as Philadelphia, Chicago, New Orleans, Scranton, San Francisco and Detroit, as was the more clannish Mafia itself.

Things were moving rapidly as the century drew to a close. The old Mafiosi were on their way out and mobsters such as Monk Eastman and 'Kid Twist' Zwerbach were soon to take their final bows.

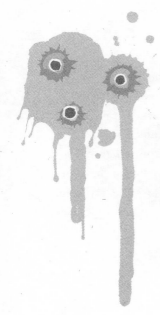

CHAPTER 4

THE MAFIA MOVES TO AMERICA

In 1880, near the railroad station at Lercara Friddi, Sicily, an English businessman called John Forester Rose was kidnapped by a bandit leader called Antonio Leone and held for a ransom of £5,000. While the authorities dithered, one of his ears was cut off and sent to them in a parcel – at which point the British government began to pay attention. The negotiations, though, took time, and Leone, growing impatient, cut off the other ear and delivered it with a note saying that Forester Rose would be history unless the ransom money arrived very soon. The British duly paid up and recovered their hapless – and by now earless – national. But so strong was their protest to the Italian government that it was forced to send an army after Leone. The bandit and most of his followers were subsequently killed in a battle. But one of them, Giuseppe Esposito, escaped and made his way to America, to New Orleans, where there was a substantial Italian community, and where he is said to have bought a fishing boat, named it *Leoni* and had the bandit's flag flown at its mast.

Posing as a fisherman, Esposito also began shaking down the prosperous shopkeepers and restaurateurs in New Orleans' Italian community, forcing them to invest in a fleet of small boats for his legitimate 'business'. He organized a gang of his own, in imitation of Leone's, and called it the 'Black Hand'. In the process he ran foul of another Italian who also seems to have been in the protection business, one Tony Labruzzo. Labruzzo shopped Esposito to the Italian consul and the New Orleans police chief put two of his best men, brothers David and Mike Hennessy, on the case. They soon arrested Esposito, who was rapidly deported back to Palermo where he was sentenced to life imprisonment.

ESPOSITO'S LEGACY

There were, however, repercussions. Tony Labruzzo was assassinated before Esposito came to trial and two other brothers, saloon-keepers Charles and Tony Mantranga, soon took over the Black Hand. They started out with the usual kind of racket: the provision of dock-hands, under duress, to Joe and Pete Provenzano, grocery store owners who had a monopoly on the unloading of fruit ships from South America. Then they decided simply to take over the monopoly, and even started going after the Provenzanos' grocery stores. Suddenly there were armed men from both sides on the streets. Two men on the Provenzano side were killed and many were wounded in an ambush.

The police chief in New Orleans was David Hennessy, one of the two brothers who had arrested and deported Giuseppe Esposito some years before. He liked the Provenzanos and was anxious to see their attackers brought to book as quickly as possible. So he corresponded with the central headquarters of the carabinieri in Rome, asking for the names and photographs of Leone's old gang. He was warned off by an anonymous letter, but he persisted. In October 1890 he was shot and killed while walking home from work.

The killing of Chief of Police David Henessy at New Orleans, 15 October 1890

Feelings in New Orleans ran high as 11 Italians, already listed in Hennessy's files, were arrested and a further ten were added to those behind bars. Seven of the accused were tried together on the charge of Hennessy's murder in February 1891. But it was soon clear that both the judge and jury had been tampered with. Though there were witnesses to the crime, and though one of the defendants had actually confessed to attending a Mafia meeting at which Hennessy's death had been decreed, the judge released two of the accused in the early stages, and the jury did the same for the rest. There were celebrations in the Italian community that night. A group of Sicilians trampled the Stars and Stripes in the mud and then hung it upside down beneath the Italian flag.

Advertisements were quickly placed in the newspapers of 14 March summoning 'all good citizens' to a mass meeting 'prepared for action'. A mob gathered. One of the sponsors of the meeting handed out guns. The mob stormed the parish prison, tore open the gates and 11 of the 12 men still behind bars were promptly lynched.

From this point, the Mafia in New Orleans went quite quiet. But there was another flare-up in 1907, when Walter Lemana, the seven-year-old son of a wealthy Italian businessman, was kidnapped for a $6,000 ransom and then killed. Four of the gang were quickly caught, and one of them was hanged. But during the course of the proceedings it became clear that businesses in the Italian community had been paying protection money to Sicilian gangs for years.

Mafia Killings 1

Police Chief David Hennessy, New Orleans, 16 October 1890
The murder of New Orleans Police Chief David Hennessy is considered to be one of the first recorded Mafia killings in America. During the late 1800s, New Orleans was a city of corruption and vice. Everyone was on the take, and that included officials. Even the

city's mayor, Joseph Shakespeare, who had been elected on an anti-corruption platform, was known to receive regular illicit payments from the gambling dens and brothels.

For years, countless waves of immigrants had been pouring into the city, with Italians firmly fixed at the bottom of the pecking order. Mixed in with these migrants were members of the Camorra and Mafia, who jostled for position in the city's underworld. Two rival families – the Provenzanos and the Mantrangas – vied for a larger piece of the criminal pie.

Police chief in the city at the time was David C. Hennessy. Descriptions of Hennessy vary widely. In 1881, he made headlines when he captured and arrested the notorious Sicilian Giuseppe Esposito, who had become one of the first crime bosses in America. Although Hennessey was respected in New Orleans and seen as an honest cop trying to put a lid on the gang problem, others viewed him as a crooked opportunist hoping to manipulate the underworld for his own purposes. Certainly Hennessy was no wallflower. In 1882 he had killed a rival officer in a shoot-out. The incident had cost him his job. Then, as a crony of Mayor Shakspeare, he had found his badge reinstated, and been appointed Chief of Police.

One of Hennessy's first tasks as chief of a force that was corrupt and riddled with political appointees was to lop off some of the dead wood. As a result, scores of lawmen lost their jobs. Next, he moved to crack down on the gambling dens and casinos – but only those not owned by members of Shakspeare's constituency. Evidently the clean-up went only so far.

Hennessy was also manoeuvring among the gangs. In an attempt to neutralize the more powerful of the two families – the Mantrangas – he had agreed to testify on behalf of the Provenzanos if they promised to reveal all they knew about the Mafia.

Hennessy was never able to testify. On 15 October 1890, he was shot down on his way home. From his hospital bed, he was able to

provide only three words of information as to the identity of his killers: 'Dagoes did it' ['dago' being an insulting word for Italians].

But this was all Mayor Shakspeare needed to hear and he leapt at the chance to eliminate a painful thorn in his side. Immediately he ordered the police force to round up as many Italians as they could. Accounts differ as to how many were arrested in the witch-hunt, but figures range from 100 to 250 – a number well beyond the 'usual suspects'. Only nine of them went to trial.

The trial was a fiasco from the start and both sides were accused of bribery and jury-tampering. In the end the judge had no alternative but to return an overall verdict of not guilty.

New Orleans was stunned. Agents of the mayor jumped on the bandwagon and after a mass meeting the jail was stormed. When the smoke cleared, 11 prisoners were found dead.

Yet, even at the time, opinion was divided as to who had killed Hennessy. Some dismissed Mafia involvement and believed the chief's death to be the work of either ex-lawmen or gamblers who had suffered as a result of Hennessy's clean-ups.

Nevertheless, anti-Italian sentiment lingered in New Orleans for years, with other ethnic Italians falling victim to the public mood. But the incident had further legacies too. The term 'Mafia', once known only by a few, was now a household word. It's also said that because of the murders the American Mafia made it a hard and fast rule never to kill a cop. The price was just too high.

THE MAFIA IN NEW YORK

Nearly one and a quarter million immigrants left southern Italy for the United States between 1900 and 1910. A high proportion of them were from Sicily, driven from the island of their birth by poverty, the relentless grind of semi-slavery, the oppression of landlords and high taxes. Many of them made their first landing in New York, and it is New York's police records that provide the clearest glimpse of Sicilian gangs operating behind the camouflage of their own communities, and at the same time preying on them.

THE FIRST GANG WARS

Born in Austria in 1882, Max Zwerbach was only two when his family emigrated to New York, hoping for a better life. Zwerbach's father had nurtured dreams of his two sons Maxwell and Daniel (later known as 'Kid Twist' and 'Kid Slyfox' respectively) joining him in the family tailoring business, an honest trade. Their nicknames give a clue as to how little his dreams came true.

Max spent his youth in the slums of New York's Lower East Side. Living in poverty and amid crime, it's not surprising that he was soon getting into trouble. Petty offences such as bicycle theft and shoplifting escalated into more serious infractions and before long Max could be seen swaggering around town, the leader of his own fledgling gang.

A growing reputation for brutality and cunning brought Kid Twist to the attention of Monk Eastman, leader of the ferocious Eastman Gang. As a strong-arm for the Eastmans, Kid Twist rose through the ranks, swiftly becoming one of Monk's second lieutenants alongside another hoodlum, Richie Fitzpatrick.

During this period, the Eastmans tried to gain control of the Lower East Side, which meant bloody conflict with the Five Points Gang, headed by Paul Kelly (formerly Paolo Antonio Vaccarelli). But on 3 February 1904, Monk was arrested for robbing a man on 42nd Street and Broadway and was soon on his way to Sing Sing prison for a ten-year term. The Eastman Gang was left without a leader.

With Monk no longer around, Zwerbach and Fitzpatrick now went for each other's throats in a bid for the vacant position. True to his name, Kid Twist managed to lure the gullible Fitzpatrick to a bar on Sherrif Street to 'discuss peace'. Fitzpatrick soon realized that he had been set up and tried to flee, but he was gunned down by one of Zwerbach's men. Zwerbach was now head of the Eastman Gang.

Under his leadership, the Eastman gang tightened its grip on the New York underworld, making money from the usual rackets but adding new ones such as forgery, election fraud and mass extortion. Despite this, it was his amorous ways that would spell the end his reign. Although he was married, he had become entangled with Carroll Terry, a Canadian singer working at Coney Island's Imperial Music Hall.

Terry had once nurtured dreams of becoming an opera singer. But, alone in New York and with her funds depleted, she ended up living with Louis Pioggi, aka 'Louie the Lump', a low-level thug in the Five Points Gang. At some time in 1908 Terry decided she'd had enough of the Lump and took up with Zwerbach.

On 14 May 1908, Kid Twist and his right-hand man, Vach Lewis (aka 'Cyclone Louie', an ex-wrestler and sideshow strongman), set off for Coney Island to catch Terry's act. Underworld gossip has it that they ran into Pioggi in a waterside bar before the show, and amused themselves by forcing him to jump from a second-storey window at gunpoint. Pioggi's ankle was damaged. So was his already wounded pride.

After the show, at around 8.30 p.m., Kid Twist, Cyclone Louie, Terry and her friend Mabel headed over to an Italian restaurant on Oceanic Walk. After dinner, when the four of them walked out of the restaurant, Pioggi was waiting in a nearby doorway. It took six shots to fell Cyclone Louie, ex-strongman that he was. Kid Twist received only one bullet, but this was a direct hit behind his right ear. Terry survived to sing again, while Kid Twist dropped like a stone. He was only 24. Legend has it that before the shooting, Pioggi called Paul Kelly of the Five Points Gang, requesting permission to kill Kid Twist. Apparently a truckload of Five Pointers showed up to assist Pioggi in the hit. Whether or not this was true, Max 'Kid Twist' Zwerbach had been dealt with and was no longer a thorn in the Five Points' side.

A few months after Zwerbach's killing, Jack Zelig was released from Sing Sing prison having served a two-year sentence for thieving. Keen to rejoin the Eastman Gang he agreed to kill Frank 'Chick' Tricker, now leading the Five Points, in revenge for Zwerbach's murder. However, with little taste for violence, his nerve failed him at the last minute and he failed to shoot his intended victim. Ashamed and in disgrace he left New York to start a new life in Chicago. But things didn't go well there either and he was almost killed by some gamblers he was trying to swindle. This brush with death changed him and he returned to New York in early 1909 as a harder, tougher and more violent man with a wicked temper and a cruel streak. Over the next year or so, Zelig demonstrated his new-found appetite for violence. This show of power reunited the various elements of the Eastman Gang, with 'Big' Jack Zelig as its leader.

Born Zelig Lefkowitz on 13 May 1882, his upbringing wasn't typical for a hood; his family was fairly comfortable and he had been given every opportunity in his early life. But, surrounded by poverty, he gravitated to the gangs of the Lower East Side and by the time he was 20 was running one of the toughest gangs in the city. Zelig was big and intimidating, standing over six feet tall and with rugged features. His real skill was as a good thief, specializing in pickpocketing, rather than as an out-and-out thug. However, during his rise up the gang's ranks, his skill in choosing men who could do the dirty work for him had made him one of the most feared men in New York City.

Ironically, Zelig was also known for his integrity (compared to other gangsters) and he became a respected leader in gangland, often referred to as the 'Big Yid' ('yid' is an insulting slang word for a Jew). From 1910 until 1912, Manhattan's Jewish district was Zelig's oyster. Merchants paid his agents for protection, and bought tickets whenever the gang threw a dance (or 'racket', in the parlance of the day). He rented his men at hefty rates to union leaders and politicians. Anyone who refused the work risked violent consequences. But he also made his fellow Jews safer from street crime than ever before. He chased away pimps, obstructed the drug trade, and sent any hooligans who assaulted Jews straight to the hospital. These acts of altruism would cause social workers, judges and journalists to revere him for decades afterwards.

The Eastmans specialized in the protection racket, particularly for gambling dens and brothels, and labour racketeering, and for a while things ran fairly smoothly under Zelig. In 1912, however, the old Eastman/Five Points rivalry resurfaced and the streets of Lower Manhattan were witness to shootings, stabbings and bomblings. Matters came to a head in June 1912 during a brawl between gang members in Chinatown. The perpretators were all arrested. As Zelig left the courthouse later that day, he was shot in the head and taken to hospital in a bad way. However, he was made of tough stuff, and recovered before being arrested, bailed and sent to Hot Springs to recover.

While he was away, New York was rocked by a huge gangland scandal. Another of the Eastmans' rackets was to act as thugs for Lieutenant Charles Becker, one of the most corrupt cops in the New York Police Department. One of Becker's numerous money-making schemes was to skim profits from illegal gambling joints. A casino owner, the hapless Herman 'Beansy' Rosenthal, was foolish enough to complain about Becker's activities to both District Attorney Charles Whitman and to the newspapers. Becker's constant graft was keeping people like him down, he said. What was an honest crook to do?

Several days later, on 12 October 1912, Rosenthal was shot dead in the doorway of the Metropole Hotel in Times Square. Suspicion immediately fell on Becker. He was accused of contracting Zelig, who had sent his right-hand men, 'Lefty Louie' Rosenberg, 'Whitey Lewis' Seidenschner, Harry 'Gyp the Blood' Horowitz and Francesco 'Dago Frank' Cirofici to take care of Beansy. Zelig, conveniently absent from the city when all this was going down, was called as a witness in the trial against Becker. The crooked cop, of course, had a lot to lose and it was no coincidence that Zelig never made it to the witness stand. Contacted by phone on 5 October 1912, two days before the trial was due to start, Zelig was called to a meeting on 14th Street. It was while he was on his way, riding the Fifth Avenue streetcar, that Zelig was shot behind the ear by petty hood Phil 'Boston Red' Davidson and died immediately.

Some mob historians believe it was all a frame-up. Becker, they hypothesize, was innocent and Zelig was actually planning to testify on the cop's behalf and not against him. We may never know. Davidson claimed that Zelig owed him money, but there is little doubt that the killing was ordered to stop Zelig testifying against Charles Becker.

When the dust settled the Eastman Gang was in ruins. Not only was Zelig dead, Lefty Louie, Whitey Lewis, Gyp the Blood and Dago Frank had all been executed by electric chair. Even Becker went to the chair – the only officer in the history of the NYPD to do so.

Mafia Killings 2

Edward 'Monk' Eastman, New York, 26 December 1920

He was the last of the old-time gangsters – a thug who did things with brass knuckles, a notched club and a knife. During his time, he was one of the most notorious and powerful mobsters in New York. Yet when Edward 'Monk' Eastman was buried in 1920, he went as a hero, with full military honours.

Monk was a brute and looked the part. Slovenly in appearance, he had thick, heavy features, cauliflower ears and stringy unkempt hair. His body bore the scars of the numerous knife fights and gun battles he'd been in. And to top all this, Monk wore a bowler hat several sizes too small.

Called 'Monk' because of his monkey-like appearance, Eastman was leader of the gang that bore his name. Making money from opium, illegal gambling and the usual mayhem, the Eastmans blundered around New York's Lower East Side, butting heads with the rival Five Points Gang headed by Paul Kelly. They also worked for the politicos at Tammany Hall, coercing voters and stuffing ballot boxes with rigged votes.

Monk had numerous run-ins with the law, but he could generally rely on the intercession of his Tammany friends to get him out of a jam. By 1903, however, things had really begun to heat up with the Five Pointers. Gun battles erupted on the streets, and several innocent bystanders were killed. The politicians at Tammany Hall were starting to get flak about their dubious connections and washed their hands of the gangs.

So in 1904, when Monk was arrested for attempted robbery, there was no reprieve and he was sentenced to ten years in Sing Sing. He served five, but when he came out in 1909 things had changed. He had become addicted to opium and his old gang was now split into factions, none of whom wanted to share with their old boss. There was just no room for Monk in the new power structure.

With no alternative, Monk returned to petty crime – but when in 1917 the United States entered the Great War, he enlisted. No doubt he found fighting in the trenches a breeze compared to some of the street battles he'd participated in back home. At any rate, Monk was in his element and tales of his heroism circulated among the troops.

At the end of the war Monk was hailed as a hero, and it was generally thought that he'd turned over a new leaf. But that was no dice – Monk was Monk. In the early morning of 26 December 1920, after enjoying a Christmas dinner at a gathering where the booze flowed freely, Monk got into an argument with one of his companions in crime – Jerry Bohan, a crooked Dry (Prohibition) agent– most likely over money. Following Bohan out on to the street, Monk called him a rat. Bohan retorted by filling Monk full of lead. That was it for Monk Eastman.

The men of Monk's former regiment had not forgotten all the gangster had done for them, however. Chipping in for his funeral, the GIs of O'Ryan's Roughnecks, the nickname of the infantry division he fought with, gave Monk a military send-off, complete with uniformed escort. It could be said that with the entombment of Monk, the Eastmans were finally well and truly buried.

THE WOLF AND THE OX

Most often, one must assume, New York's police force paid little attention to crime in the teeming Italian sections of the city. But murder was another matter, especially a series of murders such the ones which which occurred in 1902 and 1903. The male victims were found in barrels, crates or sacks and in many cases their tongues had been slit in two. They were clearly talkers who'd broken the Mafia law of *omertà* – manly silence. A Sicilian gang boss called Giuseppe Morello was immediately suspected. He was running a counterfeit ring, sending his product all over the United States, and the police were already on his track, together with that of his chief lieutenants, known to them as Lupo 'the Wolf' and Petto 'the Ox'.

From the age of ten, Ignazio Lupo had worked in a grocery store in Palermo, Sicily. At the tender age of 21, he had shot and killed a business rival named Salvatore Morello. Although he was subsequently convicted of 'deliberate and wilful murder', Lupo had already fled.

Arriving in New York in 1898, he opened a grocery store on East 72nd Street in Manhattan with a cousin named Saietta. After a brief sojourn in Brooklyn, he moved back to Manhattan, where he set up a small import business on Prince Street (in the area now known as Soho). Across the road was a saloon owned by Giuseppe 'the Clutch Hand' Morello, another immigrant from Corleone, Sicily, and head of the Morello crime family.

In 1903, Lupo married Salvatrice Terranova, half-sister to Morello. Her brothers Vincenzo and Ciro Terranova and Nicolo Morello were also part of the Morello gang. Lupo became underboss. His name –

Mugshots of Ignazio Saiettaa, aka Lupo 'the Wolf'

Lupo – means 'wolf' in Italian, so he became known as Lupo 'the Wolf'. Together they became the leading Mafia family in New York City.

Lupo developed a fearsome reputation. He was the last person seen with Brooklyn grocer Giuseppe Catania, who was found floating in the river under the Bay Bridge with his throat cut from ear-to-ear in July 1902. The body was badly mutilated. No warrants were issued in the case. However, the motive for the killing was traced back to a trial in Palermo some 20 years earlier where Catania's testimony had sent a number of men to jail for many years.

The following year, the body of a man with 17 stab wounds was found stuffed in a barrel in a vacant lot near Little Italy on Manhattan's Lower East Side. The victim wore earrings, which strongly suggested that he was Sicilian. His throat had been cut so savagely that his head was nearly severed from his body. His genitals had also been cut off and stuffed in his mouth. To Homicide Detective Sergeant Giuseppe 'Joe' Petrosino, later head of New York Police Department's special Italian Squad, this was all too reminiscent of Catania's murder.

The case began to open out. The barrel was identical to one found near where the murder had been commited, a pastry shop on Elizabeth Street, owned by Pietro Inzerillo. The body in the barrel was not immediately identified, but the police received an anonymous letter from someone who claimed to know the victim and claimed that he was related to Giuseppe de Primo, a member of the Morello gang who had recently been sent to prison for counterfeiting. The detective travelled to Sing Sing to see De Primo. When shown a photograph of the dead man, the convict immediately identified him as his brother-in-law Benedetto Madonia. He had recently visited De Primo with a man named Tomasso Petto – better known as Petto 'the Ox', enforcer with the Morello gang.

It seemed that Madonia had been a member of a counterfeit ring and had been murdered when money had gone missing. Petrosino's agents rounded up the Morello gang. In Morello's house they found a letter from Madonia saying that he could no longer remain in the dangerous business of distributing fake money and was going to return to his family in Buffalo. A search of Lupo's apartment revealed a dagger and three pistols. It seemed like an open-and-shut case.

However, the court dismissed charges against most of the gang due to lack of evidence. Only Petto was charged with murder, but even he went free after Madonia's wife, son, and brother-in-law refused to testify against him. Two years later, Petto was found dead outside his home with 62 stab wounds to his body.

Lupo was rearrested on counterfeiting charges, but these too were eventually dropped. In January 1904, he was arrested for carrying a concealed weapon described as 'a big blue barreled revolver of the latest kind', and later that year he was arrested for the kidnapping of Antonio Bozzuffi, the son of wealthy Italian banker John Bozzuffi who had previously had dealings with the Morello gang. Brought face to face with Lupo in court, Antonio Bozzuffi said he did not recognize him.

In December 1908, Lupo's business, by then based in an impressive shop on Mott Street in Little Italy, went bankrupt in suspicious circumstances and he disappeared along with Antonio Passananti, another member of the Morello gang who had paid Lupo large sums of money while running his wholesale wine business into the ground. When the wine importer Salvatore Manzella also went bankrupt, he claimed his business had collapsed because Lupo had been extorting large amounts from him over the previous three years. Manzella had kept paying up because he feared for his life.

In upstate New York, not far from a farm belonging to the Morello gang forger Salvatore Cina, Lupo hid out from the creditors on his Mott Street business. After moving back to Brooklyn, Lupo walked into the receiver's office with his attorney and claimed that his business had failed because he had been blackmailed. He was arrested for extortion in the Manzella case, but was released when Manzella failed to appear at his arraignment. Lupo was then immediately rearrested for counterfeiting.

Mafia Killings 3

Detective Lieutenant Giuseppe 'Joe' Petrosino, Palermo, 12 March 1909

Born in 1860 in Salerno, southern Italy, Giuseppe Petrosino was sent to live with his grandfather in New York at the age of 14, but when his grandfather was killed in a streetcar accident, the judge in the Orphans' Court took the boy in.

In 1883, Petrosino joined the NYPD where he was befriended by Theodore Roosevelt, then police commissioner. Roosevelt promoted him to detective sergeant and Petrosino subsequently became the first Italian-American head of the Homicide Division. In this position he came up against the Black Hand gangs, Mafiosi and Camorristi, who murdered those who would not succumb to their extortion. He came to public attention over the Morello barrel murders.

In an attempt to wipe out the Black Hand gangs, Petrosino was promoted to head up the newly formed Italian Squad. Hailed as the 'Italian Sherlock Holmes', he set off for Palermo with special permission from his boss, Police Chief Joseph Bingham, to dig out the criminal records of Black Hand suspects in the United States. He travelled, under conditions of intense secrecy, as Guglielmo De Simone, with an address at the Banco Commerciale in Palermo. But someone talked – and there is said to have been a meeting of the Black Hand in New Orleans which sent word forward that he was coming to one of the most powerful chieftains in Sicily, Don Vito Cascio Ferro.

Don Vito shot down Petrosino as he walked across Marina Square in Palermo in March 1909. He boasted publicly about it. It was a matter of honour and a demonstration to all of Don Vito's untouchability. News of the assassination caused a sensation in New York. Petrosino's body was shipped back to Manhattan, where an estimated 250,000 people turned out for his funeral.

REIGN OF THE MORELLOS

Giuseppe Morello, or the 'Old Fox' as he was known, was an early Mafioso operating in New York. Heading a gang originally referred to as the 107th Street Mob, he was one of the most powerful crime bosses of his day – the legendary *Capo di tutti Capi*, 'Boss of all Bosses'.

Morello had entered the Mafia while still in Sicily. At some point in the early 1890s, alledgedly to avoid accusations of murder and counterfeiting in his native Corleone, he travelled to the United States, settling with his family and its business in New York. Morello's gang specialized in the use of the old Black Hand extortion racket – threatening violence on fellow Italians until a pay-off was made. But Morello also had a hand in smuggling and counterfeiting. He was arrested in 1900 for passing phony $5 bills, which at the time were described as roughly executed and of poor quality. He later improved his counterfeiting process, however, and was able to produce near perfect replicas. Morello would launder these phony bills through his restaurants, saloons and other establishments – one of the first crime bosses to launder money in this way.

Morello and his lieutenant, the sinister Ignazio Lupo 'the Wolf', were dangerous individuals responsible for countless murders. Their specialty was the 'barrel murder', so called because the victim would be stuffed into a barrel after death. The 1903 murder of Benedetto Madonia was one of the first examples of this Mafia-style punishment.

In 1909 Giuseppe Morello and Lupo were eventually imprisoned for 25 and 30 years respectively for counterfeiting, while 12 other gang members were sentenced to shorter terms. The $2 and $5 bills, from which they made thousands of dollars, were originally printed in Sicily and shipped over to New York in boxes that supposedly contained olive oil, cheese, wine, macaroni, spaghetti and other prime Italian produce. They were sold for 30 or 40 cents apiece to agents who then distributed them around the country. Despite the lengthy sentences, both Lupo and Morello were paroled in 1920, just in time to benefit from the opportunities offered by Prohibition.

But during Giuseppe's incarceration, the Morello mob, now overseen by his half-brothers, the Terranovas, began to lose territory to rival gangs. In 1916 Nicolo Terranova was gunned down and when Morello was released from prison in 1920 he also found himself a marked man. Salvatore D'Aquila, at one time a subordinate Morello, owned many of the rackets in New York City. Now with his old boss released, he found that he was reluctant to relinquish the power he had connived so long to gain.

D'Aquila ordered his gunman Umberto Valenti to eliminate Morello and his associates, including rising boss Joe Masseria. Valenti was only partially successful, but eliminated one of Morello's half brothers, Vincent Terranova, before he himself was killed by Masseria.

Masseria now assumed control of the Morello gang, with Morello taking a subordinate position to his former underling. Now 63 years old, Morello was a wily strategist who had seen his fair share of gang struggles, and his opinions were greatly respected. He assisted Masseria as he moved to consolidate his powerbase and to eliminate rivals, including Salvatore Maranzano of the Castellammarese, a faction that was backed by the Sicilian Mafia.

On 15 August 1930, however, Morello was killed as he worked in his East Harlem office. He was one of the first victims of what was to become the infamous and bloody Castellammarese War, a conflict which directly ushered in a new era of organized crime and the creation of the Commission (a ruling body for the Italian Mafia) and the National Crime Syndicate (the ruling body for all mobs).

Petto 'the Ox' had retired to Browntown, Pennsylvania, where he was shot down in 1905, shortly after De Primo had been released from Sing Sing. Pietro Inzerillo suffered a similar fate following his incarceration. So much for the hunted. The hunters suffered the same fate and Joe Petrosino was gunned down and killed as he probed further into the dealings of the Mafia gangs. His assassination, at the hands of Don Vito Cascio Ferro, provoked horror in the United States but bought Don Vito plaudits and respect.

By the time of Don Vito's ascendancy to what may have been the *capo di tutti capi* of Sicily, many immigrants were beginning to filter back to the island from the United States, bringing with them news of democracy and the easy pickings to be had. The idea of long-distance co-operation across the Atlantic must have grown. The First World War, though, was soon to put the idea on hold. Though Mafiosi in Sicily, like Don Calogero Vizzini, are said to have made a fortune from war shortages, crime rates in the United States fell dramatically as its young men went off to fight.

After the war, too, there were further delays. A quota system was introduced in the United States, and this stemmed immigration from Sicily. But the island had problems of its own. In 1924, Mussolini's prefect, Cesare Mori, took over. Like Mussolini, Mori had not the slightest interest in due process. He strung Mafia leaders up from lamp-posts. He besieged whole towns where their presence was suspected. In the little town of Gangi, he arrested, captured and convicted 100 Mafiosi, including a woman, the so-called Queen of Gangi, who dressed like a man. He put behind bars leaders like Don Ciccio Cuccia and Don Calogero Vizzini; and though some were released for lack of evidence, the Mafia took the severest beating in its entire history. Murders on the island declined by three-quarters, and the population was struck dumb. When Mori offered a prize for the best essay on how to destroy the Mafia, not a single entry was received.

It took the arrival of the Second World War and the toppling of Mussolini for the idea of transatlantic co-operation to be revived – and it was, with a vengeance. In the interim, the baton of crime was passed to America, where the Sicilian Mafia was to grow exponentially through the unique medium of Prohibition.

'OUR THING'

What Joe Valachi started in court in Washington, D.C. in 1963 was well and truly finished in 1984 when Don Tommaso Buscetta began to speak about the inner workings of the Mafia to Palermo magistrate Giovanni Falcone. Though even then the word Mafia had only recently been added to the Italian criminal code. According to author Peter Robb in his remarkable book *Midnight in Sicily*, in the 1970s the *Oxford English Dictionary* was still insisting that the Mafia was: 'often erroneously supposed to constitute an organized secret society existing for criminal purposes.'

Buscetta forced a change in the dictionary's definition. He exposed everything to Falcone: the chains of command, the inter-gang wars, the deep connections between America and Sicily. He also described the oath that had to be taken by every Mafia recruit. It is worth quoting in full here, for it has odd pre-Christian echoes of the cord which passed between the body of Don Calogero Vizzini and his successor that day at Villalba. It also gives the real name of the Mafia for the very first time. Buscetta said: 'The neophyte is brought to a secluded spot, which could even be someone's home, in the presence of three or more Men of Honour of the family. Then the oldest of those present informs him that the purpose of *questa cosa* – this thing – is to protect the weak and to eliminate the oppressors. Then a finger is pricked on one of the hands of the person being sworn in and the blood is made to fall on a sacred image. Then the image is placed in his hand and is burned. At this time the neophyte must endure the fire, passing the sacred image quickly from one hand to the other until it goes out, and he swears to remain faithful to the principles of the Cosa Nostra (Our Thing), stating solemnly: "May my flesh burn like this holy picture if I am unfaithful to this oath."

'This in broad outline was the method of swearing in used when I became a member of the Cosa Nostra. After the swearing-in, and only then, the Man of Honour is introduced to the head of the family, whose post he did not know about beforehand, knowing even less about the existence of the Cosa Nostra per se', said Buscetta.

Until that moment in 1984, the real name of the Mafia that had grown within the Sicilian state had never been known to any outsider. From then on, neither it, nor the existence of the Cosa Nostra in America, could be denied.

Mafia Killings 4

Umberto Valenti, New York, 11 August 1922

As an enforcer for gangleader Salvatore D'Aquila, Umberto Valenti had quite a reputation. In his time, it was said that he was responsible for more deaths in New York than any other man. Though this may have been journalistic hype, Valenti was not a man to be taken lightly. When he went up against Joe 'The Boss' Masseria, however, Valenti clearly found himself in a different league.

Not much is known about Valenti's early life, other than the fact that he was born in Sicily in 1891. By 1914 he was heavily involved in Salvatore D'Aquila's gang – an offshoot of the old Giuseppe Morello mob.

D'Aquila had once been a captain for Morello, but had since moved on. When Morello went to prison in 1910, control of his operation fell to underlings Nicolo, Vincent and Ciro Terranova and Joe Masseria, with the two mobs frequently at odds. Masseria, in particular, was a wily customer, but his plans had to be put on hold in 1916 when he too went to jail. It was during this period that Valenti forged his reputation.

The year of 1920 was a good one for organized crime. Not only was it the first year of Prohibition, it was also when Morello and Masseria were released from jail. Both men were anxious to pick up where they'd left off and reaffirm their power base.

D'Aquila now had his old rivals to deal with again and decided to take some strategic action. Unsure of Valenti's loyalties, D'Aquila ordered him to prove himself by assassinating Morello and Masseria, as well as other high-ranking capos in the old Morello gang.

Valenti's first hit went well enough. On 7 May 1922, he assassinated two Morello bosses on the same day – Vincent Terranova and Silva Tagliagamba. Both men were killed easily enough, but when Valenti went after Masseria things started to unravel.

The following day Valenti tried to take down Masseria in the middle of the street. A battle erupted, with bullets ricocheting everywhere, and though no actual gangsters were killed, unfortunately several innocent bystanders were.

Two days later Valenti tried again. As Masseria left his home, two gunmen opened fire. Masseria dodged their first volleys, ducking and weaving like a boxer. The killers continued firing and managed to put a couple of bullets through his hat. Cutting their losses, the hit men fled the scene, driving their getaway car through a group of union workers and killing two of them. Masseria, though dazed, was still alive. With two attempts on Masseria's life ending in failure, Valenti's stock was plummeting. His intended victim, though, was gaining quite a reputation.

On 11 August, Masseria retaliated. Calling Valenti to a meeting on 12th Street, Masseria said he was willing to talk peace. When Valenti arrived, however, it was patently obvious that there was to be no peace-talk. Hat in hand, Valenti fled down the street but was gunned down as he jumped on to the runningboard of a taxi. He died a short while later.

A teenage witness to the killing described how one gunman stood out from the rest, calmly firing his gun at Valenti as he sprinted down the road. The story goes that it was Salvatore Luciano who coolly pulled the trigger that day, putting an end to Valenti's life. Salvatore would later be better known as Lucky – Lucky Luciano.

PART THREE

PROHIBITION: RUM RUNNERS AND BEER BARONS

It has been said that Prohibition did more for organized crime than any other single event, and though historians still debate this today, there's undoubtedly some truth to the statement. What is uncontested is that the Volstead Act that took effect in 1920, banning the manufacture and sale of alcohol, opened the door to increased profits for all the gangs and kept that door nicely wedged open for more than ten years.

Smart mobsters – and even the not-so-smart ones – quickly realized the money-making potential that was now available to them and acted accordingly. These were formative years for the big names. Gangsters such as Lucky Luciano, Bugsy Siegel, Meyer Lansky, Dutch Schultz and Al Capone were on the rise, and the world of the criminal gangs would never be the same again.

CHAPTER 5

THE 'NOBLE EXPERIMENT'

President Calvin Coolidge called the Volstead Act, which brought in Prohibition on 17 January 1920, 'the greatest social experiment of modern times'. But what it was, in fact, was the last stand of rock-ribbed White Anglo-Saxon America against the tide of beer- and wine-drinking immigrants it imagined to be polluting the clean, clear water of the States. It had been presented as a patriotic issue by those who had ruthlessly campaigned for it during the First World War – and now they were victorious. Germans drank beer, they'd said; we are at war against Germany. Thus, to be consistently patriotic, we must also wage war against beer. The same soon went for the Italians and their wine, for the dirt farmers avoiding taxes on spirits with their illegal stills, and it certainly went for the saloons across the country where the lower sort of worker drank away the pain of underpayment, unemployment and appalling conditions, both at work and at home. Besides, the keepers of saloons were notorious as organizers of the local vote for any politician with the ability to pay for them. They were major polluters of the Founding Fathers' body politic – and they had to go too.

It was clear, from the very beginning, that it was an act of monumental moral and political stupidity. Not only did the Act have a number of

loopholes – such as the production and prescription of 'medicinal' and 'agricultural' alcohol and of wine used for religious purposes – it was never backed by ordinary citizens. And it was they, who, by exercising what they saw as their God-given right to go on drinking, handed power to the rum-runners and speakeasy operators and those who controlled them. They voted them, in effect, into office as a sort of underground government. Not for nothing was Al Capone in Cicero, Illinois, nicknamed 'The Mayor of Crook County'.

The process by which Americans gradually – and fatally – lost their capacity for moral indignation began virtually immediately. Within an hour of Prohibition's arrival, six armed men in Chicago made off with $100,000-worth of whisky that had been earmarked for medicinal use. Within a matter of weeks, 15,000 doctors and 57,000 retail druggists had applied for licences to sell this same kind of hooch for any ache and pain they could find. In 1917, before any of the states had voted to turn themselves dry – as many did, one by one – Americans had consumed two billion gallons of hard liquor, and everyone who had any kind of capacity to do so was suddenly racing to make sure that they went right on drinking them. One of the biggest of the early bootleggers, a Chicago lawyer and pharmacist called George Remus, who moved to Cincinnati to set up his business, was soon bringing in $20 million a year. It would have been $40 million, but the other $20 million had to go to bent cops and Prohibition agents, to biddable judges and politicians.

THE CORRUPTION OF POLITICS

Remus and others like him were helped enormously by the fact that the White House was by now occupied by perhaps the most corrupt administration in America's history: that of Warren Harding. A blowhard womanizer from Marion, Ohio, Harding had always been a useful tool for corrupt party politicians in his home state. He'd become a senator in 1915, and then the last minute compromise candidate for president at the Republican convention in 1919. He campaigned mostly from his own

front porch in Marion, projecting a dream of the past: of an America of small towns and simple values, God-fearing and centred on the family.

When he arrived at the White House, he brought with him a family of his own, his campaign managers and poker-playing cronies, who promptly turned the business of government into a machine for lining their own pockets. His Attorney General, Harry Daugherty, for example, was always on hand to block investigations and organize pardons – open, in fact, to any scam at all through his bagman Jess Smith. They gathered over the booze upstairs at the White House with the president. Members of Congress were often found drunk on the floor of the House and the library of the Senate was reckoned to be the best bar in Washington, D.C.

Remus and the rest were also assisted by the fact that Prohibition agents were not made part of the United States' civil service. Instead, their recruitment was handed over to local politicians and became part of their 'bag', their area of patronage. The agents were also paid a minimum salary, one that was virtually an open invitation to corruption. But both politicians and agents were only part of a long line of people who were now queuing up for their share in the spoils. Corruption was little by little becoming a quintessential part of local, as well as national government – and nowhere more so than in Chicago.

'BIG BILL' THOMPSON

Prohibition arrived in Illinois, thus in Chicago, in 1918 under the mayoralty of 'Big Bill' Thompson. The son of a native Bostonian who'd made a fortune in real estate in the 'Windy City', Thompson never finished high school and left home aged 14 to become a brakeman on the Union Pacific Railroad. He then became an apprentice cowboy in Cheyenne. His father bought him a ranch in Nebraska, but after he died, 'Big Bill' returned to Chicago, became a star sportsman at the Chicago Athletic Club, and decided, on a bet, to run for city alderman on the Republican ticket in 1900.

By 1915, this tub-thumping man had been elected mayor and inherited all the shady connections between politics and crime that past

Democratic administrations had spawned. The rackets of the Chicago gangs – prostitution, gambling, slot machines, labour racketeering and so on – had always been shared evenhandedly between the inner city wards, whose bosses provided political protection. In return, at election time, the gangs made sure that as many of the votes as possible – real or not – went the right way. This was an arrangement that suited everyone. Violence was kept to a minimum, and the pickings were good for all – particularly for 'Big Jim' Colosimo, who controlled most of the slot machines and brothels in the city.

DIAMOND JIM'S

Big Jim Colosimo loved the high life. Diamond stick pins, linen suits, expensive food and fine music – he wanted it all. His restaurant on Wabash Avenue, called Diamond Jim's, regularly entertained the elite of Chicago, blue bloods and criminals alike. The restaurant had a lavish six-course meal for those who could afford the $1.50 price tag and offered patrons a floor show that featured both ragtime and opera. It's no wonder they called him 'Diamond Jim'. But Big Jim just got too comfortable, and by 1920 he was obsolete.

Credited with organizing Chicago's underworld and initiating what would become known as the infamous Chicago Outfit, Colosimo started his criminal career in the city's First Ward, picking pockets and committing petty crimes. Like so many of his contemporaries, he ultimately branched out into gambling, racketeering and vice. Marrying into the business, Colosimo wed bordello madam Victoria Moresco in 1902 and the pair expanded the prostitution aspects of Colosimo's criminal empire, ultimately owning over 200 brothels.

But all this wealth brought some unwanted attention and in 1909 Colosimo became the victim of a racket that he'd employed frequently himself – Black Hand extortion – where a threatening letter featuring a drawing of a black hand demanded payment if the victim was to avoid consequences such as bodily harm, kidnapping or murder. He knew the game, he knew he'd have to keep on paying or expect more threats and

escalating violence. To counter this, he brought in a torpedo contract killer from New York, Johnny 'The Fox' Torrio, Victoria's nephew. Torrio took care of Colosimo's extortion problem in a most effective and permanent manner. Remaining in Chicago, he became Colosimo's right-hand man, adding immeasurably to the efficiency of The Outfit.

With Torrio effectively running the organization, Colosimo had the opportunity to pursue other interests and started frequenting his restaurant more often and spending time with his new wife. By 1920 he had divorced Victoria and married a young singer, Dale Winter, who performed as a lyric soprano in his restaurant.

Colosimo's folly occurred in 1920, when Prohibition took effect. Torrio recognized the windfall that the 'Noble Experiment', as it was called, would offer The Outfit and urged Colosimo to take advantage of this criminal goldmine and start bootlegging. But Big Jim wasn't interested. The operation was fine the way it was; why risk things by branching out into the unknown?

Clearly Colosimo was getting in the way of progress. On 11 May 1920, he arrived at his restaurant, ostensibly to deal with a shipment of whiskey. As he was waiting for the delivery to arrive, Colosimo was gunned down by an unknown assailant. Collapsing onto the tiled floor, he died in the lobby of his own establishment. Though no arrests were made for the killing, it's believed that among the assassins was Frankie Yale, also over from New York and acting on orders from Johnny Torrio. With Colosimo's death, Torrio assumed complete control of The Outfit.

Colosimo's funeral, just like his life, was a big deal – one of those extravagant gangster send offs associated with the 1920s. The cortège filed through the streets of Chicago, taking Big Jim past his beloved restaurant one last time, while mourners and the curious crowded the street. Diamond Jim was finally laid to rest in a stately mausoleum at Oak Woods Cemetery – and once he was gone, the door to Prohibition was kicked wide open by The Chicago Outfit.

Softened up by the activities of gangs like Colosimo's, Chicago was there for the taking, and Mayor Thompson immediately became an enthusiastic participant in the cosy arrangement between politics and crime in the city. Little by little, he turned Chicago's city government into a miniature version of the Harding administration that was to come. With protection from above – a venal governor of Illinois called Ed Small – Thompson turned City Hall into a personal cash cow. Every permission, every licence, every job now came at a price – even the garbage collectors had to pay $5 a year to his Republican Fund for every horse and cart. Meanwhile, he appointed a series of corrupt police chiefs, wound down Chicago's Morals Division, and made sure that the cops regularly took 'advice' from his ward-level political chieftains. He also created in each ward what were called 'honorary precinct captaincies' – one of which was awarded to Colosimo in 1919, the year before his killing.

Colosimo was killed because he just didn't get it – and his bodyguard Johnny Torrio did. Prohibition had come and Johnny Torrio, a friend of George Remus, just knew that moving heavily into booze would make them more money than anyone could imagine. What's more, he had a relative in town at the time who not only agreed with him, but could also get rid of Colosimo's opposition once and for all: that relative was a young hood from New York called Alfonso Capone.

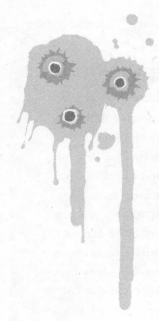

CHAPTER 6

AL CAPONE'S CHICAGO

Neapolitan in background, Al Capone was born in 1899 in New York and grew up into a resourceful small-time hood, working in the rackets and as a bouncer in a Brooklyn brothel where a knife fight gave him the nickname 'Scarface'. If he'd stayed in New York, he might never have amounted to much. But in 1920, when on the run from the police, he got the all important invitation from Chicago. Nominally, he became Johnny 'The Fox' Torrio's bodyguard – but he was, in effect, his hitman. Sent by Torrio to make Jim Colosimo's acquaintance at his saloon headquarters one night, Capone coolly gunned him down.

From then on, it was a partnership: Torrio and Capone took over Colosimo's brothels, and then moved immediately into large-scale bootlegging under the protection of the mayor and his police. When, in 1923, Bill Thompson decided not to run for mayor again, leaving the way open to a Democratic candidate, they simply upped sticks and moved their operation to the suburb of Cicero, where the next local elections were conducted more or less literally at the point of their hoodlums' guns. Cicero soon became a modern version of a Wild West frontier town, full of speakeasies and brothels. It had greyhound racing and what was probably at the time the highest stakes casino in the world.

Al Capone: one of the most recognizable crime figures in history

With their own turf secure, Torrio and Capone were now ready to move back in to claim the main prize, Chicago. This brought them into direct competition with the mainly Irish gang of 'Deanie' O'Banion, a genial ex-choirboy and journalist who served only the finest liquor and ran his business from the city's most fashionable flower shop. For a while

both sides stayed their hand. But then, in November 1924, in revenge for a trick which got Torrio a police record (and eventually nine months in jail), O'Banion was killed in his shop by three of Torrio's men after they'd arrived to order a funeral wreath.

Mafia Killings 5

Charles Dean O'Banion, Chicago, 10 November 1924

O'Banion was something of an enigma. He had been a choirboy in his childhood and as an adult went to mass every Sunday, dropped money in the poor box, and worked in his own flower shop.

But O'Banion was also an audacious and flagrant criminal. A major player in Chicago during the Roaring Twenties, he was associate and adversary of Johnny Torrio and Al Capone. Between the three of them they owned Chicago, and the other mobs, the Genna brothers included, had to be content with what was left. With his lieutenant Hymie Weiss, O'Banion was largely who James Cagney based his performance on in the movie *The Public Enemy*. When he hitched back his shoulders and curled his lips into that predatory sneer, the audience could be sure that murder would soon follow.

O'Banion ran the North Side of Chicago, with the gang's headquarters in his flower shop. Called Schofield's, it was the place the gangsters went to when buying those large floral tributes for their fallen comrades. The shop was a front, of course, but O'Banion came to love pottering among the plants and pruning them.

In 1920, with the dawn of Prohibition, it had been Torrio's idea to divide the city among the gangs. The division would allow everyone to get their fair share, while keeping a potential powder keg under control. After all, there was money to be made, but only if everyone played the game.

The plan worked well enough until about 1923, when the

various mobsters began to chafe under the arrangement. As the year progressed the Gennas were making serious inroads into O'Banion's territory, while he, always happy in a heist, started hijacking whisky deliveries meant for the other mobs. Still trying to keep a lid on things, Torrio ceded O'Banion prime turf in the South Side, also throwing in a share in his nightclub, The Ship, to sweeten the deal.

But the capper came in 1924. Spending some time at The Ship, O'Banion learned that 'Bloody' Angelo Genna had racked up a whopping gambling bill of over $30,000. Capone was inclined to let the matter drop, but not O'Banion. Supposedly, he got on the phone to Angelo and demanded payment of the debt within the week. It was an affront to the Genna boss, but it also made a handy excuse to force the issue. A vote was taken and the mobsters were unanimous – O'Banion would have to go.

It happened in the flower shop. O'Banion was in the back room, preparing wreaths for recently deceased mob 'fixer' Mike Merlo. The memorials were expensive and O'Banion had been asked to oversee them himself. He wasn't overly surprised then when the bell rang and three men, one of whom is believed to have been enforcer Frankie Yale, entered the shop. One of the men took O'Banion's hand in a fraternal grasp, then wouldn't let go. He was trapped, while the two other men drew their guns and shot him in the chest and throat. He died almost instantly.

With the murder of O'Banion, Chicago exploded in one of the bloodiest gang wars in mob history. His death didn't mean the end of the North Siders, not by any stretch of the imagination. The North Side Gang, now under the leadership of Hymie Weiss, was about to take a very sharp knife and run it down the belly of Chicago. A wound like that would be pretty deadly; in fact, it would mean the end of a lot of gangsters.

Henry Earl J. Wojciechowski, or Hymie Weiss as he was better known, is said to have been the only man that Al Capone ever feared. During

the 1920s Chicago was rife with criminality derived from Prohibition. The city had been divided into sections, with Johnny Torrio and Al Capone running the South Side and the Genna brothers controlling Little Italy. Following O'Banion's death, his friend and lieutenant Weiss was determined that someone was going to pay. The North Siders were an extremely loyal bunch and Weiss in particular had a gallant side. The gang, for instance, shunned the prostitution rings that the other mobs found so lucrative. Weiss had a vile temper, though, one that could explode without warning. Because of the frequent debilitating migraines he experienced, it's now believed that he was suffering from cancer. Weiss's agony no doubt led to the wild outbursts he was known for.

Perhaps aware that he was ill, Weiss may have decided he had nothing to lose in going after the South Siders and the Gennas. The mayhem started immediately and for several years Chicago bled.

The crime reporters of the time had a field day. Headlines on mob warfare in 1925 alone included:

- 24 January – 'Johnny Torrio, wounded by Weiss, heads to Italy, leaving the South Side gang to Capone'
- 27 May – 'Angelo Genna is killed by North Siders Bugs Moran and Vincent Drucci'
- 13 June – 'Mike Genna is shot down by police'
- 8 July – 'Antonio Genna is murdered in the street'

As a result, the surviving Gennas headed to New York, while the residue of their gang was taken over by Salvatore Amatuna then Joe Aiello, an enemy of Capone. More tellingly, Capone increased his security. On 10 August 1926, Weiss and Drucci battled it out with Capone men at the Standard Oil Building, while 20 September brought another bold attack, this time at Capone's headquarters at the Hawthorne Inn at Cicero.

As things were getting out of hand, Capone proposed a truce and had a delegate, Tony Lombardo, meet with Weiss and Bugs Moran. Capone did not attend the meeting, but participated over the phone. At first things went well enough, with Capone offering Weiss territory in the South Side. But Weiss's demands were high; he expected nothing

less than two of the murderers of Dean O'Banion – Albert Anselmi and John Scalise. So far, Anselmi and Scalise had done nothing disloyal to Capone, so his reply to Weiss was brief and to the point – he wouldn't do that to a dog. With that, the conference was at an end.

Frustrated by the outcome of the meeting and seeing no other way out, Capone ordered Weiss's assassination. The hit was meticulously planned. Capone's men rented the building next to the North Side hangout – Schofield's Flower Shop – in preparation. This was the very place where O'Banion had met his demise. Other locations were rented across the street from the shop, giving the gunmen optimum vantage points. On 11 October 1926, when Weiss arrived at Schofield's along with North Side ally Patrick Murray and several others, the gunmen opened fire. Murray was killed instantly and Weiss, hit several times, collapsed. He died on his way to the hospital.

Weiss was buried not far from his pal Dean O'Banion, and with his death the North Siders were inherited by Drucci and Moran. But it wasn't over – not by a long shot – and the battle for Chicago continued.

Mafia Killings 6

John Scalise and Albert Anselmi, Chicago, 7 May 1929

John Scalise and Albert Anselmi seemed to be joined at the hip. Though Anselmi was Scalise's senior by around 17 years, the two Sicilians were inseparable, with Scalise the dominant one.

Scalise arrived in Chicago in the early 1920s, with Anselmi arriving in 1924. Anselmi spoke no English and Scalise's knowledge of the language was limited, but command of the language was not really required for the jobs the two were contracted to perform. Almost immediately, both men attached themselves to the Genna Gang in Chicago. It was while working for the Gennas that they formed their life-long friendship. From there they gravitated to Capone and the South Side Gang.

Once with Capone, the pair honed their craft and were responsible (along with Frankie Yale) for the death of North Side crime boss Dean O'Banion. In fact, it was the lives of Scalise and Anselmi that North Sider Hymie Weiss demanded in reparation for O'Banion's murder. Capone said no dice.

Throughout 1925 the battle between the South Siders and the North Siders raged in the city of Chicago. In June of that year, Scalise and Anselmi, along with Mike Genna, waylaid and attacked North Siders Vincent Drucci and Bugs Moran. After a long battle and pursuit by the police, Genna was killed while several officers were also gunned down. The Murder Twins – as they came to be known – were taken into custody.

Over the next few years the pair went to trial twice for the murder of the officers. The original ruling sent them to jail for 14 years, but they must have had a good lawyer and no doubt some political pull through Capone, because their case was retried and they were acquitted. To Scalise and Anselmi it must have seemed that they could get away with anything, including murder. Scalise even rose to the position of vice president of the Unione Siciliana under the presidency of Joseph 'Hop Toad' Giunta.

What happened next remains the subject of some controversy. Supposedly, while Scalise, Anselmi and Giunta were attending a gathering, a violent argument broke out and all three men were murdered. The party may or may not have been a ruse to lure them to their deaths.

But a more sensational version of the story has now become a part of the Capone legend, undoubtedly growing with each retelling. In this account, Capone bodyguard Frankie Rio happened upon the startling revelation that Scalise and Anselmi had planned on betraying and murdering Capone. Turning the tables on the pair, Capone threw an elaborate party at which Giunta was also in attendance. Apparently after an extravagant meal had been enjoyed, and speeches had been

endured, Capone pulled out a baseball bat and proceeded to beat the trio mercilessly. That done, several underlings then drew their guns and finished the job.

Whatever the case, Scalise and Anselmi were dead and their remains were shipped back to Sicily for burial. The Twins had died together and now they were going home together.

QUASHED DREAMS

During the battle of Chicago, half of O'Banion's old enemies – the Terrible Gennas – had either been murdered, or fled to New York. For a while, leadership of the limping remnants of the Genna gang fell to Salvatore 'Samoots' Amatuna, a Sicilian-American gangster with aspirations to be head of the Unione Siciliana. This was a cultural and beneficent group that had started legitimately in New York and Chicago in 1893 to provide health insurance and social care for those newly arrived from Sicily, but it had since developed deep criminal connections.

Amatuna was a cut above the usual gangster, and definitely added a much-needed touch of class to the brutish Genna clan. For one thing, he understood the importance of good public opinion. After all, it didn't cost Amatuna much to buy his companions a suit when he was having one made up for himself, or to treat the street kids to a haircut when he visited the barber. People tend to remember little touches like that. They take the sting away when it's time to draw a gun.

The Unione Siciliana was the linchpin in Amatuna's bid for power. Leadership of the Unione would give him control of more than the Genna gang. It would also give him clout with Al Capone and Johnny Torrio in the South Side, as well as the average (and beleaguered) Italian immigrant who had made his way to the city in hopes of a better life.

So Amatuna – handsome, debonair and armed with a tenor singing voice with which he would often entertain his friends in his Bluebird Café on Halsted Street – was about to make an alliance by marrying Rose Pecorara, the sister-in-law of past Unione president Mike Merlo.

Although Merlo was dead by then, he had been one of the most honoured leaders of the Unione, a man both respected and beloved. Amatuna, who was by now the president himself, had great plans – but they were never to be realized.

On 10 November 1925, Amatuna was getting his hair cut in a barber shop when two men burst in and shot the place up. Amatuna was hit and though he didn't die right away, it was only a matter of time. At the hospital, with Rose by his side, Amatuna hoped to hold out long enough to wed her. But it was not to be. By the time the priest arrived, it was too late for marriage. Instead Amatuna received the last rites.

There is a picture of Salvatore Amatuna, one of the few known to exist, showing the man in the morgue, a mortician's number on his chest. His eyes are open, and his lips are pursed. It's a picture of the man and of the quashed dreams of Salvatore 'Samoots' Amatuna.

The death of O'Banion, who was buried in high style, triggered an all-out war for control of the Chicago liquor trade, with Torrio and Capone pitted against O'Banion's lieutenants and heirs, Hymie Weiss and Bugs Moran, and against the four brothers of the Sicilian Genna family, who had a licence to make agricultural alcohol. The going soon got too hot for Johnny Torrio, and he retired to Naples in 1925, taking $50 million, it's said, with him. But Capone was made of sterner and more cunning stuff. He gradually eliminated the Genna family and as he did so bought politicians and judges, journalists and police brass, until he was in control not only of all enforcement agencies and public opinion, but also of City Hall. He made massive donations to the 1927 campaign of Mayor 'Big Bill' Thompson, who'd decided to run again. With his man safely in office, Capone held court to all comers in 50 rooms on two floors of the downtown Metropole Hotel, where he projected himself to reporters as an eccentric businessman and philanthropist. He even set up soup kitchens in Chicago at the beginning of the Great Depression.

In 1929, having already got rid of Hymie Weiss, he was finally ready to move against his last surviving enemy, Bugs Moran. Word was passed to Moran that a consignment of hijacked booze could be picked up at a

garage on North Clark Street on 14 February, but soon after his people arrived, so did Capone's torpedoes, two of them in police uniform. Six of Moran's men died in what became known as the St Valentine's Massacre, along with an unfortunate optometrist who liked hanging out with hoods. Moran only escaped because he was late for the appointment. As for Capone, he was on holiday that day in Biscayne Bay, Florida, and on the phone to the Miami DA at the time of the slaughter at the SMC Cartage Company garage.

THE ST. VALENTINE'S DAY MASSACRE

On a snowy morning on 14 February 1929, seven men – most of them members of George Bugs Moran's North Side Gang – gathered inside a garage in Chicago's Lincoln Park area, apparently awaiting the arrival of a truck of bootleg whisky. The location was a known hangout for the gang.

At approximately 10.30 a.m. a squad car pulled up in front of the garage. Two men wearing police uniforms and carrying guns stepped out. They entered the garage and demanded Moran's men drop their weapons and face the wall – this was a raid. The 'policemen' then opened a back door and let in more men dressed in suits, ties and hats and carrying weapons.

Shortly after that the armed group opened fire on Moran's gang. Machine guns and rifles were used in the bloody attack, and over 70 rounds of ammunition were sprayed into Moran's men and the back wall.

The job done, some of the killers exited through the rear door of the garage. But the rest – the two 'policemen' and two of the 'civilians' – left through the front entrance. The civilians were forced out at gunpoint, their hands raised as if under arrest. To any onlookers it appeared that the police had matters well in hand.

Alarmed by the commotion, Jeanette Landesman, ironing clothes in a nearby boarding house, sent a lodger over to investigate. The lodger returned a short while later, ashen-faced, and told Jeanette to call the police – something terrible had happened.

Crime scene photo of the St Valentine's Day massacre, 1929 – this event shocked the USA and public opinion began to turn against Prohibition

When the real police arrived, they found a gruesome scene. The St. Valentine's Day Massacre, as it was later dubbed, was the bloodiest hit in Chicago mob history and unquestionably the most infamous gang assassination of all time. Six of the victims died immediately, but one – Frank Gusenberg – was miraculously still alive and trying to drag himself to the door. When asked by police who did it, Gusenberg refused to talk. He died three hours later.

There were no survivors and no one was brought to trial, but the chain of events seemed clear. This hit was just the latest in the long line of skirmishes that Bugs Moran's North Side Gang and Al Capone's South Side Gang had been engaged in for years. The costs were high on both sides. On that morning in February, Capone had also made a bid for supremacy against Moran. The only problem was that Moran wasn't there.

The investigation seemed to drag on for years, with the police pursuing several leads, but strangely never following through. It was not until 1934 that a low-level hood, Byron Bolton, was able to fill in the details.

According to Bolton, in October or November of 1928 Capone and some of his men sat down at a Wisconsin resort and planned the hit, intending to kill Moran and several of his gang. The strategy was for Bolton to keep a look-out near the garage and, the moment Moran appeared, to alert the hit team waiting at the Circus Café. That morning, when a group of Moran's men arrived at the garage, Bolton mistook one of them for Moran. The target apparently spotted, Bolton gave the signal and the cars began to arrive.

But Moran was late in reaching the garage, and when he pulled up and saw a police car there he ducked into a coffee shop instead. Bumping into another of his men along the way, he was told to avoid the garage as it was being raided.

This mistake didn't really matter, though – the hit did the trick and Moran's operations were dealt a deadly blow. But it also brought a lot of unwanted attention to Capone, even though he was in Florida at the time and had an alibi. In 1930 Capone became Public Enemy Number One, and by the end of 1933 he was in jail serving an eleven-year stretch.

Capone was never again able to regain the power he had wielded during his Chicago heyday. He died in his own in bed in 1947. And the famous massacre wall, the one that the victims were facing when they were shot? It's now part of the Mob Museum in Las Vegas, minus a few souvenir bricks – which have been taken as gruesome mementoes.

Mafia Killings 7

Jack 'Machine Gun' McGurn, Chicago, 15 February 1936

Jack McGurn was Capone's bodyguard and one of his chief enforcers. Nicknamed 'Machine Gun', because he used a Thompson sub-machine gun during jobs, his real name was Vincenzo Antonio Gibaldi, and he was reputedly the brains behind the St Valentine's Day Massacre.

McGurn had started out as a professional boxer, but gravitated to the Capone franchise mob, the Circus Gang. With his cool

professionalism and willingness to pull the trigger, McGurn was quick to catch the attention of Capone, who welcomed him into his inner circle. McGurn proved invaluable to Capone and uncovered several plots against the mobster's life, heading off would-be killers before they could make the hit.

McGurn was part-owner of a speakeasy – the Green Mill Jazz Club, on the corner of Broadway and Lawrence – and there's a story about how he dealt with a performer who wanted to work for another joint. Comedian and singer Joe E. Lewis was offered a better deal at another club and decided it was time to move on. McGurn suggested that Lewis should think again, but Lewis threw in his job anyway. So McGurn sent over some thugs to have a little talk with the comedian. Though the mobsters slit Lewis' throat and removed part of his tongue, Lewis miraculously survived. It would be several years, however, before he was able to speak or entertain again.

This gruesome incident aside, McGurn's greatest claim to fame was as the architect of the St Valentine's Day Massacre. Probably one of the triggermen in the legendary hit, McGurn was charged with seven counts of murder, but was able to beat the rap. He'd spent the entire day with his girlfriend, Louise Rolfe, or so he said. Rolfe's corroborating statement got McGurn off the hook and after that she was known as McGurn's Blonde Alibi.

After Capone went to prison, McGurn's clout began to diminish. Named Public Enemy Number Four in 1930, he was becoming a risky commodity. The Outfit's new boss, Frank Nitti, found it advisable to distance the gang from McGurn, who was drawing too much attention to the mob. Nitti didn't like McGurn anyway.

With no assignments to support him, McGurn turned to professional golf for a while, but his days were numbered. There's really no such thing as a retired gangster, and he had started to hit the bottle pretty hard. Who could tell what valuable information he might give away?

On 15 February 1936, McGurn was gunned down while spending the day bowling at the Avenue Recreation Bowling Alley. A Valentine card had been left in McGurn's name at the front desk of the alley. Because of this card there has been some speculation that the murder was in retaliation for the St Valentine's Day Massacre, a hit that went down exactly seven years and one day before Jack's death. It's more likely, however, that Frank Nitti had McGurn rubbed out to keep him from talking and the Valentine's card was just colourful camouflage.

Mafia Killings 8

Joe Aiello, Chicago, 23 October 1930

Fifty-nine – that's the number of bullets they plugged into Joe Aiello in 1930. That definitely seems like overkill, but Aiello brought it all on himself. He just seemed to have a one-track mind. No matter what anyone else was talking about at the time, he would inevitably steer the conversation back to his pet subject – whacking Al Capone.

It's not as though Aiello didn't have enough to do without starting trouble with Capone. By 1925 he controlled the remnants of the Genna brothers' old gang, which brought in lots of dollars from the home-made stills of Chicago's Little Sicily; and in 1929 he finally realized his dream of becoming president of the Unione Siciliana. And that is the crux of the matter. Apparently Capone had backed Aiello's ex-friend Tony Lombardo in the bid for presidency of the Unione. After that move, Aiello seemed compelled to start yet another war in Chicago.

He had comparatively little trouble when it came to taking out Lombardo. Capone, though, was a different matter. Here's a description of just a few of his attempts:

Early 1927 – Aiello pays the chef at one of Capone's favourite eateries to put prussic acid into the big guy's soup. The chef tips off Capone, and the whole Borgia-like escapade falls apart.

Later in 1927 – An Aiello machine-gun nest is discovered directly across the street from Capone's favourite cigar store.

25 May to 24 September 1927 – A total of eight Aiello men or hirelings are butchered in the war. In desperation, Aiello offers $50,000 for the head of Capone, but all that does is pile up more bodies on his own side.

April 1929 – Aiello tries to use Capone gunmen Albert Anselmi and John Scalise to kill their boss. Capone's spies reveal the plot and the Murder Twins are killed instead.

In 1927, when Capone found out that Aiello was being held at the South Clark Street police station on a weapons charge, he made a grand show of power, intended to put Aiello in his place. He sent down a 25-strong goon platoon to make its presence felt at the courthouse and generally spread intimidation around in a broken-nosed kind of way. The press had a field day in expectation of a bloody shootout. Flashing their guns, a couple of the gangsters were disarmed by the police, then hustled into the courthouse where they proceeded to put the fear of Al into Aiello. The whole thing was getting very bloody – and costly. Just how many more men could Aiello afford to lose?

Finally, on 23 October 1930, Aiello decided to skip town for a little while, and was holed up in the house of Pasquale 'Patsy Presto' Prestogiacomo, when the boom was finally lowered. With his bags packed, and supposedly on his way to Mexico City, Aiello was shot as he headed for a waiting cab. Staggering around the corner of the house, he encountered another machine-gun nest with an unobstructed view of the quarry. That was it, of course, the fifty-nine bullets. When the barrage of slugs finally stopped, Aiello's black trench coat was like a sieve and the wall of Prestogiacomo's house was a crumbling mess. Aiello had finally been outgunned and outgooned.

In the end, Capone was brought to book, not by the cops or the FBI – despite the myth of Elliot Ness and *The Untouchables* – but by the internal revenue service. In 1931, he was tried for tax evasion and sentenced to jail for eleven years. By the time he came out eight years later, the Mafia had moved on and become more sophisticated. And Capone was not only old hat, but half mad from tertiary syphilis. He died in his bed eight years later on his Florida estate. Bugs Moran would outlive him by ten years.

Mafia Killings 9

Edward 'Easy Eddie' O'Hare, Chicago, 8 November 1939

In 1932 the mighty Al Capone – Chicago's Public Enemy Number One, and perhaps the most notorious gangster of all time – was sent down for tax evasion. After the bloody calling card that was the St Valentine's Day Massacre, the Feds were very motivated to bring Capone in, but not just any old way. No, they wanted something that would stick, a charge that would send Big Al down for good, or at least long enough to neutralize his power. So IRS Agent Frank Wilson came up with the plan of targeting Capone's income as a means of bringing him down. It was a brilliant scheme, and for Capone, ultimately inescapable.

And that's where Edward O'Hare comes into the picture. O'Hare, otherwise known as 'Easy Eddie', was a mob lawyer and business manager for Capone. He was also as crooked as they come. O'Hare was not only partnered in a lot of the rackets on the South Side, he was also privy to some very interesting details regarding Big Al's books, business transactions and the code that all this information was written in.

When he saw the zeal with which the IRS was pursuing Capone, O'Hare didn't have to give it much thought. In a heartbeat, he sold Capone down the river. The story goes that O'Hare had a very good

reason for betraying Capone, even an altruistic one. It seems that he did this terrible deed so that his son, Butch, would be allowed to attend Annapolis, the highly prestigious naval academy, without fear of reprisal or expulsion.

It may be true that Annapolis was part of the bargain, but undoubtedly O'Hare also received other rewards for this act of treason – immunity, for one. After all, if Capone was going down, then it was time for all good rats to jump ship – starting with the sneakiest one.

While still working for Capone, and making money from the dog track they owned together plus all the other Outfit rackets he was involved in, O'Hare provided the IRS with all the information they needed to form a case against Big Al. But that's not all O'Hare did. Learning that the Outfit had got to the jury for Capone's trial, he contacted Agent Wilson with this interesting bit of news. So at the last minute Capone's jury was switched out with a new one, and Capone ended up in Alcatraz.

Miraculously, O'Hare somehow managed to survive for a number of years. But on 8 November 1939, eight days before Capone was scheduled for release, O'Hare was shot while driving his Lincoln along Ogden Avenue. The killers were never identified.

As a curious side note, O'Hare's son Butch went on to become one of the greatest heroes of the Second World War. In fact, Chicago's O'Hare International Airport is named after him. In Butch's case, it seems that the apple fell pretty darned far from the tree.

CHAPTER 7

THE RICHEST PICKINGS

What happened in Chicago happened in more or less the same way in New York – except that there the pickings were even more lucrative. Like Chicago, New York is reasonably near the Canadian border, but has the added advantage of being on the Atlantic Ocean. So the gangs who came to control the liquor trade had New York City's docks at their disposal, as well as the coves and inlets of Long Island. They controlled not only the distribution side in America's largest city, but also their product's major points of entry into the United States.

New York had always been the single most important point of entry for another important commodity: immigrants. Millions of people, on the run from poverty, persecution, authoritarianism and famine in Europe, made their first landfall at Ellis Island before starting new lives in the swarming streets and tenements of the city. They tended naturally to cling together in their own neighbourhoods, with the new arrivals learning the ropes from their own kind. There were, of course, overlaps, as well as inevitable frictions as they rubbed shoulders with communities of other nationalities. The gangs that rose up in the districts where each succeeding wave of immigrants settled were both soldiers in inter-community wars and necessary enforcers of peace.

It was, first of all, a matter of real protection. Given that poverty and crime often go hand in hand, soldiers were necessary to defend the vulnerable. Businesses within the turf had to be guaranteed and disputes had to be settled via some system that ensured at least a minimal amount of justice. This became the role of the strong-arms, who found more than enough promising raw material for their armies in young men hungry for money and advancement in the brave new world.

By the time of the First World War, the Irish and German immigrants of the nineteenth century had by and large settled in. The Germans had gone into business or migrated westward while the Irish had moved into politics and saloon-keeping – though many had also joined the police, where employment was regular and there were great opportunties for earning extra money on the side. But the newer arrivals, among them Italians, Jews and a second wave of poor German immigrants, were yet to make their mark. It was from them that the gangs – and the Mafia – of the modern period emerged, and the word 'protection' took on its contemporary meaning: that of protection against the 'protectors'.

Protection in this sense, of course, had always been a specialty of the Sicilian Mafia, but it was also a natural outgrowth of the local gangs' function, whatever their nationality. It was boosted by two further elements which the immigrants came across largely for the first time: industrialization and the rise of the trade union movement.

LABOUR RACKETEERING

Both before and after the First World War, the fledgling trade unions in New York set about organizing any industry they could find, from clothing workers in sweatshops to stevedores in the docks, using the only weapon they had against the employers: strikes. The employers responded by hiring scab labour and/or sending in goons to intimidate the strikers. Both sides, in other words, found themselves in need of solid muscle: the unions to protect their striking workers and to beat off scabs, and the employers to keep out union organizers and to bring the strikers to

heel. The gangs, in other words, became necessary warriors on both sides in a struggle that not only crossed community borders, but was also city wide. And they used this to their considerable advantage.

What the gangs chose to do was to play both sides against the middle, to make themselves necessary to both employers and trade unions so that in the end they were able, little by little, to take over percentages – often large percentages – of both. The period after the First World War saw a rapid increase in the Mafia's ongoing and serpentine involvement in American trade unions and in a huge range of seemingly legitimate businesses which paid dues to 'the friends'. This system of two-way protection became known to law-enforcement officers as labour racketeering, and had a profound effect on the growth of what came to be the American Cosa Nostra in New York. In opening up the city, it broke down the barriers between immigrant communities and made possible the co-operation of Jews, Germans and Italians in crime.

Jacob 'Little Augie' Orgen and his gang were labour sluggers – hoods hired out as muscle both to the unions and to the corporations during labour disputes. Pictures of Orgen show him with a prominent scar on his left cheek, just below the eye. The mark looks like one of those duelling scars that military officers from a previous generation used to sport. The difference was that Orgen had gained his wound in a street fight.

In the early days, the Little Augie Gang shared the labour rackets in New York with Johnny Spanish and, of course, Nathan 'Kid Twist' Kaplan. Kaplan eliminated Spanish in 1919, the same year that Orgen went to prison, and Orgen in his turn dealt with Kaplan in 1923, subsequently assuming control of New York's union rackets.

Mafia Killings 10

Nathan 'Kid Dropper' Kaplan, New York City, 28 August 1923

In his early years, Nathan 'Kid Dropper' Kaplan used to run a 'drop con'. A wallet of phony money would be planted on the sidewalk. Dropper would 'find' the wallet then, supposedly unable to spare the time to locate the owner and claim the reward, would sell it on to some likely mark eager to collect the reward for himself. Of course, there was no real owner and the sucker would be stuck with a wallet full of worthless bills.

It was a simple scam, strictly kid's stuff, but by the 1920s Kaplan had graduated to bigger things. He was one of the many who cut their teeth in Paul Kelly's Five Points Gang, along with his buddy Johnny Spanish who was reportedly the first to use an automobile in a hold-up. Though today Kaplan is credited with running his own gang by around 1910, newspapers of the time refer to him as belonging to Spanish's gang. Regardless, Kaplan and Spanish would soon become the worst of enemies, supposedly over the affections of a woman.

In 1911 Kaplan and Spanish were sent to prison for seven years. When Kaplan was released in 1918, the Five Points Gang was history, but by this time Kaplan really did have his own mob, Kid Dropper's Rough Riders, and was anxious to flex his muscles.

The newest racket of the day involved the labour unions, and the mobs hired out their men as strong-arms for both the unions and the businesses. 'Labour slugging' – protection from strike-breakers – was big bucks at the time and Kaplan wasn't the only one involved in the racket. His old enemy, Johnny Spanish, and Jacob 'Little Augie' Orgen were also in on the act. Once again, violence erupted in the streets, with Kaplan and Spanish, especially, locking horns. In 1919 Kaplan finally managed to eliminate Spanish, while Orgen was sent to jail on a charge of robbery. For a while, Kid Dropper was

the only game in town.

The party couldn't last forever, and by 1923 Little Augie was out of prison. His gang had not been idle while their boss was incarcerated and consequently the 'Little Augies' had formed quite a power base. Kaplan would need to watch his step.

In early August 1923, Kaplan was arrested on the charge of carrying a concealed weapon. On 28 August, he appeared at the Essex Market Court for arraignment. Before noon that day, Kaplan climbed into a taxi which had arrived to transfer him out. He was surrounded by a police escort who were ready for any trouble. But they weren't prepared for little Louis Cohen as he walked up behind the car and reached up to the back window. Standing on tiptoe, the diminutive Cohen fired blindly into the cab, hitting Kaplan twice and killing him. Cohen was a low-level thug for the Augies and if he'd been promised any kind of protection for pulling the trigger on Kaplan, he was to be tragically disappointed – he got a minimum of 20 years in Sing Sing. Now that Kid Dropper had been dropped, Little Augie Orgen controlled the labour rackets.

The Little Augies contained a number of up-and-comers in the underworld, such as Louis 'Lepke' Buchalter, Jacob 'Gurrah' Shapiro and Jack 'Legs' Diamond. Diamond was to become quite a celebrity in the 1920s, but Buchalter and Shapiro would prove more formidable. Buchalter, a shrewd tactician, would later assume leadership of the National Crime Syndicate's murder wing – Murder Incorporated.

By the mid-1920s, however, the labour rackets were beginning to change. Orgen had his hand in other things, of course, bootlegging included, but found that membership in the unions had begun to drop. What's more, the fear of Bolshevism was leading to increased scrutiny of all labour movements. This extra attention was beginning to shine a spotlight on the gangs, and that was something no one wanted.

Arnold 'The Brain' Rothstein – mob ruler, gambler and brilliant

Average net paid circulation of THE NEWS, Oct., 1928:
Sunday, 1,579,667
Daily, -- 1,268,047

Vol. 10. No. 113   56 Pages

DAILY 📷 NEWS

NEW YORK'S   PICTURE NEWSPAPER

EXTRA EDITION

New York, Monday, November 5, 1928

2 Cents

ARNOLD ROTHSTEIN SHOT

Story on page 3

ONE GAMBLE HE LOST!—Arnold Rothstein, kingpin of the gambling world and one of Broadway's most famous and mysterious figures, was shot and perhaps fatally wounded last night in the Park Central hotel. Although close to death, he refused to name his assailant. Unpaid gambling debt of $280,000 is blamed for his plight. He's shown in his office, where he posed as insurance broker. —*Story on page 3.*

(NEWS photo)

ARRAIGNED. — Vincent T. Rice, 17, yesterday was held without bail on charge of homicide for the slaying of Alice Joost, 15-year-old high school girl of Port Richmond, S. I. He showed no interest in proceedings, his attention centering on his appearance. Here he is in the prisoners' pen as he waited for arraignment. —*Story on page 3.*

DEATH ENDS TRANSCONTINENTAL RECORD FLIGHT.— While Eleanor Wadell waited for him to arrive at Roosevelt field yesterday, the body of her sweetheart, C. B. D. Collyer, with that of Harry Tucker, lay in the wreckage of their celebrated plane, the Yankee Doodle, in Arizona. Photo shows Collyer in cockpit and Tucker leaving cabin.—*Story on page 3.* (By Associated Press)

PETTING KILLER PRIMPS IN COURT   PAGE THREE

Daily News front page, 5 November 1928, reporting the fatal shooting of Arnold Rothstein at the Park Central Hotel, Manhattan

strategist – urged the Orgen gang to use a tactic of infiltration instead. Working inside the unions, he advised, would allow for a more subtle control of labour, give Orgen access to union coffers and still allow for a hefty pay-off from the corporations. The gambit would also have more benefits in the long run than simple labour-bashing, which could only be effective for a while.

The plan appealed to Buchalter and Shapiro, both protégés of Rothstein, but Orgen liked to do things the old-fashioned way by knocking heads together. Clearly the gang could have no future with Orgen in charge and in any case the wily Buchalter had plans of his own.

On 16 October 1927, Orgen was walking down Norfolk Street, accompanied by Jack Diamond as bodyguard. As the two neared Delancey, a car pulled up beside them, a window opened, and Buchwalter and Shapiro filled Orgen with lead. Diamond was also hit but managed to survive; a lucky escape which fuelled his reputation as the man who could not be killed.

Buchwalter and Shapiro now had control of Orgen's operations. Many years later, however, Buchwalter's own number would come up and he would go to the electric chair in 1944.

By the time Prohibition arrived, with its huge new opportunities, the seeds of a powerful alliance had been sown, an alliance that was symbolized by the first meeting of two of the most important men in American crime history: Lucky Luciano and Meyer Lansky.

Mafia Killings 11

Jack 'Legs' Diamond, Albany, New York, 18 December 1931

Jack Moran, more famously known as 'Legs' Diamond, was quite the hotshot in the Jazz Age. A Prohibition celebrity, Diamond was always in the newspapers or on the newsreels – and that's just the way he liked it.

Jack Diamond embarked upon his criminal career in a small New York street gang, but in 1917 was caught up in the military draft and did a short stint for Uncle Sam. Finding army life not to his liking, Diamond went AWOL – a little excursion that sent him to Leavenworth prison in Kansas for several years.

Once he was released, Diamond spent some time with Arnold Rothstein's mob before joining Little Augie Orgen's operation. But Diamond was less than successful in his role as Orgen's bodyguard. He was not able to save Orgen when the mobster's lieutenant, Louis Buchalter, came gunning for him in the fall of 1927. Orgen dropped like a stone that day, but Diamond was merely wounded. It would be just one of many attempts on Diamond's life – five in total – all of which earned Diamond the nickname the 'Clay Pigeon'.

Whether or not Diamond had anything to do with Orgen's demise is unknown. He certainly profited from the gangster's downfall, though, when Buchalter gave him a slice of Orgen's old operations.

Diamond now cut out on his own, running bootlegging and drug rackets. He opened a night spot, the Hotsy Totsy Club, on Broadway between 54th and 55th streets and became known as a flamboyant man about town. His new girlfriend, Kiki Roberts, was a Ziegfeld girl, no less. But Diamond was soon in competition with rival mobster Dutch Schultz and when word reached Dutch that Diamond had hijacked a truckload his illicit alcohol, they became sworn enemies. After yet another failed attempt had been made on Diamond's life, Dutch allegedly moaned, 'Ain't there nobody who can shoot this guy so he don't bounce back?' Apparently, not yet.

After a trip to Europe, ostensibly to recover from the latest attempt on his life but also to scout out alcohol and drug suppliers, Diamond endured several more attempted assassinations while he struggled to renew his operations. But his time was fast running out.

The end came while he was temporarily residing in Albany, in upstate New York. Diamond was in town successfully defending

himself against a kidnapping rap and had flopped at a boarding house. Just before dawn on the morning of 18 December 1931, Diamond, who had been celebrating his acquittal, returned to his room tipsy and exhausted and threw himself onto the bed. A short while later two men broke into the room and as one of them held Diamond down, the other shot him three times in the head.

The killers of Legs Diamond were never identified. Suspicion has fallen on Dutch Schultz, who certainly gets points for trying, but it has also been speculated that Diamond's murderers were members of the Albany police force. The police in Albany had crime in that town all sewn up. Fearing that he would move in on their rackets, the cops may well have shown up that morning in December to take Diamond out of the competition.

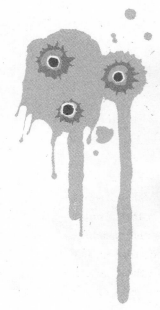

CHAPTER 8

THE SICILIAN AND THE JEW

Meyer Lansky, born Maier Suchowjansky in Grodno, Poland, arrived in New York in about 1916, at the age of 14. He seems to have taken a job as an engineering apprentice. But he was soon part of the rough-and-tumble of the Lower East Side's streets, running with the Jewish gangs and fighting for both territory and survival. It was then, some time around 1917, that he somehow ran across Lucky Luciano.

The second member of what was to become the most important partnership in the history of the Mafia was born Salvatore Lucania, and arrived in New York from Sicily with his parents at the age of ten. Almost immediately in trouble with the police for theft and, soon afterwards, drug-peddling, he seems by the time he met Lansky to have graduated into a torpedo for 'Little Augie' Orgen. He was almost certainly already a 'made man' inside the family of an old fashioned Sicilian Don called Giuseppe Masseria.

The story of how the two men met is variously told: Lansky was defending a prostitute who had been beaten up. He outfaced Luciano in a street rumble; or they met in a prison cell with Bugsy Siegel. However it happened, Luciano later said of their first encounter: 'We had an instant kind of understanding. It may sound crazy, but if anyone wants

Meyer Lansky became one of the most influential members of the Cosa Nostra

to use the expression "blood brothers", then surely Meyer and I were like that.'

Luciano soon co-opted Lansky into Little Augie's gang as a strategist during the early days of Prohibition. But it wasn't long before they outgrew Orgen's gang and were looking for new opportunities, together with a friend of Luciano's called Vito Genovese. They decided to move into booze with a man who Lansky is supposed to have met at a bar mitzvah, a man who was to take the rough street edges off them both: the legendary Arnold Rothstein.

Prohibition made the three of them increasingly powerful. Luciano later claimed that he personally controlled every New York police precinct and had a bagman deliver $20,000 a month to Police Commissioner Grover A. Whelan. He also boasted about the company he moved in: the politicians and stars he met at parties and the gatherings at the Whitney family estate on Long Island. The politicians, even presidential candidates, courted him for campaign funding and help at election time. The beautiful people wooed him for World Series baseball tickets, girls, dope and drink.

Rothstein was one of a kind. If the Mafia has glamour, then it was he who first injected it, dressing in wing-tips, fedoras, top hats, tuxedos and silk suits. If the mob is associated with fancy casinos, then it was he who opened the first of them in New York City, and brought craps in from the streets to the brushed green baize. If it is synonymous with Prohibition and the running of booze, Rothstein was the first big thinker, bringing shipfuls of it from Europe in the very early days. And if it is pleading the Fifth Amendment that comes to mind, then that was all A.R. too: his own lawyer took the right to plead the Fifth all the way to the Supreme Court and saw it turned into law.

Rothstein was not a poor boy off the streets like the other early Jewish gangsters, men like Lansky and 'Dutch' Schultz. His father – religious, generous to charities and politically well-connected – had a dry goods store, a cotton plant and a house on New York's Upper East Side. But from the age of 15 Rothstein seems to have been attracted to the roister

and turbulence of the downtown neighbourhoods: the gambling, the rackets, the booze. He may have meant to go straight, but it was his father in the end who made up his mind for him. When Arnold married a *shiksa* (non-Jew), he was disinherited, declared dead – and that was that.

Arnold made his way first as a gambler, and that remained till his death his greatest love. It was through gambling that he first became a legend in the underworld when, faced with a ringer, a pool shark specially brought in from Philadelphia to teach him a lesson, he beat him, and all those who'd bet on him, in a 40-hour session, by sheer will.

Doors at this point began to open to him and he soon became a protégé of Big Tim Sullivan, the political boss of the Lower East Side. With Sullivan's help he opened a glamorous midtown casino, and became the key to the door for rich New Yorkers wanting a good time.

Making more money from the casino than he could spend on himself – and holding court every night at Lindy's diner on Broadway – Rothstein now entered a new career as an underworld banker, backing any project that took his fancy: drugs, brothels, fixed fights. If Gatsby in F. Scott Fitzgerald's *The Great Gatsby* is based on Cincinnati bootlegger George Remus, then Rothstein appears as Meyer Wolfhiem, the man who in the novel fixed the 1919 World Series – although, in reality, Rothstein had refused to do it. He said it was a fine idea, but would create too much mayhem if the story ever came out.

He did, though, agree to back the first major booze-running operation after the passing of the Volstead Act, though only on condition that he was more than an investor: this time he had to be boss. He bought speedboats to transfer the booze from ships waiting in international waters; he paid off the police every step of the way to New York; and he employed as soldiers and drivers a great many men who were soon to become kingpins of the city's Mafia: Siegel, Luciano, Lansky, Schultz, Louis Lepke, 'Legs' Diamond, Frank Costello (born Francesco Castiglia) and more.

Rothstein did it for the money, but also for the good times – which weren't to last. On Sunday, 24 November 1928, he took a phone call

at Lindy's asking for a meeting about a gambling debt he owed to a Californian. The game had been rigged, in his view and he'd refused to pay. But he went to the meeting at the Park Central Hotel without a gun, of course, since that was against etiquette, and was later found in the lobby, shot in the stomach. He died at the Polyclinic Hospital a few days later, after a visit from his estranged wife.

***

It wasn't just in New York that the Mafia's control of criminal activities was becoming more sophisticated and deeper rooted in everyday life. In Chicago, the influence of one Al Capone was on the rise and rise.

The last day in the life of Alfred Lingle was like something straight out of a Hollywood movie. On 9 July 1930, he left the Sherman House Hotel on Clark and Randolph Streets and headed to catch the 1.30 p.m. train from Illinois Central Station to the Washington Park racetrack. Meeting a police friend along the way, Lingle told him he thought he was being tailed. Despite this, he carried on to the Randolph Street Tunnel, a subway that leads to the train terminal. It was packed at that time of day. Lingle stopped to buy a racing form, while a priest mingled with the crowd. Unfolding the paper, Lingle looked up as two men in a car waved to him, calling out 'Play Hy Schneider in the fourth'. Two other men, one dark and one fair-haired, fell in step beside him.

As Lingle made his way through the tunnel, a cigar clamped in his mouth, the fair-haired man lifted a .38 and shot him in the back of the head. Pandemonium ensued. The killer bolted, discarding some grey gloves he'd been wearing. One witness started in pursuit, but the 'priest' who had been lounging in the station blocked his path.

The killer, unable to navigate his way through the crowd, was forced to double back past Lingle's body, the cigar still clamped in the lifeless mouth. Then, jumping over a guard-rail, he disappeared into the bushes.

This was quite an operation, one that reeked of a mob set-up, with at least five hitmen involved – a number that includes the strategically

placed 'priest' and the two men in the car who fingered Lingle to the killer. The murder was professionally planned and professionally carried out, and when it hit the papers all hell broke loose.

So who was this Lingle guy? As far as the average citizen of Chicago was concerned, he was simply a 'legman' for the *Chicago Tribune*. Legmen sniffed out hot crime stories, then phoned them in to the paper where a journalist could write them up.

Immediately after his murder, however, Lingle became something more than a legman. In death, he was transformed into a martyr, a symbol of the crusading newspaperman who had uncovered a story so sizzling that the mob – probably Capone – had to take him out. The papers even offered a $55,000 reward for Lingle's killers. A little while later, once things had cooled down a bit and some real journalists had done some digging, another side of Alfred Lingle began to emerge – one very different to that of the brave newshound.

Though Lingle only made $65 a week, he had several huge bank accounts and expensive homes, and took luxury vacations in Cuba with his wife and children. He was known to make very large bets on the horses and eat at high-class restaurants and, most damning of all, he boasted one of those diamond-encrusted belt buckles that Al Capone liked to give his buddies. In fact, he was wearing it when he died.

Pennies began to drop everywhere. Lingle was not the upstanding, hard-hitting, crusading newspaperman that everyone thought he was. Lingle was a louse, a mob go-between who was playing several games at once. Tight friends with Police Commissioner William F. Russell, Lingle would give the mobs the heads-up whenever a raid was planned, or even get Russell to call off busts when it was advantageous; he would extort money from the gangs, threatening busts on speakeasies and clubs if he wasn't given a share of the profits; he would sell promotions to ambitious young police officers; and he was rumoured to own a piece of every barrel of liquor sold in Chicago. All of these schemes provided Lingle with a very healthy pay-off. It looks like he really earned that belt buckle from Capone.

So, really, it could have been anyone who murdered Lingle – or at least anyone who could pull off a very professional job. After all the suspects were sifted through, police – and undoubtedly Capone as well – came to the conclusion that the mastermind behind Lingle's murder was undoubtedly ex-Capone man turned North Sider Jack Zuta. The reason probably had to do with the price Lingle was extorting for the reopening of a North Side property, the Sheridan Wave Club – but by the time the bulk of this had been revealed, the press had lionized him as one of their own going down in a blaze of glory and Lingle had received a funeral worthy of a war hero.

'NOBODY'S GONNA ZUTA ME'

As Jack Zuta sat in the Chicago Police Department, he must have been wishing that he could turn back time. Some days earlier, he had authorized the murder of Alfred 'Jake' Lingle, a definite irritant in his side. Now the double-dealing Lingle was dead, but for some reason the press and public had decided to make a hero of him and the whole situation was getting way out of hand. Zuta may have been wondering what all the fuss was about – Lingle was just a $65 a week legman as far as the public was concerned. To those in the know, of course, Lingle was an extortionist and a rat.

But Lingle had also been in pretty thick with the all-powerful Capone, and now here was Zuta, stuck in the middle of Capone territory, enduring a police grilling. What's more, he had no safe way of making it back to his home turf.

Zuta – mob accountant and greaser that he was – always had his own interests at heart, so he begged for a ride back to the North Side from one of the cops who had picked him up in the first place – Lieutenant George Barker. Barker agreed, after a certain amount of wheedling on Zuta's part, and Zuta and three pals who had been picked up with him got into the lieutenant's car, Zuta cowering in the back seat.

Once they were in the car, though, the race was on. As Barker drove, another automobile pulled up beside them and one of the occupants – in true 1930s gangster style – jumped out onto the running board and started blasting away. Bullets hailed through the car windows, and Barker was forced to stop in order to return fire. It was a shoot-out in the street, and several innocent bystanders were wounded or killed. When at last it was all over, the attackers careened off, smoke spewing from an engine that had been specially modified to provide camouflage. Zuta, who had been slightly wounded, hobbled off briskly, losing himself in the crowd. But there was no doubt that Capone was royally upset.

Immediately Zuta made himself scarce and headed for a spa in Wisconsin, where he could relax, at least for a while. He could enjoy the scenery, listen to the music at the local dance palace, and watch the dancers cut a rug, all without the fear of Capone's goons showing up. Or so he thought.

This blissful period of peace was excruciatingly short-lived. At the beginning of August, a witness at the local drugstore later testified that she heard Zuta using the store phone, and demanding that someone had better get up there damn quick to get him out. Later that night, after the desperate call from the drugstore, Zuta put in an appearance at the local dance hall. Enjoying a drink of ginger beer and sitting next to the self-playing piano, Zuta began listening to music. Just as he dropped a coin into the machine and began to enjoy that jazzy number 'Good For You, Bad For Me', the door to the dance palace burst open.

Later, such names as Dean Stanton and Tony Accardo – both Capone men – would be bandied about in connection with the incident. But that night most of the people in the establishment didn't know who the men were. All they saw were the guns – a machine gun, a rifle and a number of pistols. No doubt they also watched as Jack Zuta was shot in the mouth, stood up and tried to run, then was pelleted with more gun blasts and collapsed dead on the floor.

Just as there was fallout after the murder of Jake Lingle, so there was fallout after the death of Jack Zuta. Zuta had kept meticulous records of all his mob transactions – everything from notes about bribes to civic officials to compromising photos of millionaires and politicians. The city was aghast at the corruption that was uncovered when Zuta died.

But Al Capone? He got what he was after, and he wasn't going to let anyone forget it. One time, when he heard a bounty had been placed on his head, Capone reportedly quipped, 'Nobody's gonna Zuta me.'

CHAPTER 9

NEW YORK AND PROHIBITION

Prohibition in New York was a farce. By 1922 there were at least 5,000 speakeasies in the city and by 1927 over 30,000 – twice the number of legal bars, restaurants and nightclubs there'd been before Prohibition began. According to the writer Robert Benchley, there were 38 on East 52nd Street alone – as well as fancy nightspots like the Stork Club, opened in 1927 by an Oklahoman bootlegger called Sherman Billingsley with money provided by Frank Costello. The Stork Club, in which the famous columnist Walter Winchell sat to observe the scene every night of the week, was only ever closed once in its entire history – one more time than MacSorley's saloon in Greenwich Village, which was a favourite watering-hole of police and politicians. MacSorley's didn't even pretend to change its famous beer for the permitted 'near' beer. It just kept on doing what it had always done, right out in the open.

What New York City had too, of course, was 17,000 policemen, backed up by 3,000 state police, 113 supreme court judges and 62 county prosecutors. It also had federal agencies, not to mention Prohibition agents by the hundred. But so corrupted was the whole system of law enforcement by the huge amount of money made by bootleggers and speakeasy operators that successful prosecutions against any of the

big players were extremely rare. In any case, no support came from the Mayor's Office, which was occupied until 1929 by the Tammany Hall fixer and ward-heeler par excellence, Jimmy Walker, and precious little was available from State Governor Al Smith, who thought Prohibition was a nonsense and often said as much.

The result was that everyone got in on the act, an act that was being increasingly controlled by what was to become the New York version of Cosa Nostra. Longshoremen, fishermen, cops, judges and cab drivers all got to dip their beaks: not only into the liquor it provided, but also into the deep lake of money that soon spilled over the banks of all propriety. The 'Big Six' of New York's bootlegging boom of the early 1920s included Lucky Luciano, his childhood friend Meyer Lansky, Busy Siegel, Louis Buchalter, Jacob 'Gurrah' Shapiro and Abner 'Longy' Zwillman. Together, they dominated the illegal liquor trade on the East Coast. But Lucky was the biggest one of all; at the age of 28 it is estimated that he grossed over $12 million a year. Mind you, what with the costs of paying off politicians, law enforcement and other Mafia gang members, he is unlikely to have turned much of a profit. However, he lived the high life, using his money, influence and reputation to rub shoulders with big name politicians, businessmen, movie stars and sports stars.

Mafia Killings 12

Rocco Perri, Hamilton, Ontario, 23 April 1944

Self-styled as Canada's greatest bootlegger, Rocco Perri was brazen about the title. He would hold court in his home in Hamilton, Ontario, granting interviews to newspapers and flaunting his position to the cops. And what's more, he was able to get away with it.

Although Perri admitted to being a bootlegger, this wasn't enough, under Canadian law, to put him behind bars. The cops required some proof; Perri had to be caught in the act to make the charges stick. During the 1920s that just hadn't happened. Though

Rocco did a little time in 1927 for perjury, there wasn't much more than that to bring him in.

It's hardly remembered today, but a form of Prohibition existed throughout the late teens and into the 1920s in a number of Canadian provinces. The problem, at least as far as the temperance organizations were concerned, was that the ban was not nationwide. Certain provinces, such as Quebec, voted Prohibition down pretty sharply, while the provinces that initiated it had a confusing array of laws in place that were full of loopholes. Perri took advantage of these and shipped the good stuff into the United States, but sold it in Canada as well, making double the money.

Perri's partner in crime was his common-law wife, Bessie Starkman, a formidable woman who was one of the few females to hold sway during the heyday of organized crime. Some claim she was the actual force behind the throne of the Perri empire, that Perri rarely acted without her instructions.

This seems unlikely, however, as Bessie was thoroughly disliked by the Perri goons, and lacked the finesse, charisma and people skills to run the Perri organization herself. Bessie was so disliked, in fact, that on 13 August 1930, she was killed, probably by members of the Perri establishment. Perri, heartbroken and almost collapsing at the cemetery, gave Bessie a lavish send-off worthy of any mob boss of the period. And then he went right back to work.

Throughout the 1930s Perri aligned himself with another strong woman, Annie Newman, and branched out into extortion, gambling and other rackets. But it would be the Second World War that finally took the wind out of his sails. Frank Zaneth, an operative in the Royal Canadian Mounted Police who had been hounding Perri for years, was at last able to apprehend the gangster under the War Measures Act, arresting him as a suspected fascist and enemy alien. It was an excuse, of course, a loophole that allowed Zaneth to bring the mobster in. Perri was well acquainted with loopholes.

He didn't get out again until 1943, and like so many other mobsters before him found that things had changed since he'd been in jail – Petawawa this time. For one thing, the Buffalo family – the Magaddinos – had expanded their territory into Perri's old stomping ground of Hamilton, Ontario.

So, on the balmy spring morning of 23 April 1944, Perri went out for a walk, and was never seen again. Some said he had just 'disappeared' himself, and that he survived into the early 1950s. It's more likely, however, that Perri was given cement overshoes and is currently residing at the bottom of Hamilton Bay. The Magaddinos then had nothing left to worry about.

There were some small benefits that arrived in New York, and elsewhere, as a result of Prohibition: they included women being welcomed to speakeasies after having been largely barred from saloons, and the invention of the cocktail, concocted to disguise the often foul taste of the alcohol available. But the minuses far outweighed the pluses and the biggest minus of all was that America, in a sense, lost its innocence. Defying the law under Prohibition became fashionable for students, for flappers, for the respectable middle classes, as an expression of personal freedom, while the mobsters behind the scenes who provided the means to defy the law became, in effect, romantic heroes. In other words, there was collusion not only between crime and politics, but between crime and society itself. Prohibition, as critic Karl Kraus once said about psychoanalysis, turned out to be the disease of which it purported to be the cure. This might have been a lesson that America could have taken into its future international campaigns, against communism and against drugs, but it was never learnt. And the Mafia again proved the beneficiary.

With everyone's attention, up to highest national level, on booze, the Mafia was by and large allowed to get on with its business as usual: spreading its tentacles deeper and deeper into the trade unions

'Legs' Diamond (second from left) and associates

and produce markets, into construction, gambling, slot-machines, prostitution and, for the first time, heroin (something that may have been suggested by Arnold Rothstein). There was little interference from the police; as for the federal agencies, even the customs service, which was highly active in New York State, never managed to uncover more than about five per cent of the illegal booze that poured over the border from Canada and out from the rum-runners' boats off-shore. This is about the same record that the combined federal agencies have today with cocaine and heroin.

The only real threat came from other gangs, from competitors in the free-for-all that was Prohibition. Trucks were regularly hijacked, shipments were stolen and patches invaded. These were people, after all, playing for huge stakes, and there were plenty of young hoods on the lookout for a bigger share of the profits. There just wasn't any discipline and the more mayhem there was, the worse it became for the common

enterprise, since both police and politicians were duty bound to sit up and take some notice at that point.

It was because of this that Lansky and Luciano, together with their friend Vito Genovese, began to discuss a grand strategy aimed at bringing the warring gangs of New York together under a unified command. But first they had to create a power base of their own, one they could bring to the negotiating table. Lansky probably had enough clout by now as a behind-the-scenes manipulator to bring the Jewish gangs onside. But Luciano had to secure the Sicilians. More perhaps than any other one man, Lucky Luciano created the modern face of the Mafia: making vast profits from drugs, operating across borders, invisible, bolstered by international agreements and alliances and ruled by representative councils.

However, at this point there remained one major obstacle to Luciano's assumption of power. The most important criminal power brokers in New York, even during Prohibition, were two old-style Mafia bosses, and he would need to break with the old ways if he was to achieve absolute power and control.

THE CASTELLAMMARESE WAR

The most powerful Sicilian bosses in New York during the 1920s were two old-style Mafia dons, Giuseppe Masseria and Salvatore Maranzano, who had been sent by Don Vito Ferro from his base in Castellammare del Golfo in Sicily in a bid to take control of operations in the United States. As the two vied for supremacy of the Italian-American Mafia, particularly in its exploitation of Prohibition, the bloodshed escalated. In the last years of the Roaring Twenties, New York became embroiled in what was to become one of the most significant battles within Mafia history – the Castellammarese War. The battle was a big one, and it changed everything.

Of the two warring rivals, Masseria had the more lofty ambitions. He wanted all the gangs of New York under his rule as *capo di tutti capi*. His

Game over: gunned down in a Coney Island restaurant, Joe Masseria clutches the ace of spades – the death card

quest for the brass ring would plunge the city into a bloody battle that would never be forgotten and would ultimately cost him his life.

As a lieutenant in the Morello mob, Masseria challenged and defeated rival mobster Salvatore D'Aquila in the early 1920s. Although D'Aquila had tried to deal with Masseria in 1922, sending gunman Umberto Valenti to do the job, Masseria had miraculously survived the attempt made against his life. He had literally dodged Valenti's bullets, and the only casualty in the attack was his fedora hat. After this failed assassination, Masseria was considered bullet-proof.

Masseria then took control of Morello's old gang, with former boss Morello working under him, and leveraged his position. In 1928 D'Aquila was murdered, and Masseria was running a healthy chunk of New York's underworld. Others may have referred to him simply as 'the man who could dodge bullets', but Masseria was still aiming higher.

In his self-proclaimed role as the boss of all bosses, Masseria put the muscle on the other mobs. But Salvatore Maranzano of the

Castellammarese faction refused to play the game. He had plans of his own and Masseria, with his demands for gold, was just getting in the way.

The hits went rapidly back and forth between the two sides until finally the Masseria faction began to crack. Masseria's men could see the writing on the wall and one by one they jumped ship. One particular man, who as a Masseria soldier, some say even *consigliere*, had often been at the centre of this rivalry, was Lucky Luciano. For all his status – and perhaps because of it – Maranzano decided to teach Luciano a lesson the old Sicilian way and induce him to change his allegiance. Luciano was picked up, strung up by his thumbs from the ceiling and tortured. Maranzano slashed him across the face with a knife, inflicting a wound that needed 55 stitches and left one side of his face permanently drooping. He was 'lucky' to have lived. He was finally released, but by then Maranzano had decided on a deal: the murder of Masseria in return for the number two spot in the Maranzano family gang. Masseria was subsequently gunned down one afternoon at a Coney Island restaurant.

Mafia Killings 13

Giuseppe 'Joe the Boss' Masseria, New York, 15 April 1931

It is said to have been Masseria underling Lucky Luciano who finally took the bull by the horns and decided it was time to put his boss out of his misery. Throwing his lot in with Maranzano, Luciano agreed to eliminate Masseria in return for control of his operations and a seat at the big table in Maranzano's gang. But according to several sources, the conflict between Masseria and Maranzano was not popular with the other Mafia gangs, who felt it was interfering in their businesses. The *New York Times* and *New York Herald Tribune* always claimed that Luciano was not involved, but there would have been no shortage of others in the queue for the job.

The story goes that on 15 April 1931, Luciano met Masseria for lunch at the Nuova Villa Tammaro restaurant in Coney Island. After lunch, the two broke open a deck of cards and started to play. Some time during the course of the afternoon Luciano excused himself and got up to go to the bathroom. While he was gone, and after the mysterious disappearance of his three bodyguards, several men stepped through the doorway and shot Masseria as he shuffled the deck. No one was convicted of the crime.

With the death of Masseria, Luciano hoped that a new age would be ushered in by Maranzano, and that the old, traditional ways of the Mafia would be left behind. He was wrong.

By the summer of 1931 the Castellammarese War was over and the body of Joe 'The Boss' Masseria was cooling in a morgue somewhere. Salvatore Maranzano took up his position as the new boss – the *capo di tutti capi* of New York City.

But Luciano was not at all happy. He had risked much to join Maranzano – he'd betrayed his old boss and backed an unknown. His hope was that Maranzano's victory would end a conflict that had lasted too long, and that Maranzano, unlike Masseria before him, would modernize the Mafia and its businesses.

At the time, the mobs were overrun with what were known as 'Moustache Petes' – old-world Mafiosi who clung to dated and sometimes meaningless traditions and who often sported bushy black moustaches which had been popular in turn of the century Sicily. Hard-line Petes wouldn't do business with non-Italians and would never get involved in drugs, for example. Some wouldn't associate with non-Sicilians, and even then preferred only those from their own villages.

The Young Turks, as Luciano's generation was called, readily broke bread with other gangs and incorporated different ethnic groups into their mobs. The Broadway Mob, to which Luciano belonged, included names such as Frank Costello and Joe Adonis, but also Bugsy Siegel and

Meyer Lansky – gangsters of Russian-Jewish extraction. Old-fashioned sectarian notions only hindered the gangs' ability to make money.

Luciano, then, expected a lot from Maranzano. He had also been led to believe that the days of the overriding Mafia boss had died with Masseria. But Maranzano proclaimed himself the *capo di tutti capi* of the New York Sicilian families. Luciano, Lansky and Genovese had other ideas. A few months later, in 1931, four of their men, posing as internal revenue investigators, arrived at Maranzano's Park Avenue headquarters, demanding to see both the boss and the books. Maranzano was stabbed and shot to death in his inner office.

Mafia Killings 14

Salvatore Maranzano, New York City, 10 September 1931

Following the death of his rival Masseria, Salvatore Maranzano envisioned himself as the ruler of a new Roman Empire – a latterday Caesar. The press had dubbed him 'Little Caesar', like Edward G. Robinson in the 1931 movie of the same name.

Maranzano inaugurated his new world order at a banquet held in late April 1931. During the celebration he rewarded his supporters, such as Luciano, by dividing New York up between them. But he also took the opportunity to assert his authority; like Masseria before him, Maranzano declared himself *capo di tutti capi*. This was not what Luciano had signed up for.

On 10 September 1931, Luciano sent over some hired guns to Maranzano's offices at the Helmsley Building on Park Avenue. These were non-Mafiosi, men that Maranzano did not recognize – such was the price of his closed mindedness. Posing as Internal Revenue agents, the gunmen had no trouble entering the building and were ushered in to see the boss. Once inside, the killers quietly closed the door behind them and put an end to Little Caesar's reign.

THE NEW YORK COMMISSION

In victory, Luciano and Lansky adopted Maranzano's idea of bringing order and central control to what became known as 'the five New York families'. But instead of making anyone the *capo di tutti capi*, they established a board of directors, the New York Commission (later known as the National Crime Syndicate) and an enforcement arm, which came to be called Murder Incorporated – in essence heralding the arrival of organized crime. In this, Luciano was the first among equals. It was he, above all, who took the now unified Mafia, both Jewish and Italian, into a whole new era. An associate later said of Luciano and Lansky: 'If they had been President and Vice-President of the United States, they would have run the place far better than the idiot politicians.'

By this time, they had almost certainly learned a lot from the foreign banks and trading houses which had helped to finance shipments of booze that had fed Prohibition America. They may also have learned from Joseph Kennedy, father of President John Kennedy, how he concealed his occasional forays into rum-running behind a protective shell of companies. But between them, Lansky – whose first love remained the casinos he'd seen as a young man with his boss Arnold Rothstein – and Luciano, who after the war became the American Mafia's representative in Europe, did more to expand the New York mobs' reach and influence across the United States and beyond than anyone else. It was Luciano who first shifted the Mafia into drugs. And it was Lansky, the grand strategist, who moved the Mafia's money and power into Las Vegas, funding movies and setting up legitimate businesses all across the country. Lansky said in the 1970s (and perhaps only he really knew): 'We're bigger than US Steel.'

CHAPTER 10

THE NATIONAL CRIME SYNDICATE

The Mafia became much more organized following the setting up of the National Crime Syndicate. Its presence was not confined to New York and Chicago. There were at least 20 families involved in illicit Mafia-related activities in cities across America, including Buffalo, Detroit, Philadelphia, Boston, Kansas City and, of course, Los Angeles. While New York was divided up between the notorious 'five families', other cities tended to be dominated by a single one.

The Purple Gang was the most notorious mob in Detroit during the Roaring Twenties. Chicago had the South Siders and the North Siders, as well as various bottom-feeders. New York was lousy with mobs, gangs who either learned to cooperate with each other or were demolished. In Detroit it was the Purple Gang, and they had the city all sewn up.

Loosely controlled by four brothers – Abe, Joseph, Raymond and Isadore Bernstein – the gang had its fingers in all the money-making operations of the day: extortion, bootlegging, prostitution, narcotics, gambling, theft, hijacking, murder and, of course, abduction. They'd even been named as suspects in the kidnapping and murder of the baby son of aviation hero Charles Lindbergh. But so had half the underworld of the time.

As the Purple Gang grew in power, they began to get sloppy. But if an entire city has instant amnesia caused by the threat of a tommy gun, it's hard for the cops to make a case stick and with just about every public official on their payroll the Purples decided they could afford to let things slide a bit. After all, they thought, they were practically invincible. They were wrong.

The situation began to fall apart for the gang when Joseph Lebowitz, Isadore 'Izzy the Rat' Sutker and Herman 'Hymie' Paul came over from Chicago to escape the ire of Al Capone. Once in the city, the three newcomers joined up with a subgroup of the Purples called The Little Jewish Navy. They now dubbed themselves the Third Avenue Terrors and after a while started to flex their muscles, disregarding territorial divisions and hijacking whisky shipments. The Terrors were trying to go into business for themselves.

In 1931 the Bernstein brothers decided it was time to put the Terrors in their place – permanently. On 31 September they called them to a meeting at the Collingwood Manor apartments, supposedly to talk business. Everything seemed on the up and up. After all, the Terrors' buddy, Sol Levine, was going to be there. What could possibly go wrong?

The Terrors would soon find out. After pleasantries had been exchanged and everyone was settled, the Purple Gang representatives – Harry Keywell, Irving Milberg and Harry Fleisher – drew their guns and opened fire on the three from Chicago. Their guns still smoking, the Purples exited the apartment and took off in a getaway car idling in the street outside. And as far as the Purples were concerned, that was that.

Except that by now Detroit had had enough and the authorities were under pressure to lower the boom. Three of the killers, Bernstein, Keywell and Milberg, were soon rounded up – although Fleisher was never caught. During the trial, Sol Levine – terrified of the Purples, but even more so of the police, apparently – put the finger on the gang and the defendants were sentenced to life in Marquette prison. With three key members gone, the Purple Gang withered away and Detroit heaved a huge sigh of relief.

Across on the east coast, in Boston, Charles Solomon – colourfully known as 'King' Solomon – was the pre-eminent bootlegger during the 1920s. Of course, he had other interests as well – narcotics, gambling, and pandering (procurement). But for Solomon, the demon rum was king, and he used his fleet of ships to bring in the hard liquor from Central America and Canada. Solomon sold prime stuff then, not the homemade rotgut that some bootleggers would foist on their hapless customers. And, for 'King' Solomon, court was his nightclub, the Cocoanut Grove on Piedmont Street, one of the most popular spots in the city.

Solomon owned the Grove from 1927 until his death in 1933, and it was a classy joint. Decorated in a South Sea island theme, the Grove featured swaying palm trees and a roof that would slide back in order to enhance the atmosphere. Many's the time the King could be found there, surrounded by celebrities and taking care of mob business. After leaving the Grove, Solomon would do the rounds of Boston's other hot spots.

Mafia Killings 15

James 'Buddy' McLean, Boston, 31 October 1965

It was known as the Irish Gang War – a mob battle that started in Boston, Massachusetts in 1961 and didn't end until 1967, when one of the mobs was completely wiped out and an estimated 60 hoods had been killed.

James 'Buddy' McLean was the boss of the Winter Hill Gang – one of the most infamous and successful gangs in the United States. McLean was a charismatic and respected leader, one who wasn't afraid to roll up his sleeves and get his hands dirty with the rest of his men. Though he had an angelic face, with 'the map of Ireland' all over it as they say, McLean was a scrapper and had won the respect of Boston's Italian mob, headed by Raymond Patriarca.

The Winter Hill Gang was called an Irish mob, but the gang included other ethnicities. An Italian-American member was Alex Petricone. As an example of art imitating life, Petricone later became an actor. Look for him in *The Godfather, Part I*, acting under the name of Alex Rocco and playing the Bugsy Siegel-inspired character Moe Greene.

On Labour Day 1961, friends of McLean were having a party with some of the McLaughlin Brothers, Boston's other notorious 'Irish' gang. The gathering was a drunken bash, and during the bleary-eyed festivities, George McLaughlin made a pass at Petricone's girlfriend. A beating ensued for McLaughlin, and he was dumped onto the lawn of the nearest hospital, more dead than alive.

George McLaughlin did survive, but his brother Bernie was furious. He went to McLean, demanding restitution. He wanted George's attackers rubbed out, and he wanted that pronto; but he needed McLean's assistance and go-ahead. McLean tried to calm the situation; besides – he pointed out – George got what was coming to him, he should just walk it off.

This remark didn't sit too well with Bernie McLaughlin and after several attempts to get McLean to change his mind, he took action. A few nights later, while McLean and his wife were sitting in their living room, Mrs McLean saw some movement outside, around the family car. McLean went out, brandishing a gun, and chased two men off his property. He also found an explosive device attached to the bottom of his vehicle.

That was too much for McLean and on 31 October 1961, aided by Petricone, he took Bernie McLaughlin out as the mobster left the Morning Glory Bar in Charlestown. McLean was arrested and there were dozens of witnesses, but astoundingly none of them had any recollection of the event and McLean did no time for the killing. All that could be pinned on him was illegal possession of a weapon, for which McLean got two years.

The first volleys had been fired in Boston's Irish Gang War. Over the next few years, casualties were high, especially for the McLaughlin gang. The McLaughlins were all but collapsing and it was clear that their days as a significant mob force were coming to an end.

Allies of the gang took one last potshot, however, and on 3 1 October 1965, shortly after his release from prison, James 'Buddy' McLean was shot dead as he left the Tap Royal bar on Broadway.

The war would rage on for several more years, but despite this, the McLaughlins were pretty well dried up. And McLean's old gang? Although McLean was now dead, the Winter Hill Gang was just getting started.

As a major power in Massachusetts, Solomon was a Boston representative at the Atlantic City conference that took place in 1929. The conference was an early mob summit and anyone who was anyone in gangland was there. The get-together was hardly clandestine, and throughout the festivities the press were on hand to snap shots of Enoch 'Nucky' Johnson, Meyer Lansky, Dutch Schultz and Charlie Luciano. While there was plenty of entertainment at the conference, it was not all play and no work. The meeting represented the first large step toward the real organization of crime and paved the way for the creation of the National Crime Syndicate.

Unfortunately, the spirit of co-operation, peace and brotherly love which the conference tried to engender did not translate itself to Boston. During the late 1920s and early 1930s, several rival groups contended for supremacy in the city. Making a lot of noise was Philip Buccola, boss of what would later become Boston's powerful Patriarca family. Buccola (a gangster who lived to be 101) had his enforcers and wise-guys making the rounds, wiping out the competition as they went along. As the Buccola goons made their way to the Cocoanut Grove and Solomon's seat of power, the King's days as top dog were put in jeopardy.

The hit came in the early morning of 28 January 1933, after Solomon had left the Grove and headed to the Cotton Club to dance away the night. In attendance were a couple of chorus girls whom Solomon was entertaining for the evening. At some time during the celebrations, Solomon excused himself and headed to the men's room. So did two broken-nose types and during a scuffle which could be heard on the dance floor, Solomon received several slugs in the chest and neck. That was the end of Charles Solomon.

No one registered any astonishment when Buccola advanced his position in the city and became the rising star in Boston. The king was dead, long live the king.

Since then the city has had a long history of mob activity, particularly in the Irish-American neighbourhoods of Somerville, Charlestown, South Boston and Roxbury. There have been numerous gang wars over the years with power changing hands regularly. But the early 1960s witnessed the arrival of the Winter Hill Gang, which made much of its money through the fixing of horse races. With soaring profits on offer, a new war for dominance began between the Winter Hills from Somerville and the Charlestown Mob. The violence escalated over the years and was not over until at least 1967, by which time the Irish Mob War, as it became known, ended with the eradication of the Charlestown Mob.

Mafia Killings 16

Donald Killeen, Boston, 13 May 1972

This is the story of Donald Killeen and of the notorious double-dealing James 'Whitey' Bulger, who offered up Killeen as payment in a deal with the devil (or the Winter Hill Gang, in this case). This act of treachery completed, Bulger then embarked upon a bloody campaign that eventually won him complete control of Boston's underworld.

It could be said that it all began when Kenneth Killeen, Donald's younger brother, bit off the nose of Mickey Dwyer of the Mullen

gang. As Dwyer was rushed to emergency, Killeen boss Donald picked up the nose, wrapped it in a napkin and sent it to the hospital for reattachment to the unfortunate Dwyer. But the nose episode was just an excuse for the start of yet another gang war in Boston.

In the 1960s and early 1970s, the Killeens owned the southern part of Boston, termed Southie. The Mullens, however, had other ideas; there were plenty of them and it was just a matter of time before the two gangs came to blows. When the shooting began, the city of Boston was knee deep in dead hoods.

Although the Killeens were the dominant gang, the Mullens were determined, and before long the Killeens found themselves backed into a corner. That's when Whitey Bulger, Donald Killeen's bodyguard, decided he needed to rethink his allegiance.

Going to Winter Hill leader Howie Winter, Bulger made it clear that he could put an end to the war – one that was costing numerous lives, not to mention money – by taking out his own boss, Donald Killeen. If he could finish off Donald, he reasoned, then the rest of the Killeens would topple like dominoes. All Bulger wanted in return was a position in Howie's mob. Winter could then absorb the remnants of the Killeens and the Mullens into his own gang. This way, everybody would win. Everybody except Donald, of course.

On 13 May 1972, Donald Killeen was at home, celebrating the fourth birthday of his young son. He went outside to fetch a toy train set that he'd hidden in the trunk of his car, but got fifteen bullets in the face instead. It's said that it was Whitey Bulger who pulled the trigger that day and then sped off in a waiting car.

With Donald Killeen gone, Howie Winter sued for peace with the Mullens and successfully took control of Boston's criminal world – but by 1979 Whitey Bulger had wrested leadership of the Winter Hill Gang from him, and the city had another new leader.

Mafia Killings 17

Richard J. Castucci, Revere, Massachusetts, 29 December 1976

Sam Giancana is reputed to have said that the mob and the CIA were basically two sides of the same coin. Whether or not that's true, there have undoubtedly been CIA agents – and FBI agents for that matter – who were more interested in pursuing their own agendas than upholding the law. In fact, some agents have gone so far as to actively assist the mob.

Take Agent John 'Zip' Connolly of the FBI, who accepted bribes, falsified records and became involved in racketeering – and that's just for starters. Connolly was in league with Boston mobsters James 'Whitey' Bulger and his buddy, Stephen 'The Rifleman' Flemmi, and consistently tipped them off on relevant FBI proceedings. It could almost be said that Connolly was a mole for Bulger.

That's where Richard Castucci enters the picture. He was no angel; a member of the Patriarca family, he owned several notorious clubs and ran high stakes gambling games. But for all that, Castucci, a family man, was nowhere near as bad as Whitey Bulger or Stephen Flemmi. Some time around 1970 Castucci got himself into financial trouble, owing large sums to loan sharks and to the Patriarcas. So, as a solution to his financial woes, Castucci became an informer to the FBI in exchange for a pay-off.

Castucci got hold of some hot information regarding Bulger's mob, the Winter Hill Gang; he had discovered where two wanted members of that gang, Joseph McDonald and James Sims, were hiding out. He passed his knowledge on to the FBI, as was part of his agreement. Connolly, of course, found out about the tip-off and forwarded the information to Bulger.

Predictably, the end for Castucci was unpleasant. On 29 December 1976, Bulger, Flemmi and another Winter Hill member – John Martorano – lured him to an apartment in Somerville, Massachusetts and put a bullet in his head. They then rolled the

body into a sleeping bag and hid it in the trunk of Castucci's Cadillac Sedan de Ville. When he was finally found in the aftermath of a snowstorm, his body had frozen.

The FBI immediately suspected Bulger and Flemmi of the murder and initiated an investigation, but Connolly immediately began to deflect the investigation away from his Winter Hill pals and toward the Patriarca family. Because of this cover-up, the FBI did not pursue Whitey Bulger for the murder of Richard Castucci.

The truth, however, was clamouring to be heard. When Stephen Flemmi was at last arrested in 1995 he decided that his best defence was to do a little deflecting of his own. Flemmi put the finger on Connolly and revealed the whole dirty business about Bulger and Connolly's arrangement.

Today, Bulger, Flemmi and Connolly are all behind bars. As a side-note, in 2009, the family of Richard Castucci received a cash settlement of over six million dollars from the Federal Government because of Agent John Connolly's failure to do his duty.

THE MASSACRE OF KANSAS CITY

Later that year came a massacre in Kansas City. Though it is now largely forgotten, at the time it caused quite a ruckus. When it was all over, and four police officers plus a prisoner they were transporting lay dead, mob boss John Lazia really should have known that his time was up too.

Lazia, together with prominent politician Tom Pendergast, ruled Kansas City in the early 1930s. Pendergast took care of the official aspect, greasing wheels and making sure that the right people (and that meant Pendergast people) held the right jobs. Lazia and his underboss Charles Carrollo, meanwhile, oversaw the more colourful angles. Pendergast, of course, got his fair share from all the operations.

It's said that Kansas was the best-run corrupt city in the country, due in no small way to Lazia. As part of his understanding with Pendergast, Lazia kept a lid on violent crime, while Pendergast turned a blind eye

The fatal shooting of Frank Nash and his police escort in front of Union Railway Station, Kansas City, 1933

to the less 'serious' (and more profitable) crimes of bootlegging and gambling. From his desk at the police station (no less), Lazia kept tabs on all illegal activity in Kansas City: no crook could enter the city without his say so, and no crime could be committed without his OK – or else. For a while, the system worked exceedingly well.

This state of affairs changed in early 1933, however, when the Lazia regime sustained several dents to its prestige. That year saw the kidnapping of an important heiress (not a Lazia-approved crime), plus the rise of several local hoods who had begun to muscle their way into the mobster's territory.

But things really span out of control in the city in June that same year. Bank robber Frank Nash was going to be transferred to Leavenworth prison after years on the run. Several of Nash's friends decided they wanted to spring the convict and planned to hijack the convoy as it arrived at the city's Union Station.

The group approached Lazia for approval, and the mobster gave them the thumbs up. He also supplied them, it's said, with additional gunmen – apparently Adam Richetti and 'Pretty Boy' Floyd among them.

Pretty Boy Floyd – there's a name from criminal legend! It's now thought that Richetti and Floyd did not actually take part in this particular adventure, but it makes for a great story.

What happened next was absolute chaos. By the end of the hijacking four law inforcement officers were dead, and so was Nash. But maybe Nash had been the target all along.

After the massacre, Kansas City was agog and Pendergast found it expeditious to distance himself from Lazia. When the mob boss was indicted on tax evasion charges in 1934, Pendergast was nowhere to be found and Lazia was sentenced to a year in jail. What's more, Pendergast now began to put his support behind another gang. The writing was on the wall for Lazia.

On 10 July 1934, Lazia was shot down while returning to his lavish apartment after a night on the town with his wife and his bodyguard. The coroner later reported that the gangster had been killed by one of the guns that had been used in the massacre – an inside job. It was no shock to anybody, then, when Charles Carrollo, Lazia's second in command, became the next big thing in Kansas City.

The Kansas City Massacre was as much of a disaster for the mobs as it was for the city, the police department and the civic authorities, and in the weeks and months afterwards the underworld experienced a lot of heat. The most logical solution to this problem, as far as the mobs were concerned, was to remove the focal point of all this attention.

There are legendary figures of the Roaring Twenties and Dirty Thirties, gangsters who spring to mind in the context of bold bank robberies, bullet-riddled cars and smoking machine guns. Pretty Boy Floyd, Bonnie and Clyde, Machine Gun Kelly – they personify the period. But there's one of this crowd, one of the bloody and lawless, who today is apparently remembered only by a few – Vernon Clate Miller. Back in the day, though, Miller was a force to be reckoned with and for some, including important members of the National Crime Syndicate, Miller, as the only gunman identified from the Kansas City Massacre, was in part to blame for a crackdown on organized crime in the area.

So, who was Vernon Miller? You wouldn't know it from the way he died – he'd been trussed up and dumped on a dirt road – but at one time he was a highly respected individual. A member of the National Guard who had fought Mexican rebel Pancho Villa, Miller also did his bit 'over there' and came back as a decorated war hero, lionized for his bravery. Once Stateside again, Miller took up the position of sheriff in his home of Huron, South Dakota, and was known to be tough but honest.

And then things suddenly veered off in an entirely different direction. Maybe it was shell shock from the Great War, or maybe Miller was suffering from an advanced case of syphilis as one source indicates (though there is no further verification on that, so it may just be embellishment). Either one of these conditions could have caused Miller's mind to rapidly deteriorate.

In any case, one fine day in August 1922, Miller embezzled $6,000 from the treasury of Beadle County in North Dakota, and skipped town. After that, it was all downhill for Vernon Clate Miller. To start the criminal ball rolling, Miller dabbled in bootlegging like everybody else at that time; and then he got into gambling, making friends with Louis Buchalter. But as with the other desperados – Floyd, the Barkers, Parker and Barrow – it was bank robbery that really gave Miller a sense of purpose. And as his criminal career progressed, he became more and more unpredictable; something was certainly amiss in the mind of Vernon Miller.

Between 1927 and early 1933, Miller took part in no fewer than eight bank robberies. He and his gang were responsible for at least 27 gunshot deaths or injuries – a number of them members of Miller's own mob, of course. In the Kansas City Massacre alone, when Miller's gang tried to free bank robber Frank Nash from law enforcement officers, five people were killed. By now, Miller had become one of the FBI's most wanted, and the cross-country manhunt was on.

But the Feds were not the only ones after Miller. And that's how Vernon Clate Miller, legendary gangster and public enemy, ended up dead on a dirt road on 29 November 1933. When an autopsy was

performed on the pulpy residue, it became evident that Miller had been tortured, then strangled – a true gangland-style slaying. No doubt he would have much preferred to go out in a blaze of bullets, Thirties style.

Mafia Killings 18

Charles Binaggio, Kansas City, 5 April 1950

Charles Binaggio was a mobster and political fixer in Kansas City. Originally attached to the corrupt but effective James Pendergast's political machine, Binaggio broke out on his own in the mid-1940s when the Pendergast ship began to sink.

Backing his own man for governor – Forrest Smith – Binaggio had plans for Missouri. First, he wanted to get control of the police forces of Kansas City and St Louis – just a few men in highly placed positions. Once he had the cops in his pocket, Binaggio intended to declare the state wide open to gambling. Putting the word around, Binaggio took up subscriptions – mob money – to get his man into position and in 1948 Forrest Smith became Governor of Missouri. Now everything was in place – pretty soon there'd be plenty of loot to go around.

There would have been, except it now seemed that suddenly Forrest Smith was developing a conscience. It couldn't have come at a worse time. Some sources indicate that Smith began to stall Binaggio regarding the gambling, telling him that he would have to wait six months for the new administration to get its sea legs. Other sources say that Smith went even further, and actually blocked Binaggio's Police Board choices. Whatever the tactic, the gambling plans had to be put on the shelf. There were now a lot of very unhappy gamblers demanding that somebody pay their money back. Binaggio was about to find out what the price would be.

Binaggio spent the afternoon of 5 April 1950 in his garden, pottering around his roses. After dinner he said farewell to his wife

and daughter and headed to the Last Chance tavern on Southwest Boulevard, an establishment he partly owned. According to Binaggio's bodyguard, Nick Penna, Binaggio received a call about 8 p.m. and then excused himself. Taking his second-in-command, Charles 'Mad Dog' Gargotta, with him, Binaggio told Penna that he'd only be gone for about 20 minutes. Penna was never to see Binaggio alive again.

The next morning the bodies of Binaggio and Gargotta were found sprawled in one of the rooms of the Democratic Club on Truman Road. An open door and the sound of running water had alerted a cabbie to the scene, and the police were called in.

So, who shot Binaggio? The theory is that the killing was likely an outside job – some contract killer brought in from New York or Chicago. The hit certainly looked professional – four clean shots fired point blank at Binaggio's head. Gargotta had put up more of a fight apparently and had made a run for the door. But it was futile. A single shot had stopped Gargotta in his tracks and then the murderer had moved in for the kill. These killings marked the end of the political career of Charles Binaggio.

THE AMERICAN BOYS

With plenty of criminal Mafia action in all the major cities across the United States, now more organized since the birth of the National Crime Commission, there was lots of work to be had throughout the country. It was not unusual for gang members from one city to operate in another, fulfilling one contract or another and then hightailing it back home.

Gus Winkler was a safe-cracker, torpedo and freelance hood during the days of Prohibition. The highlight of Winkler's criminal career was undoubtedly becoming a pal of 'Scarface' Capone. Though Gus was considered a gutless wonder, he'd somehow made it into Capone's good books and was used by the mob boss for special cases, including the

assassination of Frankie Yale and that hit of all hits, the St Valentine's Day Massacre.

Starting out in the St Louis gang Egan's Rats, Winkler hooked up with Fred 'Killer' Burke and Bob Carey. When things fell apart for the Rats in 1924, Winkler ended up in Chicago, by way of Detroit. It was some time during this period that he lost an eye during a mail robbery. A vain man, Winkler hoped to polish his image and took to wearing glasses in order to camouflage the disfigurement.

Mafia Killings 19

William 'Dinty' Colbeck, St Louis, 17 February 1943

Colbeck was a member of St Louis's notorious Egan's Rats during the Roaring Twenties. Fiercely loyal to boss William Egan, Colbeck had done a stint in the Great War. After serving with the 89th Infantry Division, he took the skills he'd learned in battle and put them to use for the gang. Unfortunately, it was Colbeck and his itchy trigger finger that engulfed St Louis in a gang war that left the city reeling.

In the early 1920s the city was divided between several gangs – Egan's Rats, the Cuckoos, and the Hogan Gang being the main mobs. The Rats were the dominant gang and lorded it over the others in their bootlegging and bank robbery enterprises. In 1921, though, a couple of Hogan men decided to put an end to all that and took out Rat leader William Egan. Colbeck was shortly on the scene and, reputedly hearing Egan's last words, could name his killers. Now, this may have been true, or it may have been a convenient way for Colbeck to assume the mantle of leadership. In any case Colbeck was determined – Egan's death meant war.

Shortly after the slaying, St Louis was indeed a war zone, and members of both mobs shot it out on the streets, running down anyone unlucky enough to get in their way. Costs were mounting too, and Colbeck soon found that the Rats' bootlegging funds were

drying up. The gang took to bank robbing and postal hold-ups to rustle up some funds, but it was clear that Colbeck was not the boss Egan had been, not by a long shot. Unable to command anywhere near the loyalty that the old boss had, Colbeck found himself increasingly isolated, and paranoia set in. As a pastime, Colbeck took to picking off his own men.

When Rat member Ray Renard was arrested for robbery, then, he figured he had nothing to lose and likely everything to gain by spilling the beans. Based on Renard's statements, Colbeck and the core of the gang were sentenced to 25 years.

Colbeck lingered in prison until 1940, when at last he was paroled and out on the streets again. With the sweet smell of freedom in his nostrils once more, Colbeck got to thinking that maybe he could pick up where he'd left off; he could put the old gang back together and rule St Louis once more.

But like so many others before him, Colbeck didn't realize that everything had changed since 1924. The mobs didn't operate the same way, that was for sure, and none of the current hoods felt like making room for Dinty Colbeck.

Really, Colbeck should have known what was coming next. On the night of 17 February 1943, he was gunned down while driving his car on Destrehan Street. With the demise of Colbeck and with the other Rats either dead, in prison or moved on, St Louis had seen the last of Egan's Rats.

Winkler, Burke and Carey came to the attention of Al Capone, who referred to them as 'The American Boys'. But the gang were enterprising and pulled numerous heists on their own, holding up armoured cars and robbing banks in New Jersey, Wisconsin, Los Angeles and Ohio. Revenue from these robberies would allow Winkler to act as something of a gangland broker for criminal enterprises and to open an underworld safe-house for mobsters on the run.

Winkler was described as self-obsessed and talkative, and it was undoubtedly this chatty quality that would later get him into trouble. The end came for him on 9 October 1933, when he was shot down on Roscoe Street. Like so many others, Winkler's killers were never identified, and could have been just about anyone in the syndicate. Winkler, trusted by no one, had made it clear on more than one occasion that he was out for himself no matter what. Though he'd apparently enjoyed a certain amount of protection from Capone, once Scarface was sent up the river, the new boss of the Chicago Outfit, Frank Nitti, had no use for Winkler.

Suspicion about the killing has also fallen on Roger Touhy and his Chicago gang. In December 1932, Winkler had participated with the Touhy mob in a mail robbery worth $250,000. Winkler had worried that the gang was after him because he hadn't divided the loot to their liking.

Mafia Killings 20

Roger Touhy, Chicago, 16 December 1959

Roger Touhy's story sounds like a Hollywood movie; a rags-to-riches-to-rags rollercoaster ride that featured it all – bootlegging, conmen and Al Capone. But the story also includes the tormented Touhy in a legendary case of injustice that still shocks to this day.

Touhy started out an honest enough guy. After serving in the navy during the First World War, he returned stateside again and put his all into trying to make an honest buck. But in the 1920s when everybody was raking in millions from bootlegging, Touhy gave in and jumped on the bandwagon. It wasn't long before he had his own gang.

Bootlegging in Chicago was a pretty dangerous way to make a buck, and it wasn't long before Touhy came into direct contact with those illustrious mobsters Al Capone and Frank Nitti. Inevitably conflict broke out between the two gangs, and once again Chicago was a war zone.

Now the story really picks up speed. Like so many mobsters of the time, the Touhy gang went in for ransoming other hoods – it was a fast way to supplement their income and spread the dollars around. Capone, meanwhile, happened to know this guy – one John 'Jake the Barber' Factor – who'd spent some time in England. While in Europe, Factor (who was the half-brother of the famous Max Factor) had pulled off several truly sizzling scams, including one involving the British royals – a swindle that netted Factor millions. Another sting actually broke the bank at Monte Carlo.

On the run and in Chicago, Factor sought protection from Al Capone. The authorities wanted to ship Factor back to England for trial, but he was far too wily for that and he came up with a cunning plan. Factor would fake his own kidnapping and put the blame on the Touhy gang. This way he would be obliged to stay in the United States in order to testify at the trial, and Capone would get the Touhy gang out of his hair.

It was the old 'two birds with one stone' gambit, and it paid off. Roger Touhy was framed and charged with snatching Jake Factor, a kidnapping that hadn't actually taken place. With a prosecuting judge snugly in his pocket, Capone made sure Touhy was found guilty and slammed with a heavy sentence. In 1933 poor Touhy got 99 years for a make-believe felony.

Being incarcerated for something you didn't do, for 99 years, is enough to break anybody, but Touhy rolled up his sleeves and began a frankly heroic campaign to win back his freedom, launching one appeal after another – all of them slapped down. Then, in 1942, after nine years inside, Touhy began to get desperate and he and several other inmates staged a bold prison break. For a brief but glorious time, Touhy was on the outside and a free man. It didn't last. A few months after the break, Touhy and the others were picked up and thrown back in jail. He got an additional 199 years tacked onto his sentence! Capone may have had something to do with that.

Made of stern stuff, this setback seemed to inspire Touhy to work even harder. Finally, after latching onto a motivated and brilliant lawyer, he managed to dig up an honest judge and his case was reopened.

At long last, the much put-upon Touhy was exonerated of a crime he had not committed. But there was still that pesky business of the 199 years for the prison break. The obliging judge reduced that sentence down to three years and finally, in 1959, Roger Touhy was released from prison, having served nearly 26 years.

Now that he was out, Touhy decided it was high time to settle a few scores. By this time Capone was dead, so there was not much Touhy could do about him. But there was still Factor, living like a king in Vegas. There were also other members of the Chicago Outfit who needed taking down a peg or two – Tony Accardo and Paul Ricca, to name just two. Touhy and his inventive lawyer planned on launching a suit against all of them, demanding the staggering sum of three hundred million dollars in compensation. It wasn't likely such a suit would get anywhere, but it would certainly shine a very bright light on all the activities of Factor and the mob – and that was something the Outfit could not allow to happen.

So, less than a month after he was released from prison and before his case went to court, Touhy was gunned down on the steps of his sister's house in North Lotus Avenue. He was only shot in the legs, but it was enough; he died an hour later from blood loss.

Before his untimely end, Touhy wrote a book, *The Stolen Years*, about his amazing life.

In any case, on 9 October 1933, Winkler went down and he went down hard – a total of 72 bullets and buckshot pellets passed through his body, ensuring that he would never get up again. And Winkler's link to the St Valentine's Day Massacre? It was his wife, Georgette, who later

revealed his connection with that epic slaughter. During Winkler's criminal career, the blonde and beautiful Georgette had acted as his right hand, often vetting his contracts. After his death, Georgette attempted to publish her memoirs – a work that outlined her husband's relationship to the mob. But the piece was considered too hot at the time and remained unpublished until its discovery 60 years later, when it blew the lid off the massacre.

Mafia Killings 21

Francesco Ioele (Frankie Yale), New York City, 1 July 1928

Francesco Ioele, better known as Frankie Yale, gave Al Capone his first job. Though based in New York, Frankie also did favours for Capone and Johnny Torrio in Chicago; it was Frankie Yale who bumped off both Big Jim Colosimo and Dean O'Banion for his Chicago pals. But in 1928, when Yale crossed Capone, he found he'd made a grave error.

Yale was a crime boss and enforcer. Like so many other mob figures, though he could be generous, he was an extremely violent man. He once brutally beat his own brother and is considered responsible for the decapitation of crime boss Ernesto Melchiorre. By the 1920s Yale had expanded his operations into labour racketeering, extortion and bootlegging. He even marketed a 'Frankie Yale' brand of foul-smelling cigars that he forced shopkeepers to sell.

The friction between Capone and Yale started around 1925. In that year Capone successfully backed Tony Lombardo for the leadership position of the Unione Siciliana. Lombardo instituted some reforms within the Unione which probably cost Yale some graft. In retaliation, Yale put his backing behind Joe Aiello, a rival of Capone.

By 1927 the situation had deteriorated to such an extent that Yale felt it was time to teach Capone a lesson. Yale used to act as a rum-runner, bringing shipments of booze from Canada into the

United States. The liquor would then be sent off to supply some of the other gangs, Capone's included, with hooch they could sell to the speakeasies in their territories. In the spring of 1927, however, some of the shipments meant for Capone began to vanish.

Capone smelled a rat, and sent in James D'Amato to infiltrate the Yale's gang and investigate. D'Amato's findings confirmed Capone's suspicions – Yale was responsible for the hijackings. To make matters worse, once Yale discovered D'Amato's treachery, he had him killed.

Nothing now could save Yale. On 1 July 1928, while sitting in his bar, the Sunrise on 14th Avenue and 65th Street, he received a mysterious call requesting that he return home immediately. The caller must have been persuasive, because Yale leapt up and jumped into his car. As he sped along New Utrecht Street, a car containing four men pulled up alongside him. The occupants, rolling down their windows, opened fire on Yale. Flooring the accelerator and careening down 44th Street, Yale lost control of his car and smashed into the front of a house. The impact killed him and threw his body out onto the street amid the broken glass and twisted steel.

The Thompson sub-machine gun that had been used to dispatch him was later found in an abandoned car. The sub-machine gun was already gaining popularity in Chicago, where it was referred to as a 'Chicago Typewriter' but Yale's kiling was the first time it had been used in a New York gangland war.

Capone's use of the sub-machine gun to kill Yale was intended to send a message to the New York underworld. When the gun was found, there would be no mistaking where the hit on Frankie Yale had come from – it was Chicago style.

GENOVESE'S FOLLY

During the early 1930s the hits kept coming, with one killing followed by another, then reprisals and so on. Some killings were almost routine, for everyone except the victim of course, but some had repercussions.

The hit on Ferdinand Boccia haunted mobster Vito Genovese for decades. Boccia's corpse kept popping up at the most inconvenient times, forcing the gangster to relocate twice and delaying his elevation to crime boss by two decades. Evidently 'The Shadow', as Boccia was known, had a score to settle.

Genovese and Boccia were members of the Luciano mob in the mid-1930s. The pair devised a plan to milk a visiting Italian out of a small fortune in a crooked card game. Boccia introduced Genovese to the mark and during the course of the game the gangsters managed to relieve the gentleman of a cool $150,000. The only problem was that when it came to dividing the money, Boccia, as the man who had supplied the victim, thought he was worth more than the amount Genovese had allotted him. This was a big mistake on his part.

Some time in 1934, possibly 19 September, Genovese had Boccia shot as he sat enjoying a cappuccino in a Brooklyn coffee shop. The killers were probably Cosmo 'Gus' Frasca and George Smurra. The pair then dumped Boccia's body into the Hudson River, where it bobbed quietly for three years.

In the meantime, in 1936, mob boss Lucky Luciano was sentenced to 50 years in prison, and while he was gone Genovese managed to take up the mantle of godfather for the Luciano mob. But his first tenure as boss was to be short-lived. Apparently a body had just been discovered floating in the Hudson and now there was this small matter of murder to be dealt with – Boccia had returned. Not waiting around to be arrested, Genovese caught the next boat to Naples.

Mafia Killings 22

Louis 'Two Gun' Alterie, Chicago, 18 July 1935

One of the slickest moves to come out of the Roaring Twenties was the 'ambush murder'. In this type of hit, snipers would rent a location across the street from a joint their victim was known to frequent.

Then, when the mark showed up, the assassins would lay waste to him in a spray of bullets. The technique was precise and methodical, one that was sure to guarantee success. One of the pioneers of this method of killing was Louis 'Two-Gun' Alterie.

Louis Alterie was a member of Dean O'Banion's North Side gang. Although he lived and worked throughout the 1920s in Chicago, Alterie's heart – he always said – was in the West, where he loved to put his feet up at his ranch. The descendant of Spanish and French ranchers in California, Alterie saw himself as a cowboy and tended to dress the part. Tall, with dark slicked-back hair, he must have cut quite a figure when he was all duded up in his ten-gallon hat, cowboy boots and diamond-studded belt, especially when standing next to some torpedo from New York looking all slick in pinstripes and a fedora.

Alterie also loved to let loose like an outlaw in a saloon. Case in point: when Dean O'Banion was killed, Alterie told all and sundry, including the press, that he wanted to meet the killers out in the street somewhere and shoot it out, Western style. After this outburst the rest of the North Siders convinced Alterie to retire for a while – they had enough on their hands with Al Capone and didn't need any extra scrutiny from the press and the police.

Alterie laid low for a while on his ranch, punching cows and lassoing longhorns. But Two-Gun being Two-Gun, it didn't take long before he got into an altercation or two. One such event, a gangland shooting in Glenwood Springs, led to Alterie's arrest and, after his conviction, he was banished from Colorado for a period of five years.

Alterie headed back to Chicago. It was now 1933, and America was in the middle of the Depression. Though the North Siders were still limping along, their power had been greatly depleted. Despite this, Alterie was able to slip easily once more into the life of a racketeer, making a tidy sum through the labour unions. But Alterie hadn't counted on the Chicago Outfit. Though Capone was in jail,

his mob had the city all sewn up and they weren't looking to share their labour profits with Alterie.

On 18 July 1935, as Alterie and his wife were leaving their hotel, shots rang out from across the street. Alterie spun round, arms in the air, then fell to the ground, hit by a total of nine bullets. He died later that day on the operating table, a victim of an ambush, the very technique he had pioneered. Louis 'Two-Gun' Alterie had gone to that big ranch in the sky.

MURDER INCORPORATED

During the 1930s the American press became increasingly fascinated by the Mafia and its gruesome activities. Because the mob was something that most members of the public could not really see, demand for such stories grew, particularly in New York and Chicago. While the creation of the National Crime Syndicate was a good story, the setting up of its enforcement arm, dubbed Murder Incorporated by the newspapers, was a great one.

Originally a gang formed in New York in the early 1920s by the Jewish mobsters Meyer Lansky and Benjamin Siegel, this was a loose coalition of Italian and Jewish gangsters, based in the Brooklyn neighbourhoods of Brownsville, East New York and Ocean Hill. They were recruited by the Syndicate when Louis 'Lepke' Buchalter and later Albert Anastasia, the so-called 'Lord High Executioner' because of his love of violence, took over its leadership.

Although its members were involved in a variety of illicit activities including loan sharking, prostitution, gambling, bootlegging and labour racketeering, they became infamous for their role as the New York syndicate's so-called 'execution squad'.

Louis 'Lepke' Buchalter was one of the members of the National Crime Syndicate dubbed 'Murder Incorporated' by the press

The group's headquarters was a 24-hour coffee shop called the Midnight Rose Candy Store, located under the No. 3 subway at Saratoga and Livonia Avenue in Brownsville, Brooklyn. It was run by a little old lady called Rosie Gold. No one knows how many killers were included in the group, but it is said they were responsible for anywhere between 400 and 1,000 killings in some ten years, earning between $1,000 and $5,000 per contract. The story has it that Rosie Gold kept a row of payphones along the back wall of the shop; the members of Murder Inc. would pass the time sipping on her malted milks until one of the phones rang, giving the details of the hit. No mobster was safe if Murder Inc. was involved.

Pretty Amberg was truly one of the most hated gangsters in New York. In fact, Amberg wasn't pretty at all, but he could not have cared less about his looks. Supposedly once offered a job in a circus as the missing link, far from being offended by this, Amberg claimed bragging rights on the offer.

He was a loan shark and bootlegger and ran some rackets in Brooklyn with his brothers Joseph and Hyman. He liked things on the tough side and would reputedly spit into diners' soup bowls as he entered a restaurant. He also had a nasty habit of killing transients on the street. Once sarcastically described by author Damon Runyon as being in the laundry business, Amberg would stuff his victims into a bag and tie them up with wire in such a way that they would strangle themselves as they struggled to get out. For a while, the Brownsville area of Brooklyn was littered with laundry bag corpses. All in all, Pretty Amberg was a gruesome customer.

The Ambergs' rackets stayed modest for a while but as the brothers began to rake in the money, interest from the other mobsters grew, including such heavyweights as Owney Madden and Legs Diamond. Dutch Schultz took a fancy to their operation and once commented to Amberg that it might be a good idea if they went into business together. Amberg was less than enthusiastic about this idea and suggested that Schultz take his own gun and shoot himself with it.

But the Ambergs were also getting into competition with Louis 'Lepke' Buchalter and Jacob 'Gurrah' Shapiro for what was becoming increasingly valuable territory. Madden, Diamond and Schultz (especially Schultz) were dangerous enough, but when the Ambergs started locking horns with Buchalter, they were taking on the Syndicate's most dangerous individual.

The Amberg gang began to disintegrate pretty rapidly after that. Brother Hyman had already died in 1926, killing himself after a failed prison escape attempt. Joseph and Louis were still around – though not for long. In September 1935 Joseph and his bodyguard/chauffeur Morris Kessler were killed in what was to be one of the first major jobs for the murder organization. They were gunned down while collecting protection money from a Brooklyn auto repair shop.

Pretty Amberg was soon to follow them. Less than a month later, on 23 October 1935, he met his demise. His body had been bound with wire and set ablaze inside a car. As it turned out that week in October was a busy one for Murder Incorporated. Buchalter and his buddies also rubbed out the legendary mobster Dutch Schultz the very next day.

Nowhere in the United States was really free of Mafia influence, particularly not anywhere with a touch of glamour. New York, Chicago, Las Vegas, San Francisco and, of course, Los Angeles – if there was money, there was always someone ready to exploit those who had a lot of it.

Jack Gordon was a star in New York; he was also a star in Los Angeles. Lighting up the silver screen in second-feature flicks such as *Jungle Raiders* and *Gambler's Choice*, Gordon worked as a bit-part actor and extra in Hollywood. But he wasn't really an actor (as a viewing of any one of his performances will confirm); he was actually Irving 'Big Gangi' Cohen, a low-level hood who at one time had worked for Walter Sage out in the Catskills.

Both Sage and Cohen were occasional hired killers, but mainly made their living by picking up money from slot machines and dropping it off to the mob. The only problem was that Sage developed sticky fingers and started skimming a little money off the top. That's when a contract was

put out on Walter and three gunmen from Murder Incorporated – Abe Levine, Jack Drucker and Pittsburgh Phil – were sent over some time in 1937 to take care of the situation. The killers conscripted Sage's buddy Cohen to help them. That way, when they took Sage out for a little ride, he wouldn't expect a thing.

The day arrived and Drucker and Cohen went off with Sage in a car; Phil and Levine followed behind. As they were driving, Cohen suddenly reached forward and held Sage down as Drucker proceeded to stab him with an ice pick. Some reports indicate that Drucker also got a little over-zealous and accidentally stabbed Cohen in the arm too; but the job was done and Sage was very, very dead.

Now they had to get rid of the body. The plan was to weigh Sage down with a slot machine, in an ironic gesture, and toss him into deep water. As soon as the car stopped moving, though, Cohen leapt from the back seat and ran off screaming into the woods. He was either appalled by what he had done or thought that he too was a target. Maybe it was a little of both. Where Cohen went nobody knew and as long as he stayed quiet, no one was likely to come after him, so they let him run.

So it was a surprise in 1939 when Levine, attending a matinée performance of a new boxing flick, *Golden Boy*, happened to catch a glimpse of Cohen in a crowd scene. He squinted, looked twice. Yes, it was Cohen all right. It seems that after his 'escape' Cohen had made a beeline for Hollywood, where he had managed to find work as an extra.

Now, everyone knew where Cohen was, and Sage's body was found in Swan Lake in the Catskills in July 1937. Abe Levine, who had decided to turn informer, started to name names in a big way and implicated Cohen in the killing of Sage. Cohen was picked up by the police.

Cohen went to trial for the murder of Sage, but gave such an emotional and convincing performance (probably his best) that the jury acquitted him. He was a free man and returned to Hollywood to further his career by appearing in other B flicks, such as *Prison Train*, though he does have a small part as a gangster in *Some Like It Hot*, which must have been typecasting.

Mafia Killings 23

Peter Panto, Lyndhurst, New Jersey, 14 July 1939

'Where is Peter Panto?' The cry went up through the docks. It had been a mob killing, for sure, since most disappearances on the docks were connected with the mob. The shipping companies, the unions, and the foremen were all mobbed-up, no question. It was precisely this that Panto was fighting against – corruption on the piers and in the unions, the lack of security, the abysmal and dangerous working conditions. But at that time, if you took a stand on the waterfront you were butting heads with Albert Anastasia and Murder Incorporated. Needless to say, you didn't stand very long.

No doubt about it, shipping offered an unquestionable fortune to the mob at that time. Not only did the mob control the unions, demanding payment from workers just for the privilege of working, but they muscled the shipping companies as well, using the threat of strikes to get what they wanted. The Mafia could also freely help itself to cargo the ships brought in, literally lifting whole boatloads of goods and bringing in contraband from all over the world.

Peter Panto was an Italian immigrant, a dockworker trying to make an honest living through back-breaking and irregular work on the piers. He was also an activist, a voice for workers' rights, who had started a rank and file movement to improve working conditions and to challenge the mob. Because the two, of course, went hand in hand; nothing could ever improve on the piers while the mob was calling the shots.

In the summer of 1939, the movement was picking up traction. Peter's first rally in June of that year saw a promising 350 in attendance. The next meeting, a mere two weeks later, exploded in size and a whopping 1,500 crowded in to hear Peter speak. Word was getting out.

All of this raised some eyebrows in the mob, of course, and Anastasia and his union boss brother Tough Tony applied the thumb screws to the labour leaders. Something had to be done about Panto. Intimidation, threats, smear campaigns – all were used to put the fear of the mob into Panto, but none had any effect.

On the evening of 14 July 1939, three members of Murder Inc. – Mendy Weiss, Tony Romanello and James Ferraco – paid a visit to Panto and hustled him from his home into a waiting car. Panto battled like a demon, biting into Mendy Weiss's finger – apparently he hit bone – but it was all for nought, of course. After all, this was Murder Incorporated. The three thugs garrotted Panto and dumped his body into a pit of quicklime.

When Panto did not return home, angry friends, relatives and stevedores demanded that something finally be done. The phrase 'Where is Peter Panto?' was taken up by protestors and simple dockyard workers alike, and the question was scrawled on the walls of the wharfs.

In January 1941 Panto's remains finally showed up buried in a limepit in New Jersey, and everyone understood exactly what had happened to him. Though he hadn't stopped corruption and mob involvement in his lifetime, Peter had helped to light a fire that could never go out. 'Where is Peter Panto?' He's in the hearts of all those who stand against injustice and the mob.

Mafia Killlings 24

Irving 'Puggy' Feinstein, New York City, 5 September 1939

Irving 'Puggy' Feinstein put up a heck of a fight but, of course, he didn't really have much of a chance. He had been lured to a meeting by three of Murder Incorporated's most notorious killers, and these

were guys who took a great deal of pride in their work.

Feinstein was strictly low-level, a bottom feeder who could have happily spent a long and fulfilling career running second-rate rackets out of Brooklyn, but for one mistake he made some time in the late 1930s. Apparently he ripped off Vincent 'The Executioner' Mangano, who was top dog of the Mangano family. People don't generally walk away from things like that.

Whatever it was that Feinstein did is now lost to history, but it probably consisted of working in an unauthorized territory or not paying street tax. Anyway, the offence was grievous enough to have Mangano underboss Albert Anastasia himself put the finger on him. And that was it – Feinstein's days were now strictly limited edition.

Murder Incorporated sent its best, most prolific boys to do the job; and the best, of course, meant the worst. Irving's killers are known to have been Martin Goldstein, Abe 'Kid Twist' Reles and Pittsburgh Phil, the most hated members of the murder-for-hire clique. Phil especially was a fiend, and used to volunteer for as many jobs as he could, just for kicks.

Poor Feinstein. He was brought to Reles's house on East 91st Street in Brooklyn and murdered by the ghastly trio, supposedly while Reles's mother-in-law was in an adjoining room. The elderly lady must have been very deaf; how else she could have missed all the commotion is anybody's guess.

During the proceedings Feinstein battled for his life, but taking chunks out of Pittsburgh Phil's finger was a very unfortunate move, because it just made his death all the more tortuous. At last, when Feinstein was no more, the trio of murderers took his pitiful remains out and burned them.

Enforcers like Dutch Schultz often came to a bloody end

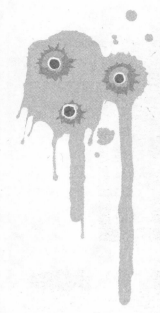

CHAPTER 11

A NEW ERA

Prohibition finally came to an end in 1933 and it is instructive that many of Prohibition's major players immediately went into legitimate business in precisely the commodity out of which they'd made such huge amounts of money.

Joseph Kennedy became the American distributor of Haig & Haig Whisky and Gordon's Gin, Frank Costello set up Alliance Distributors, selling the same brands he'd made popular illegally. Samuel Bronfman, the biggest Canadian bootlegger, founded a company called Seagrams, and Luciano, Lansky and one of their torpedoes, Benjamin 'Bugsy' Siegel, started up Capitol Wine and Spirits, which specialized in high-end wines and liqueurs.

The Mafia, or Cosa Nostra, identified for the first time in 1984 by the aforementioned Sicilian don Tommaso Buscetta, went on, of course, to many other things. But the best way to tell this part of the organization's history is to go both backward and forward, and look at the career of one of the men who helped create the all-important Commission and its body of enforcers, Murder Incorporated: Dutch Schultz.

As for Lucky Luciano, who used to have breakfast with Lansky at a delicatessen on Delancy Street every day he could, he was jailed in

An FBI photo of 'Lucky' Luciano

1936 on a trumped-up charge of racketeering in prostitutes, and was put out of circulation in Sing Sing prison. He later said that he'd been double-crossed by President Roosevelt, for whom he'd brought out the vote in 1935. Roosevelt, through an intermediary, had offered to rein in, on Luciano's behalf, the investigations of Judge Samuel Seabury. He didn't. As president, he encouraged them further, and Luciano became his number-one victim and was sentenced to between 30 and 50 years in prison. But his finest hour was yet to come.

THE DUTCHMAN

'Dutch' Schultz wasn't Dutch, he was German; and his last name wasn't Schultz, it was Flegenheimer. His father kept a saloon and livery stable in what was known as Jewish Harlem, but deserted his family in 1916. Whether this sent his son Arthur off the rails is uncertain, but a life of crime was to beckon at an early age. Coming out of jail at the age of 16, following an 18-month stretch for burglary, Arthur borrowed the name of a legendary member of the old Frog Hollow Gang, and got down to business.

A chorus girl had once said that he looked like Bing Crosby with his face bashed in. Dutch was no beauty, but he didn't have to be. By the mid-1920s, after riding shotgun on Arnold Rothstein's liquor trucks, he'd put together the toughest gang in New York, mainly operating in the Bronx. They ran protection for some of the fanciest uptown restaurants. They were into slot machines and the numbers racket; liquor, restaurants, labour unions, gambling, and fixing any horse race or boxing match they could. By the beginning of the 1930s, Dutch, who had a reputation for miserliness, was said to be making $20 million a year.

Mafia Killings 25

Vincent 'Mad Dog' Coll, New York City, 8 February 1932

Vincent Coll worked for a while in Dutch Schultz's mob during the 1920s. Schultz found him a useful enforcer – he seemed to have little conscience and plenty of gall, a combination that Schultz found advantageous, at least for a while.

But Coll was a loose cannon, to say the least. He earned the nickname 'Mad Dog' from the accidental killing of a young child, five-year-old Michael Vengalli. Coll had been trying to whack mobster Joseph Rao, but when he sprayed the street with bullets in one of those epic shoot-outs of the time, several small children were hit in the barrage and little Michael was killed. After that incident, police officials considered Coll something less than human – a mad dog.

Coll would often improvise while carrying out jobs for Schultz, a trait his boss did not appreciate. On one occasion, going beyond his orders, Coll killed speakeasy owner Anthony Borello because he refused to carry Schultz's hooch. Another time, again without Schultz's authorization, Coll robbed a dairy, helping himself to the hefty cashbox. Schultz was furious at all the unwanted heat these activities brought. But Coll thought he was worth it. In fact, he thought he was worth much more and when confronted about his

faux pas, his reaction was to demand Schultz take him on as partner in his mob. Schultz, not very politely, refused.

The animosity with Schultz building to epic proportions, Coll now struck out on his own, kidnapping mob bosses for profit. This was a risky prospect, to say the least, but Coll reasoned that his plan had to pay off, at least in the short term. The gangs would be unable to call the police for help – for obvious reasons – and they'd have to cough up. But inevitably Mad Dog was antagonizing some very powerful figures in New York's underworld.

One such figure was Hell's Kitchen boss Owney Madden. Coll angered Madden by pulling his kidnapping racket on Madden's friend, gangster George DeMange. DeMange was released after the ransom was paid, but Coll may as well have painted a big red target on himself.

Inevitably, Coll tried his kidnapping gag once too often. In 1932, apparently trying to put the squeeze on Madden once again, Coll contacted him from a public telephone in the London Chemists drugstore on West 23rd Street. As Coll stood in the booth, a car pulled up and three men got out. Stepping into the store, the men opened fire on Coll, filling him full of lead. Coll, hit at least 15 times, collapsed in the booth. The Mad Dog had been put down.

Coll's killers were never identified, but both Dutch Schultz and Owney Madden had one less enemy. By the end of that day in February, the man who dared to prey on the mobsters was gone.

Mafia Killings 26

Charles 'Vannie' Higgins, Brooklyn, New York City, 19 June 1932

On certain nights during the late 1920s and early 1930s, the sound of Charles 'Vannie' Higgins' aeroplane could be heard in the skies over the northeastern states of America as he flew from New York to

Canada and back. Higgins used to run rum with his plane. He used other methods of transport too, of course, including trucks, taxis and boats, including his famous vessel *The Cigarette*. But it was the plane he loved and he would often fly it himself.

Higgins had cut his criminal teeth in 'Big Bill' Dwyer's gang in the 1920s and when he struck out on his own, earning himself the reputation as one of the most prominent bootleggers of the Prohibition era, he came into conflict with Dutch Schultz during the bootlegging wars of Manhattan. Everybody seemed to bump shoulders with Schultz. Higgins apparently sided with 'Legs' Diamond and Vincent Coll against Schultz and the streets would regularly erupt with their gun battles.

Higgins had numerous run-ins with the law and was arrested many times. He was only convicted once, however, and this only resulted in a fine, not a jail term. It seems that whenever Higgins went to trial witnesses would go missing, or find that they suddenly had to leave on some spurious excuse. Higgins had a number of highly placed friends who always came through in a scrape.

One of his connections was Joseph H. Wilson, warden of New York's Great Meadow Maximum Correctional Facility upstate in Comstock. Warden Wilson had conscripted the prisoners to clear a landing field for Higgins and the two men spent the day reminiscing, no doubt with the lifers milling about just yards away. New York Governor Franklin Delano Roosevelt didn't care for Warden Wilson fraternizing with the likes of Higgins, a known gangster, but the warden let it roll off his back – his friends were his own business, he told the future president.

But Vannie Higgins's overriding concern was his family, and shortly after his visit with Warden Wilson he was compelled to make the ultimate sacrifice for them. On the night of 19 June 1932, Higgins attended a recital of his seven-year-old daughter's dance class at Prospect Park in Brooklyn, surrounded by family members

along with some enforcers.

As Higgins and company were leaving the building after the performance, a car pulled up on the darkened street. Several men carrying guns stepped out and began shooting. Acting fast, Higgins pushed his family aside and ran down the street, drawing the gunmen's fire. After collapsing on the ground, he was taken to the nearest hospital. He held on for about 15 hours, enduring several blood transfusions, but really his death was a foregone conclusion. Refusing to name his assailants, Higgins died, still swearing he would get his killers.

Though Higgins may have known who killed him, his murderers were never identified – but when Brooklyn DA William O'Dwyer began proceedings against Murder Incorporated in 1940, Higgins was named as just one of the many targets of that organization. Higgins may have lived a gangster, but in the end, it could be argued, he died a hero.

Dutch Shultz simply beat up or got rid of anyone who stood in his way. He out-muscled his competition – arriving in the numbers racket, for example, by simply calling a meeting, laying his .45 on the table and saying 'I'm your partner.' When 'Legs' Diamond had to leave New York after killing a drunk, Dutch took over his liquor trucks and, when Legs objected, he had him killed.

He avoided arrest by paying off the police and providing campaign funds and votes to all the politicians who mattered – particularly district attorney William Copeland Dodge. But a noose of prosecutions gradually settled around his neck. Dutch beat the rap on a tax-evasion charge in Syracuse in 1933, but in 1935 he faced another, this time put together by special prosecutor Thomas Dewey. His lawyers eventually succeeded in having the trial moved to a little upstate town, but the consensus was, in Lucky Luciano's words, that 'the loudmouth is never coming back.'

Schultz, though, spent months in Malone, New York, before the trial, schmoozing the inhabitants, dressing modestly and even converting

to Catholicism in the town's little church. When he got off, he told reporters: 'This tough world ain't no place for dunces. And you can tell all those smart guys in New York that the Dutchman is no dunce.'

The 'smart guys in New York', though, didn't want the Dutchman on their turf any more. Fiorello La Guardia, who'd succeeded Jimmy Walker as New York's mayor, sent a message warning him not to come back, and started literally breaking up his gambling empire – he had himself photographed on barges taking a sledgehammer to Dutch's slot machines. Thomas Dewey started preparing another case, this time against Dutch's restaurant rackets. His operation began to leak at the seams as other mobsters moved in on it.

He was exiled to Newark, New Jersey, where he set up his headquarters in a restaurant called the Palace Chop House. Then, sometime in late autumn 1935 – after having had to kill one of his own lieutenants for conspiring with Luciano – he called a meeting of the Syndicate and demanded the assassination of Thomas Dewey. The Syndicate refused: it was far too high-profile. Dutch said, fine, he'd kill Dewey himself – and so signed his own death warrant. In October, with his lieutenants, he was gunned down in the Palace Chop House by assassins from Murder Incorporated. He was 33.

Mafia Killings 27

Abraham 'Bo' Weinberg, New York City, 9 September 1935

'Bo' Weinberg was a lieutenant in Dutch Schultz's mob. For a long time he was Schultz's right-hand man and his most trusted enforcer. But Schultz was an erratic soul, and as his underworld power grew, so did his eccentricities. In 1933 he was indicted for tax evasion. It was time for him to take a little vacation. For a while he went on the lam and Weinberg ran the Schultz mob in his absence.

Weinberg had done a number of extremely delicate pieces of work for Schultz, allegedly including the assassinations of 'Legs'

Diamond, 'Mad Dog' Coll and, one theory suggests, Arnold 'The Brain' Rothstein. However, as he took control of the Schultz gang, Weinberg's concerns began to grow. Schultz was an expensive commodity. While on the run he'd been racking up bills, and when he finally came out of hiding to face the music in 1934, his legal fees were eating up profits.

So Weinberg approached the National Crime Syndicate – the underworld ruling body – and offered to cut a deal with them. He feared that Schultz's gang would soon unravel and that Charlie 'Lucky' Luciano and the Syndicate would divvy up the remains of the Dutchman's enterprises. Why not meet them in the middle? Maybe this way Weinberg could still retain control over the majority of the mob's operations. Luciano felt slightly differently about things, though, and began to make moves to distribute Schultz's regime among the members of the Syndicate.

Imagine everyone's surprise, then, when in 1935 Schultz was back, his trials ending in acquittal. By acting like a good citizen – donating bags of toys to orphans, giving money to charity and kissing babies – the Dutchman had managed to sway the jury, much to the astonishment of the judge.

Schultz was astonished too when he came back to his empire and found things significantly altered. Not to worry, Luciano explained, they'd only been minding house while Schultz was otherwise occupied, and now things could go back to normal. The idiosyncratic Schultz reportedly teared up when he heard Luciano's side of things, but Luciano knew there was more going on with Schultz than met the eye.

The Dutchman now had a major score to settle with Weinberg. No points for guessing what happened next. On 9 September

New York Mayor Fiorello La Guardia sends a message to Dutch Shultz warning him to close down his gambling empire

1935, after leaving a nightspot somewhere in midtown Manhattan, Weinberg disappeared and was never seen again. A story exists – and they always do – that it was Schultz who put a bullet into Weinberg's head that night. In any case, it's widely believed that Schultz had Weinberg encased in cement – either totally or just his feet – and then dumped in the river. As his body has never been recovered, it can probably be said with accuracy that Bo Weinberg sleeps with the fishes.

Mafia Killings 28

Dutch Schultz, New Jersey, 24 October 1935

Without doubt this was the biggest contract in the history of Murder Inc. As a bootlegger, gangster and racketeer during the late 1920s through the mid-1930s, Schultz was one of the big ones, right up there with Lucky Luciano, Bugsy Siegel and Al Capone. His was a name embedded in mob lore and he had a reputation to be reckoned with.

Fearless, ambitious and intelligent, Schultz was a unique individual, to say the least. Half the underworld thought he was nuts. Charming and affable one minute, Schultz could erupt with a violent temper the next. He could also kill a man as coolly as he lit a cigarette. Any up-and-comer who dared to lock horns with the Dutchman soon thought better of it, if they could still think at all. Schultz battled with the likes of Mad Dog Coll and Legs Diamond and came out on top.

But Schultz hadn't reckoned on the zeal of special prosecutor Thomas Dewey, who had a mission to get rid of mobsters like Schultz no matter what the personal risk. In 1935 Schultz was tried twice for tax evasion. Putting his vast fortune into his court battles, he launched a huge goodwill campaign that made him seem like a

kind-hearted citizen wrongly placed in the hot seat. Schultz was ultimately triumphant in court and his second trial ended in acquittal. But Dewey wasn't done yet and he began to build a case against the Dutchman that was rumoured to include accusations of racketeering and murder. If convicted of this last item, Schultz could go to the electric chair.

Schultz brought his grievance to the National Crime Syndicate – Luciano, Siegel, Louis Buchalter, et al. He had a job for Murder Incorporated, he said – he wanted them to take care of Dewey for him and he was willing to pay whatever it cost. Unquestionably, this request caused some raised eyebrows among the members of the Syndicate. Eliminating someone of Dewey's standing would bring a reprisal that none in the underworld would survive.

The decision was made not to assassinate Dewey. Instead, Luciano had a better idea and he put it to a vote – after Schultz had left the room, of course. On 24 October 1935, as Schultz was dining at the Palace Chop House in New Jersey, several gunmen entered. He was in the rest room when the killers opened fire. Shot in the gut, he managed to stagger to a table where he collapsed into a chair. At first it seemed that his chances of survival were good but, after the bullet had been removed, infection set in (the bullets had been treated with rust, an old mob trick), and Schultz spent 22 hours in agonized delirium, muttering incoherently. With ravings such as 'don't let Satan draw you too fast', Schultz's deathbed ramblings have become entrenched in his legend, and read like psychedelic poetry.

But in all his ramblings Schultz made no mention of who shot him – in this respect, he was true to his Mafia roots.

PART FOUR

THE 1940S-1960S: CRIME GROWS UP

By the 1940s, the tommy-gun battles that had marked earlier decades were officially over for the most part and it could now be said that the mob was wearing a suit and tie. The Mafia and all its associate gangs of various nationalities had their fingers in a number of respectable enterprises, and organized crime was run very much like a business.

But that doesn't mean that the mob had lost its teeth, not by a long shot. The way that Bugsy Siegel and Albert 'Lord High Executioner' Anastasia were removed from the picture showed that no one was too important to escape reprisals. And then, of course, there was the rumoured Mafia involvement in the assassination of President Kennedy in Dallas, in November 1963.

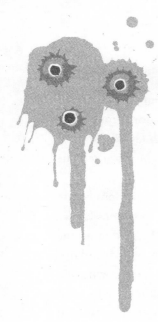

CHAPTER 12

THE MAIN MEN

Whether because of their opposition to the unpopular Prohibition Era of the 1930s, or the mob's move westwards towards the glamourous destinations of Las Vegas and California in the 1940s, or the fantastic sepia coloured photographs that inhabit the magazines, books and internet sites today, the Mafia has become part of the world's entertainment landscape through books, TV series and blockbuster films. The big names in the early 1940s – Lucky Luciano, Louis Lepke, Meyer Lansky, Bugsy Siegel, Alberto Anastasia and Vito Genovese – not to mention some of the cops, like Donnie Brasco, who faced them – are still big names today Why such ruthless and often greedy killers should have such a glamorous reputation is a subject of much debate, but the main men listed below have left a legacy that is impossible to ignore.

LOUIS LEPKE

Louis Lepke, short for 'Lepkele' or 'Little Louis', was born Louis Buchalter in Williamsburg, Brooklyn in 1897. His father, the owner of a hardware store on the Lower East Side, died of a heart attack when he was 13, and his mother moved soon afterwards to Colorado. Little

Louis, then, came of age in the streets. He hung out with hoodlums, and was soon in trouble with the law. He was sent out of town to live with his uncle in Connecticut, and then to a reformatory, from where he soon graduated, around the time of his 21st birthday, first to New York's Tombs prison, and then to Sing Sing, where he acquired the nickname 'Judge Louis'.

Back on the streets again in 1923, he went into the protection business with an old pal, Joseph 'Gurrah' Shapiro – they were known as 'the Gorilla Boys' and specialized in bakeries. But they didn't hit the big time until they went to work for Arnold Rothstein, who dealt large in both liquor and drugs – or so it was said. Soon they were moving into the union rackets, backing the workers against the bosses with goon squads, and vice versa – and then taking over from both. They started out in this with a real expert, 'Little Augie' Orgen, as their principal mentor. But by 1927, Orgen simply stood in their way. So on 15 October, they gunned him down in front of his clubhouse on Norfolk Street on the Lower East Side. By the beginning of the 1930s they ruled the labour roost. They controlled painters, truckers and motion-picture operators, they were expanding their drugs business and they still took in $1.5 million a year from bakeries. They were now known, not as 'the Gorilla Boys', but 'the Gold Dust Twins'.

In 1933, with the setting up of the Syndicate, Lepke became a board-director and one of the founding members of Murder Incorporated, its enforcement arm of contract killers, among whom was a Brooklyn thug called Abraham 'Kid Twist' Reles. That same year, though, Lepke was indicted by a federal grand jury for violation of anti-trust laws. And though he ultimately beat the rap on this one, the Feds began closing in with narcotics charges, and the Brooklyn DA's office with an investigation into racketeering. In the summer of 1937, he, along with 'Gurrah' Shapiro, went on the run, and Lepke soon became the most wanted man in US history.

While he was hiding he made attempts to silence the potential witnesses against him, but the heat on the streets became too great.

In August 1940 he gave himself up, with the understanding that he'd face federal narcotics charges rather than a state indictment for murder. He was sentenced to 14 years and shipped to the penitentiary at Leavenworth, Kansas.

However, Abe Reles, one of the executioners he'd hired in the old days, began to sing. For six months Reles was held at a hotel in Coney Island as he gave evidence at trial after trial. On 12 November 1941, his dead body was found, but it was too late for Louis Lepke. Reles had already appeared before a grand jury hearing to give evidence against him, evidence that could be – and was – used in court.

Louis Lepke and two of his lieutenants, Mendy Weiss and Louis Capone, were tried for murder and condemned to death. They went to the electric chair in Sing Sing prison on 4 March 1944. The murder of Reles – which got Alberto Anastasia and Bugsy Siegel off the hook – was probably arranged by Frank Costello.

ALBERT ANASTASIA

The eldest son of a railroad worker, Umberto Anastasio began calling himself Albert Anastasia after his first arrest – 'to save the family from disgrace', his brother Anthony said. With three of his nine brothers, he began working on board freighters after his father died in the First World War. They jumped ship in New York in 1919.

Employed as a longshoreman, Anastasia was 19 when he was convicted of killing another worker on the Brooklyn waterfront. He spent 18 months in the death house in Sing Sing before winning a retrial. By then, four key witnesses had disappeared and he walked free. But in 1923 he was sent away for another two years for carrying a gun.

Anastasia used strong-arm tactics to take control of the International Longshoremen's Association. This brought him into contact with Giuseppe 'Joe the Boss' Masseria, the most powerful boss in Brooklyn. Masseria's top aides were Frank Costello and 'Lucky' Luciano, who worked with Vito Genovese, Meyer Lansky and 'Bugsy' Siegel.

During the Castellammarese War, Albert Anastasia joined the other young turks to rid organized crime of the old-style 'Moustache Petes'. The war ended when Luciano lured Masseria out to lunch at a restaurant on Coney Island. When Luciano went to the bathroom, Anastasia, Genovese, Siegel and Joe Adonis came rushing in, guns blazing, killing Masseria.

When Luciano had first told him of the plan, Anastasia hugged him and said: 'Charlie, I have been waiting for this day for at least eight years. You're gonna be on top, if I have to kill everybody for you. With you there, that's the only way we can have any peace and make the real money.'

This was extraordinarily eloquent for Anastasia. Short and thickset, he was normally a man of few words and his Italian was scarcely better than his English. He had left school at 11.

The National Crime Syndicate, also known as the Commission, had been set up, in part, to prevent the infighting that had caused the Castellammarese War. The men at the top realized they needed some serious muscle if they were to be taken seriously, so Murder Incorporated was set up under the command of Louis 'Lepke' Buchalter and Anastasia, now underboss in the Mangano crime family.

Its team of celebrated killers included Harry 'Pittsburgh Phil' Strauss, Frank 'the Dasher' Abbandando, 'Buggsy' Goldstein, Harry 'Happy' Maione – known for his permanent scowl – and Vito 'Chicken Head' Gurino, who practised his aim by shooting the heads off chickens. Anastasia was also active. By this time, he had earned a new nickname, 'The Executioner' for his work. According to some reports this was because he enjoyed watching his victims die. He had established a reputation for being especially brutal and cruel.

In 1932, he was indicted on charges of murdering a man with an ice-pick, but the case was dropped due to lack of witnesses. The following year, he was accused of murdering a man in a laundry, but again no witness could be found.

Italian-American Mafia boss Albert Anastasia smiling in a park. Italy, 1940s

When Dutch Schultz found himself the target of special prosecutor Thomas E. Dewey, he demanded that Murder Inc. hit Dewey. Anastasia came up with a plan. One of his men would walk up and down the street where Dewey lived, wheeling a pram. When there was no one about, he would pull out a sub-machine gun from under the blankets and cut Dewey down. However, Luciano, Lansky, Costello and Adonis were against the idea as it was in direct violation of the rules under which the organization had been set up. They were only to kill one another, not prosecutors, policemen, FBI agents, journalists or civilians, as it risked bringing down too much heat on them. Instead, Schultz was to be hit, and Anastasia arranged it.

Murder Inc. came to an end when one of its top lieutenants, Abe 'Kid Twist' Reles, was arrested for a number of murders and turned state's evidence. His testimony led to the arrest, trial and execution of lieutenants Louis Capone and Mendy Weiss, along with Pittsburgh Phil Strauss, Happy Maione, Dasher Abbandando, Buggsy Goldstein and Louis Buchalter, who was already in jail for narcotic trafficking and extortion.

Reles' testimony was also used to build a case against Anastasia. However, Reles fell to his death from the window of a hotel in Coney Island, where he was being held under ironclad police protection.

Mafia Killings 29

Abe 'Kid Twist' Reles, Coney Island, New York, 12 November, 1941

Abe 'Kid Twist' Reles was a high roller in the Syndicate's assassination wing, Murder Incorporated. Louis Buchalter, Jacob Shapiro and Albert Anastasia ran the organization, but Reles and his gang – the Boys from Brownsville – were the main executioners. When someone needed rubbing out, Reles and his boys did it with relish. But Reles

has another claim to fame: he's the stool pigeon who finally brought down the murder squad.

Reles and his gang liked to ply their trade in creative ways. Generally contracted for out-of-town killings so that they couldn't be traced to the victim, the group would tail the mark for a while before getting down to the hit. Once ready, they would use a variety of methods to get the job done – Reles favoured using an ice pick, for instance.

So efficient was the assassination squad that they became notorious during the 1930s and it's believed that Murder Inc. was responsible for nearly one thousand killings, many of them unsolved. All that changed in 1940, though, when Reles found himself implicated in a murder dating all the way back to 1933.

Hauled up on murder charges, it didn't take long for him to decide what to do. Facing conviction and execution, Reles concluded his best bet was to name names, a lot of names – all the names. Thanks to Reles and his near-eidetic memory, the authorities were able to close a lot of gaps, lowering the boom on Mendy Weiss, Louis Capone, Dasher Abbandando, and even Louis Buchalter himself, to name but a few. All of the aforementioned were sent to the chair.

And Reles wasn't done yet. He was about to put the finger on Albert Anastasia as well – though not if Anastasia had anything to say about it, of course.

Reles was being sequestered at the Half Moon Hotel on Coney Island. There was practically a brigade of cops keeping an eye on the mobster. But that didn't stop Reles from falling to his death from a window of the hotel on the morning of 12 November 1941. Coincidentally, or not, he died the day before he was to testify against Anastasia.

The official ruling of the time was that Reles had climbed out of the window – either as a prank or to try to escape – and that he'd accidentally fallen. But nobody actually believes that. It's far more

plausible that Anastasia bought off the cops and had his men take care of Reles or that the cops did the job themselves. The mug-shots of Reles before his death show a man whose eyes are round with terror. Reles was a marked man and he knew it.

After his literal fall from grace, Reles became known as 'the canary who could sing but couldn't fly'. And what came of the charges against Albert Anastasia? With Reles no longer around to testify, they were dropped.

Dewey did manage to put Luciano away on pimping charges, but in 1942, Anastasia developed an audacious plan to get Luciano out of jail. With the United States now on a war footing, there was a danger that the longshoremen could disrupt the war effort. Many of them were Italians, and therefore enemy aliens. Through Anastasia and his brother, union boss Anthony 'Tough Tony' Anastasio, Luciano would be able to guarantee that there would be no problems on the waterfront.

But first Anastasia planned a little sabotage of his own. To draw attention to the danger America faced, he had his brother arrange a fire on the French liner *SS Normandie*, which had been seized by the United States government and was being converted into a troop ship. It burned and capsized in New York harbour. Luciano was then transferred from Dannemora, one of the toughest prisons in the system up on the Canadian border, to the more conducive Great Meadow Correctional Facility, closer to New York. In 1946, Thomas Dewey, now governor of New York, pardoned Luciano, who was released and deported back to Italy with a suitcase containing a million dollars, allegedly supplied by Meyer Lansky.

Anastasia earned his United States citizenship by serving in the US Army as a technical sergeant training GI longshoremen in Pennsylvania. He remained underboss of the Mangano crime family, but frequently argued with the boss, Vincent Mangano. For 20 years he remained

loyal. But in 1951 he formed an alliance with Frank Costello, head of the Genovese family. Vincent Mangano then disappeared and to this day his body never been found. The same day, the body of his brother, Philip, was found shot to death in a swampy area near Sheepshead Bay. While he never admitted to the murders, Anastasia took over the family with the approval of the Commission.

After the war, Anastasia bought into a dress factory and purchased a house overlooking the Hudson River in Fort Lee, New Jersey. He lived there with his wife and son behind a chain fence, guarded by a 'chauffeur' and watchdogs. He also bought a house in Italy for his aged mother and sister.

In the early 1950s, Anastasia was summoned by the US Senate Special Committee to Investigate Crime and by the State Crime Commission to answer questions about organized crime. Anastasia refused to say how he made a living, on the grounds of self-incrimination. He refused to tell them anything else either. In 1952, the federal government began deportation proceedings against him on the grounds that he had lied on his naturalization papers and had used fraud to obtain a 'certificate of arrival' from the Immigration and Naturalization Service. He had also said that he had never been arrested and had only used one name, Umberto Anastasio, neither of which was true. It was alleged that for many years he had taken part in activities he knew to be prohibited by state and federal laws. But the courts ruled against the government and the case was dropped in 1956.

Several attempts had already been made on his life. When underboss Willie Moretti was killed in a restaurant in Cliffside Park, New Jersey, in October 1951, Anastasia was supposed to have been with him. A few weeks later, Anastasia was at a party in Newark, celebrating the acquittal of associate Benedicto Macri on a murder charge, when he had to flee out of the back door as gunmen came in through the front.

Mafia Killings 30

Guarino 'Willie' Moretti, New Jersey, 4 October 1951

Moretti was quite a card. If there was any humour at all in a situation, he could find it. He loved a good story and was known to tell quite a few in his time. So when the Kefauver hearings started in 1950 and suspected Mafia members were called in to testify, Moretti found that he just couldn't help himself – some stories were too good to keep under his hat. And that's when Vito Genovese took it upon himself to cut Moretti off in mid-sentence.

Moretti had long been a member of the Luciano family and was a well respected 'made man'. It's said he was pals with such luminaries as Dean Martin, Jerry Lewis and Frank Sinatra. The story goes that when Sinatra was trying to break his contract with Tommy Dorsey but the band leader wouldn't agree, Moretti showed up at Dorsey's and stuck a gun down his throat to persuade him to change his mind. Needless to say, Sinatra was released from his contract. No doubt Moretti had a great laugh over that one.

Unfortunately, Moretti was a little too fond of a good time. What with all the booze and the parties, the nightclubs and the late nights, some time during his life he had contracted syphilis. For years, though, he was able to keep his illness under control and act as an effective Mafioso.

But by the time the Kefauver hearings began, Moretti had definitely gone into decline. Syphilis causes mental degeneration and Moretti's behaviour was becoming aberrant. He'd started to bet on imaginary horse races and to ramble on endlessly when telling his famous stories. When other mobsters, such as Frank Costello and Meyer Lansky, were called to testify at the hearings, each one refused, pleading the Fifth Amendment. Moretti, however, seemed to treat the Kefauver hearings as a bit of a lark, a chance to show off and have some fun. He had the senators at the hearings in stitches

on more than one occasion. Clearly Moretti was starting to falter. Who could say what secrets he might give away?

It was Vito Genovese who went to the Commission for permission to put Moretti down. The argument was bitter, but in the end it was decided – Moretti had to be dealt with and his death would be a mercy killing. But, of course, Genovese had another motive: with Moretti out of the way, he would be one step closer to total control of the Luciano family.

On 4 October 1951, Willie Moretti met some friends for brunch at Joe's Elbow Room in Cliffside Park, New Jersey. He had quite a pleasant day planned and was even expecting to meet up with Dean Martin and Jerry Lewis later. However, some time during the course of the meal, when the waiting staff were conveniently in the kitchen, Moretti's companions pulled out their guns and put an end to him. It's said that he was hit a number of times in the face and that such shots were signs of respect. But with friends like that, who needs enemies?

Meanwhile, Anastasia developed a greater passion for murder than ever. After watching a young Brooklyn salesman named Arnold Schuster on television, talking of his part in the arrest of America's most prolific bank robber Willie Sutton, Anastasia said: 'Hit the guy … I can't stand squealers.' In March 1952 Schuster was shot outside his own home, twice in the groin and once in each eye. Anastasia had now violated the founding rule of Murder Inc., first outlined by Bugsy Siegel: 'We only kill each other'.

In 1954 he was indicted on two counts of income tax evasion. The first trial ended with a hung jury. Before the retrial, the body of Vincent Macri, Benedicto Macri's brother, was found stuffed in the boot of a car in the Bronx. A few days later, Benedicto himself was found floating in the Passaic River. Another key witness was Charles Lee, a New Jersey plumbing contractor who had received $8,700 for work he had done

on Anastasia's home. He and his wife went missing, and their home in Miami, Florida, was found splattered with blood. The government case now in tatters, Anastasia accepted a plea bargain and spent just one year in a federal penitentiary.

At the time, Vito Genovese was trying to take over the Luciano family, but Anastasia supported his rival, Frank Costello. Normally Meyer Lansky would also have supported Costello, but Anastasia was trying to muscle in on his gambling operation in Cuba. It seemed likely that something had to give.

Mafia Killings 31

Anthony Carfano, New York City, 25 September 1959

Anthony 'Little Augie Pisano' Carfano had been a member of the Luciano mob in the 1930s (and went back even further than that). He later became a heavy hitter for Frank Costello when the mobster took over Lucky Luciano's operations. A loyal soldier, Carfano threw in his lot with his old boss, Costello, when Vito Genovese was muscling him out of the Mafia.

On the evening of 25 September 1959, Carfano went to New York's Copacabana nightclub to unwind a little. Things had been pretty tense for him lately, with a murder attempt on Costello and Genovese hanging over him. Besides, the Copacabana on East 60th Street was one of the hottest night spots in the country.

Carfano didn't go to the Copa alone, though. Janice Drake, a former beauty queen, was with him. Carfano had a long history with Janice and her husband, Allan, because he had helped to build up Allan's career. He was a second-rate comedian, but with the backing of Carfano he was getting some pretty sweet gigs. It was only when Carfano ran foul of Genovese that things started to dry up for Drake.

While Allan was out on the road with his act, hitting the hot spots, Carfano would check up on Janice to make sure she was

coping. He would also take her out on the town and buy her pearl bracelets. Yes, Carfano and Janice were more than just friends.

That night – Carfano's last – he and Janice were enjoying the food and each other's company, when he got a phone call. It's speculated that this call was from Frank Costello and he was giving his friend a heads up: 'Augie, they're gunning for ya; get out of there in a hurry!' So Carfano left the Copa post-haste and took Janice with him. The pair slipped into Carfano's car – a beautiful black Cadillac – and Carfano hit the gas. But Genovese had foreseen such a possibility, and had some torpedoes planted in the back seat of the car, waiting. Exit Little Augie Pisano.

The bodies of Carfano and Janice were found slumped in the front seats of Carfano's vehicle, which was parked somewhere near LaGuardia Airport. Carfano had fallen sideways, and Janice was next to him, her head leaning against the passenger window, her open eyes staring off at nothing. For poor Janice it had been just a case of being in the wrong place at the wrong time. As for Carfano, he had discovered the heavy price of loyalty.

Mafia Killings 32

Thomas Eboli, Brooklyn, New York City, 16 July 1972

When Tommy Eboli became head of the Genovese family in 1969 he must have thought that he had it made. After all, not only had the Genovese family once been the Luciano family, but it was still one of the most powerful mobs in the country. The only thing was, Eboli hadn't counted on Carlo Gambino, who had some ideas of his own concerning that particular branch of the Mafia.

Eboli had an interesting life. As well as being a made man and running rackets, he had also once been a fight manager – in fact, he had handled the boxing career of future mob boss Vincent

'The Chin' Gigante. One time, during a match, when he didn't like a decision the referee had made, Eboli climbed into the ring and physically attacked the man. Supposedly Eboli had arranged for the other boxer to take a dive, but the referee wasn't in on the fix.

Eboli paid his dues, slowly working his way up through the ranks until 1959 when his time finally came. That was the year that Vito Genovese was set up by the mob and sent to prison on a narcotics charge. This was Eboli's big chance, and he was promoted to the position of acting boss, along with Michele Miranda, Gerardo Catena and Philip Lombardo. Even though the role was shared, it gave Eboli a taste of power, and he found that he liked it.

So when Genovese died in prison and Eboli became the sole leader of the family, he figured it was time to flex his muscles a bit. In 1972 he started a narcotics scheme and borrowed a whopping sum of four million dollars from Carlo Gambino to get the ball rolling.

Trusting Gambino wasn't the smartest move Eboli could have made. Shortly after he had started to set things up, the police abruptly – and conveniently – got wind of the operation and swooped down. Eboli's cohort in the drug game, Louis Cirillo, was arrested and both the narcotics and the money that Eboli had borrowed were confiscated.

Now, of course, it was suddenly imperative that Carlo Gambino get his money back – every red cent of it. And naturally Eboli couldn't scrape the funds together. On 16 July 1972, Tommy Eboli exited his girlfriend's apartment at around one o'clock in the morning. As he climbed into his car, a truck pulled up from nowhere and he was shot five times in the neck and head.

Now that Eboli was gone, Gambino lost no time with his next move and nominated a buddy of his – Frank Tieri – to the role of boss of the Genovese family. That was no surprise, since Gambino had been moving behind the scenes, placing trusted pals of his into positions of power for a while. Tommy Eboli had been just another pawn who had fallen for Carlo Gambino's gambit.

On the morning of 25 October 1957, Anastasia entered the barber's shop of the Park Sheraton Hotel. His bodyguard Anthony Coppola parked the car in the underground car park, then took a stroll. While Anastasia relaxed in the barber's chair, two masked men raced in. The shop's owner was told: 'Keep your mouth shut if you don't want your head blown off.'

Pushing the barber out of the way, they opened fire. The first volley brought Anastasia to his feet, but he did not turn towards his killers. Instead, in his confusion he lunged at their reflection in the mirror. Grabbing for the glass shelving in front of the mirror, he brought it crashing to the floor. There were two more shots – one in the back of the head.

Anastasia was not afforded the lavish funeral normally given to a crime boss. There were just 12 mourners. No Mass was said for him, though his brother Salvatore, a Catholic priest, had visited the cemetery beforehand and blessed the grave. Anastasia's obituaries in the newspapers said he had been responsible for at least 63 murders.

Eight years later, a Mafia soldier called Joe Valachi claimed that the killing had been ordered by Anastasia's old associate, Vito Genovese, on the grounds that Anastasia had been invading his turf. The members of the Commission had agreed. In the old days, of course, at this point they would have got in touch with Murder Incorporated – and Alberto Anastasia himself.

Overleaf: Plain-clothes detectives examine the barber shop of the Park Sheraton Hotel, New York, where the body of Albert Anastasia lies partially covered.

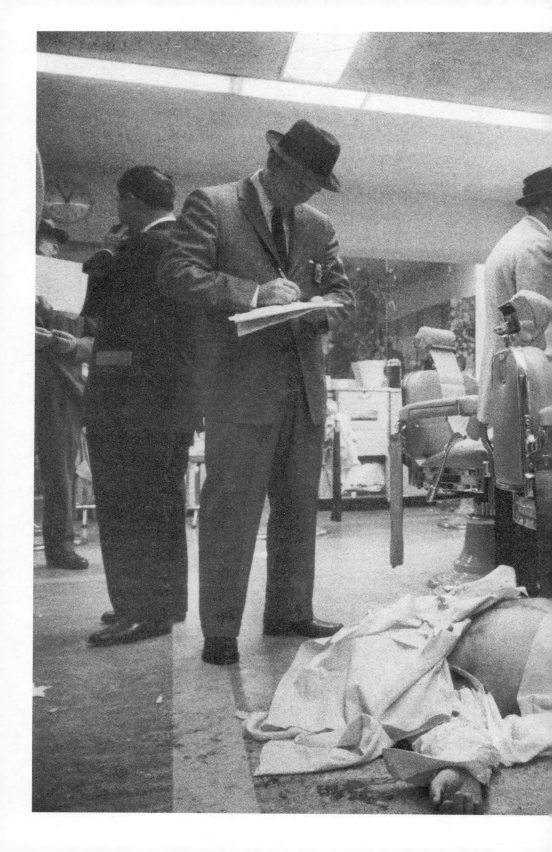

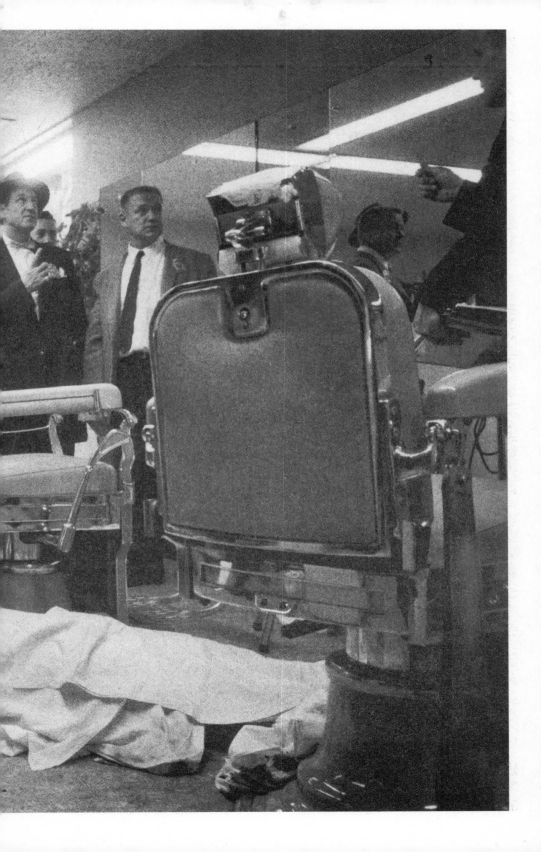

AN INNOCENT MAN

Anthony 'Tough Tony' Anastasio was another of the four brothers who jumped ship in New York in 1919. While elder brother Albert pursued a career in homicide, Tony took control of Brooklyn Local 1814, a position he held for three decades. He also rose to become vice-president of the International Longshoremen's Association, running the Brooklyn waterfront with an iron fist. He only had to mention 'my brother Albert' to make his point.

And he was ever loyal. Once he confronted a reporter from the *New York World-Telegram and Sun* and asked: 'How come you keep writing all those bad things about my brother Albert? He ain't killed nobody in your family … yet.'

At Albert's behest, Tony had organized the burning of the SS *Normandie*. He also prevented any further sabotage on the waterfront, stopped the enemy receiving details of sailings and helped US Navy Intelligence, who were operating on the dockside.

When Lucky Luciano was leaving for Italy, Tough Tony ensured that only top gangland figures were allowed aboard the *Laura Keene*, docked at Brooklyn's Bush Terminal, to bid him farewell. Reporters and other onlookers were held back by 50 longshoremen carrying menacing bailing hooks.

After Albert's murder in 1957, Tony's influence waned. However, Carlo Gambino, who succeeded Anastasia as head of the family, allowed him to retain control on the waterfront.

Fearing that Vito Genovese was out to kill him, Tony talked to the FBI. According to a memo dated August 1962, he told agents: 'I ate from the same table as Albert and came from the same womb but I know he killed many men and he deserved to die.'

In 1963, Tony Anastasio died of a heart attack in hospital. On the day of his funeral, all work was halted on the Brooklyn docks. Although he had a police record stretching back to 1925 with

charges ranging from assault to murder, he had been cleared on every count and died an innocent man.

Valachi – one of that vanishingly rare species, a Mafia witness – also revealed for the first time two things about the American Cosa Nostra: first, that the *capi* themselves had no direct involvement in crime of any kind, but only through intermediaries; and second, that its profits were already by that time being laundered through legitimate businesses.

Mafia Killings 33

Lawrence Mangano, Chicago, 3 August 1944

'Dago' Lawrence Mangano was a member of the Chicago Outfit. In charge of the Near West Side, he quietly rose through the ranks until he found himself almost on a par with the ambitious Anthony 'Big Tuna' Accardo. That, of course, was a situation which couldn't last long.

In the 1930s, Mangano dealt with gambling, a goldmine for gangs once Prohibition had been repealed. At the end of his life he would be branded Public Enemy Number Four, at a time when the United States, and Chicago especially, was awash with gangsters. In fact, Mangano was only a few notches below Outfit boss Frank Nitti.

Like so many mobsters of the time, Mangano had the cops in his pocket – all except one, Captain Luke Garrick. Mangano took care of Garrick, though – one day in 1928, the captain's home in Summerdale Avenue was destroyed by a bomb. After that Garrick, who survived the blast, fell nicely in line like all the others. It was a minor incident in the career of Mangano, but it shows the lengths to which he was willing to go.

In 1941, the Chicago Outfit began to implode. They'd been shaking down the Hollywood moguls, demanding money to ensure

the entertainment unions wouldn't strike. The revelation of this racket caused quite a stir, especially when top Hollywood figures such as Harry Warner of Warner Brothers testified.

Frank Nitti began to lose his grip at the thought of having to go back to prison again. He suffered from claustrophobia, and just couldn't bear the idea of being caged in a confined space. So on 19 March 1943, Nitti blew his brains out.

Paul Ricca and Louis Campagna, also top men in the Outfit, were brought down by the Hollywood scandal, and were packed off to prison. The setback to the Outfit was staggering. It really only left Tony Accardo and Lawrence Mangano as the top contenders for Al Capone's old crown.

The end for Mangano came on the evening of 3 August 1944. He had been out on the town in suburban Cicero with Mike Pontelli, his chauffeur (and bodyguard) and Pontelli's then girlfriend, Rita Reyes. As the group was heading home, driving along in Mangano's car, Mangano noticed a vehicle following behind them.

Not worried in the least, Mangano thought it was just the cops looking for a shakedown; he could easily buy them off. So on Mangano's instructions, Pontelli pulled the car over and stopped on Blue Island Avenue. Mangano got out, money in hand, but when the other car pulled up, the occupants opened fire and splattered Mangano all over the road. Circling round, they came back and finished off Pontelli too.

Mangano survived, but not for long. Astoundingly, there were around two hundred shotgun pellets in his body. With the death of Mangano, Tony Accardo was uncontested in his bid for the leadership of the Chicago Outfit.

Mafia Killings 34

Vincent Mangano, Jamaica Bay, Long Island, 19 April 1951

Vincent 'The Executioner' Mangano was boss of one of New York's five Mafia families. But there was also another executioner in the Mangano family – Albert Anastasia. These two together in the same gang never saw eye to eye, and since Anastasia was also one of the leaders of Murder Incorporated, it was a foregone conclusion which executioner would come out on top.

The Mangano mob made its wealth through gambling, labour racketeering and the waterfront. Mangano controlled the waterfront through Albert Anastasia and his labour boss brother 'Tough Tony' Anastasia. Because of the two brothers, all goods coming into port on a daily basis were pretty much up for grabs and Mangano could lift whatever he wanted.

However, Mangano severely resented Anastasia's moonlighting for the murder squad. He undoubtedly also felt threatened by Anastasia's elevated position in the group, one which allowed him to pal around with Lucky Luciano and Frank Costello, to name just two. Mangano and Anastasia would verbally duke it out on a regular basis, sometimes nearly coming to blows. But both knew the score – best to lie low and put up with things as long as it was convenient. It was just a matter of time, though, as to who would strike first. This prickly state of affairs lasted until 1951.

Later, Anastasia claimed that Mangano had forced his hand, that he had put out a contract on him and left him no choice. Apart from that, Anastasia had nothing to say, not to the police, nor the Commission. But everybody knew the score. In the battle for the Manganos, Anastasia had staged a little family coup.

The first to go was Mangano's brother, Philip, naturally enough also in the mob. His waterlogged body was found in a marsh in Jamaica Bay on 19 April 1951. He had been shot three times. Later

that same day it was pretty clear that Vincent was also missing. Both Mangano brothers were gone within hours of each other, though Vincent's body has never surfaced.

Now Anastasia had to move swiftly to consolidate his position. Meeting with the Commission and backed by Frank Costello, Anastasia persuaded the group to give him control of the Mangano family. He must have been pretty convincing because when he left the table that day, the entity known as the Mangano family was history – it had become the Anastasia family. Albert 'The Executioner' Anastasia had really arrived.

BENJAMIN 'BUGSY' SIEGEL

Bugsy Siegel was there right at the beginning of the new-look New York Mafia. He was in the jail cell, so one of the stories went, where Lucky Luciano first got together with Meyer Lansky. He was one of the four gunmen who murdered Giuseppe Masseria and one of the four 'internal-revenue agents' who were in at the kill of Salvatore Maranzano, the ruthless would-be *capo di tutti capi* of the city's underworld. He was also appointed, along with Meyer Lansky, to the board of the Unione Siciliana, one of the first attempts at a commission to guide the power of the Mafia nationwide. He may not have understood much about the politics – he started out as a small-time car-thief and driver of booze-trucks, after all – and he left that sort of thing to Luciano and Lansky. But he knew all the right people. He was presentable, and in 1935 must have seemed the ideal choice to spearhead the New York families' expansion of operations to the West Coast.

'Bugsy' Siegel

Mafia Killings 35

The Two Tonys, Los Angeles, 6 August 1951

Loose and wild, Tony Brancato and Tony Trombino, were desperados, living audaciously – and they died sprawled out on the front seat of a car somewhere near Hollywood Boulevard in one of the most infamous hits in mob history.

Tony Brancato was regarded by most as a low-level hood from Kansas City, but that's not how he saw himself. As far as he was concerned, he was going places and Kansas City just wasn't big enough to hold him. That's why he headed over to the bright lights and fast times in Los Angeles to work for Mickey Cohen, one of the big cheeses out there. His brother Norfia also worked for Cohen and there seemed to be a prospect that Norfia could get him a real sweet gig.

As soon as Tony Brancato hit the coast, he began to make himself unpopular, muscling in on other people's rackets and generally stirring up a lot of noise. It wouldn't do. Cohen had a lot of problems of his own, what with tax charges and a war with another LA mobster, Jack Dragna. For Cohen, control of the entire city was at stake, and he didn't have time to babysit Norfia's little brother.

So Tony Brancato struck out on his own for a bit, did a little freelancing, not really getting anywhere. Then he got the brilliant idea of bringing his old pal Tony Trombino down from Kansas City. Once Trombino hit town, the two pals let loose, getting into robbery, narcotics, murder. . . They were even suspected of murdering Bugsy Siegel – but so were a lot of others. Leaving a trail behind them a mile wide, the Tonys didn't care how they pulled off their jobs and it showed. By the end of their career they had been arrested a total of 46 times.

The two Tonys never seemed to realize that some targets were off limits. On 28 May 1951, together with some other gangsters,

they held up the sports betting concern of the Flamingo Hotel in Las Vegas, run by Mickey Cohen. The total haul of the heist was $3,500. It was not much of a pay cheque, but the truth was that with the Flamingo job, the Tonys had bitten off more than they could chew. The Flamingo, built by Bugsy Siegel, was and always had been a mobbed-up operation. Basically, then, the Tonys had just ripped off the mob. After that Jack Dragna got into the picture and it was pretty much a done deal as far as the Tonys were concerned.

Jimmy 'The Weasel' Fratianno was given the contract, along with Charlie 'Bats' Battaglia. And on the night of 6 August 1951, the end came for the two Tonys as they sat in their car in a side street just off Sunset Boulevard, waiting to hear the details of a big score that was supposedly coming their way. It was just a lure of course.

The cops never found out who killed Brancato and Trombino until Fratianno flipped in 1977 and named the Tonys as just one of the hits he'd done. It's to be hoped that the Tonys enjoyed spending that $3,500 before their inevitable demise.

Teaming up in southern California with a local mob led by Jack Dragna, Siegel ran drugs and operated a string of gambling clubs and offshore casino-ships on behalf of his New York bosses both before and during the war. With the help of his pal, actor George Raft – and with his rough edges smoothed off by a divorced millionairess called Countess Dorothy di Frasso – he was at ease in the best Hollywood circles. He was on first-name terms with people like Jean Harlow, Clark Gable and Gary Cooper – and a magnet to every starlet. He fitted right in.

Gambling and stars: it was this combination that was to lead to Siegel's one major contribution to Mafia history. In 1945, he suggested to his bosses the idea of building a casino and hotel in the Nevada desert at a place called Las Vegas. He put together $3 million, some of it reportedly from Howard Hughes, and the Commission soon organized a loan to match his investment. The place, he said, would be called

The Flamingo – a name suggested by his girlfriend Virginia Hill. There would be a grand opening, with all of Hollywood's royalty present for the glamorous event.

However, word soon got back to the Commission that money had been disappearing during The Flamingo's construction, some of it salted away abroad. A decision was taken at an informal meeting of bosses in Havana, Cuba, that Siegel would have to repay with interest the East-Coast Mafia investment as soon as the hotel–casino opened. Trouble was, the grand opening that Siegel had planned turned out to be a disaster. Bad weather kept planes grounded at Los Angeles airport and the stars never showed. In two weeks, The Flamingo was closed after losing $100,000.

Bugsy couldn't pay, and his old friends in New York could no longer protect him. It was a matter of business; an example had to be set. So, on the night of 20 June 1947, Siegel was gunned down as he sat in the living-room of Virginia Hill's Los Angeles house on North Linden Drive. The final bullet, the 'calling card', was fired into his left eye. Just five people attended his funeral.

But Seigel had been popular with Mickey Cohen, an associate who had helped him set up the hotel and who ran its sports book operation. Cohen, who had previously worked for the Chicago Outfit, was renowed for his violence and reacted badly to the killing. He went to the Roosevelt Hotel, where he believed the assassins were staying, started shooting in the air and demanded that the shooters meet him outside. Cohen's time in Las Vegas had not been without incident and his activities had attracted the attention of the authorities and other gangs.

After its initial closure, the Flamingo started up again under new management. It was soon followed by two more Las Vegas casinos: the Tropicana, controlled by Frank Costello, and the Thunderbird, controlled by Meyer Lansky.

Mafia Killings 36

Gus Greenbaum, Las Vegas, 3 December 1958

The scene was a 1950s bedroom. The shade of a chrome floor lamp hovered like a spaceship over the bed. Light from a television flickered, while the piercing 'off-the-air' signal whined unendingly. Next to Greenbaum was a heating pad, something to take the chill off the night. The only thing was that Greenbaum couldn't feel that chill at the time. Greenbaum would never feel anything again: he was dead.

It must have been the Vegas curse. That's the thing that got both Greenbaum and Bugsy Siegel. Undoubtedly many a gambler has fallen victim to the curse on some level or other – gambling away their pay cheques, their mortgages, their sanity. Greenbaum and Bugsy lost more than that, though. They lost their lives.

Mere hours after Siegel had been executed for mismanaging the Las Vegas Flamingo Hotel, the Chicago Outfit brought in Greenbaum, along with Moe Sedway, to turn the prospect round. The pair did just that, and in spectacular fashion, bringing the casino into the black to the tune of $4,000,000 within the first year. Of course, it helped that Siegel wasn't around to skim the profits any more.

Greenbaum seemed to have the magic touch when it came to Vegas, and the Outfit and Meyer Lansky liked what they saw. In 1955, Outfit boss Tony Accardo and mob accountant Jake Guzik asked Greenbaum to take over management of the Riviera as well, another mobbed-up casino that was losing money. Greenbaum, however, turned them down. He was tired of the game, he said, and wanted to rest. He was looking forward to spending the rest of his life just pottering around and living off his ill-gotten gains. 'Sure,' Guzik said, patting Greenbaum on the back; then the mobsters headed back to Chicago. Seven days later, Greenbaum's sister-in-

law was found murdered in her home. Greenbaum got the message and took over the Riviera for his good buddies in the mob.

But maybe Guzik should have listened to Greenbaum and let him retire. The strain of running things in Vegas was beginning to tell on Gus and he took to seeking out recreation – heavy recreation – that consisted of gambling, alcohol, narcotics and female companionship. The mob weren't pleased, but they could have overlooked all of it as long as the casinos stayed in the black. The trouble was, in order to pay for all of these expensive pastimes, Greenbaum had begun to skim from the till just like Bugsy before him.

According to Johnny Roselli, it was Meyer Lansky who put the contract out on Gus Greenbaum. No surprise there – Lansky was the gambling tsar. On 3 December 1958, Greenbaum and his wife, Bess, were found murdered in their home, Greenbaum was still curled up in front of the TV. It was strange that Mrs Greenbaum had also been killed – the mob doesn't usually kill family members. Maybe Lansky just wanted to underline the message – in red ink. Or perhaps it was the Vegas curse.

Mafia Killings 37

Abner Zwillman, New Jersey, 16 February 1959

Some Mafiosi seem to be somewhat forgotten today. Known only to few today, in his time Abner Zwillman was one of the most important mobsters in New York's underworld and a member of the Syndicate. He was referred to as the Al Capone of New Jersey.

Zwillman worked the rackets – gambling, labour slugging and bootlegging – with some legitimate businesses such as nightclubs thrown in. Reports say that he controlled about 40 per cent of all the booze that was smuggled into the United States from Canada – that's a lot of whisky! The Zwillman mob was making a bundle.

Zwillman also dabbled in the movie-making industry, partially running the Projectionist Union and payrolling the overbearing movie mogul Harry Cohn. It's fairly common knowledge that Cohn had mob connections, and Zwillman lent the mogul quite a hefty sum. But the money wasn't without strings, of course. Expecting the loan to be repaid – and with plenty of interest – Zwillman also demanded that Cohn give his girlfriend a movie contract. Zwillman's girlfriend at the time was no ordinary starlet, but the original platinum blonde herself – Jean Harlow. Zwillman reputedly gave the beautiful Harlow a jewelled bracelet and a red Cadillac, among other gifts. Now that's travelling in style.

But when the 1950s came along, Zwillman, like so many other gangsters, began to feel the pinch. In mid-1950 he was called to testify at the Kefauver hearings and from 1953 to 1956 he endured investigation, indictment and trial for tax evasion. The Feds were finally trying to get tough with organized crime and Zwillman was one of their targets.

The heat was really on in 1959 when Zwillman was called to testify before the McClellan Senate Committee. Zwillman was reportedly despondent and there were those – Meyer Lansky, for one – who feared he would crack under the pressure and give the whole game away. Apparently, Lansky went to the Syndicate.

On 26 February 1959, Zwillman was found in his basement hanging by a cord from the ceiling. The official ruling on his death was suicide – after all, Zwillman had been pretty low, what with the McClellan investigation and his recent tax troubles. But a ruling of suicide would definitely not explain the bruises that were found on his body, particularly his wrists. On the contrary, such marks seemed to indicate that the mobster had been bound prior to being killed and then strung up after death.

One story says that Lucky Luciano, by then exiled and living in Italy, confirmed that Zwillman had been murdered. Maybe only

Meyer Lansky could corroborate that statement, but murdered or not, Zwillman wouldn't be testifying any time soon.

THE GENTLE DON

It's not easy to imagine that the world of the Mafia was any place for men with a softer side. But one man did stand out from the crowd and earned the nickname 'the Gentle Don' in honour of his attempts to use diplomacy rather than extreme violence to get what he wanted in life.

Angelo Annaloro was born in Villalba, Sicily, and went as an infant to the United States in 1911. His father, Michele, ran a grocery store in south Philadelphia. Young Angelo first came to the attention of the police when he turned in an extortionist who had tried to extract protection money from his father.

When he turned to crime, he changed his name, taking the maiden name of his paternal grandmother. Police records from the 1930s reveal that he gave his name as Angelo Bruno when he was arrested on illegal gambling and bootlegging charges. He was introduced to Philadelphia Mafia boss Salvatore Sabella by Michael Maggio, owner of the cheese factory in which he worked. In his thirties, Bruno became a made man.

When Sabella stepped down at the end of the Castellammarese War, Joseph 'Bruno' Dovi pushed aside John Avena to take over the family. He was succeeded by Joseph Ida. Under his regime, Bruno graduated from small-time bookmaker and gambler to major numbers writer and loan-shark, and was made *capo*. With underboss Marco Reginelli and *capo* Peter Casella, he ran the Greaser Gang whose bookmaking, gambling and loan-sharking operations turned over $50 million a year.

In 1953, a police raid uncovered 17,000 numbers slips in Bruno's headquarters. Convicted, he was fined and given two years' probation.

Angelo Annaloro was nicknamed 'the Gentle Don' due to his preference for diplomacy over violence

But that did not stop him gambling and loan-sharking and he managed to escape several other prosecutions.

Mafia Killings 38

Jack Whalen, Sherman Oaks, near Los Angeles, 2 December 1959

He should have had everything. Jack Whalen, aka Jack O'Hara, stood 6 feet tall with 1950s-style matinée idol looks. Whalen could have been a movie star; he *should* have been a movie star. It would have been better than tangling with Mickey Cohen – one of Los Angeles' most notorious mob bosses.

As a youngster, Whalen had gone to a private military school where he'd hobnobbed with the offspring of the wealthy and played polo in between classes. In the Second World War he had been a hero, a bomber pilot. And when he returned from overseas he had married into one of the richest families in Los Angeles. There was no reason why he couldn't have had it all. He must just have been drawn to the seamier side of life.

Whalen was pretty tough; he could smash heads together – and often did – with the best of them. He relied on his muscle to get the job done and was so tough that he'd take care of business without using a gun. They called him 'The Enforcer'. Truth be told, Whalen was practically a mob all by himself.

Like others of the time, Jack Whalen had tried to muscle in on some of Mickey Cohen's territory when that gangster went to prison. This, of course, didn't sit too well with Mickey and by 1959 Jack had taken things too far.

Just before midnight on 2 December 1959, Jack Whalen burst into Rondelli's restaurant. Present at one of the tables that night were Joe Mars, George Piscitelle and Sam LoCigno, flunkies for Mickey Cohen – and Cohen himself. Whalen was looking for

Piscitelle and LoCigno, he said, they owed a bookie client of his nine hundred bucks and he was there to collect.

Arriving at Cohen's table, Whalen began to rough up Piscitelle and LoCigno, demanding the dough. Shortly afterwards, someone at the table pulled out a gun and shot Whalen right between the eyes. He went down about as hard as you'd expect, and expired soon after.

So, who pulled the trigger that night? Mickey Cohen hadn't seen what had happened, or so he said. As soon as Whalen started on Piscitelle and LoCigno, Cohen dived under the table and stayed there until things died down – literally.

During the investigation, several guns were found in a trash can outside the restaurant, almost as if they'd been planted there. But what's even more interesting is that a few days after the murder, Cohen stooge LoCigno showed up at the police station and confessed to the killing. The case went to trial but, try as they might, the prosecution could not pin Whalen's death on Cohen.

After a guilty verdict and an appeal, LoCigno eventually got life; it's more than likely he got a hefty pay-off from Cohen too. But that's a lot better than what Jack Whalen got.

When Ida was deported to Italy, he had to choose between Bruno and Antonio 'Mr Miggs' Pollina as his successor. He chose Pollina. By then Bruno had his own loyal following, so Pollina sought to eliminate his rival. He gave the contract to underboss Ignazio 'Natz' Denaro. But Denaro told Bruno, who appealed to the Mafia Commission in New York. It was a dangerous move. If the Commission had found against him, he would have written his own death warrant. However, by asking for the Commission's arbitration, he had shown them respect.

Pollina had not asked permission to whack Bruno, who had already forged an alliance with Carlo Gambino. The Commission found in Bruno's favour, naming him the new boss of the Philadelphia mob and

giving him permission to whack Pollina. Instead, Bruno forced him into retirement. This was typical of 'the Gentle Don', who sought to resolve disputes by diplomacy rather than murder.

By the mid-1960s, the Commission was headed by Carlo Gambino, who gave Bruno a seat. Bruno's alliance with Gambino enhanced his status and for two decades he maintained a 'Pax Mafia' in Philadelphia. As the Gentle Don kept violence to a minimum, this was largely tolerated by the authorities. Neil Welch, who later became special agent in charge of the FBI's Philadelphia office, said that for years the Bureau did not pursue Bruno with great vigour.

Bruno maintained a front as a legitimate businessman, running the Atlas Extermination Company in Trenton, New Jersey and the Aluminum Products Sales Corporation in Hialeah, Florida, as well as retaining an interest in a casino at the Plaza Hotel in Havana, Cuba. Nevertheless, he chalked up further arrests for interstate tax conspiracy and filing false income tax returns.

When family member Nicky Scarfo stabbed a longshoreman over a seat in a restaurant, Bruno banished him to Atlantic City, then a depressed area. But in 1976 laws were passed to allow gambling there, in an attempt to revive the city. The rush was on to build casinos. Bruno had contacts in several steel companies in Pittsburgh and the Philly mob took a major hand in the construction work. They then moved in on all aspects of the gambling industry. Suddenly Scarfo was cock of the walk.

By then Bruno's hold on the family was weakening. He spent two years in jail for refusing to testify before a grand jury during an investigation into corruption in Atlantic City involving a number of high-ranking officials. Instead of maintaining his monopoly, he allowed New York and New Jersey families to move in on his casinos in New Jersey. He also refused to become involved with the lucrative drugs trade. This caused resentment among the younger soldiers and *capos*.

In 1979, the 69-year-old Bruno was not in the best of health and faced indictments for racketeering. His *consigliere*, Anthony 'Tony

Bananas' Caponigro, conspired with New York and New Jersey crime families to have Bruno wasted. He consulted Frank 'Funzi' Tieri, the acting boss of the Genovese family. Tieri gave his word that he would support Caponigro in front of the Commission.

On the evening of 21 March 1980, Bruno's driver, John Stanfa, took his boss home. As Stanfa pulled up outside Bruno's house at 934 Snyder Avenue, Philadelphia, a man was waiting in the shadows. Stanfa pushed the button, lowering the passenger window next to Bruno. The man in the shadows moved swiftly towards it. He pulled a 12-bore shotgun from under his coat, put it to the back of Bruno's head and pulled the trigger. As Bruno slumped lifelessly, the gunman ran to a waiting car and sped off.

Stanfa was wounded when some pellets hit him in the arm. He was later charged with perjury relating to the testimony he had given in front of the grand jury investigating Bruno's shooting. At Bruno's funeral, the cortege consisted of 17 limousines and 35 other cars. More than a thousand people filled the pavements outside the church.

Mafia Killings 39

Philip Testa, Philadelphia, 15 March 1981

The body of slain mob boss Angelo Bruno had hardly cooled when his underboss, Philip 'The Chicken Man' Testa, became head of the Philadelphia mob. Not that Testa had had anything to do with the Gentle Don's demise – that had been the work of Antonio Caponigro, who would pay a terrible price for his transgression – but that didn't stop Testa benefiting from Bruno's death.

Testa's tenure as godfather should have been a successful one. He intended to take the best of Bruno's regime – the late mobster's sense of tradition and honour – and add some new, badly needed improvements. Testa planned on opening up Philadelphia to mob-

sanctioned drug trafficking, something that had been banned under the old boss, as well as inducting some fresh blood into the fold. As soon as Testa grasped the reins he brought in a whole flock of fledgling mobsters who took the oath, pricked their fingers and became fully-fledged Mafiosi.

As many as nine men – Salvatore 'Chuckie' Merlino, Frank Narducci Junior, and Testa's son, Salvatore, among them – received their made men buttons one night in 1980 or 1981, in an initiation ceremony that featured the traditional burning of saints' cards as part of the ritual and undoubtedly ended in unbridled celebration.

Testa had done everything right, in other words. Everything should have worked. But blood had been spilled and the smell of death was in the air. There was now no holding back the dogs of war.

Greed – it was the same thing that had inspired Bruno's murder. Peter Casella, Testa's underboss, didn't want what Testa was selling – the drug opportunities (Casella had been in trafficking himself), the new mobsters in the club. Casella wanted more.

Once again, a member of the Philadelphia mob committed murder without the full permission of the Commission. The story goes that Casella whipped up a bomb that sported 20 sticks of dynamite and had finishing nails embedded in it. When Testa came home to his house on West Porter Street, south Philadelphia on the morning of 15 March 1981, the device was detonated as soon as he set foot on his porch and opened the front door. The explosion was devastating and was felt nearly three miles away. Despite being blown straight into his kitchen, Testa was still alive, at least initially; he died several hours later, after being rushed to the hospital. It hadn't even been a year since the death of 'Gentle Don' Bruno.

The war was just getting started in Philadelphia.

Caponigro was summoned before the Commission, who said they had not given permission for the hit, nor had they even considered it. He turned to Tieri who, he said, had sanctioned the killing. Tieri denied it. As Caponigro had killed a Commission member without the Commission's consent, he was sentenced to death. On 18 April 1980, his body was found in the boot of a car in the South Bronx. He had suffered 14 bullet and knife wounds. His executioner was Joe 'Mad Dog' Sullivan, a Bronx enforcer.

But the effects of the Don's death did not end there. Over the next five years, 28 members or associates of the 60-strong Philadelphia family would die. After Caponigro's death, Bruno's underboss Philip 'The Chicken Man' Testa took over the family with Scarfo as his *consigliere*. A year later, Testa was returning home when a remote-controlled bomb blew up his house. Testa's underboss Pete Casella claimed that he had been made boss at a meeting with Paul Castellano and Fat Tony Salerno. Scarfo discovered that he was lying. In exchange for allowing the Gambinos and the Genovese to operate in Atlantic City, Scarfo obtained their backing to become boss of the Philly mob and Casella went into retirement in Florida.

Then war broke out with Harry 'the Hunchback' Riccobene. War continued on and off for the next 20 years until the family was stabilized under Joseph 'Uncle Joe' Ligambi in 2001 – it was a far cry from the 20 years of profitable peace Angelo Bruno had given them.

Mafia Killings 40

Robert Riccobene, Philadelphia, 6 December 1983

The war in Philadelphia continued. Mob bosses Angelo Bruno and Phil Testa had met their ends in 1980 and 1981 respectively. Control of the Philadelphia family had been awarded to Nicodemo Scarfo, through a deal he'd brokered with the Gambino and Genovese families, for partial interest in the gambling mecca of Atlantic City.

Not everyone was pleased with this state of affairs, however. Chief among Scarfo's detractors were the Riccobene brothers – Harry, Mario and Robert – since Scarfo was expecting the Riccobenes to pay tribute, something they'd never had to do before. It seems that under Bruno and then Testa, the Riccobenes had held special status, been independents and hadn't had to share their wealth. Now with Scarfo calling the shots all that was about to change. Harry, naturally enough, had other ideas.

Little 'Nicky' Scarfo was a ruthless operator. Whereas Don Bruno would use murder as a last resort, violence was always the opening move for Scarfo. It was no surprise, then, when Scarfo decided it was time for Harry Riccobene to go. But he didn't expect the Riccobenes to fight back.

It was open war in Philadelphia, the kind of knock-down, shoot-'em-up bloodbath that used to explode in Chicago during the 1920s and 1930s. Gunmen drove through the streets and bodies were dropping everywhere. Once, while Harry was making a call from a phone booth, the Scarfo faction happened by and shot him five times. That wasn't enough to take out Harry, though – the 70-year-old managed to knock the gun from his assailant's hand and was still standing after the incident.

Failed attempts like this were getting under Scarfo's skin, and he ordered the boys to step it up a bit. Though they managed to hold their own for quite a while, the Riccobenes couldn't stand up to the rest of the Philly Family. It didn't help that by 1983 Scarfo, Harry and Mario Riccobene were in prison. With two top players gone, the Riccobenes weren't able to hold out much longer.

It was the last volley in the battle for Philadelphia. On 6 December 1983, Robert Riccobene was returning to his mother's house in Southwest Philadelphia after a shopping trip. As the pair stepped out of their car, Scarfo's men opened fire. Robert turned to run, but didn't get very far and fell dead as he tried to hop a fence.

He had been shot in the back of the head and right in front of his mother, which was a supposed breach of Mafia rules. It shows how far things had gotten out of hand.

The Riccobenes had been subdued, and Little Nicky Scarfo was busy carrying out business from his prison cell. But Nicodemo Scarfo was just getting started.

THE BEGINNING OF THE END

Born in 1940 in the tiny mountain village of Caccamo, some 30 miles from Palermo, John Stanfa belonged to a Mafia family. Two of his brothers and one brother-in-law were also Mafiosi. After a car bomb in the Palermo suburb of Ciaculli killed seven policemen and military personnel, said to have been part of a bloody war between rival clans in the city, the authorities stamped down on the Mafia, prompting 1,200 arrests. Aware of the danger, Stanfa and his wife emigrated to the United States, settling in Philadelphia.

Mafia Killings 41

Salvatore Testa, Philadelphia, 14 September 1984

If there was anyone that Salvatore Testa should have been able to trust it was his godfather, the Godfather – Nicodemo Scarfo. Testa had known Scarfo all his life and looked on him as a father. He should have had nothing to fear from the man, but nobody was safe with Scarfo.

Salvie Testa was the son of Philip 'The Chicken Man' Testa, that same Chicken Man who had run the Philly family after the death of Don Angelo Bruno, and who was later himself murdered in a nail bomb attack. It's said that Salvatore was a Mafia blueblood, that he'd

been born and bred for the life. They called him the Crown Prince of the Philly Mob. Standing over 6 feet tall and darkly handsome, he looked the part.

After the death of Salvie Testa's father, Scarfo took over the Philadelphia family and a new regime – one of violence, intimidation and fear – was initiated. Testa became a *capo* in this new regime, standing right beside Scarfo. After all, he was the son of a late mob boss, and Scarfo's godson.

When Scarfo went to war with the Riccobene brothers, Testa was there, dishing it out with the rest of them. Testa was a specific target of the Riccobenes, and received several dangerous wounds in that war, even surviving a hit while eating clams in a south Philadelphia pizza parlour. He was shot eight times, but recovered, with scars that were marks of his loyalty to Little Nicky Scarfo.

It wasn't all one way, though; Testa struck fear into the hearts of the Riccobenes and was never as happy as when he was finally able to take revenge on the men who had murdered his beloved father, Philip. In all, it's said he was responsible for at least 18 deaths.

As the 1980s rolled on, Testa was everywhere and the media were beginning to take notice of the handsome, charismatic gangster. The press were starting to refer to the mob prince as a rising star in the Mafia.

Little Nicky Scarfo was taking notice too, and he didn't like what he saw. Testa was becoming too popular and getting awfully close to the top. The jealous and unstable Scarfo was beginning to view him as more of a threat than a godson.

Sometime in 1984, then, Little Nicky Scarfo ordered the hit on a man who had been like flesh and blood to him – Salvatore Testa. At a Mafia funeral, Testa was singled out and given the kiss of death.

On 14 September 1984, Testa was lured by his best friend to the Too Sweet candy store in Southwark, Philadelphia, ostensibly for a meeting. Once inside, he received two shots to the back of his head

and died immediately. His corpse was found later by the side of a dirt road in New Jersey.

During the early 1980s, the Philly family existed in an atmosphere of paranoia and treachery, thanks to Scarfo's mismanagement of the mob. Over the next few years, Nicodemo Scarfo would be tried on a number of charges – including Salvatore Testa's murder – and as a result, is likely to spend the rest of his life in prison. Among those who testified against him were members of Scarfo's own Philly family – mob men who no longer felt any loyalty to the man who had ordered the murder of his own godson.

After several months, Stanfa returned to face the music and was sentenced to eight years. When he got out in 1987, Scarfo was in jail and the Philly mob was in tatters. Stanfa adopted a low profile, spending some time in Sicily. When he returned, Anthony Piccolo was acting boss, but the Gambinos and the Genovese backed Stanfa to take over, with Piccolo as his *consigliere*.

Stanfa was as bad a boss as Scarfo. He increased the street tax that other thugs were required to pay to Cosa Nostra and sent old-time mobster Felix Bocchino out to collect it. When 73-year-old Bocchino was shot dead in his car, the press said it was the first Mafia hit in Philadelphia in seven years. It became clear that a bunch of young turks led by 'Skinny Joey' Merlino were responsible. Stanfa struck back with a botched hit on 'Mikey Chang' Ciancaglini. At that time, Merlino was in jail.

Stanfa beefed up his operation by bringing Rosario Bellocchi and Biagio Adornetto over from Sicily. He also patched it up with Merlino. Skinny Joey, Mikey Chang and Adornetto became made men. But when Adornetto made a move on Stanfa's daughter, Sara, Bellocchi was sent after him with a shotgun and Adornetto fled.

Meanwhile, Merlino was making trouble. He liked to bet. When he won, he would collect his winnings; when he lost, he refused to pay up.

Stanfa decided to go to war with him, but Merlino struck first. Stanfa's underboss, 'Joey Chang' Ciancaglini, was shot up in his social club. He survived, but was so badly injured that he was forced to retire.

In jail, Merlino made friends with Ralph Natale, a serious rival to Stanfa. Stanfa ordered a hit on Merlino. He had a lucky escape when a bomb failed to detonate. Then, in August 1993, Merlino was injured while Mikey Chang was shot dead. Stanfa thought he had taught Merlino a lesson. But he was wrong.

Three weeks later, Stanfa's car was stuck in traffic when a van pulled up alongside. The doors opened and shots came raining down on Stanfa's car. His son was hit in the face, but Stanfa and his driver managed to escape. In a tit-for-tat retaliation, two top Merlino associates were hit. One vital member of the Merlino faction, Tommy 'Horsehead' Scafidi, then defected to Stanfa.

Merlino went back to jail for parole violation. Stanfa then discovered that they had an informer in their midst – the rat was caught by two bullets in his head. Nevertheless, on 17 March 1994, Stanfa and 23 of his men were indicted on racketeering charges that included murder, murder conspiracy, extortion, arson, kidnapping and obstruction of justice. Not only did the FBI have their informants inside the Philly mob, they had also been bugging Stanfa since he had first taken over as boss. Bellocchi and others turned state's evidence to escape long prison sentences. For Stanfa, there was no one left on whom he could inform. In November 1995, he was sentenced to five consecutive life sentences.

THE LAST DON

Born to Italian-American parents, Joey Massino was brought up in Maspeth, a working-class area of Queens, New York. He dropped out of high school and went instead into the lunch-wagon business, selling snacks and soft drinks at factories and construction sites. But his trucks were a cover for illegal gambling, loan-sharking and selling stolen goods. He soon became known to the police as a rookie wiseguy.

A burly 5 feet 9 inches, he ate too many of his own sandwiches and doughnuts. His weight ballooned to 250 pounds and he became known as 'Big Joey'. In 1960, he married Josephine Vitale and his brother-in-law Salvatore 'Good Looking Sal' Vitale became his right-hand man.

A teenage friend was the nephew of Philip 'Rusty' Rastelli, a *capo* in the Bonanno family who was based in Maspeth. Rastelli was the kingpin of a hijacking operation that pulled off five or six road robberies every week in the New York area. Also maintaining a thriving 'roach coach' business, Massino and his team successfully branched out into hijacking. As a protégé of Rastelli, Massino was 'made' in the Bonanno crime family.

Most heists took place with the gang blocking the truck and a team member jumping on to the running board and sticking a gun in the driver's face. Massino used a different method. Thanks to his loan-sharking business, he could organize 'give-ups', when a teamster, or truck driver, could not afford to pay. That is, the truck driver handed over the goods without fuss. Using this method, he is thought to have got away with $100,000 worth of coffee, $500,000 worth of clothing on its way to Saks Fifth Avenue and $2 million worth of Kodak film.

The key to his success was organizing 'drops' – empty warehouses or lots where the contraband could quickly be offloaded on to smaller trucks for delivery to fences or pre-arranged clients. Massino's contacts were so good that he organized drops and fences for other hijackers. Soon he was running an underground clearing house for stolen goods – everything from lobsters to air conditioners. This brought him into contact with another hijacker, John Gotti. They became neighbours when Massino moved his family out to Howard Beach in Queens.

However, the FBI were on his trail. On one occasion, they thought they had him cornered in a warehouse full of stolen goods. But as they rushed in at the front door, Massino vanished out the back, down a pre-planned escape route. Another time it was discovered that he was off-loading expensive suits via a rope line from the warehouse to a clothes

shop when a customer dropped in for a cut-price purchase. 'He was smart and feared and nobody would give him up,' said one agent.

FBI agent Patrick F. Colgan spotted a hijacked truck outside a diner in Maspeth one night. He tried to follow it, only to be blocked by a car that then sped off. When the car caught up with the truck, Massino jumped out of it and climbed up on to the truck's running board. He had a word with the truck driver, then leapt back into the car and took off.

Colgan assumed that Massino had told the driver to dump the rig and then try to escape. He managed to catch up with the truck before that happened and was holding the driver, Ray Wean, at gunpoint when Massino turned up and asked what was going on. Colgan told Massino that he was under arrest, but Massino said that he needed to relieve himself first. He then drove off. Two days later, Massino gave himself up. He stood trial on his first felony charge for theft from an interstate shipment. While Wean was convicted and spent a year in prison, Massino's attorney argued that his client had innocently stopped to find out if Wean, a casual acquaintance, was having trouble. He was acquitted.

While Carmine Galante was in jail in the 1970s, Rastelli took over as boss of the Bonanno family. But when Galante was paroled, Rastelli was in jail, and he took over again. Nevertheless, Massino remained loyal to Rastelli and visited him in prison. This enraged Galante and Massino feared that Galante might whack him. But before this could happen the Commission gave Rastelli permission to take out Galante. Massino was outside the restaurant as back-up when the hit was made.

Massino had previous experience of murder. He and John Gotti had killed and dismembered Paul Castellano's daughter's boyfriend, Vito Borelli, after he said that Castellano looked like Frank Perdue, the well-known purveyor of poultry. Joseph 'Do Do' Pastore, a cigarette

Joseph Massino appeared as a defendant in the Rastelli-Bonanno family trial, September 1986

smuggler and loan-shark, was also whacked by Massino because Massino owed him $9,000. With Galante dead, Rastelli became boss of the Bonanno family again. But he was in jail, so he made the *capo* Salvatore 'Sally Fruits' Ferrugia acting boss. Massino was also promoted to *capo*, but the Bonanno soldiers knew that Massino had the direct line to Rastelli.

In May 1981, Massino heard from a Colombo soldier that three Bonanno *capos* – Philip 'Phil Lucky' Giaccone, Alphonse 'Sonny Red' Indelicato and Dominick 'Big Trin' Trinchera – aimed to take over. Massino consulted Paul Castellano and Carmine Persico, who told him to 'do what you have to do'.

The three renegade *capos* were invited to an 'administration meeting' in a Brooklyn social club run by the Gambinos. Weapons were traditionally not carried at these events, so it was all the more of a surprise to them when they were gunned down by masked men.

At the time, undercover FBI agent Joseph Pistone had penetrated the Bonanno family under the alias Donnie Brasco. By then, he had collected enough evidence to put the key players away for a long time. When Massino discovered this, he ordered a hit on Dominick 'Sonny Black' Napolitano, who had nominated Pistone.

DONNIE BRASCO

Undercover FBI agent Joseph Pistone spent six years infiltrating the Bonanno crime family. Brought up in Paterson, New Jersey, he joined the FBI in 1969. In 1974, he was transferred to New York to work on the truck hijacking squad. With a Sicilian heritage, fluent Italian, and the ability to drive an 18-wheel truck, he was perfectly positioned to infiltrate the hijacking gangs. Raised in a working-class area and the son of a bar owner, he also knew 'the life'.

The FBI erased all record of Pistone's former life and constructed a new identity for him as Donald 'Donnie the Jeweler' Brasco, a

small-time burglar. This gave him a non-violent reputation, so he would not be asked to hurt people. But he had to learn the street value of gems, and how to pick locks and dismantle alarms.

His undercover work started off as a six-month assignment and kept getting extended as he earned the trust of Dominick 'Sonny Black' Napolitano and Benjamin 'Lefty Guns' Ruggiero, who told him: 'As a wiseguy you can lie, you can cheat, you can steal, you can kill people – legitimately. You can do any goddamn thing you want and nobody can say anything about it. Who wouldn't want to be a wiseguy?'

In the 1970s, the US and Italian mafias had set out to control the world heroin trade, but there was friction between the American wiseguys and the Sicilian 'Zips' who came to the States. Pistone exploited this rift.

Pistone nearly lost his life when Bonanno soldier Tony Mirra accused him of stealing $250,000 from the crime family. Pistone had three meetings with Mirra and representatives of the family and was eventually found to be innocent, though Mirra was later killed for introducing Pistone to the family. Then came the time for Pistone to become a made man. For this he would have to kill someone. Fortunately, the guy he was supposed to whack had disappeared.

In 1981, when Joseph Massino took out the three *capos*, the FBI decided that it was too dangerous for Pistone to continue. When he was pulled out, the top mobsters were offering $500,000 for a hit on Donnie Brasco or his wife and children before he could testify. Pistone and his family were relocated and given 24-hour protection.

Meanwhile, two FBI agents paid a night-time call on Fat Tony Salerno, boss of the Genovese family and member of the Commission. He was told that if Pistone or his family were harmed or threatened, there would be massive retaliation.

'Get the word out, Tony,' he was told. 'Leave Pistone alone.' Salerno replied: 'We don't hurt cops; we don't hurt agents. Hey, you boys have a job to do, you got my guarantee.'

For his undercover work, Pistone was given a $500 bonus by the FBI. He retired in 1996, but continued to live under an assumed name for his own protection. 'It's not the wiseguys I'm most worried about,' he said. 'They respect me. They know I just did my job. I never entrapped anyone, never got them to do something they wouldn't have done anyway. But there's always the chance of running into someone who thinks he's a cowboy, you know, someone who doesn't like what you did.'

He wrote a book about his undercover work called *Donnie Brasco: My Undercover Life in the Mafia*, which was published in 1988. This was made into the 1997 movie *Donnie Brasco*, starring Johnny Depp as Pistone and Al Pacino as Ruggiero.

When the first wave of indictments was handed down in the wake of the Donnie Brasco investigation, Massino's name was not on the list. He had been wary of Pistone from the beginning and had always been cautious about government surveillance. He would not even let people refer to him by name. Instead, when they spoke about him they were to tug their ears – hence his nickname, 'The Ear'.

Nevertheless, he figured it would only be a matter of time before he was arrested, so he went into hiding. He still managed to run the family during this period – first from the Hamptons on Long Island, then from his hideout in the Pocono Mountains in Pennsylvania.

However, in July 1982, Massino was indicted for conspiracy to murder the three *capos*. Two years later, Rastelli was released from prison. He and Joseph Massino then arranged the murder of Cesare Bonventre, a Bonanno soldier, because he had failed to help Massino while he was on the run. By this time, most members of the Bonanno family considered Massino to be the boss, although Rastelli remained titular head.

After consulting a lawyer, Massino handed himself in on 7 July 1984, confident that he could beat the rap. He was released on $350,000 bail. But more indictments followed.

He was charged with labour racketeering and conspiracy to murder Do Do Pastore. He and Rastelli had controlled Teamsters Local 814, where they ran a scam in moving and storage. Found guilty, he was sentenced to ten years.

Although Wean and Pistone testified against him, Massino was cleared of the murder charges. He was found guilty of a 1975 hijacking, but it fell outside the RICO act's five-year statute of limitations, so he was cleared of that as well.

A LIFE SENTENCE

When Rastelli died in 1991, Massino became boss of the Bonanno family. He was released the following year, at a time when other crime bosses such as John Gotti, head of the Gambino family, were either in or on their way to jail. So the newspapers started calling him 'the Last Don'. In true godfather style, he held court at the Casablanca restaurant in Maspeth. But then, to save himself, his underboss Salvatore Vitale agreed to testify against him. Others followed.

Mafia Killings 42

Alphonse Indelicato, Dominick Trinchera, Philip Giaccone, New York City, 5 May 1981

Even though mob usurper Carmine 'Lilo' Galante had been dealt with in July 1979 – his body crumpled on the back patio of Joe and Mary's Restaurant in Brooklyn, a burning cigar still in his mouth – Bonanno boss Philip Rastelli was really not much better off than before. He was, after all, still in prison. And what's more, certain members of the family were not at all happy with the new division of power, the most vocal of these being *capo* Alphonse Indelicato.

One thing was clear to Rastelli – the battle for the Bonanno family was not yet over.

Rastelli relied heavily on his two allies, Dominick 'Sonny Black' Napolitano and Joseph Massino, to run things for him while he was in jail. They were extremely loyal to Rastelli. This was a good thing, because Indelicato had allies of his own.

They were known as the Three Capos – Alphonse 'Sonny Red' Indelicato, Dominick 'Big Trin' Trinchera and Philip 'Phil Lucky' Giaccone – and they were significant players. Indelicato realized that with Rastelli languishing in prison and with the Machiavellian Galante out of the way, leadership of the Bonanno family was still very unstable. If he acted now, what was there to stop him from becoming head of the Bonannos himself? It was worth a try.

The only problem was that any move Indelicato could make would undoubtedly start another Bonanno war, and nobody wanted that. Not him. Not Rastelli. And not the Commission. Talks of peace were attempted and with the intervention of the Commission, the Three Capos were convinced to bury the hatchet, at least for a while. But the concord didn't last, and it wasn't long before the Three Capos were voicing their dissatisfaction again.

Napolitano and Massino had to act quickly. A meeting was called at the Embassy Terrace Catering Hall in Gravesend, Brooklyn. And that's when it all went down.

It happened on 5 May 1981. Indelicato, Trinchera and Giaccone arrived at the hall, but Indelicato didn't like the way things looked. He'd taken the precaution of scattering his men in different hideouts throughout the city. That way, if things blew up, the rest of his gang – the Red Faction – would not be wiped out all at once.

It didn't really matter though, because once the door closed on the Embassy Terrace basement, and the Three Capos were trapped in the killing room, all hell fatally and forcefully broke loose. Nine men closed in and, pulling out weapons, blasted into the *capos*.

Big Trin was shot in his ample belly. He was followed to the floor by Giaccone. Indelicato tried to run, but was shot down before he could make it to the door. Smoke filled the room, and blood tattooed the floor. The Three Capos were gone and the Bonanno family could be at peace again – at least until the next murder was decreed.

Among the shooters that day was Montreal mobster Vito Rizzuto. The Montreal family was on the rise.

On 9 January 2003, the FBI picked up Massino at his home in Howard Beach, to face 19 federal charges. More charges soon followed. FBI assistant director Pasquale J. D'Amuro said: 'Massino is the most powerful mobster in the country.'

He went on trial the following year, facing charges related to seven murders, loan-sharking, arson, gambling, money laundering and extortion. The trial lasted for nine weeks and featured more than 70 witnesses, including Massino's brother-in-law and six other members of the Bonanno family. He was convicted on 11 counts, including the murders of the three *capos* and Dominick Napolitano.

Mafia Killings 43

Gerlando Sciascia, New York City, 19 March 1999

The hit on Gerlando Sciascia was a delicate job that required finesse and subterfuge. One false step and the results could mean war – a bloody battle between the Bonanno family and the powerful Rizzutos of Canada. If it did come down to war, the repercussions would be international; the Rizzutos were an influential link to the Sicilian Mafia. Bonanno boss Joe Massino was well aware of all this, but as far as he was concerned he had no other choice – Sciascia had to go.

For a long time, outsiders regarded the Rizzutos as simply an offshoot of the Bonannos. The Montreal family funnelled kilos of narcotics into the United States via Canada and ran some very lucrative rackets in Quebec and Ontario, but other than that, the Rizzutos were just a branch of one of New York's five families, not a power in their own right. That, however, was not the view held by Vito Rizzuto, who exercised significant authority in Montreal. As far as he was concerned the Rizzutos didn't need to rely on the waning influence of the Bonannos. Tall, handsome, dapper and imposing, Rizzuto was a born leader and as such was beholden to no one, not even Joe Massino.

Gerlando Sciascia was the liaison between the two families. Residing in Montreal for a while, Sciascia (also known as George from Canada) was a *capo* with the Bonannos. With contacts in both families, George was the perfect bridge between the two separate worlds – at least that's what Massino intended. But there may have been a few things that hadn't occurred to Massino. Born in Sicily, Sciascia came from the same village as the Rizzutos. In the clannish world of the Mafia, close ties are everything.

Sciascia's true position became crystal clear when his second-in-command – Joseph LoPresti – was murdered. LoPresti was a Bonanno made man, and no doubt pretty adept at keeping Massino up to date on Sciascia's comings and goings. LoPresti's murder hadn't been sanctioned by Massino and Sciascia's excuse was that he had been removed because of drug use. The careful Massino thought otherwise and began to reconsider the Sciascia situation.

On 18 March 1999, Sciascia received a note at his headquarters, a small jewellery store in the Bronx, telling him to meet DeFilippo at a Manhattan diner. At the diner, fellow *capo* Patrick DeFilippo told Sciascia that they were driving to a different location and the three men climbed into mobster John Spirito's SUV. As Spirito drove the vehicle, DeFilippo shot Sciascia in the head with a silenced gun.

The gunmen then drove to a deserted Bronx street, where they left the body on the road. The idea was to make the killing look like a drug deal gone wrong.

But Vito Rizzuto wasn't buying it. He realized, or at least strongly suspected, what had really gone down that day in March. By the end of the 1990s the Rizzutos ceased funnelling money into the coffers of the Bonanno family; there would be no more tribute from Canada. The Montreal family had just solidified its formidable power.

The FBI was not finished with Massino. He was also to be tried for the 1999 murder of a Bonanno assassin named Gerlando 'George from Canada' Sciascia, who had been in on the murder of the Three Capos. This time the US Attorney General John Ashcroft sought the death penalty.

When the authorities also made it clear that they planned to strip him of all his assets, leaving his family homeless and penniless, Massino reconsidered his position and began to co-operate, giving evidence against Vincent 'Vinny Gorgeous' Basciano, who had become acting head of the Bonanno family.

In 2005, Massino pleaded guilty to the murder of Sciascia and received a life sentence on top of the life sentence he had received for his previous convictions. However, his forfeiture was lowered from $10 million to $9 million. Basciano was also sentenced to life imprisonment while other top players ended up in jail with long sentences. The Bonanno family never recovered from the investigative work of Donnie Brasco.

Mafia Killings 44

Dominick Napolitano, Brooklyn, New York City, 17 August 1981
The last thoughts of a marked man are not often known. And when

they are, it's usually evident they've been reduced to one single, desperate plea – the desire for life. But Dominick Napolitano was different, a cut above the usual mobster. We know this because of Joseph D. Pistone, referred to by the Mafia as Donnie Brasco.

Pistone was a Fed, an FBI agent who'd worked on infiltrating the mob for six years. When Pistone – Brasco – was introduced to Bonanno *capo* Napolitano, the two became fast friends. Napolitano had interests outside the 'club' and he and Brasco would often pal around together, going out for coffee, or playing tennis. Sometimes they'd talk as they fed Napolitano's valuable homing pigeons.

But all the time that he was getting closer to the Mafia and to Napolitano, Pistone was compiling evidence which would eventually indict more than 200 mobsters, and convict more than 100 of them.

In 1981 Napolitano decided it was time to promote Brasco and he gave him the contract on Bruno Indelicato. With the job completed, Napolitano promised, Brasco would finally become a made man. At that point the FBI pulled the plug on the operation. It was a no-win situation. Pistone, of course, could not commit the murder; but to refuse the contract would mean his own death. You can't say no to the mob. So Donnie Brasco, then, quietly disappeared.

Now that the game was up, the Feds approached the *capo*. If news of the Brasco deception were to reach the Bonannos – which it inevitably would – Napolitano's life wouldn't be worth a plug nickel. But if Napolitano were to become an informant, the government could offer him protection.

And this is when Napolitano – Mafia man though he was – showed his true mettle. He refused to break *omertà*. Though his life could now be counted in mere days, Napolitano would not betray the mob. Nor would he run.

On 17 August 1981, Napolitano was summoned to a meeting. It was 'the' meeting, and he knew it. Handing his keys, his ring and the care of his beloved pigeons into the hands of the bartender of

the Motion Lounge in Williamsburg, Brooklyn, an establishment he owned, Napolitano phoned his girlfriend to say goodbye, telling her that all this wasn't Brasco's fault – he had just been doing his job. After that he headed to the home of Bonanno associate Ron Filocomo in Flatlands. Once he arrived, he was pushed down a staircase into the basement, then the shooting began. Reportedly the first bullet missed him, and Napolitano demanded that the killers fire again, and this time make a good job of it. The door to the basement remained closed.

When Napolitano's body was found in Arlington, Staten Island, his hands had been cut off – a symbol that he had welcomed an infiltrator into the Mafia. But Dominick Napolitano went to his death with his back straight, his shoulders squared and bearing no ill-will to his friend Donnie Brasco.

THE LOST DON

Born in Chicago to Italian immigrants, Joey Lombardi dropped out of school early. He committed his first theft at 18 to finance an operation for his mother. Known for his humour – earning him the nickname 'the Clown' or 'Pagliacci' – he changed the last letter of his name to an 'o' when he joined the Outfit. On the streets he was known as 'Lumpy', because he was so good at giving people lumps on their heads.

Lombardo made his way up the crime ladder as a jewel thief, a juice loan collector and a hitman. Quickly rising to become *capo* of the Grand Avenue crew on Chicago's North Side, he had 30 soldiers under him and ran the same streets in the Grand-Ogden area as Tony 'the Ant' Spilotro and Tony Accardo's Circus Café Gang.

At the age of 25, Lombardo owned a construction company. Over the years, he also owned a trucking company, was said to be a worker for a hot-dog stand manufacturer, and had hidden holdings in restaurants and real estate. Meanwhile, he was racking up arrests for burglary and loitering, though in each case he avoided conviction.

In 1963, his name was linked with John 'No Nose' DiFronzo, later boss of the Chicago Outfit, in a West Side loan-sharking ring. Lombardo and five others were accused of abducting a factory worker who owed $2,000, tying him to a beam in a basement and beating him unconscious. In court the man could not identify his assailants and Lombardo walked free – his 11th acquittal following 11 arrests.

Lombardo's activities included loan-sharking, illegal gambling and selling pornography. He even ran a ring dealing in stolen furs that operated at four Midwestern airports, including O'Hare. His men wore overalls so that they looked like airport workers.

Identified as a rising star, Lombardo was one of a thousand guests invited to a party honouring West Side overlord Fiore 'Fifi' Buccieri at the Edgewater Beach Hotel. This was 'the largest assemblage of mobsters ever staged in Chicago', the police said. They were entertained by crooner Vic Damone and a 20-piece band.

While the Chicago mob moved into Las Vegas, Lombardo stayed at home in the Windy City making so much money that he was a regular reader of the *Wall Street Journal*. He oversaw Tony Spilotro and Frank 'Lefty' Rosenthal in Las Vegas and liaised with Allen Dorfman, whose father had introduced Jimmy Hoffa to the mob. Dorfman ran the Teamsters' pension fund, which was used to buy new casinos.

Meanwhile Lombardo was also keeping his hand in as a hitman. In 1973, two men carrying shotguns walked into Rose's Sandwich Shop on Grand Avenue, lined the customers up against the wall and picked out disgraced police officer Richard Cain. He was Sam Giancana's bagman and did other work for the mob, while acting as an informant for the FBI. The gunmen put their shotguns under Cain's chin and blew his head off. One of the trigger men was said to be Lombardo.

In 1974, Lombardo, Spilotro and Dorfman were charged with defrauding the Teamsters' pension fund of $1.4 million. The money was being siphoned through the American Pail Company, a front organization run, some say unwittingly, by 29-year-old Daniel Seifert. Tony Accardo, who was then running the Chicago Outfit, told Lombardo to take Seifert

out. He was shot dead by four masked gunmen in front of his wife and child. Lombardo was said to be one of the trigger men. Without Seifert, the fraud case fell apart and the defendants were acquitted.

According to FBI informants, Lombardo had authorized the killing of Indiana oilman Ray Ryan, a millionaire, when he stopped paying off one of Lombardo's associates. Another informant asked Lombardo's permission to whack a man who had damaged his disco in Schiller Park. 'Break the guy's arms, legs and head instead,' Lombardo replied. 'But if the problem occurs again, do whatever you have to do.'

Lombardo and James 'Legs' D'Antonio were sitting in a car outside when the police went to raid an illegal gambling den. They sped off. Officers pursued them. After a six-minute high-speed chase, they stopped the car and tried to walk innocently away, while Lombardo threw some notebooks over a fence. The police arrested the two men and recovered the notebooks. They contained the licence plate numbers of the cars that were chasing them and a number of off-colour jokes. What do you expect? Lombardo's nickname was, after all, 'The Clown'.

Six thousand dollars were found in his pocket; another $6,000 in his shoes. In court, explaining their frantic flight, Lombardo said: 'I had $12,000 on me. Those guys might have been robbers or killers.' He was found guilty of resisting arrest.

The FBI put a phone tap on all the lines from Dorfman's office, seeking to prove the Outfit's ownership of several casinos in Las Vegas. Instead they listened in on a bribery scheme. The Teamsters would sell a plot next to the Las Vegas Hilton, to US Senator Howard Cannon of Nevada, at a knockdown price. In return, he would kill a bill deregulating the trucking business.

Lombardo, Dorfman, Teamsters' president Roy Williams and others were indicted. As the trial progressed, jurors were approached by menacing strangers. Nevertheless, they found the defendants guilty of 11 counts of bribery, fraud and conspiracy. While out on bail awaiting sentence, Dorfman was killed by a shotgun blast. Apparently the mob thought he was too soft to serve time and might inform on them.

Lombardo told the judge: 'I never ordered a killing. I never OK'ed a killing. I never killed a man in my life. I never ordered or OK'ed any bombing or arson in my life.'

The judge praised his eloquence and sentenced him to 15 years. From behind bars, Lombardo continued to protest his innocence. 'I have no faith in the system,' he said.

Soon after, Lombardo was convicted of skimming almost $2 million from Las Vegas casinos and was sentenced to another 16 years, running concurrently. Tony Spilotro was also facing trial. He and his brother Michael were found in a shallow grave in Indiana. The man who was supposed to have disposed of the bodies, John Fecarotta, was then killed for his incompetence.

Lombardo was paroled in 1992, only to make his most public joke yet. He put a small ad in a number of Chicago papers that said: 'I never took a secret oath with guns and daggers, pricked my finger, drew blood or burned paper to join a criminal organization. If anyone hears my name used in connection with any criminal activity please notify the FBI, local police and my parole officer, Ron Kumke.'

Nevertheless, back in the old neighbourhood, Lombardo still played the big-time mob boss. His pal Chris 'the Nose' Spina lost his job as a foreman at the First Ward sanitation yard in 1993, when the city alleged he was spending all his time chauffeuring Lombardo around town while he was clocked in at work. In 1997, a Cook County judge reinstated Spina – with back pay. 'He's seen as a spy of the Clown,' the *Chicago Tribune* reported.

After several years, DNA evidence tied the death of Big John Fecarotta to mob enforcer Nick Calabrese, who was already serving time in Michigan. Confronted with this, Calabrese flipped and told the FBI the inner workings of the Outfit. He gave details on 18 gruesome gangland murders and the FBI started Operation Family Secrets.

In 2003, the FBI approached Lombardo in the masonry shop where he worked and took a saliva swab and a hair sample. They were hoping to match the DNA to a strand of hair found in a ski mask left in the getaway

car used in the Seifert murder. Agents also warned Lombardo that his life was in danger.

Lombardo was indicted for his role in at least one murder, as well as for illegal gambling and loan-sharking. But before the arrest warrant was issued, he disappeared. While 14 other defendants appeared in court, everyone wondered where the 'Lost Don' was.

The *Chicago Tribune* put a photo of a cigar-chomping man on the front page of their Metro section under the headline: 'Have you seen this "Clown"?' But it wasn't Lombardo, just someone who looked like him.

The Clown then wrote to the judge, claiming he was innocent and spelling out terms for his surrender. He signed himself: 'Joe Lombardo, An Innocent Man'. In the letter, he made it clear that he was not going to flip. It was a message to the mobsters who might be on his tail.

A $20,000 reward was put on Lombardo's head and after nine months he was captured following a visit to his dentist – who just happened to be Tony Spilotro's brother, Patrick.

Lombardo pleaded not guilty. In court it was revealed that he was suffering from atherosclerosis, but had not seen a doctor. 'I was unavailable,' he explained.

Unusually, Lombardo took the stand in his own defence, claiming that he was in a police station reporting the loss of his wallet at the time of Seifert's slaying. But employees of an electronics store identified Lombardo as the man who had bought a police scanner used during the murder, and Lombardo's fingerprint was found on the title application of the car used.

He was found guilty of murder, racketeering, extortion and loan-sharking. At his sentencing, he complained: 'I was not given a fair trial and now I suppose the court is going to sentence me to life in prison for something I did not do. I did not kill Daniel Seifert and also I did not have anything to do with it.'

He was right. He did get life. It was 33 years to the day since Daniel Seifert had been killed. Seifert's son Joseph was in the courtroom. It was his turn to laugh.

THE CHICAGO OUTFIT

Unlike the 'Five Families' who competed for turf in New York, the Chicago Outfit ran all organized crime in the city. But like all Italian-American crime families it was still answerable to the Commission.

Also known as the Chicago Crime Syndicate, the Outfit started in 1919 when a Black Hand gang under 'Sunny Jim' Cosmano tried to shake down a chain of brothels run by 'Big Jim' Colosimo. At this, Colosimo called for back-up from his wife's cousin Johnny Torrio, a saloon and brothel keeper in New York. Within a month, 18 of Cosmano's gang had been gunned down. Cosmano himself was wounded by a shotgun blast and fled the city.

Torrio had brought with him a New Yorker of Neapolitan descent named Al Capone. With Prohibition now in force, Torrio wanted to go into bootlegging. Colosimo was against it, so he too was gunned down.

The largely Irish North Side Gang were Torrio's rivals in the bootlegging business. Their attempt on his life left Torrio badly wounded and he returned to Italy, leaving Capone in charge. Capone set about expanded the Outfit, wiping out George 'Bugs' Moran, Earl 'Hymie' Weiss and all who opposed him. He also introduced the principle that, unlike the New York families, you did not have to be Italian to join.

When Capone went to jail for tax evasion in 1931, his underboss Frank Nitti took over. But he was only a frontman. Former Neapolitan Camorrista Paul 'the Waiter' Ricca was acknowledged as boss by the Commission and ran the Outfit for the next 40 years.

Together Nitti and Ricca moved in on Hollywood. The studios paid them off to avoid labour unrest. But in 1943 they were indicted. Nitti shot himself rather than go to prison. Ricca then became the official boss with his enforcer Tony 'Big Tuna' Accardo as underboss. Accardo was also dubbed 'Joe Batters' by Capone after he killed two men with a baseball bat while Capone looked on.

Mafia Killings 45

James Ragen, Chicago, 15 August 1946

James Ragen was an anachronism, a hangover from the rough-and-tumble days of the 1920s who held his own against larger and more sophisticated groups in Chicago. A co-founder of the athletic club/street mob Ragen's Colts, he steadfastly remained an independent when that gang was absorbed into the Syndicate via the Chicago Outfit in the 1930s.

After Prohibition was repealed in 1933, the mobs concentrated their efforts largely on gambling to supply the vast income that booze had once given them. One such source of revenue was provided by the General News Service, which swiftly communicated gambling and racing results to the entire country. With instantaneous race results wired throughout the nation, bookies had inside knowledge of racing winners while they were still taking bets. The possibilities for profit were enormous. Run in the 1930s by publisher Moses Annenberg, with Ragen as his assistant, the service was worth a fortune.

In 1939, though, Annenberg was indicted for tax evasion and sold the racing wire to Ragen. Though the mob may have had a foothold in the service during Annenberg's day, Ragen was determined to run the operation without Syndicate interference and rake in the profits for himself. He became one of the most powerful gambling figures in the country.

The smell of filthy lucre inevitably reached the sensitive noses of the Syndicate. During a time when supposedly a 12-year-old couldn't slice bread in Chicago without the mob's say-so, there was no way the Outfit was going to let an independent like Ragen get the better of them. At first the mob attempted to start rival wire services, then they tried to buy Ragen out. When neither of these plans panned out, the Outfit got serious. Ragen was wily, he'd

survived for years on the mean streets of Chicago and he knew how the mob operated. So he contacted journalist Drew Pearson; Ragen had a story to tell.

Pearson communicated with the FBI and as the Feds took down Regan's statements they found out just how deeply entrenched the Outfit was in all of Chicago's day-to-day businesses. The mob had representatives everywhere, some of them very highly placed. The information was dynamite, but it apparently went nowhere.

It seemed as if the Feds were sitting on their hands. Backing away from Ragen, they claimed that the responsibility for the Chicago Outfit rested with the city of Chicago itself – in other words, it was a municipal and not a federal problem.

Ragen's next move was to hire bodyguards, but it wasn't enough. On 24 June 1946 he was shot while driving down the street in his car. Much to the dismay of the Outfit no doubt, Ragen survived this first assault and was taken to hospital, but while trying to recuperate he died suddenly on 15 August. The coroner stated that a vial's worth of mercury had been found in Ragen's stomach, an amount sufficient to kill three men. But no murder charges could be brought, apparently, because of the slim and incomprehensible reason that it could not be ascertained whether Ragen had died as a result of the gunshots, or the mercury poisoning.

After three years in jail, Ricca took a back seat, leaving Accardo as acting boss. Meanwhile the Outfit took in new recruits including Fiore 'Fifi' Buccieri and Salvatore 'Sam' Giancana, who helped Frank Sinatra build his career. Giancana also gave his support to John F. Kennedy, who was elected as US president in 1960.

With the aid of union leader Jimmy Hoffa and old-time mobster Meyer Lansky, Accardo used the Teamsters' pension fund and the Outfit's casinos to launder money. Accardo was officially a *consigliere* until his death in 1992, but ran the Outfit using a series of front bosses,

who included Giancana, Samuel 'Teets' Battaglia, Jackie 'the Lackey' Cerone, Joseph 'Joey Doves' Aiuppa, Joseph 'Joe Nagall' Ferriola and Sam 'Wings' Carlisi.

John 'No Nose' DiFronzo – aka 'Johnny Bananas' – took over in 1993, followed by Angelo J. 'the Hook' LaPietra, who got his soubriquet from his method of torturing his victims. He would hang them on a meat hook then burn them with a blowtorch. During that era Lombardo was either underboss, *consigliere*, or – some say – the real boss of the Chicago Outfit.

MEYER LANSKY

One of the problems with writing about the Mafia in America is that it was described for decades as non-existent, a mirage. So the roots, for example, of the trade in heroin and cocaine in which the United States and many other Western countries are now enmeshed remain buried, out of sight, although there is a general view today that Meyer Lansky and 'Lucky' Luciano started the Mafia on this road in an organized way. It is said that Lansky himself became hooked on heroin after his son was born crippled, and then did cold turkey in a hide-out in Massachusetts, watched over by a hood called Vincent 'Jimmy Blue Eyes' Alo, ever after a close friend.

After that, though – and after Luciano's imprisonment – Lansky increasingly took to the shadows, living apparently quietly in a tract house in Miami, as he moved the Mafia into gambling operations in Las Vegas, the Bahamas and Cuba.

In 1970, after hearing that he faced tax evasion charges, Lansky, by now 68, fled to a hotel he owned in Tel Aviv, Israel, before being extradited, by order of the Israeli Supreme Court, back to the United States. In the end, he was acquitted of all charges. In the late 1970s and early 80s he could be seen walking his dog along Miami's Collins Avenue or having a meal in a diner with his old friend 'Jimmy Blue Eyes'. He died from a heart attack in 1983, at the age of 81.

Lansky was the last of his kind and, by the time he passed on, the Jewish mobs had become a thing of the past. Like the Irish and German immigrants before them, the Jewish community had passed into the mainstream. Only the Sicilians, the five families set up by Lansky and Luciano remained: the Geneveses, the Gambinos, the Luccheses, the Bonannos and the Colombos. They remained, at least in part, because they retained close ties with the island from which they derived, the last great redoubt of the Mafia and the site of its rebirth: Sicily.

Meyer Lansky was eventually acquitted of all charges

CHAPTER 13

LUCKY LUCIANO, DON CALÒ AND THE INVASION OF SICILY

Lucky Luciano was about to stage the greatest coup of his life, and from an unlikely place: his cell in Sing Sing Prison. When the United States entered the Second World War against the Axis powers – one of them Italy – immigrant Italians soon found themselves with divided loyalties. There was sabotage in the New York docks where many of them worked, interruption and theft of war supplies and spying. Officers of US naval intelligence, knowing that the ultimate authority in the docks belonged to the Mafia through its control of the longshoremen's unions, then approached Luciano to co-opt his help in the matter. Luciano obliged. From then on, on his say-so, the sabotage and the delays stopped. The war effort went on unimpeded.

However, Luciano had another service to offer his new friends. Word began to go out to immigrants from Sicily to help the authorities – to identify for them the best places to land on the island, the nature of the ground that would have to be traversed by any invading army and the safest paths and routes. Messages were also sent in Luciano's name to key figures in the Sicilian Mafia, instructing them to co-operate with the Americans when they arrived. Fully five months before the final landing, Luciano – who'd been born Salvatore Lucania near Villalba – launched

an appeal against his 30- to-50-year sentence for prostitution-running on the grounds of 'services rendered to the nation'.

Though Luciano was not yet to get out of prison, everything went according to his master-plan. When American forces landed in central and western Sicily in early July 1943, 15 per cent of the soldiers were of Sicilian birth or descent. They carried with them not only the American flag, but others emblazoned with the letter 'L' for Luciano. These soon appeared all over the island as the Americans advanced with the help of expert Mafia guides – one was even dropped, it is said, from a reconnaissance plane at the doorstep of the priest in Villalba, who just happened to be the brother of the island's *capo di tutti capi*, Don Calogero Vizzini.

Ten days after the landing, Don Calò was picked up behind the lines in Villalba by American tanks and whisked away. He was made an honorary colonel in the US Army, but became known to the footsoldiers as 'General Mafia'.

Don Calò played his part well. The Sicilian Mafia had for 20 years been brutally put down by Mussolini, so they could be shown to the naive Americans to be demonstrably 'anti-fascist'. They were released at his behest from Mussolini's jails as the Americans advanced and installed in top positions in almost every municipality under the military administration they left in their wake. Don Calò and other Mafia bosses had lists of fascist sympathisers and collaborators with the Germans in their areas. Communists were clearly unacceptable. Who else, after all, was there to trust but the fellow freedom-fighters who had prepared the ground and cleared the passes for their American liberators?

With Don Calò at their side, encouraging Italian soldiers to desert, it took the American force just seven days to conquer central and western Sicily. General Patton called it 'the fastest blitzkrieg in history'. There were negligible casualties, as the Italian army seemed to melt away from their positions alongside the Germans. The British, under General Montgomery, were not so fortunate. It took them five weeks to battle their way up the island's east coast, with thousands of losses.

When the Allies went on to the Italian mainland, they were soon met by another Mafia representative, Vito Genovese. Genovese had escaped to Italy from New York in 1937, on the run from a murder charge, and had become a close friend of the Italian dictator Benito Mussolini. He'd made major donations to the Fascist Party and had been awarded the title of Commendatore, one of Italy's highest honours. He'd also, so it was said, generously provided Mussolini's son with cocaine and organized the killing of a New York anti-fascist newspaper editor through the good offices of Carmine Galante.

Mafia Killings 46

Carlo Tresca, New York City, 11 January 1943

Ever since the anti-Italian backlash that accompanied the death of Captain David Hennessy in 1890 (possibly a Mafia murder), the Cosa Nostra had steered clear of politicos and other high profile public figures. The consequences were just too severe.

However, just like everything to do with the Mafia, there are a couple of notable exceptions to this rule. One of these exceptions probably occurred in Dallas in 1963. Enough has been written on the assassination of President John F. Kennedy to fill a whole bookstore but there is compelling evidence to suggest Mafia involvement in the murder. Another death, one that took place in 1943, was undeniably a Mafia slaying – the murder of Carlo Tresca.

Tresca was an Italian-born anarchist, newspaper editor and activist. Born in Sulmona, Tresca had fled Italy in 1904 to avoid impending arrest, bringing his ideals and strength of purpose with him. A principled man, Tresca fought ceaselessly for his beliefs – empowerment of workers, justice for the downtrodden and, of course, the ideologies of anarchism. Tall and handsome, he was a

Mussolini, 'Il Duce', put down the Sicilian Mafia for nearly 20 years

riveting speaker, and a powerful voice against Fascism for Italian-Americans. This was particularly important throughout the 1930s and the opening years of the Second World War.

Tresca's fiery oratory undoubtedly made certain factions uncomfortable, though, both in the United States and in Italy. Mussolini reportedly sent Fascist operatives to deal with him in 1926, using bombs. They failed.

But Tresca had his fair share of enemies in the United States as well, among them Frank Garofalo, underboss of the Bonanno family. Tresca wrote fervently against the Mafia, and shortly before he died had penned a piece that brought Garofalo to task. Tresca knew he was at risk; he had lived with danger all his life. Ultimately, though, he could only be what he was – tireless and crusading.

Undoubtedly his outspokenness brought Tresca to his death. On 11 January 1943, he left his newspaper office at around 9:45 in the evening. Just as he crossed the road, a black car pulled up beside him and a man in a trenchcoat got out. Moments later, Carlo Tresca was lying dead in the street, a bullet in his head.

For a long time the murder of Tresca was considered a mystery, with alleged responsibility veering between Fascist agents operating in America and Italian communists. But the assassination was very well-orchestrated, smooth and clean; historians now know that the murder of Carlo Tresca was a Mafia hit. In fact, the evidence is fairly clear as to the identity of the man in the trenchcoat that dark January evening: Carmine 'Lilo Galante, decades before his audacious takeover of the Bonanno family. In the death of Tresca, Galante would have been operating under orders from Frank Garofalo, and therefore Joseph Bonanno himself.

But Tresco's achievements demand that he be remembered for far more than the way he died. He was a man of worth, one who stood his ground, and not just another notch on the gun of Carmine Galante.

With the Allies headed towards Rome, Genovese quickly saw the light and he reappeared as the official interpreter and adviser to the US military governor of Naples, Colonel Charles Peretti, who was already, Lucky Luciano was later to say laconically, 'a good friend'. Peretti proved an invaluable fixer, particularly to a group of senior American officers, through whom he bribed his way into the black market. Soon 60 per cent of all food unloaded by the Allies in the port was disappearing into the hands of Genovese's network of corrupt American soldiers and local Camorra men, and though Genovese was shipped back to the US in 1944, by that time he had already paid more than one visit to Sicily with Colonel Peretti to see Don Calò. His network in Naples, furthermore, remained in place – to be taken over by Lucky Luciano when, finally released from his American prison and deported, he settled in the city in 1948.

With Sicily now under Allied control, there were headaches for the military government – and for the landowners who as ever ruthlessly controlled for their own benefit both the land and the rural poor. In the cities there were food riots, and in the countryside demonstrations for land reform. Meanwhile, in the north of Italy – and to a degree in Sicily – the communists had emerged from under cover after their long battle against fascism and were entering politics as an organized force for the first time. The Christian Democratic Party, founded with a ringing endorsement from the Pope and hidden backing from the Americans, was not yet the strong bastion against communism that it would become.

The landowners, then, needed help, and so did the military government. And it was in this atmosphere that they both turned, once more, to the Mafia, who were not only anti-communist in precisely the way the military government demanded, but were also by now dreaming – as were huge numbers of Sicilians – of separation from Italy, of becoming a British colony or America's 49th state.

In September 1944, Don Calò demonstrated the Mafia's credentials as solidly anti-communist when his men bombed and shot up a joint

communist and socialist meeting in Villalba. This was even though he had permitted the meeting 'as long as neither the Mafia nor land reform were discussed'. Within two months, the US consul in Palermo was secretly reporting to his boss, US Secretary of State Cordell Hull, that Don Calò was having meetings with both military and Mafia figures about nominating a Mafia boss as the head of an insurrectionary separatist movement.

In the end, the movement, which at its height had over half a million supporters, fizzled out. Early in 1946, even before the new Italian constitution had been approved, the provisional government announced that it was giving Sicily a high degree of autonomy: its own elected parliament, the right to collect its own taxes and control over the money that from then on – and for 30 years into the future – was to flow to it from Rome. This was an offer the Mafia simply could not refuse: money, and plenty of it, in return for votes. It already had gathering control over local politics and the beginnings of a deal with the Christian Democrats. But if separatism died in the hearts of men like Don Calò, anti-communism did not, particularly in one of the most enigmatic characters of modern Sicilian history, Salvatore Giuliano.

SALVATORE GIULIANO

Salvatore Giuliano was a bandit. A peasant from Montelepre, he had killed a carabiniere in 1943, at the age of 20, when stopped by a patrol while carrying contraband grain. Four months later he killed another during a police raid and a few weeks later he organized a prison breakout which was to form the basis of his gang. There were many gangs like Giuliano's in Sicily at the time, and most of them were quickly put down. But Giuliano's survived and became famous, mostly because of his daring and charm. Known as the 'King of Montelepre', he played host to the national and international press. He dispensed popular justice, he was flamboyant and handsome and he even had a brief fling with a Swedish photojournalist. He was also mysteriously well connected. He

met with the chief prosecutor of Palermo and with Vito Genovese during one of his visits. He had contacts with police and politicians. It remains to many a mystery how he could have survived for the seven years he did after that first killing of his – unless it was in the interests of some very powerful people to keep him alive.

One group of powerful people who made his acquaintance was almost certainly the Mafia. For in the brief insurrectionary period of the separatist movement Giuliano was made a colonel in the separationists' army, probably at the request of Don Calò. He was also strongly anti-communist, and that suited the Americans' purposes well. In addition to robbing the rich – he once took a diamond ring off the Duchess of Pratameno's finger in her Palermo palazzo – he also raided and firebombed the offices of what he called 'the vile reds'. So it must have been among his worst nightmares – as well as those of the Mafia, who were quietly moving into an alliance with the American-backed Christian Democrats – when, in the first elections for the new Sicilian parliament in April 1947, the United Left – not the Christian Democrats – won.

Giuliano had written to US President Truman about the need 'to stem the communist tide in Sicily' and Truman had announced that Italy was in the front line of the battle against this world threat. Bandit and president, in other words, were of one mind. On 1 May 1947, Truman's secretary of state, George Marshall, wrote to the US ambassador, saying that the communists should be excluded from the national government, and on the same day Giuliano killed as many of them as he could find.

Still nothing is known for certain about what came to be called the massacre at Portella della Ginestra. The documents relating to it have never been published, and an Italian senator who saw them declared it would cause 'a national catastrophe if they ever came to light'. All that is known is that when 1,500 or so villagers met in an open space outside the town of Piana degli Albanesi to celebrate May Day, Giuliano's men opened up on them from the flanks of a mountain above, killing 14 and wounding 65. There were rumours that they were armed with the latest American weapons and even that some of the men were dressed

in American uniforms. But, as to who gave the order for the massacre, it is – in the words of a 1972 parliamentary commission – 'absolutely impossible to attribute responsibility either directly or morally to this or that party or politician.'

After the massacre, though, Giuliano's local usefulness seems to have come to an end and most of his gang were caught and disposed of one by one – several of them, according to the writer Norman Lewis, 'being added to the scrupulously kept list of those – now amounting to over five hundred names – who had slipped on the stairs of the Ucciardone prison.' By June 1950, Giuliano was alone except for his cousin and right hand Gaspare Pisciotta. There was said to have been an offer of amnesty for both men, even of an American military plane to fly them away to the United States. But Giuliano did not go and on 4 July in a Mafia safe house in Castelvetrano – where he, by report, spent his time reading Shakespeare and Descartes – he was shot dead by his cousin as he lay sleeping.

Immediately a cover-up began. Giuliano's body was taken outside by the carabinieri and pumped full of bullets as if he'd died in combat. By the time the world's press arrived, a fog of lies already surrounded the death, including one suggestion, faithfully reported, that some 350 men of the newly set-up Banditry Suppression Taskforce Command had been involved. This scenario, however, soon fell apart. For one thing, the blood from Giuliano's body seemed to have run uphill from his corpse and for another, Pisciotta proved all too ready to claim responsibility.

In the end, for all the attempted cover-up, Pisciotta was charged with Giuliano's murder and put on trial in Viterbo on the mainland, where he announced early in the trial that he'd killed Giuliano at the request of Italian Minister of the Interior, Mario Scelba who, with a group of landowners, had also been behind the massacre at Portella della Ginestre. Pisciotta said that later he'd reveal all. But he would not have the chance. He died after being poisoned in Ucciardone prison on 8 January 1954 – the same day that Christian Democrat Scelba was sworn in as Prime Minister of Italy.

CHAPTER 14

THE MAFIA AT CORLEONE

Don Calò died of a heart attack in early 1952, and with his death there began to ebb away for ever the old rural traditions of the Sicilian Mafia, which had always been more concerned with power and influence than with money. Though the title of *capo di tutti capi* passed to his successor in Villalba, Giuseppe Genco Russo, the future increasingly belonged to men like Luciano Leggio and Totò Riina, young killers from Corleone who'd learned a new attitude from those American gangsters who'd either stayed in or returned to Sicily after the War. Leggio, the senior of the two men, was an estate manager and hitman for his boss in Corleone, Dr Michele Navarra. Both had been implicated in 1948 in the murder of a brave young trade unionist and labour organizer called Placido Rizzotto, who had disappeared soon after the 1947 election. Rizzotto had somehow contrived to win the local council for the left, despite Navarra's attempts to rig the poll by issuing several hundred certificates for blindness or extreme myopia to local women, so that they would have to be accompanied to the voting station by his men. Retribution was swift. Rizzotto was taken at gunpoint outside the town and hanged from a tree by Luciano Leggio. Then his body was thrown into a hundred-foot-deep crevasse. A shepherd boy who'd reported

what he'd seen was given something by the good Dr Navarra to calm his nerves – and promptly died.

Both Navarra and Leggio were later charged with the deaths, thanks mainly to a captain of the carabinieri from northern Italy who'd been assigned to Corleone: a young man who was later to play a crucial role in the uncovering of post-war Mafia activities, Carlo Alberto Dalla Chiesa. Leggio was acquitted for lack of evidence and though Dr Navarra was sentenced to five years' exile in Calabria, he was – thanks to his friends in the Christian Democratic Party – welcomed back to Corleone after just a few months to the strains of the town band.

THE END OF THE OLD WAYS

By this time Lucky Luciano had set up his new home in Naples and he was quickly instrumental in bringing together Vito Genovese's old Camorra network and members of the Sicilian Mafia in what was to become one of their chief post-war money spinners: cigarette smuggling. The Italian government had awarded itself a monopoly on the sale and distribution of cigarettes, but the cigarettes almost everyone wanted were American. The Mafia provided them, just as they'd provided the booze during Prohibition. Gross profits amounted, it was said, to at least $1 billion a year.

The other big money spinner for the Sicilians was land speculation and construction. With money pouring into the island from the mainland for post-war reconstruction and development, it was child's play to find out from crooked politicians and bureaucrats which areas were next in line to get planning permission. These would then be bought up wholesale at agricultural rates by building companies headed by Mafia front-men – front-men who weren't bothered at all by the quality of what they actually put up. The profits here were not as great as in cigarette smuggling, but they still amounted to well over $100 million a year.

The old businesses of the traditional Mafia went on, of course: protection rackets, grain smuggling and control over commodities in

short supply. Dr Navarra started a bus company with the American military vehicles he was allowed to commandeer. Luciano Leggio seems to have made much of his living from butchering stolen cattle. But the future, and Leggio knew it, lay not in the countryside but in Palermo, where the politicians and the money were. The countryside was becoming increasingly poor and depopulated: between 1951 and 1953, 400,000 Sicilians emigrated to Australia, Argentina and elsewhere and there were no longer enough labourers to work many of the huge hereditary estates.

There was also an up-and-coming new business to get into: heroin. Luciano seems to have set up his first heroin processing plant in Palermo in 1949, using morphine base smuggled in from the Lebanon. As the number of heroin addicts tripled in the United States, he was a regular visitor to the Sicilian capital. He was busily suggesting to those who would listen, not only a serious investment in the drugs trade, but also the setting-up of a central commission, or cupola, of the sort he'd set up in America, to direct Mafia activities and keep the peace between factions. He wanted the Sicilians, in other words, to do two things based on the US experience: to go international and to grow up.

Luciano Leggio and his right-hand-man Totò Riina agreed. But first they had to create a power base of their own in Corleone. So after an argument with Dr Navarra over involvement in a dam project, which would have made Liggio a fortune in protection and speculation, they killed him in 1958 after ambushing his car. They then set about exterminating, one by one, every member of his faction they could find. Between 1958 and 1963 the modest town of Corleone became one of the murder capitals of the world.

One man, though, was watching events very closely: a man who was later to do more than anyone else to bring down the Mafia in Sicily. His name was Tommaso Buscetta, the highest Mafia figure ever to break the code of *omertà* and become a witness for the state. He had by now helped to set up the commission Luciano had suggested, and he later said of Dr Navarra's murder that it was 'the underlying cause of the crisis that

afflicted the Mafia organization [from then on].' By killing for personal gain, Leggio had set a precedent in which the Mafia's traditional codes of conduct stood for nothing. For Buscetta, that was the beginning of the end.

JOE BANANAS VISITS SICILY

Leggio and Riina were playing for big stakes. The year before they killed Dr Navarra, at the height of a major war over control of Palermo's wholesale meat market, a visitor from the United States had arrived to be met like a visiting statesman at Rome airport, complete with a red carpet, by the Italian Minister for Foreign Trade, Bernardo Mattarella. This was apt enough, since Mattarella had grown up with his visitor in Castellamare del Golfo outside Palermo – and doubly apt, perhaps, in as much as a young Christian Democrat protégé of his, a 'made' Mafia man called Salvo Lima, was about to become Palermo's mayor. Giuseppe Bonanno, known as 'Joe Bananas', the head of one of New York's five families, was his visitor, and he was on his way to Palermo for a summit meeting with his Sicilian counterparts.

The meeting took place at the Grand Hotel et des Palmes in Palermo between 10 and 14 October 1957. The highpoint seems to have been a dinner hosted by Lucky Luciano at the Spano restaurant midway through the visit. The guestlists at the meeting and the dinner were slightly different, but Joe Bananas and his *consigliere* Carmine Galante, who supervised a heroin network for the Bonanno family, were present at both. The subjects under discussion were the same: the setting up of the Sicilian Commission and the establishment of a heroin supply-and-sale network in which the Sicilians and the Americans would be equal partners. At the dinner, Luciano introduced the Americans to family boss Salvatore 'Ciaschiteddu' (Little Bird) Greco, his nominee for head of the Commission, and also to a group of young likelies, among them Tommaso Buscetta. At the meeting, three more heads of families were present, including Don Calò's successor as *capo di tutti*

capi, Giuseppe Genco Russo. Both Buscetta and Leggio may also have been there.

Whoever attended the meeting, though, the upshot was the same: the establishment of the Commission, under Salvatore Greco, was agreed and a joint partnership with the Bonanno family in the smuggling of heroin was cemented – subject to the agreement of a meeting of the New York Commission later in the year. Within a matter of weeks, as a gesture of good faith, untraceable Sicilian assassins had gunned down the brutal and stupid Alberto Anastasia, one of the founders of Murder Incorporated, in a New York City barber's chair. But the approval of the American Commission had not been secured – at least not until later. The summit meeting held the following month in Appalachin, New York, was due to address the matter. In the event, the meeting was raided by the police, and for the first time senior American Mafia figures were exposed.

Lucky Luciano decided that the project should go ahead anyway. In fact, he had already begun it, with the establishment of the so-called French Connection.

THE FRENCH CONNECTION

One of Luciano's problems was that there was a lack of skilled chemists in Sicily and Naples. Both Sicilians and Neapolitans were expert smugglers – and there was never any problem finding couriers to take the refined heroin into the United States, usually via Canada. But organizing a sophisticated chemical laboratory capable of turning morphine base into refined heroin was quite another matter. So Luciano had turned early on to the organization that controlled the docks at Marseille, the secret Union Corse – and in so doing had taken hold of another present gifted to organized crime by the Americans.

At the end of the war, the Americans had faced exactly the same problem in France that they had in Italy: the rise of the communists who, as in Italy, had fought with the socialists as partisans. Now there

The docks at Marseille became the base for the French Connection

was a growing fear in America that the well-organized and increasingly popular communists would seize power in a *coup d'état*. So the CIA and the State Department decided to seize the bull by the horns and take on the communists in one of their most important strongholds: the city of Marseille.

Marseille was the most important port in France, and its docks were controlled by communist-led unions who provoked civil unrest in the form of demonstrations and street battles. The CIA poured money and agents – including a psychological warfare team – into the city. They also recruited old allies in their fight against the communists, particularly among the Union Corse, many of whose members had been Resistance fighters and/or American agents.

Antoine Guerini had worked as a contact man for British and American intelligence, and had been an important conduit for the Allies' parachute-drops of arms during the German occupation. Now he was put in charge of a force of Corsican strong-arms hand-picked by him, whose job it was to secure control of the docks for the socialists whom the CIA were backing. He was soon successful, and with control of the port now in his hands and an army of enforcers at his back, he went on to take over one of Marseille's bigger businesses, the heroin trade.

Marseille became one of the key links in the heroin trail that led from the Middle East through Sicily and on to the United States. The Sicilians provided the morphine base and shipment to Marseille. They also took care of the onward journey of refined heroin to America for distribution. Gigantic profits were generated along the way, enough for everyone to share. Buying a kilo of morphine base might cost, say, $1,000, but by the time it had been refined to 90 per cent pure heroin and delivered to the US, that same kilo would have multiplied in value over 30 times. At street level, diluted with milk powder, it'd be worth fully $300,000 at early 1950s prices. The value added in Marseille, in other words, was $6,000 a kilo; the value added by a successful arrival in New York was a further $23,000 per kilo – for something that could be carried in a shopping bag, several kilos at a time.

An American Drug Enforcement Agency officer, who worked in France at the height of the French Connection, later remarked that in the late 1960s and early 1970s, 'it's no coincidence that we arrested over 40 former French intelligence officers': in other words, men who'd been as useful to the French as they'd been to the Americans.

CHAPTER 15

THE DEATH AND LEGACY OF LUCKY LUCIANO

In 1962, the visionary Luciano died at Naples airport, waiting for the arrival of a Hollywood producer who wanted to make a film of his life. It is said that there were Interpol agents there who wanted to interview him too. The official cause of death was a heart attack, but there were those who claimed that he was stricken after drinking a cup of coffee. So the possibility remains that he was poisoned, either because a film would bring his associates unwelcome publicity or because they were afraid of what he might say if arrested.

What he'd left behind, though, was to prove an abiding legacy. All the ingredients that were to lead to the domination of the Sicilian Mafia over huge swathes of the island's economy were now in place. Via its control over the countryside and over the water supply to orchards, it had moved into the island's slaughterhouses, produce markets and food-processing plants. It controlled the docks and the Palermo mayor's office. It took in perhaps 30 per cent of all the money invested in the island's development by the central government; and its tentacles reached high into the Christian Democratic Party, for whom it now regularly delivered the all-important Sicilian vote. It was also in charge of almost all buildings in Palermo. Under Salvo Lima, by

now a member of the Italian parliament, and his successor as mayor of Palermo, a Mafia ex-barber from Corleone called Vito Ciancimino, 2,500 of 4,000 building licences issued between 1958 and 1964 went to just three people, all Mafia fronts.

It also had its Commission and, with heroin, what was to become an unending stream of money – money which could be housed in banks which, because of Sicilian autonomy, were not governed by Italy's central bank. It was also well on its way to control over Sicily's tax-gathering, much of which ended up in the hands of two cousins, Ignazio and Nino Salvo – and this wasn't small money either. The commission paid to Sicilian agents was 10 per cent of all the monies taken in, three times more than in the rest of the country.

THE FIRST SICILIAN MAFIA WAR

The potential pickings, then, were huge, and after the death of Luciano the Sicilian families viciously fought each other for them in what turned out to be the final struggle between the old style and the new. The new Mafiosi, among them Luciano Liggio, had probably been influenced by the American hoods who'd returned to Sicily as a result of pressure from Senator Estes Kefauver's Special Commission, which in the early 1950s had established the existence of a nationwide crime syndicate in America known as Cosa Nostra. They brought with them not only management techniques, but also lessons in gang warfare. The Sicilians were quick to catch on.

Part of the struggle was territorial. The terms and conditions under which the Sicilian Commission had been set up made it slightly different from its American counterpart. In New York, that's to say, the word 'territory' was used metaphorically. The waste-disposal business, for example, was seen as the 'territory' of the Gambino and Lucchese families, while the docks 'belonged' to the Genoveses. In Sicily, the division between families was much more geographically-based, centred on particular towns and villages and areas in Palermo.

There were regional commissions that presided over each 'province', i.e. the territory of three contiguous families; and these in turn sent representatives to the central Cupola.

In theory, this should have worked. After all, the Sicilian Mafia was in the first place a cartel, an association of producers of a commodity called protection, and the Commission's job was on the face of it simple: to discipline each of the individual producers of protection and to restrict competition from outsiders. But there were several problems with this. In the first place, these individual producers were not stable organizations. Luciano Liggio, for example, who was to make the Corleonesi a truly formidable power, was still blasting his way to control over the competition within his own territory.

Secondly, there were inequalities of opportunity, and these were exacerbated both by the building boom in Palermo and by the Mafia's new business of drugs. The Cinisi family, for example – led by Cesare Manzella and his deputy Gaetano Badalamenti – were centred on a seaside town on the way to Palermo airport. The airport was part of its territory and this gave them a vital edge in the smuggling of any contraband. The family of Angelo and Salvatore Barbera, meanwhile, controlled an area in Palermo full of new building. This gave them a major source of extra revenue, which they were able to invest elsewhere, particularly in the new and all-important business of heroin.

As if this wasn't enough, there were inter-family deals that went wrong, investments that failed to pay off, all carried out amid a general atmosphere of secret suspicion. And the result was a gathering toll of punishment murders followed by killings in revenge: this was to be the era of the vendetta. In 1962 and early 1963, the heads of three Palermo families were killed, including Cesare Manzella and Salvatore Barbera. Angelo Barbera, on the run in Milan, was badly wounded. Finally, an attack made on the Greco family – headed by Salvatore 'Little Bird' Greco, the head of the Cupola – went badly wrong. A car bomb left outside the house of a trusted Greco lieutenant exploded while being examined – and seven soldiers and policemen were killed.

The result was a massive crackdown on the Mafia. There were arrests all over the island. Totò Riina was captured at the end of 1963, followed four months later by Luciano Liggio. So intense was police activity that the Cupola was suspended and many of the individual families dissolved. Salvatore Greco took refuge in Brazil. There were too few Mafia soldiers on the street – they were all in prison awaiting trial – for them to be able to do proper business.

In the end, two separate trials took place on the mainland: one relating to the five-year bloodbath in Corleone, and the other to the inter-family wars in Palermo. But the result in each was more or less the same. In the Palermo trial, which wound up in December 1968, 60 of the 114 defendants were acquitted and most of the rest were found guilty only of minor charges. As for the Corleone trial, the judge and jury had been effectively softened up by threats of death, and all the accused were acquitted the following year 'for lack of evidence'. The only significant aftermath was that Totò Riina was arrested again soon after his return to Corleone and exiled to a small town near Bologna in northern Italy. But he never went north. Instead, for the next 24 years, he lived 'undercover' – this being Sicily, more or less openly – in Palermo.

LITTLE DOLL

Assunta Maresca was the only daughter of Camorrista Vincenzo Maresca, whose family, the Lampetielli – known for their lightning speed with flick knives and pistols – controlled Castellammare di Stabia, a small town to the south of Naples. Pretty and spoilt, she earned the nickname Pupetta, or 'Little Doll'. She was renowned for her beauty and was jealously guarded by her four brothers, who beat her if she so much as caught a man's eye. Nevertheless, she entered a beauty contest held in a village south of Naples and became 'Miss Rovegliano'.

When an old-style *guappo*, or Camorra boss, who was ten years her senior – Pasquale Simonetti aka Pascalone 'e Nola (Big Pasquale of Nola) – began courting the buxom 17-year-old, her brothers acquiesced.

The wedding of racketeer Pasquale Simonetti and beauty queen Pupetta Maresca in 1955. After a few months, Pasquale was killed. A short time later Antonio Esposito lay dead when Pupetta took her revenge on the man who had ordered the killing.

Simonetti was a man of importance, one of the emerging bosses of the local gangs. An imposing man with great charisma, he used this to his advantage. The state authorites were hardly present in this rural area and he became a kind of lawgiver, dispensing justice in local disputes. If a son had been arrested, for example, Simonetti would be asked if he could find a good lawyer. If a girl had been dumped by her boyfriend, could he buy her some furniture to act as a dowry? Simonetti was there as an arbiter. It was said that he once summoned a boy who had seduced and abandoned a local girl and gave him a wad of money. 'This is for your wedding or your funeral – you decide,' he said.

His biggest claim to fame was that he was reputed to have slapped Lucky Luciano during a visit to the racetrack in Agnano, though not everyone believed the story. He ran the usual rackets, mainly protections,

although from his base in Nola, a town ten miles inland from Naples, he also fixed the price of fruit and vegetables in the city. But his money really came from smuggling cigarettes, a business in which competition was fierce. In 1953 Simonetti was arrested and charged in connection with attempted murder in a shoot-out over territorial supremacy with a rival gang. He was sent to prison for eight years.

He was released at Christmas in 1954 and immediately proposed to Pupetta. When they married in April 1955, the whole town turned out. There were 500 guests at the wedding breakfast. They brought envelopes stuffed with the traditional offerings of money or jewels for the new bride.

With her marriage, Pupetta acquired a new status. In the mornings, people queued outside her house, bringing gifts of cheese or wine. On his part, Simonetti was keen to regain his lost prestige and his business interests which, while he was in prison, had been taken over by his former partner, Antonio Esposito. Esposito had promised to keep Simonetti in the loop, but he did not keep his promise. The enmity grew and seemed likely to explode into the usual spiral of violence.

Esposito was the first one to act. On 16 July, in the Piazza Mercato in the centre of Naples, Simonetti was approached by Gaetano Orlando, a man he knew as 'The Ship' because of his rolling gait. Simonetti went for his gun, but 'The Ship' was too fast and shot him in the stomach. Simonetti was taken to hospital, but he told the police nothing. Pupetta rushed to his bedside to find him bleeding heavily. 'I begged him to tell me what had happened,' she said. 'He told me Esposito was behind it … That's how I knew who did it.'

Simonetti survived the night, but died the following morning, leaving Pupetta a widow at 20. Already pregnant, and afraid she might be on Esposito's hit list, she moved back in with her parents. 'I was frightened in the house on my own,' she said. 'It was like a nightmare, after starting a new life with my handsome prince, to be back living with my mother.'

She informed the police what her husband had told her about the shooting, but they did nothing. She had no proof. No one in the

market had seen anything apparently, or perhaps they were suffering a convenient lapse of memory. Pupetta was distraught; if Simonetti's murder went unpunished, it would diminish her status as the widow of an important man.

A WOMAN OF HONOUR

Esposito immediately began sending Pupetta threatening messages. It seemed that he knew her every move, so she began carrying her husband's gun – a Smith & Wesson .38 – which she had taken from his bedside as a 'memento'.

A few weeks later, the new widow was making her daily visit to the cemetery, accompanied by her driver and her 13-year-old brother, when she saw Esposito walking along the road nearby. She stopped the car. Esposito strolled up and said: 'I hear you have been looking for me.' He reached in the window and chucked her under the chin. 'Here I am,' he said. 'Get out of the car.' He began to open the door, but Pupetta reached into her handbag and pulled out Pasquale's gun. Holding it in both hands, she opened fire.

'I fired the first shot,' she admitted. 'He was going to kill me.'

Twenty-nine bullets were found in Esposito's body, and there was no sign whatever of any of the other occupants of the car, Pupetta's brother included. While awaiting trial, she gave birth to a son, Pasqualino – 'Little Pasquale' – in jail. She wrote reassuringly to her parents: 'Think of me as a girl away at college,' she said. 'Sometimes I laugh and sing.'

Flowers were showered from the balconies on to the police van carrying her to court. For the first time, microphones were allowed in the courtrooms of Naples assizes so the crowd could hear what was going on. While no witnesses could be found for the murder of Simonetti, 85 people turned up to speak in Pupetta's favour. She was unrepentant, telling the court: 'I would do it again.' With that, the court erupted with cheers.

Pupetta was found guilty and sentenced to 14 years. 'Prison was a nightmare,' she said. 'It was run by nuns, wizened old hags who were

consumed with envy. I was young. I had just got married. I had my lovely silk underwear ... they took it away and gave me a rough sack dress to wear, shapeless and several sizes too big. I threw it back at them. "You wear it!" I said.'

She did her best to give the nuns hell, refusing to have her hair cut and constantly demanding to see the governor. 'You can imagine me in the midst of all those old women rotting in jail. There were some young ones too, but they were from Calabria and Sicily – primitive girls.'

Having proved herself to be 'a woman of honour', she inherited her husband's authority. Other prisoners waited on her, bringing her clean bed linen and hot coffee and asking her for favours. She had food brought in for those less fortunate and stuck up for inmates' rights, effectively becoming the boss of the prison and earning the nickname 'Madame Camorra'. While in jail, she was bombarded with proposals of marriage. Inspired by her example, a musician composed a song called 'La Legge d'Onore' – 'The Law of Honour' – and the newspapers called her 'The Diva of Crime'.

She was allowed to keep her son Pasqualino with her until he was three. Then he was sent away to be brought up by her mother. When she was released, at the age of 31, her son was a stranger to her.

KILLED BY HIS MOTHER'S LOVER?

Some months after her release, a former cellmate introduced Pupetta to handsome Camorrista Umberto Ammaturo, who ran guns from Germany to Libya and cocaine from South America to Italy, via Nigeria. They became lovers and she gave birth to twins. But Ammaturo and Pasqualino did not get on.

The young man wanted to prove himself. He had already pulled a gun on the nephew of a Camorrista known simply as 'O Malommo' – 'the Bad Man' – and he had let it be known that once he was 18 he was going to kill 'The Ship' – the man who had killed his father. In January 1974, the day after his eighteenth birthday, Pasqualino was due to meet Ammaturo on the construction site of Naples' new flyover. He was never seen again.

Pupetta believed that Ammaturo knew something about Pasqualino's disappearance. She asked him about it repeatedly – to the point that he would beat her up for asking. If he had admitted to knowing anything about Pasqualino's death, Pupetta would have killed him. She even approached judge Italo Ormanni, who was investigating the disappearance, telling him that Ammaturo had killed her son, but she refused to sign a formal complaint. The judge was convinced that Pasqualino's body was in one of the pillars supporting the flyover, but he failed to get permission to knock it down.

Despite all this, Pupetta did not leave Ammaturo and continued to help him in his criminal activities. When war broke out between Raffaele Cutolo's Nuova Camorra Organizzata and the Nuova Famiglia faction, Pupetta's favourite brother was shot several times. He survived, but was sentenced to four years in prison, where he was again threatened by Cutolo's men.

MEDIA FIGURE

In 1982, Pupetta called a press conference at the press club in Naples. 'If Cutolo touches one member of my family, I will have his gunmen killed,' she declared. 'I will kill his lackeys, even the women and babies in their cradles ... The whole region is being strangled by an invisible force, seeping through every strata of society. That insidious force is Raffaele Cutolo. He wants to rule at any price – you are either with him or against him. Cutolo wants to become emperor of Naples, and this town is in chains because of him. All these deaths, the rivers of blood which are running through our city as people watch helplessly, all this is caused by one power-crazed madman.'

Cutolo dismissed this as histrionics. 'Pupetta should have more dignity,' he said. 'She has made a complete fool of herself.'

Behind the scenes, he started threatening her.

Later that year, Pupetta and Ammaturo were arrested for extortion and the murder of forensic psychiatrist Aldo Semerari, who had helped Ammaturo escape jail by feigning insanity. His severed head was found

between his legs. Ammaturo fled to South America leaving Pupetta to face the music alone. She was sentenced to four years. Maintaining her innocence, she claimed that Cutolo had used his contacts in the judiciary to put her away. 'I was tortured by the judges, every day of those four years,' she said. 'The first 14 years were different because I had committed a crime and it was right that I paid for it. But those four years in prison were terrible because there is no peace for an innocent person in prison.' Ammaturo was later acquitted on appeal due to lack of evidence. However, when he became a *pentito* in 1993 he admitted to the murder.

After leaving prison, Pupetta retired to Sorrento. In 1988, a film, *Il caso Pupetta Maresca*, was made about her life. The title role was played by Alessandra Mussolini, granddaughter of Benito, the Italian dictator.

In 2000, Pupetta made the newspapers again when she complained to the police that an employee had run off with the 10 billion lira – $5 million – she had won on Italy's biggest lottery. She said she had dispatched Giovanni Boscaglia, a 67-year-old small-time criminal, to play the numbers they had picked. But when they came up she did not hear from him. However, Pupetta's contacts in the Neapolitan underworld soon tracked him down. Boscaglia agreed to go to a notary public to hand over the winning ticket and sign a legal agreement that the pair would divide the winnings. But lottery officials said the ticket he handed over was a fake.

THE MANCHESTER MAFIOSA

It seems highly unlikely, but one Sicilian godmother hails from Rochdale, just outside Manchester, England. In 1979, Ann Hathaway (no relation to the Hollywood film star), then a 17-year-old dancer, met Antonio Rinzivillo in a club in northern Italy. They married, had two children and lived in Rome. Rinzivillo and his brother Gino specialized in arms trafficking, drug dealing and extortion for

Giuseppe 'Piddu' Madonia, second-in-command to Totò Riina until his arrest in 1992.

Rinzivillo was jailed for four-and-a-half years soon after they married and was in jail for all but four years of their 20-year marriage. His wife claimed that she knew nothing of his criminal activities. However, according the authorities in Sicily, she was a go-between for the Rinzivillos and their criminal network. 'She was a significant focal point through which passed all the orders and messages for other members of the organization,' said Major Bartolomeo di Niso of the Sicilian Carabinieri. 'She was a point of contact which would keep the whole machine running.'

Hathaway was taped demanding $120,000 from Rinzivillo's money launderer, Angelo Bernascone, for her brother-in-law Gino. In another tape, recorded a few weeks later in August 2005, she warned Bernascone of Gino's anger when he failed to pay, telling him: 'My brother-in-law was f*****g furious.'

On 1 October that year, Gino was heard on tape issuing a warning to Bernascone via Hathaway. He is heard telling her: 'You tell him "My brother-in-law has lost many friends and it's your fault . . . clearly people were right about you . . . Tell him "You and I are through. Full stop."' Bernascone turned himself in to the police in September 2006, saying he feared he was going to be killed.

Accused of running her husband's empire while he was in jail, Hathaway was also sought. 'You can't just arrest somebody just because you're married to someone that's got problems,' she protested. 'What's that got to do with me?'

Having fled back to England, she faced extradition. In a plea bargain, she admitted associating with the Mafia and was given a two-year suspended sentence. If her husband ever gets out of jail, she hopes he will join her in Rochdale.

CHAPTER 16

SAM GIANCANA, THE MAFIA AND THE DEATH OF JFK

In the United States, the 1960 election which brought President John Kennedy to office was decided by a few hundred thousand votes. The Democratic majority in Cook County, Illinois was the key that unlocked the door to the White House. Cook County, Illinois just happened to be Al Capone's old stamping ground, as Kennedy's father Joe, who'd been a bootlegger and associated with the Italian Mafia, knew well. Mafia boss Sam Giancana – who shared at least one lover with President Kennedy – later boasted of having swung the election there for Joe's son as a favour. Giancana and the Mafia were also involved in American-sponsored attempts to kill Prime Minister Fidel Castro of Cuba, Several of the conspiracy theories surrounding the assassination of the President Kennedy in November 1963 claim that he was killed at the behest of the American Mafia because he refused to return the favour it had done him. Indeed, by allowing his brother, Attorney-General Robert Kennedy to investigate organized crime and Teamsters Union boss Jimmy Hoffa, Kennedy had made matters much worse.

We will probably never know the truth. But then that's in the nature of our knowledge of Cosa Nostra. It exists in the shadows, and only very occasionally does it come out into the light, through

the confessions of *pentiti*, via wiretaps, at trials. The rest is silence, discretion. As Tommaso Buscetta, the most famous and highest-ranked of all the *pentiti*, said: 'In my ambience no one asks direct questions, but your interlocutor, when he considers it necessary, makes you understand, with a nod of the head, with a smile … even simply by his silence.'

Added to this is the fact that the family bosses and the members of the New York and Sicilian Commissions are far, far removed from the actual execution of any crime. They live at the top of a pyramid, outwardly respectable businessmen – sometimes, it is true, with no visible source of income – seemingly legitimate. Salvatore Inzerillo's brother-in-law Rosario Spatola in Sicily, for example, made millions of dollars from construction alone. He was said to be the fifth-highest tax payer in the whole of Italy.

Silence, remoteness, wisdom, power: these, then, were – and are – the watchwords that govern the behaviour of the senior ranks of Cosa Nostra. They were – and are – the law: a law that was regularly broken, however, by the head of one of New York's five families: Joe Bananas.

Mafia Killings 47

Jimmy Hoffa, Detroit, 30 July 1975

It may have been a summer's day just like any other; children played in the park and people went about their business as they always did. But that afternoon, Jimmy Hoffa, former president of the International Brotherhood of Teamsters union, headed to the

In October 1957, members of the Teamsters labour union (with a jackass mascot) root for the election of Jimmy Hoffa, an activist with mob connections. By the 1950s, organized criminals had infiltrated the Teamsters and corruption had become endemic.

Machus Red Fox Restaurant on Telegraph Road in Detroit. He was to meet with Anthony Giacalone and Anthony Provenzano, two union men with strong ties to organized crime. At least that was Hoffa's plan. Unfortunately, neither Giacalone nor Provenzano showed up. At around 2:45 that afternoon a car did arrive at the restaurant, Hoffa got into it . . . and was never seen again.

Theories abound as to what happened to him that day and why. Investigations have continued for years, with authorities digging through empty fields and searching suburban residences, all with no result. Hoffa is gone, and his body will probably never be found, whether it's at the bottom of a lake somewhere or maybe encased in cement at Giants Stadium. We may never know just who assassinated Hoffa that day, but we can certainly surmise, and with a fair amount of accuracy, the reason why the job was done.

During Hoffa's time the unions meant big business to organized crime, and Hoffa definitely had his connections. Senator Bobby Kennedy and his 'Get Hoffa' team had been after him for years, and in 1964 were finally able to convict him of jury tampering and bribery. A further successful charge was also offered of skimming money from Teamster pension funds and funnelling it into the mob.

Hoffa, of course, appealed his conviction but was ultimately sent to prison in 1967, leaving trusted ally Frank Fitzsimmons as temporary Teamster president. Unfortunately for Hoffa, Fitzsimmons soon proved to be less of a friend, and began to put some distance between himself and the imprisoned union boss.

In 1971 things changed when Hoffa won a pardon from President Richard Nixon, on the stipulation that he resign and refrain from re-entering union business until 1980. This arrangement suited Fitzsimmons and the mob nicely. It has been speculated that the Mafia orchestrated the release of Hoffa in return for funds into the Nixon campaign (a move meant to keep the pro-Hoffa Teamsters

pacified, something Fitzsimmons badly needed to do) so long as the ex-union leader remained out of labour politics. That last part, of course, was the important bit – Hoffa had to steer clear of the Teamsters. But the union was in Jimmy Hoffa's blood and for the rest of his life he vigorously attempted a return to Teamster leadership.

And that was the crux of the problem. Nobody wanted Hoffa back as union leader – not Fitzsimmons and not the mob. Certainly Hoffa had loaned out union money to the Mafia, but Fitzsimmons was now doing exactly the same thing, and much more generously. This was a cash cow that the Mafia was not about to let slip away. In the end, Fitzsimmons was a lot more malleable than the hard-nosed Hoffa had ever been.

So, on that day in July, Hoffa, like Bo Weinberg, disappeared into history. The man who used to brag that he didn't need a bodyguard was declared legally dead in 1982.

In the curious way that time has of healing all ills, today Jimmy Hoffa's son James is president of the Teamsters Union.

JOE BANANAS AND THE HEROIN BUSINESS

Giuseppe Bonanno – or Joe Bananas – was, by the consensus of the other members of the Commission and even his own street-soldiers, a flake. Quite apart from his heroin business, of which many of the bosses still disapproved, he was, in the early 1960s, trying to take over territory on the West Coast and in doing so was treading on other bosses' toes. There were even rumours that he was plotting against other Commission members.

As if this wasn't bad enough, in 1964 he made his own son Bill his family's *consigliere*, thus flying in the face of another Mafia tradition. More senior people had been passed over, and in any case Bill Bonanno

had been born with a silver spoon in his mouth: he couldn't even talk the language of the streets. A civil war broke out. Complaints were made to the Commission, and the boss of a minor New Jersey family called Sam 'The Plumber' Cavalcante was appointed to the job instead, either to bring the family back together or – and this may have been the Commission's intention – to split it further apart.

As it happened, the FBI had a wiretap in Cavalcante's office and were able to listen in when he had a meeting with one of his captains, who was also the business agent for a New Jersey-based union. From the conversation between the two men, the FBI found out that both Bill Bonanno and father Joe were refusing to answer summonses from the Commission. 'When Joe defies the Commission, he's defying the whole world!' exclaimed the outraged Cavalcante.

Why Joe Bananas wasn't killed remains a mystery. In October 1964 he was kidnapped by armed men off the streets of Manhattan only to reappear two years later, looking fit and well, at a courthouse in Manhattan's Foley Square. He gave himself up to a judge, but wouldn't explain where he'd been and faced a minor charge for obstruction of justice. At this point he retired to a house in Tucson, Arizona, as if nothing had happened.

Whether he continued to run his family from Tucson is unknown. What is known is that the Bonannos' New York territory, including the heroin business, was eaten away gradually in the late 1960s and early 1970s by the Gambino family, despite the fact that in 1973 Phil 'Rusty' Rastelli was elected head of the Bonnanos. He was denied a seat on the Commission. The inference was that Rastelli was weak – and this put both him and the Gambinos at odds with the murderous ex-*consigliere* of the Bonanno family, Carmine Galante.

Joseph Bonanno died in his bed at home in Tuscon on 11 May 2002, he was 94 years old. It was an unusually peaceful end for a lifelong Mafioso, once head of one of the most powerful American crime families, perhaps finally laying to rest the notion implied by his 'Bananas' nickname, which he hated all his life, that he was crazy.

Mafia Killings 48

Alberto Agueci, Rochester, New York, October 1961

It used to be thought that the Mafia banned its members from dealing in drugs. This was not because drug money was beneath them, as some sources seem to insist. Really, nothing is beneath the mob. The actual reason was the effectiveness of the Federal Bureau of Narcotics (later the Drug Enforcement Administration) and the extremely long sentences associated with drug convictions. The thinking was that the longer a thug was in jail, the more likely he would be to flip and sing like a canary.

But there's just too much money to be made from narcotics, and where there's a buck, there's the mob. So although not officially sanctioned, many a mobster was able to make a fortune from drugs. They just had to do it on the sly. And any Mafioso unfortunate enough to get caught dealing could consider himself on his own – there would be no protection from the boss. Basically, it would be the old kiss-off. And that's exactly what brothers Alberto and Vito Agueci got in the early 1960s.

The Agueci brothers had emigrated to Canada from Sicily and were part of a vast drug operation that stretched from Turkey through Sicily into France (the French Connection) and then into the United States via Canada. The brothers had set up shop in Toronto and belonged to Stefano 'The Undertaker' Magaddino's family – a mob that operated out of Buffalo, but had tentacles that reached into Southern Ontario and Montreal. One of their partners in this racket was Joe Valachi, who later became part of Mafia legend as a high-profile informant.

Some time in the late 1950s the Feds began to get wind of the drug operation, and initiated a crack-down. Valachi was arrested in 1959, and the Agueci brothers in 1961. For his own personal protection, mob boss Magaddino closed the door on them.

Alberto Agueci was enraged. He had fully believed he'd be bailed out by Magaddino and would receive the counsel of a top-notch lawyer. It was not to be. As reality slowly dawned on him, he began to lose his grip. Valachi later commented that he could tell Alberto was not going to do well in prison.

In desperation, Alberto's wife was forced to sell their lovely new Toronto home in order to bail the Mafioso out. Once he was freed, Agueci headed straight to Buffalo and Magaddino.

A mob boss who has been insulted is a dangerous enemy. The godfathers have their dignity and their standing within the Mafia to maintain. No insult can be ignored. Vengeance for any slight must be brutal and it must be swift. A message needs to be sent: 'The boss will tolerate no disrespect.'

Once Agueci had finished his tirade, and the smoke had settled a bit, Magaddino ordered two of his goons – Danny Sansanese and Freddie Randaccio – to take him out to a field somewhere and deal with him. And, Magaddino told them, don't be gentle about it.

On 3 November 1961, Alberto Agueci's pitiful remains were found in a farmer's field. He had been unspeakably tortured over a number of days – his teeth were kicked in, his eyes were burned out with a blowtorch, his genitals had been cut off and stuck in his mouth and chunks of flesh had been removed from his legs while he was still alive. Finally, strangulation had ended his torment, and then his body had been set ablaze. There was nothing else to say. Magaddino had made himself heard, loud and clear.

Mafia Killings 49

Ernest 'The Hawk' Rupolo, Jamaica Bay, New York, 27 August 1964

Ernest Rupolo had been a career criminal almost since the time he

could walk. In a very early mugshot, taken at the ago of about 20, his mouth is twisted in a crooked smirk. Already, though, there is a patch over his right eye. He had lost it in an earlier altercation and the offending bullet never exited his head; it remained there, lodged in his skull for the rest of his life, a terrible souvenir from a lifetime of violence.

A killer for hire, way back in the 1930s Rupolo had been involved in the contract that Vito Genovese had put out on Ferdinand 'The Shadow' Boccia. It's not likely that Rupolo actually killed Boccia, but he did know about it – all about it. Then, in 1944, he was picked up for the attempted murder of another mobster, Carl Sparacino. Facing a lengthy prison sentence, Rupolo decided to feed the authorities information about the Boccia killing; and his story would lead all the way to the top, to Vito Genovese of course.

No doubt about it, Rupolo was clearly a risk-taker. Of course, it might have been because of the bullet that was lodged in his brain. Maybe it had severed certain cerebral connections in his head that at one time would have given him access to common sense, or at least to the notion of self-preservation.

The accusation of Boccia's murder brought Genovese all the way back from Italy so he could stand trial. But, predictably, two of the key witnesses in the case passed away before they could testify, and Genovese was acquitted. Three years after this debacle, in 1949, Ernest Rupolo was back on the street and attempting – very vigorously – to make himself scarce.

One might imagine that Rupolo's life expectancy at this point would be pretty short. But Vito Genovese did not deal with him right away. In fact, years and years went by, and still the mob boss made no move against Rupolo. Maybe it was because Genovese had not been convicted of the Boccia murder, or maybe it was because he wanted Rupolo to suffer. Ultimately, his death did not fit into Genovese's plans. So Rupolo was allowed to languish, waiting for the inevitable, as

he made a meagre living from any small racket he could put together.

His number was finally up in August of 1964. Joe Valachi had just testified against the mob the year before, and this famous betrayal may have triggered something in Genovese, inspiring him to take revenge against all squealers, just on principle. They, of course, included Rupolo.

His body was found on 27 August 1964. The corpse was in a dreadful state. Bound at the hands, Rupolo had been stabbed and shot multiple times. With his feet encased in cement, his body had been dumped into Jamaica Bay in New York. His had been a hard-luck existence, but 'The Hawk' must have known that in the end there was no escaping his fate – even though it had been long ago, he'd still been marked for murder.

THE MOB AND JFK

Everyone who was old enough to understand the news at the time remembers the day that President John F. Kennedy was killed. It was like the moon landing, or the murder of John Lennon – an event that effectively stopped time for just a moment and seized the public consciousness.

Conspiracy theories galore exist around this event, but let's concentrate on only one of them – the involvement of the Mafia, and more specifically of Richard Cain, in the assassination of the president. Cain (aka Richard Scalzetti) had been the mob's mole in the Chicago Police Department and with his espionage experience he assisted the Mafia in its plan with the CIA to bring down Cuban president Fidel Castro. Cain was of superior intelligence, spoke five languages and worked on training Cuban exiles for the Bay of Pigs Invasion. He was also said to be a crack marksman. All of these statements, save the latter, are verifiable facts.

Further, the bespectacled and innocuous-looking Cain had an extremely tight relationship with Mafia Don Sam Giancana himself. It has even been posited that Giancana was Cain's biological father. In

short, Cain had the contacts, the know-how and the abilities to make him invaluable to the mob for this particular job.

So what was Cain's role in the death of the president? Well, the claim, supposedly from the mouth of Sam Giancana himself, was that Lee Harvey Oswald had not been alone on that terrible day in 1963. Apparently Cain was there with him. What's more, it was actually Cain who fired the bullet that ended Kennedy's life, and not Oswald. The mob's motive in the killing, of course, was to halt the Senate's investigation into Mafia operations. In other words, the mob wanted to get the government off its back.

Ten years after the assassination, the Mafia decided they could do without Cain's services, and had him eliminated too. Shortly before he died, Cain apparently contacted FBI agent William F. Roemer and began to supply him with information regarding gambling operations in Chicago. It was Cain's plan to use Roemer in order to remove powerful gambling rivals and therefore take over the city's gambling scene himself. It was a typical Cain move, trying to play both sides.

If Cain had been working with Roemer, there would have been nothing to stop him from relaying everything he knew about the Mafia's involvement in the Castro Project (as the assassination attempt against the Cuban leader was termed) and the murder of President Kennedy. There was no way the mob could let Cain live.

Cain was murdered inside Rose's Sandwich Shop in Chicago on 20 December 1973. That day, masked gunmen entered the restaurant and forced everyone present up against the wall; then, asking where the package was, shot Cain – and only Cain – through the head several times before exiting. Supposedly before the killers left they took something from Cain's pocket, but what the item was no one can say. Possibly it was only a ruse; we'll never know, because Cain's killers have not been identified. Sam Giancana was reportedly suitably upset when he heard

Overleaf: John Kennedy's possible links with the Mafia have long been the subject of whispered discussion

about the murder of Richard Cain. It would have gone badly for the killers if he had ever caught up with them, whoever they may have been.

THE CASTRO PROJECT

Momo Salvatore Giancana (more familiarly known as Sam) was a real operator, rubbing elbows with Frank Sinatra and the Kennedys and working on a contract to assassinate Fidel Castro. Giancana liked jet-setting and publicity and all the trappings that went with them. This high-profile existence didn't sit too well with the rest of the Chicago Outfit though, especially mob boss Anthony 'Big Tuna' Accardo, who tended to play his cards close to his chest. To Accardo, the only good publicity was no publicity. It was only a matter of time before his patience with Giancana would wear out.

Giancana was the street boss for the Chicago Outfit. Having worked his way up through the ranks for years, he became the face of the Chicago mob in 1957. The real power at that time, though, lay in the hands of Accardo and Paul 'The Waiter' Ricca, who controlled things from the shadows.

This didn't mean that Giancana had no authority – far from it. He was one of the most powerful mobsters in the country. But on matters of great importance Giancana would defer to the decisions of people even more powerful – Ricca and Accardo. That was how the Outfit operated.

It's part of the Giancana legend that he'd fixed the votes in Chicago during the Federal election of 1960, a strategy that gave John F. Kennedy the presidency that year. Then when the Kennedys didn't play ball as Giancana had expected – calling off the Federal investigation into organized crime – he came up with a supplementary arrangement, one that took place in Dallas on 22 November 1963. Who can say whether this is true? Countless books have been written on the assassination of JFK but no conclusive proof has ever been found.

But it is said that there are files in existence (known as the Family Jewels Documents) that detail how, as part of their Cuban Project, the

CIA approached Giancana with the offer of a contract. The Agency wanted some assistance with the elimination of Fidel Castro, and who better to take on a job like that than the Mafia?

Several attempts to poison the leader were made (apparently at the instigation of Giancana), but all were in vain. Castro survived, and any further assassination plots were soon to be deflected by the Cuban Missile Crisis.

The situation changed rapidly for Giancana after this, and in 1965 he received a year in prison for contempt of court. On his release, he found it advisable to lie low for a while and headed to Mexico, where he made a fortune operating casinos. Unfortunately he didn't see fit to share any of his gambling profits with the Outfit at this time, which was not a smart move.

The good times couldn't last forever and in 1974 Giancana was deported from Mexico and arrived back in Chicago again. What's more, he was also called to appear before a Senate Committee investigating the Castro contract that the CIA had put out.

By now Accardo had had enough: Sam Giancana had become a liability. On 19 June, he was assassinated while frying up some peppers and sausages in his basement in Oak Park, Illinois, and his secrets died with him. Of course, no one knows what those secrets are, but the story goes that some time in 1960 Joe Kennedy invited Frank Sinatra to the Kennedy compound in Hyannis Port and asked him for some help with the support of Catholic union members in West Virginia. Joe looked at Sinatra, 'You and I know the same people, and you know the people I mean'. Sinatra understood.

A few days later Sinatra invited his friend Giancana for a round of golf and in a quiet moment asked him for a favour. Giancana looked at him, nodded, and said, 'It's a couple of phone calls, and tell the old man I said hello'.

Mafia Killings 50

Jasper Campise and John Gattuso, Naperville, Chicago, July 1983

The hit on Ken Eto was going to be the job that gave Johnny Gattuso promotion to made man. It shouldn't have been too hard. All he had to do was lure Eto to a quiet parking lot, wait until he parked the car, place a gun to his head, then it would be over. Only it didn't happen that way. Although Campise and Gattuso thought they'd planned every detail, somehow after all the smoke had cleared, Eto was still standing upright. More than that, he was now ratting everyone out, and big time.

Ken Eto was a Japanese-American in the Chicago Outfit. His was not the usual ethnicity of a Mafioso, but he was a good earner, bringing in millions. He'd worked for the Outfit for years running a bolita game – a numbers racket – since 1949 and lining the pockets of his boss Vincent Solano, who was also boss of the whole North Side.

Eto was true-blue too, a reliable goodfella who could always be counted on to do his job, keep his mouth shut and generally toe the line. The last thing Eto ever wanted to do was to rat out his pals – it just wasn't part of his makeup. It was too bad Solano didn't understand that.

Everything started to unravel some time in the early 1980s when the Feds began to clamp down on Eto's bolita game. That's when Solano started getting nervous. The mob boss just didn't realize that he had nothing to worry about when it came to Eto. The best thing to do, Solano felt, was to get rid of the problem altogether.

Of course, Eto knew that it was coming; he knew he had no choice, and decided to go the way they wanted him to.

The contract eventually made its way to Jasper Campise and John Gattuso, the Abbott and Costello of Chicago's underworld.

But maybe Eto had been born under a lucky star; it just wasn't his time to go. Campise and Gattuso had everything worked out so nicely. They'd even packed the bullets themselves so they'd be more difficult to trace. And that's how everything fell apart – there just wasn't enough oomph in those slugs.

Picture it: the three of them sitting in the car, Eto waiting for the shot to be fired. Campise was sitting in the back seat, talking pleasantly about the dinner they were going to have, trying to keep Eto's suspicions under wraps. Then Gattuso raised his gun and blam – three times. Eto slumped over sideways in the car. Campise and Gattuso got of the car and headed out into the night, confident of a job well done.

But, despite the fact that he had three bullet in his head, Eto was still alive. Pulling himself out of the car, he staggered to a drugstore, where he called for an ambulance.

Of course, if Eto wasn't going to flip for the Feds before, he was certainly going to do it now. He told the FBI about everything – crooked cops, old robberies and unsolved murders. He also told them a lot about Solano. Eto even told stuff about the mob that hadn't happened yet. It was all gold. Ken Eto proved to be a most reliable informant.

For Campise and Gattuso, their days were numbered. The pair had been missing for a few days when their bodies were found in the trunk of an abandoned car in suburban Naperville on 14 July 1983. It was the foul odour emanating from the vehicle that had prompted a local resident to call the police. The two men had been stabbed repeatedly and left in the open so that they could easily be discovered, clear signs that they had disgraced the mob.

Eto spent the rest of his days in Georgia, living under an assumed name. Joe Tanaka, as he came to be called, lived to the ripe old age of 84 and died of natural causes.

THAT DAY IN DALLAS

Johnny Roselli was also thought to have been in on the CIA plan to murder Castro and Kennedy. It seems that the Mafia was really busy in the 1960s and Roselli was at the forefront.

'Hansdome' Johnny Roselli had good looks, with an impressive mane of silver hair, immaculately tailored suits and two dimples that appeared when he flashed his winning smile. He worked out of Vegas, skimming money from the casinos.

According to various sources, Johnny was either on his way to Dallas in order to abort the Kennedy assassination or he was actually one of the shooters, aiming from his position down a sewer drain.

Whatever the rumours, the mob was feeling a lot of heat from Senator Bobby Kennedy (JFK's brother) in his zealous crusade against organized crime. To the Mafia, pressure from the government meant a loss of revenue, and put the boys at the top – Sam Giancana of Chicago and Santo Trafficante of Florida – in compromised positions. This alone was more than enough to make the mob take action.

In the 1970s, all of this started to unravel and Roselli found himself in the thick of it. He appeared twice in front of Senate Committees with regard to the Castro and Kennedy affairs, on 22 September 1975 and 23 April 1976 respectively. And during all this, Roselli was not pleading the Fifth and keeping his mouth firmly shut, the way a Mafioso should do – he was being rather forthcoming with his testimony.

On 9 August 1976, at the point at which Roselli was expected to testify in front of the United States Senate Select Committee one more time, his body surfaced in Florida's Dumfoundling Bay. He had been shot and strangled, then stuffed into a barrel and tossed into the water. His legs had been cut off so he would fit into the drum; newspapers of the day wrote that Roselli may still have been alive when he was thrown into the bay, though today we know this to be incorrect. Roselli had done some talking, but once again the Mafia had had the last word.

Bobby Kennedy zealously campaigned against organized crime

CASINO

Originally from Puglia, Italy, Anthony 'the Ant' Spilotro's parents emigrated to Chicago in 1914. They ran Patsy's restaurant on the corner of Grand and Ogden Avenues, where such well-known criminals as Frank Nitti, Paul 'the Waiter' Ricca and Sam Giancana regularly dined. Patsy's car park was often used for mob meetings.

Spilotro dropped out during his second year in high school and made money shoplifting and purse-snatching. Then he teamed up with

childhood friend Frank Cullotta. They would rob Jewish kids and ride around together in stolen cars. 'Tony was the toughest kid I knew,' said Cullotta. 'He was so tough that his brother Victor used to offer guys $5 to see if they could beat him up. Usually, Victor got a taker and the guy would try to kick Tony's ass, but if it looked like Tony was gonna lose, we'd all jump on the kid and break his head.'

In a fight with some black boys, Spilotro pulled out a knife and stabbed one of them, but the victim did not press charges.

At the age of 17, Spilotro was fined $10 for stealing a shirt. He was arrested another 12 times for petty crimes before the age of 22.

When Cullotta and some other youths shot three men in a tavern, Spilotro helped them get rid of the guns. He then roped them into a scheme whereby they waited outside banks and robbed anyone carrying a large amount of cash.

By the age of 18, they were making $25,000 a month each. But when Cullotta bought a new Cadillac, Spilotro told him to get rid of it. He had already made contact with the Chicago Outfit, who wanted them to continue driving around in inconspicuous Fords and Chevrolets.

ONE OF HIS EYES POPPED OUT

Spilotro hung out with Vinnie 'the Saint' Inserro, who introduced him to Jimmy 'the Turk' Torello, Charles 'Chuckie' Nicoletti, 'Milwaukee Phil' Alderisio, Joey 'the Clown' Lombardo and Joseph 'Joey Doves' Aiuppa. Aiuppa would go on to become head of the Outfit – a job Spilotro had coveted from an early age.

On one occasion, two hold-up men named Bill McCarthy and Jimmy Miraglia had an argument with Philly and Ronnie Scalvo. The Scalvos were then found dead, along with a woman, but no one had given permission for the hit, so retribution was ordered.

Spilotro, Nicoletti and Alderisio abducted McCarthy. They took him to a workshop to torture him but he would not talk, even when they stabbed an ice-pick through his testicles. So Spilotro put McCarthy's head in a vice and tightened it until one of his eyes popped out. He

then put lighter fuel on McCarthy's face and set fire to it. Unimpressed, Nicoletti ate pasta throughout the incident.

Before he died, McCarthy gave up Miraglia's name. Eleven days later, the bodies of Miraglia and McCarthy were found in the boot of Miraglia's car.

After these murders, Spilotro hooked up with Outfit enforcer 'Mad' Sam DeStefano, collecting debts for him. As part of Milwaukee Phil's crew, he began shaking down bookies. Then he became a bail bondsman, bailing out soldiers for Lombardo, Alderisio and Torello.

By 1963, Spilotro was a made man in the Chicago Outfit, controlling the bookmaking in the northwest side of Chicago. He quickly attracted the attention of law enforcement officers and the media, who called him 'the Ant' because he was just 5 feet 2 inches tall.

The following year Spilotro was sent to Miami to work with childhood friend Frank 'Lefty' Rosenthal, a mob-backed bookmaker, handicapper and match-fixer. In 1961, Rosenthal had appeared before the McClellan Committee on Gambling and Organized Crime, where he took the Fifth Amendment 37 times – refusing even to say whether he was left-handed (the origin of his nickname).

DEADLY AFFAIR

In 1971, Spilotro was sent to run the Outfit's interests in Las Vegas with 'Fat Herbie' Blitzstein as the muscle. Once more he worked with Rosenthal, who was in charge of the skim. Spilotro's job was to siphon off as much cash as possible before it was recorded as revenue. Working with his brother, Michael, out of a jewellery store called The Gold Rush, Spilotro imposed a street tax on all criminal activities, enforcing this with five murders in which the victims were brutally tortured before they were killed. But even before Spilotro arrived in Las Vegas, the FBI in Chicago had alerted the bureau there that he was on his way. He was only in town two weeks before they had a wiretap on him. The local police picked him up every three or four months 'on general principle'. It was a hassle, but Spilotro enjoyed the publicity.

In September 1972, Spilotro had to go back to Chicago to face trial alongside 'Mad' Sam DeStefano and his brother, Mario, for the 1963 murder of real estate agent Leo Foreman. One of the killers, Charles 'Chuckie' Crimaldi, had turned state's evidence. Spilotro was worried about fellow defendant Sam DeStefano who, it was said, had cancer and was afraid of dying in jail. The Outfit bosses began to worry that DeStefano would not only jeapardize his own defence, but also those of his other crew members. In a secret meeting, the boss of the Chicago Outfit, Tony Accardo, gave DeStefano's crew permission to kill him.

Thanks to an alibi provided by his sister-in-law, Spilotro was acquitted in the Leo Foreman case. As Spilotro walked free after the trial, FBI agent Bill Roemer said quietly: 'You're still a little pissant. We'll get you yet.'

Spilotro smiled, and said: 'F*** you.'

Mafia Killings 51

'Mad' Sam DeStefano, Chicago, 14 April 1973

Sam DeStefano was a bona fide lunatic, making 'Crazy' Joe Gallo seem like a sea of calm. Born in southern Illinois, Sam DeStefano moved to Chicago as a teenager. At 18, he was convicted of rape. Convictions for extortion, bank robbery, assault with a deadly weapon and possessing counterfeit ration stamps soon followed.

In 1930, DeStefano joined Sam Giancana's West Side 42 Gang of violent thugs and bootleggers. He rose to become a major drug trafficker and loan-shark – introducing the 'juice loan', where extreme violence was used to force borrowers to repay as quickly as possible (this was the 'juicing' part – he'd squeeze his clients dry). If they couldn't pay, he would have the opportunity to go to work.

His reputation as a brutal and sadistic murderer was seen as useful by the gang, because he made them lots of money. However, his unstable mental condition also meant that while other 42 Gang members rose to senior positions in the Chicago Outfit, DeStefano

was never a made man, despite killing his own brother on the gang leader Momo Giancana's orders. He remained a debt collector and executioner, two things at which he was very good. He kept his instruments of torture in the sound-proofed basement of his home where he could enjoy hurting his victims, with his wife and three children living blissfully untroubled above.

The depravity of his actions only really came to light after his death. In his book, *The Enforcer*, FBI Agent William Roemer, who had played a big part in various investigations, labelled him the worst 'torture-murderer' in the history of the United States. But there was no shortage of stories of his actions during his lifetime.

When restaurant owner Artie Adler could not pay up, DeStefano took him to his basement and went to work on him with an ice-pick. During the torture, Adler died of a heart attack. His body was dumped in a frozen sewer and caused a blockage during the spring thaw. This amused DeStefano no end.

Debt collector Peter Cappelletti tried to run off with $25,000. He was taken to Mario DeStefano's restaurant in the suburb of Cicero, where he was stripped and handcuffed to an overheating radiator. After being tortured there for three days, he begged to be killed. Instead, DeStefano invited Cappelletti's family to dinner. After they had finished the four-course meal, Cappelletti was brought out, naked and badly burnt, and thrown at the feet of his mother. DeStefano then urinated on him. In some versions of the story, members of Cappelletti's family were forced to urinate on him too.

Usually the mob would not put up with such a noxious character as DeStefano – he was too much of a liability. But he was smart as well as crazy; his money-making abilities and his usefulness as a fixer ensured he was around a lot longer than others might have been. Things changed in November 1963, when DeStefano paid a visit to the offices of real estate agent and loan shark, Leo Foreman. There was an argument, and Foreman threw him out. On the pretext

of making peace, DeStefano lured Foreman to the Cicero home of his brother Mario, who softened him up with a hammer, assisted by Spilotro and Crimaldi. DeStefano then stabbed him 20 times with an ice-pick. When Foreman pleaded for his life, DeStefano shot him repeatedly in the buttocks, then finished him off with a butcher's knife. Even after Foreman was dead, they continued cutting lumps of flesh from his body.

In 1972, Crimaldi turned state's evidence and Sam and Mario DeStefano and Spilotro were indicted for Foreman's murder. He was already said to be crazy, but DeStefano's courtroom antics became increasingly bizarre. He turned up in his pyjamas, in a wheelchair and addressed the court through a megaphone. The trial turned into a circus when the newspapers featured it on their front pages. This robbed the other defendants of their chance to influence the jury with bribes or by coercion. And it meant 'Mad Sam' had to go.

On 14 April 1976, a meeting was scheduled at DeStefano's house in Gaelwood. Spilotro and Sam's brother Mario had been invited on the pretext that they had discovered where Crimaldi was being held by the authorities. Thirty minutes before they were due to arrive, DeStefano's wife and bodyguard said they had to go out. When his guests arrived, DeStefano started gloating about exacting his revenge on Crimaldi. Then Mario stepped aside; Spilotro was standing behind him with a double-barrelled shotgun. He fired twice. The first blast tore off 'Mad Sam's arm at the elbow. The second hit him square in the chest, killing him instantly.

It is not surprising that the murder was never brought to trial.

Frank 'Lefty' Rosenthal adjusts his tie while refusing to answer questions before the Senate Rackets Subcommittee. Rosenthal was brought before the committee for bribery and match-fixing in 1961.

Then Spilotro was indicted alongside Lombardo for defrauding the Teamsters' pension fund. This problem was solved by the murder of the only witness, 29-year-old Daniel Seifert. Both men were acquitted and Spiloto returned to Las Vegas.

Although Spilotro's job in Vegas was to keep an eye on Rosenthal and other Outfit interests, he began running a team of burglars known as the 'Hole in the Wall Gang', so-called because they often gained entry by making a hole in a wall or roof.

Meanwhile, West Coast Mafia turncoat Aladena 'Jimmy the Weasel' Fratianno testified against Spilotro and the Nevada Gaming Commission blacklisted him. He was barred from being physically present in any Nevada casino. As a result, he expanded the Hole in the Wall Gang's activities to encompass the entire tri-state area.

But the gang's burglar alarm specialist Sal Romano was picked up on another charge. He flipped, and the crew were arrested on their next outing. Hearing that there was a contract out on him, Cullotta also turned state's evidence, but his testimony was not enough to convict Spilotro on conspiracy charges.

The bosses of the Chicago Outfit were not pleased with Spilotro. As well as operating without their authority, he was gaining a dangerously high profile. Then came news that Spilotro was having an affair with Rosenthal's wife. Mafia bosses don't approve of such things. Then Rosenthal was car-bombed. Although it was thought that Milwaukee boss Frank Balistrieri – aka the 'Mad Bomber' – was responsible, Spilotro was also a suspect. FBI wiretap evidence in which Spilotro mentioned Joseph 'Mr Clean' Ferriola, then running the Chicago Outfit, had also been heard in court.

Spilotro was about to face trial for skimming profits at the Stardust casino and violating the civil rights of a government witness. A retrial of the Hole in the Wall case was also scheduled. At the same time, Spilotro's brother, Michael, faced extortion charges in Chicago. On 14 June 1986, the two men were summoned to a meeting where they believed Michael was going to be a made man. Instead they were

beaten with baseball bats and buried alive in a cornfield in Enos, Indiana, some 60 miles southeast of Chicago.

Their remains were accidentally unearthed by a farmer. The grave was just four miles from a hunting lodge owned by Mafia boss Joe Aiuppa, who was in prison at the time for skimming profits from Las Vegas casinos.

Nicholas Pileggi's 1995 book *Casino* describes the Las Vegas careers of Spilotro and Rosenthal and was used as the basis for a movie of the same name, directed by Martin Scorsese.

Mafia Killings 52

Herbert 'Fat Herbie' Blitzstein, Las Vegas, 6 January 1997

After the death of Anthony Spilotro, Herbert Blitzstein was like a man adrift and alone in a vast sea. Herbert, or 'Fat Herbie', was in a tight spot. It might seem that this hulking figure of a man – 6 feet tall and over 300 pounds – would be capable, intimidating, and able to leave his own unmistakable mark wherever he went. But Blitzstein, despite his size, had always been a wing-man, a wiseguy in the supporting cast rather than a lead player. Once Spilotro shuffled off, Blitzstein's rackets were basically up for grabs.

Blitzstein came from Chicago to Vegas with Spilotro, helping the mobster operate the Outfit's lucrative casino-skimming operations. Spilotro was the brains and Blitzstein was the very impressive muscle. Spilotro's group also ran the Hole in the Wall Gang.

Things were going well in Vegas for a while, until Spilotro got himself blacklisted at the casino. Then the law came down pretty hard, not only on Spilotro but the Outfit as well. Naturally enough, the Chicago mob removed Spilotro from its register – permanently. After a stint in prison, Blitzstein was out on his own.

Blitzstein made his way back to Vegas and seemed to be flying

under the radar for a while. But his flamboyant appearance – impeccably dressed and looking like a mobbed-up Luciano Pavarotti – gave away his occupation, and pretty soon he was running rackets again. Only this time, there was no Spilotro or Outfit to back him up.

Bringing in some solid money from loansharking and fraud, Blitzstein did not see fit to share it with the other powers operating in the free town of Vegas, including Los Angeles' Milano Brothers. This left him unguarded and open for anybody to take a pop at. And that, of course, is exactly what the Milanos did, with a little assistance from some goons from Buffalo.

The end came on 6 January 1997, when Herbie Blitzstein was found in his home, slumped over in a chair. At first glance it appeared that he had suffered a heart attack, but further investigation revealed that he had been killed by a bullet, or three.

THE RISE AND RISE OF TONY ACCARDO

Tony Accardo came to fame as Al 'Scarface' Capone's ruthless enforcer. However, Accardo was also respected for his intelligence. It was said that he had 'more brains before breakfast than Al Capone had all day'. In a criminal career that lasted more than 70 years, he never did any time in jail.

Accardo's parents were from Sicily, emigrating to the United States the year before he was born. He grew up on Chicago's West Side. Dropping out of school at 14, he became a delivery boy for a florist, then a clerk in a grocery store. These were the only two legitimate jobs he had in his lifetime.

His first arrest – for a motor vehicle violation – came in 1922.

The following year, he was fined $200 for disorderly conduct in a pool hall where gangsters hung out. Two more convictions for disorderly conduct brought him to the attention of Al Capone,

then well on his way to becoming Chicago's crime czar.

Accardo joined the Circus Café Gang, whose members included 'Screwy' Claude Maddox, Anthony 'Tough Tony' Capezio and Vincenzo DeMora, aka 'Machine Gun' Jack McGurn. The gang became allied to Capone's Chicago crime syndicate.

After delivering moonshine from the home stills in Little Sicily to the speakeasies around Chicago, Accardo quickly graduated to pick-pocketing, mugging, auto theft, burglary, assault and armed robbery, and was arrested several times.

DeMora graduated to Capone's inner circle as a hit man and, when Capone sought to expand his crew, he recommended Accardo, who quickly showed his usefulness by saving Capone's life. When an assassination attempt was made by the North Side Mob, Accardo pulled Capone down and shielded him with his body. As a result, he became his personal bodyguard.

In later years, Accardo boasted of participating in the St Valentine's Day Massacre, where seven members of Bugs Moran's North Side Gang were wiped out. Although he was never officially tied to the murders, he was seen that day in the lobby of the Lexington Hotel on Michigan Avenue – Capone's headquarters – with a machine gun. Accardo was arrested soon afterwards, but no one was ever charged. He certainly carried out other hits for Capone.

When two of the other gunmen, Giovanni Scalise and Alberto Anselmi, tried to take over, Capone invited them to a formal dinner with other gangsters. After the speeches, Accardo beat them to death with a baseball bat. This was the occasion on which he earned his soubriquet.

When Capone went to jail for income tax evasion in 1931, Accardo was given his own gang which helped run gambling in Chicago and Florida. He quickly rose to number seven on the Chicago Crime Commission's 'public enemy' list.

Paul 'the Waiter' Ricca took over the Chicago Outfit in 1943, naming his friend Tony Accardo as his underboss. Together they ran the mob

until Ricca's death in 1972, expanding their operations to Texas, Arizona, Nevada, Colorado and California, as well as Florida, Cuba and the Bahamas. They pulled out of areas such as labour racketeering, which were attracting too much attention from the authorities. Instead the Outfit moved into slot machines, which appeared in petrol stations, restaurants and bars in the area controlled by the Outfit, as well as in the casinos in Las Vegas.

SINATRA'S CONTRIBUTION

In 1946, Accardo headed the Outfit's delegation to the meeting of the Commission called by Meyer Lansky in Havana. They took over the top four floors of the Hotel Nacional. Lucky Luciano was there. Delegates paid tribute with envelopes stuffed with cash, totalling $200,000, which Luciano said he would invest in the Nacional's casino. Frank Sinatra flew in to Cuba with Accardo, it is said, carrying a suitcase containing a million dollars for Luciano.

In 1957, Accardo was at the historic Mafia summit at Apalachin, in upstate New York, to divide up the operations of Albert Anastasia following his assassination. It was held on the country estate of Joseph 'Joe the Barber' Barbara. However, the local police noticed a large number of expensive cars with out-of-state license plates turning up, so they staged a raid. Accardo and Sam Giancana fled through the woods. Giancana later complained that he tore up a $1,200 suit on some barbed wire and ruined a new pair of shoes.

For some time in the late 1950s and early 1960s, Giancana handled the day-to-day running of the Outfit. He had begun his career in the mob as Accardo's driver and they had been arrested together for questioning in a kidnapping case. But his connection with John F. Kennedy gave him too high a profile to be boss, so Ricca and Accardo stepped in and deposed him.

Even while Giancana was in charge, Accardo still kept his hand in as an enforcer. He was thought to have been responsible for the killing of William 'Action' Jackson, a juice man or debt collector for the mob,

who had possibly become an FBI informant. Jackson was stripped naked, beaten with a baseball bat and hung by his rectum from a meat hook. His knees were broken, a cattle prod was applied to his genitals and his body was punctured with ice-picks. Then he was left for three days until he died.

CHAMPAGNE LIFESTYLE

When Paul Ricca died, Accardo brought in his buddy Joe Aiuppa, who had been boss of the rackets in Cicero. Meanwhile Accardo began to spend more time with his wife Clarice, a Polish-American former chorus girl, in their 22-room mansion, which boasted two bowling alleys, an indoor swimming pool, a pipe organ, a tub carved from a single piece of Mexican onyx and gold-plated bathroom fittings said to be worth half-a-million dollars.

The Internal Revenue Service investigated Accardo and in 1960 he was convicted of tax evasion, specifically for deducting $3,994 as operating expenses for his sports car, a red Mercedes-Benz 300SL. Accardo claimed to have used the car in the course of his employment as a salesman for a Chicago beer company. The jury found this hard to believe and convicted him. He was fined $15,000, and sentenced to six years in prison. The conviction was overturned on appeal.

Accardo did little to hide his personal wealth. He held lavish parties at his palatial home, with fountains gushing champagne and violinists mingling with the guests. He also enjoyed country sports. A phalanx of Cadillacs would take Accardo and his cronies out to South Dakota, where they would shoot pheasants with machine guns. And he got his nickname 'Big Tuna' for a 400-pound fish he caught.

Accardo also liked indoor sports. Once he was taken for $1,000 by a pool hustler who wedged the table and tweaked his game accordingly. When the trick was spotted, Accardo blamed himself for being such an easy dupe. 'Let the bum go,' he ordered. 'He cheated me fair and square.'

Accardo appeared before US Senate committees three times, carrying

a cane with a tuna-fish handle. During his testimony, he invoked the Fifth Amendment 172 times – including in answer to the question: 'Have you any scruples against killing?' He continued to deny any involvement in organized crime, while admitting that he knew leading figures in the Mafia. The only time he admitted to breaking the law was years before, when he had gambled.

In January 1977, while Accardo was away, his home was broken into by some foolhardy burglars. When Accardo was told, he ordered Tony Spilotro, Aiuppa's most savage enforcer, to handle the case. The word got out and thieves and cat burglars fled the city, fearing they could be mistaken for the culprits. It took some time for Spilotro's men to crack the case, but this only made things worse because Accardo's temper continued to escalate.

A year after the break-in, Cook County began to reverberate with what they called 'trunk music'. The first burglar was found shot dead, another was castrated and a third had his face burned off with an acetylene torch. In each case, the *coup de grace* was delivered with a bullet to the head or a slashed throat. For good measure, two of the executioners were also killed. There were no further break-ins at Accardo's property.

Accardo died at the age of 86 of natural causes, a rare thing for a crime boss. He now lies in a mausoleum at the Queen of Heaven Cemetery in the Chicago suburb of Hillside, Illinois.

Mafia Killings 53

Johnny Mendell, Chicago, January/February 1978

In Chicago, the Outfit called the shots. And from 1947 to 1992 Anthony 'Joe Batters' Accardo definitely ran the Outfit. Anybody who dared lock horns with Accardo was asking for trouble. Johnny Mendell, on the other hand, was just a burglar – a very good one,

but still no match for Accardo. Unfortunately, that's not the way Mendell saw it.

On 21 December 1977, Johnny Mendell and his collaborators robbed Harry Levinson's jewellery store on North Clark Street. The thieves got in and out, leaving no evidence behind. By the time they were finished the crew had nearly cleaned out Levinson's shop, omitting only the famous 'Idol's Eye Diamond', a beautiful blue pear-shaped gem. Once Mendell and his gang had fenced the goods, they could look forward to a happy and prosperous New Year.

Unfortunately, Mendell hadn't realized that Levinson was an old pal of Tony Accardo. Concluding he wouldn't get much help from the police, Levinson contacted his friend. If anyone was able to recover the jewels, it would be the boss of Chicago's underworld, the Big Tuna himself. Accardo agreed and put the word out on the street – the goods better turn up, and fast.

Apparently the thieves obliged, because the jewels were silently and quickly returned. And that should have been the end of it. After all, Mendell had been playing it fast and loose by not checking with the Outfit in the first place. If he had, he would have known that Levinson's was off limits and saved himself a lot of grief. However, Mendell played by his own rules, not the Outfit's, and was not pleased with the way things turned out. He had put a lot of time and money into that job and now had nothing to show for it. Something was owing to him, and he knew just where to get it.

In early January 1978, Accardo and his wife had left their River Forest mansion for a vacation in California. While they were away, Mendell took the opportunity to break into their house – the personal home of the godfather of the Chicago Mafia – to steal the jewellery back.

When Accardo heard the news he was apoplectic. He was a ruthless Mafia Don, not someone to mess with; his vengeance for this slight was swift and it was brutal. One by one the Mendell crew

dropped. Some were stabbed, others garrotted, but all turned up stuffed into the trunks of cars. Mendell, whose body was found on 20 February 1978, had been tortured before he'd been killed.

In the end at least nine people were murdered, allegedly on Accardo's orders, two of whom had nothing to do with the burglary at all. It was Mendell's fatal mistake, and one he would never have the opportunity to repeat.

TURNING STATE'S EVIDENCE

Following his arrest in 1993, Anthony 'Gaspipe' Casso became the highest-ranking member of the American Mafia to turn state's evidence. Once the head of the Lucchese family, he now says that Cosa Nostra is 'not an honored society of men any more, it is a society of self-servicing scumbags that would give up their mother to turn a buck.' But he still hates himself for betraying it.

Casso's grandparents were from Naples and his father was connected. Thanks to his childhood friend Salvatore 'Sally' Callinbrano – later Anthony's godfather and a *capo* in the Genovese family – the family did not go hungry during the Depression. Callinbrano made sure that Michael Casso had regular work as a longshoreman on the Brooklyn docks as well as access to the pilfering that went on. A tough guy, Casso Sr always carried an eight-inch length of lead gas pipe that he used as a weapon. As a result, he was give the nickname 'Gaspipe', which his son inherited.

One of the younger Casso's earliest memories was visiting Callinbrano's club on Flatbush Avenue with his father, where everyone treated the well-dressed *capo* with respect. With the death of Albert Anastasia in 1957, Casso Sr took over the International Longshoremen's Association Local 1814. When Anthony graduated from the Francis Xavier

Anthony Casso, aka 'Gaspipe'

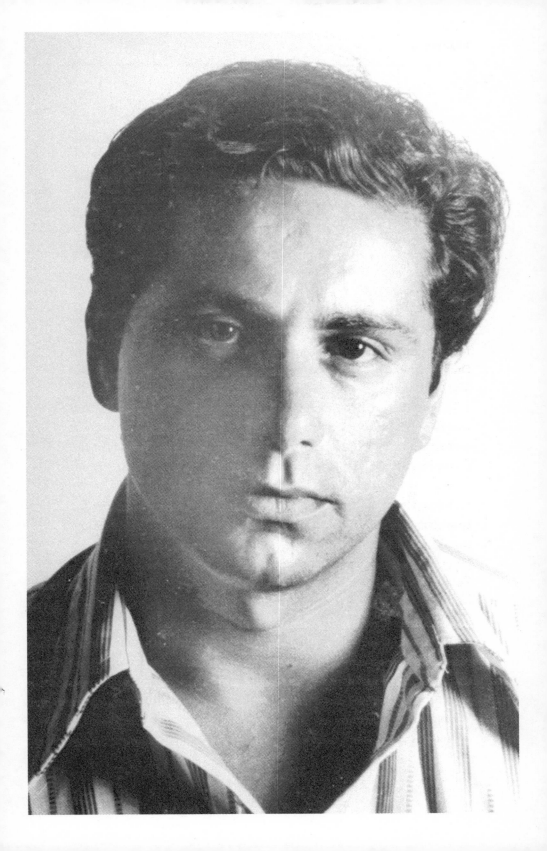

Catholic Elementary School, Callinbrano gave him a $50 bill. Later he gave him a gold, diamond and sapphire pinkie ring – an essential piece of jewellery for a made man.

On Sundays in summer, the family would go for picnics to Allendale Lake in New Jersey with the families of Joe Profaci, Vito Genovese and Albert Anastasia. There would be target practice with .22 rifles. Casso liked firearms and was a good shot.

In south Brooklyn, Casso was surrounded by the Mafia ethos. Disputes would be settled with the gun or the ice-pick and dead bodies turned up regularly, dumped in Flatbush or in the bays and estuaries around the coast.

In 1954, Casso witnessed the murder of Joe Monosco on 4th Avenue, followed by Donald Marino's murder on the corner of 5th Avenue and Sackett Street. The next year he witnessed the murder of Frank 'Shoes' De Marco in Costello's Bar. Murder was a way of life in Brooklyn.

Casso's father took him hunting at Mafioso Charlie LaRocca's farm in upstate New York. The slaughter of wild animals, Casso later saw, was part of his training for organized crime. He joined a gang named the South Brooklyn Boys and became a notorious street fighter. As a result of one of these fights, Casso was arrested for the first time.

When Casso dropped out of school, Callinbrano supplied him with a forged birth certificate so that he could join the longshoremen's union; he also found him a $250-a-week 'no-show job' on the docks. Through Callinbrano, Casso met Lucchese *capo* 'Christie Tick' Furnari and Paul Castellano, who got him another, more lucrative 'no-show job'. He also collected bookmaking money and loan-sharking receipts, sometimes heavy-handedly.

In 1961, Casso saw a junkie hassling a girl. He intervened and an argument ensued. Casso pulled out a .32 pistol and shot the man several times in broad daylight. While Casso hid out in New Jersey, his father tried to pay off the police, but did not have the $50,000 they demanded. Vincent 'the Chin' Gigante, then a *capo* in the Genovese crime family, offered to pay, but Casso did not want to join the Genovese. Meanwhile,

the junkie, who had been badly wounded, was looking for Casso, saying he would kill him. Casso returned to Brooklyn to confront him. But the junkie was also connected. His uncle was a *capo* in the Genovese family and wanted no trouble. Money changed hands. Casso was arrested, but the victim did not identify him and he was acquitted.

Casso then went into the hijacking business, arranging for drivers to give up their loads for $10,000, rather than at gunpoint. He also bribed guards so that he could steal from the piers. Soon he was so busy he brought others – including Frankie DeCicco – into the operation.

In May 1968 Casso married and moved into a garden apartment in Bensonhurst and bought his parents a retirement home in the Catskills. By this point he was robbing banks by tunnelling into basement vaults. He carried out a hit for Lucchese made man Christopher Furnari in front of other 'made' men. Then he and DeCicco gunned down a man in the street who had robbed them. Gradually, he built his own crew.

With Vic Amuso, he began importing marijuana from South America. He was soon a wealthy man. But in 1972, on the word of an informant, Casso was arrested. Through Greg Scarpa, he found out who the informant was and bought him off. This made him realize he needed information from the other side. He managed to put two crooked police officers, Louis Eppolito and Stephen Caracappa, on the payroll, along with others including an FBI agent.

SETTLING SCORES

In 1974, after a long hiatus, the Gambino family books were open again, but by then Casso had become a made man in the Lucchese family instead, and was a member of Vincent 'Vinnie Beans' Foceri's *borgata* (branch of the family), which had its headquarters on 116th Street in Manhattan and 14th Avenue in Brooklyn.

Selling marijuana and cocaine, Casso dealt with Roy DeMeo and Sammy 'the Bull' Gravano. He also took on private work. When the daughter of a friend was raped, he waited until the rapist was out on bail, abducted him, mutilated his genitals, then killed him. And when his

wife's 16-year-old nephew was killed by a member of the Colombo family, Casso demanded, and succeeded in getting his killer's death.

When Furnari became *consigliere* of the Lucchese family, he wanted Casso to become a *capo* and take over his crew. But Casso preferred to be the one soldier a *consigliere* was allowed and recommended Amuso for the post of *capo*. Casso was running a lucrative bootleg gasoline scam with Ukrainian mob boss Marat Balagula in Brighton Beach. When the Russian gangster Vladimir Reznikov tried to muscle in, Casso set him up to be hit by DeMeo's crew. 'After that, Marat didn't have any problems with other Russians,' said Casso.

When Castellano decided that DeMeo had to go, John Gotti and Frankie DeCicco gave the contract to Casso. He, in turn, approached the Testa brothers and Anthony Senter, who did the job.

The so-called Commission Case followed in 1985, when 11 top Mafiosi, including the heads of the five families, went on trial for racketeering. John Gotti decided that it was time to make his move by hitting Castellano and becoming boss. Casso was against the coup and tried to talk DeCicco out of it, but Gotti had promised to make him underboss.

For killing their boss without permission, Gotti and DeCicco were sentenced to death by the Commission. Casso and Amuso were given the contract and they were told to use a bomb. They learned that Gotti and DeCicco were going to visit a social club in Bensonhurst. When DeCicco's car arrived, Herbie 'Blue Eyes' Pate slipped a bag containing C-4 plastic explosive under it. It was detonated by remote control. DeCicco was killed instantly. Another man with him was badly injured, but Gotti was not there, he had cancelled at the last moment. They did not get a second chance because Gotti courted publicity and was almost always surrounded by the press. Meanwhile, Gotti gave a contract on Casso to a hit team led by James Hydell. Gaspipe was shot at outside the Golden Ox restaurant on Veterans Avenue in Brooklyn and sought refuge – from the assassins and the police – in the restaurant's freezer. Hydell paid for his failure to do the hit successfully with his own life.

PLEA BARGAIN GOES WRONG

The boss of the Lucchese family, Tony 'Ducks' Corallo, realized that the Commission Case was going to put the leadership of the family away for the rest of their lives. Because Casso was the family's biggest money-maker, Corallo suggested that he should be the new boss. But Casso refused and the leadership passed to Amuso, with Casso as *consigliere* and, later, underboss.

The Mafia had moved in on a $150 million deal from the New York Housing Authority to install replacement windows. In the resulting racketeering investigation, Amuso and Casso were indicted. Tipped off by a mole in the FBI, they went on the run, leaving 'Little Al' D'Arco as acting boss.

Even though he was a fugitive, Casso still ordered hits. When 'Fat Pete' Chiodo decided to plead guilty, Casso and Amuso were in danger of being implicated. The two men ordered D'Arco to kill Chiodo. When he failed, Amuso ordered, for the first time in Mafia history, a hit on D'Arco's wife, but the authorities were wise to this move and she and her children were taken into the Witness Protection Program.

Amuso was captured in a shopping mall in Scranton, Pennsylvania. This left Casso in charge of the Lucchese family. D'Arco realized he was in danger and turned himself in to the FBI. Casso continued to run the Lucchese family from the back of a van, but made the mistake of buying new mobile phones. He was arrested in the shower at his girlfriend's home in Mount Olive, New Jersey.

An attempt to bribe his way out of jail was foiled at the last moment. Casso also planned an ambush on the van that brought him back from court, as well as a hit on the judge. When these ploys failed, he offered to turn state's evidence and pleaded guilty to 72 counts of racketeering, including 15 murders – though it was thought he was personally responsible for at least 44 and had ordered many others.

Casso was sent to a special prison unit for co-operating witnesses, but he got into fights with other prisoners and bribed the guards for favours. The prosecutors decided that he was too unreliable to take

the stand against Vincent 'the Chin' Gigante and relied instead on the testimony of D'Arco and Gravano. Casso then wrote a letter claiming they were lying. Clearly, he was not a co-operative witness and was dropped from the program. Returned to a regular prison, he was kept in solitary confinement for his own protection. Having broken the terms of his plea bargain, he was sentenced to 13 terms of life imprisonment, plus 455 years.

LOUIS EPPOLITO AND STEPHEN CARACAPPA

When Casso agreed to co-operate with the government in 1994, he gave the authorities the names of two rogue police officers, Louis Eppolito and Stephen Caracappa. These men had not only been informants but had also carried out hits for the mob. They had been on the payroll of the Lucchese family between 1985 and 1993, each earning $4,000 a month.

Casso gave the men $65,000 to murder Gambino *capo* Eddie Lino in 1990. The two officers pulled him over on a road leading to the Belt Parkway in Brooklyn and shot him dead. They also set up Bruno Facciolo, a Lucchese soldier who fell out of favour with Casso by failing to visit him when he was recuperating from James Hydell's attempt on his life. Eppolito and Caracappa said they thought Facciolo was working for the FBI. Facciolo was found in the boot of a car with a canary stuffed in his mouth – the mob's traditional warning to informers.

Eppolito and Caracappa cruised Brooklyn and Staten Island looking for James Hydell. They found him in a laundromat, flashed their badges, and told him he was under arrest. Then they put him in the back of an unmarked police car, drove to a back street garage and transferred him to the boot.

Casso was waiting in the Toys R Us car park in Mill Basin. He then took Hydell to a safe house where he beat him up and dragged

him into the basement. Casso demanded to know who had ordered the hit. Hydell named Angelo Ruggiero, a Gambino *capo* nicknamed 'Quack Quack' for his uncanny ability to duck indictments.

Gaspipe sent for Gotti and Gravano to see what they had to say about it. They refused to come, but two days later two Gambino *capos*, 'Joe Butch' Corrao and 'Good Looking' Jack Giordano, arrived. They were genuinely shocked at the sight of Hydell. Casso listened to what they had to say, then pulled out a 9mm Beretta and shot Hydell 15 times before finally killing him.

The Gambino *capos* said they would report what they had seen to Gotti. Casso said that he wanted Ruggiero's head on a plate. He didn't get it. Gotti had bigger things to worry about and Ruggiero eventually died of cancer in 1989.

Eppolito and Caracappa were found guilty of eight counts of murder and conspiracy to murder, along with the obstruction of justice, narcotics trafficking, illegal gambling and labour racketeering. Eppolito was the son of a mobster, a fact he failed to mention when he applied to join the New York Police Department. His uncle and cousin had been murdered by Roy DeMeo and Anthony Gaggi. He was sentenced to life plus 100 years. Caracappa got life plus 80 years. Each was fined more than $4 million. The two continued to protest their innocence.

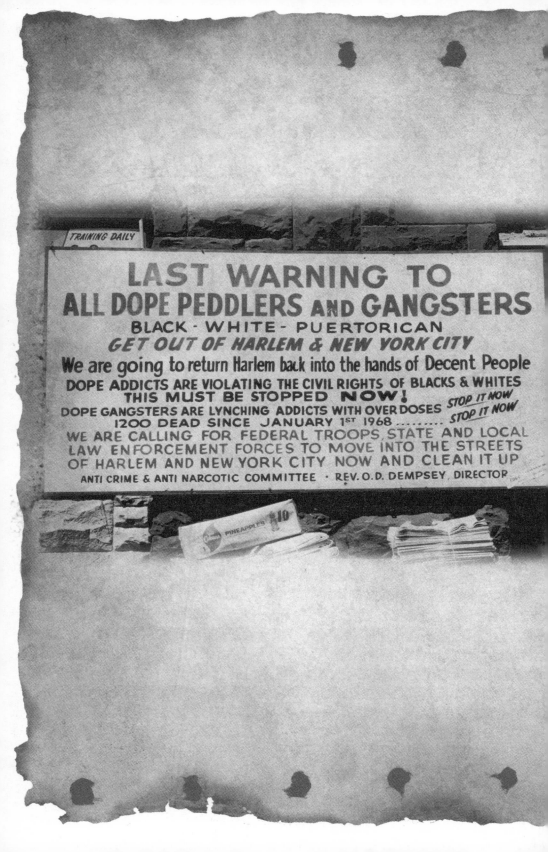

PART FIVE

THE 1970S: TAKING CARE OF BUSINESS

Notable Mafia hits during the early years of the decade include the murders of 'Crazy' Joe Gallo, Sam 'Momo' Giancana, Carmine 'Lilo' Galante, and the disappearance of ex-Teamster leader Jimmy Hoffa. But the war against organized crime was about to get serious with the passing of the RICO Act in 1970, which gave law enforcement more effective tools with which to prosecute racketeers. Soon more Mafiosi than ever before were cutting deals in order to avoid lengthy prison sentences, as well as heavy fines. And, of course, in the mob, there's only one way to treat a squealer.

CHAPTER 17

THE MAFIA TURNS AGAINST THE STATE

In 1970, after a series of summit meetings in Palermo and Milan, and after the heat from the police had died down, the Sicilian Cupola was re-established. This time it was as a triumvirate, with Luciano Leggio representing the countryside families, and two bosses from Palermo – Gaetano Badalamenti and the young head of the Santa Maria del Jesù family, Stefano Bontate – representing the rest. Within a few months, however, something would happen to mark a change in traditional Mafia practices. It was the murder – by Leggio and Totò Riina, Buscetta later said – of Palermo chief prosecutor, Pietro Scaglione.

Up until that point, Scaglione had been a good friend of the Mafia. He had 'lost' files and shelved cases, and made sure that Mafia defendants were acquitted for lack of proof, including an entire family from Joe Bananas' birthplace, Castellamare, who were arraigned for involvement in the French Connection trade to the US. It is possible that Scaglione had changed his mind about helping the Mafia and his death had been ordered by the Commission. It is also possible that he was murdered by Leggio – as a *pentito* (or turned Mafia witness) later said – for 'favouring Badalamenti' too much. But whatever the reason, it was an indication of how far certain members of Cosa Nostra were now prepared to go. No

judge had been killed in Palermo since the war – it was an unwritten rule that they should remain untouched. A gauntlet had been thrown down which announced that no one, not even the State, was invulnerable from now on.

If the murder was personal to Leggio, then it was also a significant slap in the face for the Commission – and this is the more likely explanation. Leggio, who was by now recovering from an operation for bone disease (performed by the Italian president's personal surgeon in Rome), was soon flouting its will in quite another way. His emissary in Palermo, Totò Riina, started kidnapping and holding for ransom members of rich local families. This cut right across the delicate ties the Mafia had established with both the hereditary landowners and the Christian Democrat establishment. It was a considerable embarrassment, but there was nothing the Commission could do, since both Badalamenti and Bontate were in Ucciardone prison facing charges at the time. Only when they got out again was kidnapping finally and formally banned.

It must have been with some relief, then, that the Commission heard the news in 1972 that Leggio had left the island for Milan. It took him a while to return. On the mainland he took up kidnapping again, and had a hand in the snatching of John Paul Getty III, who famously lost part of an ear before his grandfather would pay the ransom. Leggio was arrested and jailed in 1974, leaving the field open to his much more dangerous and subtle lieutenant, Totò Riina.

TOTÒ RIINA BEGINS TO TAKE POWER

Salvatore 'Totò', or 'Shorty', Riina was born in 1930, the son of a peasant family. He had little or no formal education. He only ever spoke limited Italian and hardly wrote at all.

One day his father Giovanni Riina was emptying the explosives from a wartime shell, so that he could sell the metal casing as scrap. The shell slipped from Giovanni's grasp and exploded, killing him and one of his sons, seven-year-old Francesco, and wounding another son, Gaetano.

Only Totò was left unhurt. At the age of 12, he effectively became head of the family.

Unrestrained by the firm hand of a father, Totò soon turned his back on the life of a peasant and hung about in the piazza of Corleone, telling his friends Bernardo Provenzano and Calogero Bagarella that he was not going to die poor. He and Provenzano were recruited by Luciano Leggio, hitman for the local doctor and *capomafia* Michele Navarra. The three of them did a brisk trade in stealing cattle and selling the butchered meat. They would greet each other with a kiss on the cheek, a typical Mafia gesture. Riina was warned off joining the Mafia by a local policeman, Provenzano by an older brother. It did no good.

In May 1949, after the procession of the crucified Christ in Corleone, Riina and his friends got into a fight with Domenico Di Matteo using sticks and knuckle-dusters. Ten days later there was another fight outside town. This time it ended with gunfire. Riina loosed off half-a-dozen shots with an automatic. One shot fatally wounded Di Matteo and Riina himself was wounded. He was arrested in his hospital bed.

In court, in chains, he spoke abusively to the judge and was sentenced to 12 years. Out after six years, and by now a 'made' man, he quickly attached himself to Luciano Leggio, who was determinedly rising up through the ranks of the Corleone family of Dr Navarra, the President of the Cultivators' Association of Corleone and chairman of the local branch of the Christian Democratic Party. If Navarra had problems – with trade union organizers, for example – Leggio always fixed them. In the small, sprawling village of Corleone, there were 153 murders between 1953 and 1958.

The year after Riina's release, he was invited to stay for dinner at the home of his friend Calogero Bagarella. Calogero's sister, 13-year-old Ninetta, served at table. Although at 26 Totò was twice her age, he was instantly smitten with her pretty oval face, black eyes and long black hair, which she wore in a ponytail.

Ninetta had been born into a Mafia family. From 1963 to 1968, her father Salvatore Bagarella had lived in exile in northern Italy because of

his involvement with the Mafia. Her eldest brother Giuseppe was also sent into exile and was murdered in prison in 1972.

For Riina, her family background could not have been better – by then a third brother had joined the Mafia. What's more, Calogero was in love with Riina's sister. But Ninetta was something special. While Riina was barely literate, Ninetta was an avid reader, improving her mind by poring over books from the school library. She sat in the front row in class and studied Latin and Greek. A model pupil, she saw education as a way of escaping poverty and she was determined to get a proper job when she grew up.

She also consumed novels to give herself a broader perspective. The ones she picked usually concerned the plight of the oppressed and poor and their struggle against their oppressors. 'What I read in those books,' she said, 'was life in Corleone.' She was also fascinated by Machiavelli – 'because his principle, the end justifies the means, was applied to the letter by the local police,' she said.

Despite the intellectual rift between them, Riina wooed Ninetta in the traditional way. Every morning he would wait in the narrow alleyway where she lived and follow her to school. On the way, not a word was spoken. 'For years I followed her with my eyes, for years I never gave her a moment's rest,' he said, 'until she decided to marry me.'

DEADLY FEUD

Meanwhile a feud had broken out between Leggio and Navarra, who had vetoed a lucrative construction project Leggio was involved in. Although this might have been the catalyst, the truth was that both Leggio and Riina were growing increasingly resentful of Navarra's unwillingness to move with the times. This was a point of view possibly put to them by Navarra's cousin, a Sicilian-American called De Carlo, who had fought in the war, after which he had settled first in Corleone, then in Palermo.

Upset by the perceived slight, Leggio put the squeeze on one of Navarra's lieutenants. In return, the two men were ambushed by unknown assailants, though Navarra was suspected. Riina is said to have

saved Leggio's life, though he was wounded in the arm. Honour had been satisfied, or so Navarra thought. He was wrong.

On 2 August 1958, Navarra was being driven home from Lercara Friddi, birthplace of 'Lucky' Luciano, by a doctor who had no Mafia associations. Navarra was unarmed and had no bodyguard. They were ambushed by Leggio, Provenzano and Riina, who had abandoned the traditional *lupara*, or sawn-off shotgun, in favour of Al Capone-style sub-machine guns and automatic pistols. They fired 124 bullets into the car; 92 of them hit Navarra.

A month later, they made peace overtures to Navarra loyalists and Riina was sent alone and unarmed to a Mafia meeting. 'Who's dead is dead,' he said. 'The dear departed has gone away. Let us think of the living.' Solemnly he crossed himself. Before there was an answer, Provenzano and another man appeared and opened fire with sawn-off shotguns. One of Navarra's men was shot in the face. The others fled.

In the ensuing chase through the streets of Corleone, Provenzano was hit in the head and left for dead. Two women were injured, along with an eight-year-old girl; a two-year-old girl was wounded by a stray bullet. But when the police arrived, no one had seen anything. Interviewed in his hospital bed, Provenzano claimed to have been on his way to the cinema when he collapsed unconscious. 'I have no idea what happened,' he said.

War broke out and Riina quickly became one of Leggio's most trusted killers, never hesitating to cut down Navarra loyalists and any inconvenient witnesses. The final shot was always to the mouth, to warn anyone who knew anything to remain silent. *Omertà* was absolute. A journalist asked a weeping mother walking behind a coffin: 'Who was killed?' She replied: 'Why, is somebody dead?'

During the conflict, some 50 people were murdered and there were a further 22 murder attempts. At first, victims were shot down in the streets, shops and bars, or in their homes. Then came the *lupara bianca* or 'white shotgun' (a killing done in such a way that the victim's body was never found). People simply disappeared, their bodies thrown down ravines, dissolved in lime or burnt on giant grills over open fires.

Provenzano was wounded trying to ambush Navarra lieutenant Francesco Paolo Streva in the alleyway where Ninetta lived. As he made his escape, a woman emerged to wipe up the trail of blood. Streva was ambushed again four months later. This time he was murdered and left in a ditch, together with his two bodyguards and their guard dog. Leggio and his two lieutenants, Provenzano and Riina, now controlled Corleone.

But this was not enough for Leggio. He wanted to move into Palermo. This prompted another Mafia war which became so ferocious that Leggio and his men had to go into hiding.

After they had killed Navarra, the lives and careers of Leggio and Riina became more or less inseparable. Riina was given preference over Leggio's other chief lieutenant, Provenzano; though by now Riina was living on the run, he was sent to represent Leggio in Palermo. Three years later, around the time that Leggio went to prison, Riina secretly married the sister of another Corleonese soldier with whom he went on to have four children.

DIPLOMACY MATTERS

In December 1963, Riina was caught in a police roadblock. He found himself in the Ucciardone prison in Palermo, surrounded by incarcerated Palermo dons wearing silk dressing gowns and brandishing silver cigarette holders. They looked down on the Corleonesi – which only fuelled Riina's ambition further. 'When I get out of here,' he said, 'I want to walk on a carpet of 100,000-lire banknotes.'

Six months after Riina's capture, Leggio and Provenzano were arrested. All three men refused to co-operate with the authorities and in 1969 they appeared in the dock together in Bari along with another 61 Mafiosi. Intimidation of the jury led to them all being acquitted. Riina was only found guilty of stealing a driving licence and sentenced to six months, time he had already served.

Whether Leggio was pulling the strings from behind bars cannot be known. But in 1975, when the full six-man Commission was finally re-instituted and had reinforced the ban on kidnapping, Riina reacted by

kidnapping the father-in-law of Nino Salvo, one of the two cousins who had taken the Mafia into the tax-collection business. Salve had made an extra fortune out of the money poured into Sicily after the earthquake in the Belice valley seven years earlier. The earthquake killed 500 people and left 90,000 homeless; 60,000 people were still living in Nissen huts seven years later. Not a single new house was built. The only things that the government's money seemed to have bought were roads that led nowhere and flyovers used by sheep. The roads and flyovers had been built by the Salvos.

The Salvos, then, were family – and the kidnap of the father-in-law was another severe embarrassment for the Palermitans on the Commission, particularly when he died of a heart attack before he could be returned. But then that was the point. Riina already had control over Palermo's mayor, the ex-barber from Corleone, Vito Ciancimino. Now he was announcing to the Commission and their pals that he was the only power; and, as it turned out, the Commission had neither the will nor the necessary unity to resist him. Riina had Gaetano Badalamenti thrown off the Commission – indeed, expelled from the Mafia – and had his place taken by one of his own allies, Michele 'The Pope' Greco. After Badalamenti fled to Brazil, Riina managed to persuade the Commission that, as a man living under cover and thus with special needs, he should be assigned a couple of men from the other families to help him. He acquired, in other words, a small army of killers loyal only to him who acted as spies on, and bridges to, every one of his potential rivals.

One *pentito* witness later said of Riina: 'I never saw him angry, sometimes a little flushed, but never aggressive or rude.' Another remarked that he had 'cunning and ferocity, a rare combination in Cosa Nostra.' Tommaso Buscetta, the highest-ranking witness of them all, said that although Riina looked like a peasant, he had a diplomatic manner 'and God only knows how much diplomacy matters in Cosa Nostra. He was a great persuader and he knew how to work up people when he needed to.'

Buscetta also described Riina as living Cosa Nostra 'twenty-four hours a day. Always talking and discussing. Got information on everything. Followed every family's internal affairs. Got news from his spies. Cold and attentive to the smallest detail … he never tired of making suggestions, giving orders, handing out death sentences …' By a mixture of fear and charm, Riina in the end came to hold them all in thrall. He divided and ruled them – and in the end he took them over completely.

FORMAL ENGAGEMENT

After his short spell in prison Riina returned to Corleone, where he was rearrested and sentenced to four years' exile. He was granted a few days' liberty to settle his domestic affairs and he used the time to formalize his engagement to Ninetta, who was by now a 26-year-old teacher. While he had been away she had enrolled at Palermo University, to study literature and philosophy. Travelling there by bus every day, she was accompanied by two police officers who suspected she had links to the Mafia. Then two of her brothers shot a cattle breeder who was wooing her sister. One brother was arrested and the other went on the run. Ninetta was forced to give up her studies and take a teaching post at a private institute.

Riina took his mother to meet Ninetta's mother. The two women would formally seek 'clarification' – that is, discuss the dowry and make arrangements for where the couple would live. Riina was not a rich man, but Ninetta's mother was confident that he could make money, provided he stayed out of jail.

Business concluded, drinks were served and Riina gave Ninetta an engagement ring. 'We got engaged in the intimacy of our families,' said Ninetta. 'It's not as if we said to each other "I love you" or "You're the light of my life". We were serious people.'

Riina then went into exile in San Giovanni in Persiceto, near Bologna, in northern Italy. He signed in at the police station there, but disappeared a few days later to become a fugitive again.

Meanwhile, Ninetta's brother Calogero Bagarella joined Provenzano in Leggio's hit squad to take out Michele 'the Cobra' Cavataio in the

ongoing Palermo war. Dressed in police uniforms, they shot up Cavataio's headquarters. Calogero Bagarella was shot and fatally wounded. Provenzano was wounded too, but he finished the job with a machine gun. When it jammed, he hit Cavataio's skull with the butt until it caved in. Riina made a brief appearance in public at Calogero's funeral.

Leggio was in poor health, so Riina and Provenzano went to work for the *capomafia* of Cinisi, Gaetano Badalamenti and Stefano 'the Prince' Bontate, another *capo* in Palermo. Riina seized the opportunity to learn as much as he could about the inside workings of the Sicilian Mafia. It stood him in good stead.

When Leggio moved to Milan, Riina became his representative on the Mafia triumvirate, whose other members were Badalamenti and Bontate. But Bontate mocked him for being a peasant and tried to get him arrested. Nevertheless, Riina took his place on the broader Commission that replaced the triumvirate.

ON TRIAL FOR LOVE

In July 1971, Ninetta Bagarella arrived at the law courts in Palermo. She had been accused of being the liaison between the Leggio clan and several fugitives. The police had evidence that she had arranged Leggio's various stays in hospital. The 27-year-old schoolteacher looked nothing like a Mafia wife. Eschewing austere black clothing, she wore a blue dress with yellow and red flowers printed on it, the hemline above the knee. She also sported high-heeled shoes and her diamond engagement ring.

The year before, the police had requested her passport. She had sent it to them, together with a letter calling them 'persecutors, tormentors, torturers'. This brought a charge of slander. The police then brought about her dismissal from the school in which she had taught physical education for four years. They sought to have her exiled to the mainland. She was the first woman they had tried to banish.

Ninetta brought with her a petition drawn up by the archpriest of Corleone, a colleague of Ninetta's at school, and signed by scores of residents. In it, the archpriest said that the Bagarellas were 'an exemplary

Ninetta Bagarella – beauty queen and Mafia wife

family dogged by misfortune and the law does not respect the affairs of the heart and persecutes a schoolteacher just because she is engaged to Salvatore Riina'.

Of Ninetta's 'exemplary family', a father and brother were in exile; another brother was officially a fugitive but had actually been gunned down in a hit two years earlier; and a third brother was Riina's lieutenant. However, the archpriest said: 'Her mother comes to Mass every morning and takes communion.'

In court, the presiding judge said: 'Miss Bagarella, you know it has been proposed that you be sent into exile.' In a clear, calm voice, Ninetta replied: 'I don't believe the court wants to send me into exile. If you have a conscience, if you have a heart, you won't do it. Only the women remain in our family. We have to work for ourselves and for our men, father and brothers who have been dogged by misfortune. I am a woman and I am guilty only of loving a man who I esteem and trust. I have always loved Totò Riina. I was 13 and he was 26 when I first fell in love. He has never been out of my heart. That is all I am guilty of, your honour.'

The judge pointed out that Riina was a dangerous criminal who was wanted for numerous murders.

Ninetta dismissed this: 'A pack of lies. Slander. Salvatore is innocent.'

She was then accused of belonging to the Leggio clan.

'I don't even know Leggio,' she said.

For over an hour she parried every accusation thrown at her. Her lawyer then delivered dozens of testimonials from fellow teachers, pupils and parents.

'The only thing I want is to marry Riina,' she told the court. 'I don't want our relationship to remain platonic. But I have not seen him for such a long time. I know nothing about him. I don't even know if he still loves me.'

The judge denied the petition to send her to the mainland, but ordered that she be put under police surveillance for two-and-a-half years. She was also placed under curfew from 7.30 p.m. to 7 a.m.

After the hearing, she was asked by a journalist: 'What is the Mafia?'

'The Mafia is a phenomenon created by the newspapers to sell more newspapers,' she shot back.

Hearing of her testimony, Riina said: 'I don't want any other woman. I only want Ninetta. They don't want me to marry her? Well, I will carry out a massacre.'

MARRIED ON THE RUN

Just one week before the end of her sentence, a policeman visited the Bagarella household after 7.30 p.m. Ninetta, however, was not there. The policeman was told that Ninetta had taken a job in Germany. In reality, she was with Riina. Now they were both on the run. Nevertheless, they were married by Mafioso priest Father Agostino Coppola, nephew of Frank 'Three Fingers' Coppola, a leading light of the Gambino family, although the marriage was never registered. The couple spent their honeymoon in Venice. Nine months later, Ninetta gave birth to their first child, a daughter named Concetta, at an exclusive clinic in Palermo. She gave birth to three more children

there – Giovanni, Giuseppe and Lucia. She registered the children under her own name and neither she nor Riina, who visited, was bothered by the police.

NINETTA ON RIINA

Before her trial in Palermo, Ninetta gave an interview to the newspaper *Giornale di Sicilia* in an office near the courtroom.

'I am nervous, very nervous,' she said, 'even if I am making an effort to remain calm to put my case to the judges. The flashes of the photographers' cameras don't help keep me calm. I don't like publicity,' she said.

She was unapologetic about her love for Riina. 'You think bad of me because I, a teacher, have fallen for and become engaged to a man like Salvatore Riina,' she said. 'But I am a woman. Don't I have the right to love a man and follow the pull of nature? I picked him firstly because I loved him and love ignores many things, and then because I admire and trust him. I love Riina because I believe he is innocent … I am here for him today. He has been away from me for two years. I haven't heard anything from him directly or indirectly. I am a woman and this makes me doubt his love. I feel alone and disheartened … Riina does not care about the feelings or needs of a woman.'

In court, she said the only thing she was guilty of was loving Totò Riina, Mafia boss and multiple murderer.

In 1974, Leggio was jailed for the murder of Navarra, and Riina took over the Corleonesi. He sought to dominate the heroin trade and ordered hits on a number of the policemen, judges and prosecutors who tried to stop him. Snooping reporters were equally unwelcome. In 1979, Ninetta's brother, Leoluca, killed Mario Francese, a journalist on the *Giornale di Sicilia*. Then a fresh Mafia war broke out in Sicily.

Riina and Ninetta moved into a villa in Palermo with a damp-proof

underground vault to store her furs. Although she had over a million dollars' worth of jewellery, she was existing in a sort of golden prison: she could not visit her mother, her children had to be escorted to school and, according to her sisters, she was even reprimanded by Riina for standing on the balcony.

Mafia Killings 54

Alex 'Shondor' Birns, Cleveland, 29 March 1975

Taking care of business – in Cleveland they did it with bombs. Alex 'Shondor' Birns, Cleveland's high-profile and violent Public Enemy Number One, knew this better than anyone. He had been responsible for so many bombings that it would be hard to count them all.

Maybe the reason Birns felt the impulse to use bombs went way back to his childhood, during Prohibition. At that period, ordinary people got into bootlegging, supplying local hoods with homemade rot-gut. One such ordinary person was Birns's own mother, Illon. One day, while Illon was tending to the family still, the makeshift apparatus exploded and she was killed, which must have devastated her young son.

By the time Birns was 16, he had started to fall in with the local hoods. A tough street fighter, he became a member of the Woodland Mob, before branching out on his own in the protection and numbers rackets. The money he earned was good, too, and gave Birns important contacts within the Cleveland Mafia.

Though he lived by his fists, Birns could be charming and affable when he wanted to be. He loved to drive expensive cars and dress in the latest fashions. He became great pals with the local press, and would often shoot the breeze with them. But for all this, there was no denying how tough Birns was when the situation called for it. And, of course, there were always his bombs.

Birns was very impressed by over-the-top Irish-American hood Danny Greene, who could bust it up with the best of them. In the early 1960s, Birn hired Greene as part of his mob and made use of Greene's fists (and guns) when needed. But hiring Greene turned out to be the worst move he ever made.

As the 1960s turned over into the 1970s, relations between Birns and Greene became somewhat strained. It didn't help that Birns felt Greene had reneged on a sizeable loan from him, one that he himself had borrowed from the Gambino family. So Birns put out a contract on Greene, and this being Cleveland, naturally one of the weapons of choice was a good old-fashioned bomb. It was too bad for Birns that Greene discovered the device before it could explode and decided to send it back directly where it had come from.

The end for Birns was truly terrible. On 29 March 1975, he left one of his favourite restaurants, climbed into his Lincoln and turned on the ignition. The ensuing explosion rocked the street, setting off car alarms. Glass rained down on to the pavement – the windows of nearby buildings were blown out – and people came running from all directions. Birn had been blown through the roof of his car and severed in two; his upper body lay in one place, while his legs came down somewhere else. For all that, though, the tough old mobster was still alive for a few moments before his body shuddered and he faded into oblivion. Birns had died in the same incendiary manner as many of his victims.

Mafia Killings 55

Danny Greene, Cleveland, 6 October 1977

An Irish-American mobster who gave away green pens, had a green office with a green rug, flew the Irish flag outside his home and named his gang the Celtic Club, Danny Greene saw himself as a

modern-day Celtic warrior, a Brian Boru or Cuchulain from legend. Together with another independent working outside the purview of the mob, John Nardi, he went to war with the Cleveland Mafia and blew the city apart.

To some in Greene's home turf of Collinwood on the east side of Cleveland, he was a hero, the Collinwood Robin Hood, who would distribute turkeys and hams on Christmas and Easter and never let a local family go hungry. But that was only one side of the complicated Greene. He was also a union leader who embezzled money from the Longshoreman Union's coffers, was a known FBI informant and tried to take control of the Cleveland rackets, no matter what the cost.

The local Cosa Nostra was not giving up without a fight, but for long time they didn't seem to be equal to the task of eliminating him. Every hitman they sent after Greene came back having failed, if they came back at all. There was an aura about the guy, a certain mystique, and it seemed to be growing. Greene didn't avoid the mob – he publicly taunted them, daring them to bring it on.

The story is told of how Greene confronted a branch of the Hell's Angels as they tried to set up shop in his neighbourhood. He entered their dilapidated hangout with a lit stick of dynamite by way of illustration. If the bike gang caused any trouble, Greene promised, he would blow them to kingdom come – hideout and all. He then removed the fuse from the dynamite and walked away.

Every day that Greene survived, every moment that he went against the status quo – blowing up his enemies as he did so – the prestige of the Cleveland family suffered. The situation became so dire that families from other parts of the country offered to send over help if the Cleveland mob could not tend to its own backyard. Greene just seemed to be invincible.

But he wasn't, of course. Finally, in May 1977, Greene's partner John Nardi was killed – by a bomb, naturally enough. Then, on 6 October, Greene met his own end. Exiting a dentist's surgery, he

got into his car just as the automobile next to his exploded. Losing his legs and an arm, he died instantly.

However, the death of Danny Greene initiated an investigation that brought down the top players of Cleveland's Mafia and eventually put a dent in Cosa Nostra nationwide. Though Greene was no longer around to see it, he and Nardi had beaten the mob.

BOSS OF BOSSES

In 1983, convicted killer Tommaso Buscetta, who had been on the losing side in the so-called Second Mafia War, became a *pentito*, the first senior Mafia figure to do so. He revealed that the Mafia was a single organization run by a Commission, or Cupola, headed by Riina. To divert resources from the investigation Riina organized a terrorist-style attack, known as the Christmas Massacre, in 1984. A bomb was detonated on the 904 express train in a tunnel through the Apennines between Florence and Bologna, killing 17 and injuring 267. Nevertheless, Buscetta's evidence led to the Maxi-Trial in 1986, which led to the conviction of 338 Mafiosi. Riina was given a life sentence in absentia.

Riina continued his campaign of murdering rivals to maintain his position as 'boss of bosses', while simultaneously cultivating political connections. When the Maxi-Trial convictions were upheld, he ordered the assassination of the former mayor of Palermo, Salvatore Lima, along with prosecuting magistrates Giovanni Falcone and Paolo Borsellino.

The killing of Falcone and Borsellino led to public outrage. Fearing the wrath of Riina, the acting boss of the San Giuseppe clan, Balduccio Di Maggio, fled Sicily and became a *pentito*. He told the authorities he had a rough idea of where Riina lived. Studying footage of film shot covertly in the area, he spotted Ninetta getting into a car. Next day, Riina was arrested coming out of the same building.

Although Provenzano became titular head of the Corleonesi, it was thought that the faction was run by Ninetta's brother Leoluca until

his arrest in 1995. Two years later, Riina's son Giovanni was arrested. Ninetta wrote an open letter to the Rome newspaper *La Repubblica*, saying: 'I've decided to open my heart, which is swollen and overflowing with sadness for the arrest of my son Giovanni ... At home we all miss him, our family situation has become hell, we cannot accept that a boy barely 20 years old, with no previous convictions, is first arrested, then questioned for two days and then jailed.'

Ninetta appealed to the mayor of Corleone for help. While intimidated by her presence, there was nothing he could do. In 2001, Giovanni was sentenced to life imprisonment for four murders. The following year, his younger brother Giuseppe was given 14 years for extortion, money laundering and criminal association. Then, in 2007, the widow of Paolo Borsellino filed a civil suit for damages against Ninetta and was awarded €3,360,000 compensation.

THE PIG

Giovanni Brusca was known quite simply as 'the Pig' for his unkempt appearance and unbridled appetites, which included a thirst for blood. He once admitted killing at least a hundred people, but couldn't remember the precise body count; he tortured and murdered the 11-year-old son of a fellow Mafioso who had turned state's evidence; and he detonated the bomb that killed crusading prosecutor Giovanni Falcone, resulting in a huge anti-Mafia backlash. Then Brusca turned state's evidence.

There was never any doubt that Brusca would become a Mafioso. In the 1940s, his grandfather had given refuge to Salvatore Giuliano, the bandit and fugitive leader of the Movement for the Independence of Sicily. Brusca's father, Bernardo, had risen through the ranks to become a local boss. The young Giovanni Brusca first set foot in a prison at the age of five when his father was in jail. Bernardo would eventually serve several life sentences for his numerous killings and died in prison in the year 2000.

At the age of 12, on the instructions of his father, Giovanni was delivering food and clothing to fugitives, including Bernardo Provenzano and Leoluca Bagarella, who were hiding out near his home in San Giuseppe Jato, a town halfway between Palermo and Corleone.

A local woman who had known Brusca as a youth said: 'He was a very normal teenager. He went out for pizza and to discotheques like everybody else.'

However, his free time was usually spent cleaning his father's weapons which were kept buried in the fields. At 18 he was already overweight and had sloping shoulders. It was then that he committed his first murder. He was not told why the person had to die, but he and two others let off a hail of bullets as the mark drove by. The victim was fatally wounded and died later in hospital.

The following year, Brusca ambushed a thief who had challenged the Mafia's authority. When the miscreant came out of the cinema, Brusca carefully fired into the crowd with a double-barrelled shotgun, hitting only his target. Rushing home, he hid the gun, changed his clothes, and raced back to relish the mayhem he had caused.

'I've always been very cold before, during and after the crime,' he confided in his memoirs. 'I might sometimes be reluctant to become "operative". But once I'd decided, all the worries, the fears and the doubts disappeared.'

At 19, he was fast-tracked into the organization and initiated by Totò Riina himself, whom Brusca already called *Padrino* or 'Godfather'. He then went to work as a driver for Bernardo Provenzano.

Mafia turncoat Tommaso Buscetta remembered the young Brusca as 'a wild stallion but a great leader'. Another informant, Salvatore Barbagallo, said: 'Giovanni was an excellent soldier, but he doesn't know how to think politically.' But mostly he was remembered as a ruthless butcher with little charisma.

In his memoirs, Brusca admitted: 'I've tortured people to make them talk; I've strangled both those who confessed and those who remained silent; I've dissolved bodies in acid; I've roasted corpses on big grills; I've

buried the remains after digging graves with an earthmover. Some *pentiti* say today they feel disgust for what they did. I can speak for myself: I've never been upset by these things.'

Brusca's torture sessions would usually last for only half an hour. He would break the victim's legs with a hammer and pull his ears with pliers – 'but only enough to hurt him and make him understand that we were serious'. This was rarely effective, because the victims knew that they were going to be killed anyway.

'The condemned showed superhuman strength,' he said. 'We realized that and we'd say the fateful word: *"Niscemuninne"* ("Let's get out of here"). The torturers would then strangle the victim.'

Brusca often didn't even have to know his victims. Once a boss from the neighbourhood of Agrigento asked him for a favour – to kill anyone on a certain type of tractor, in a certain place, at a certain time. Three tractors drove by and he killed all three drivers. On another occasion, he rushed a job because the victim was about to get married and he did not want to leave the would-be wife a widow.

THE FALCONE KILLING

During the Second Mafia War in the early 1980s, Brusca became a member of Riina's death squad, which introduced terrorist tactics. He would travel escorted by a truck containing men carrying AK-47s. If they were stopped by the police and the back doors were opened for a routine check, they were told to open fire immediately.

In July 1983, the death squad blew up Palermo chief prosecutor Rocco Chinnici outside his home. The car bomb they used also killed Chinnici's two bodyguards and the porter of the apartment block and injured another 20 people. The car itself was blown three stories high, before crashing back to earth.

Two weeks after the murder of Chinnici, Riina ordered Brusca to prepare another car bomb. This time the target was to be Giovanni Falcone, who was working on indictments for what would become the Maxi-Trial, at which Riina would be sentenced, in absentia, to life.

Brusca tried to keep watch on Falcone's home but, following Chinnici's assassination, the police stopped anyone parking outside the homes of prosecutors or other prominent officials. Instead, Brusca stationed himself outside the law courts, where he noticed a truck that brought coffee and pastries to the prosecutors each morning. He planned to pack an identical truck with explosives, but could not work out how to make his getaway without being caught in the blast.

Brusca's next target was Salvatore Lima, a former mayor of Palermo who had become a member of the Italian chamber of deputies. He was in the firing line for having failed to protect Mafiosi from the Maxi Trial or use his influence to get their convictions overturned on appeal. Lima was on his way to make arrangements for a dinner in honour of former Italian prime minister, Giulio Andreotti, who was visiting Palermo, when gunmen on motorcycles blew the tyres out on his car. Lima tried to escape on foot but was shot through the head.

Brusca was then contracted to kill Falcone. The judge had made the mistake of falling into a routine. Every Saturday he would fly in from Rome with his wife, then drive down the autostrada to their home near Palermo. The original plan was to blow up a bridge on the freeway, but Brusca thought it would not work. He also vetoed a plan to blow up a pedestrian underpass, because the main force of the blast would come out of the exits. Instead he chose to pack the explosives into a narrow metal drainpipe that ran under the road near the autostrada exit for Capaci. The bomb would be detonated by a remote-controlled device normally used for model aircraft. Brusca tested it by setting off old-fashioned flash bulbs, working out precisely when he had to flick the switch to blow up a speeding car.

Simulations were performed on a quiet country road outside Corleone. Metal tubes were buried and concreted over to see just how effective the explosives were going to be. After successful tests, Brusca reported back to Riina that he was 'operational'.

Twelve drums containing 770 pounds of explosive in all were placed in trenches dug under the autostrada. Then for weeks Brusca and his

men kept watch, looking out for Falcone. Twice they missed him. Once he was with his friend and fellow prosecutor Paolo Borsellino. 'If we'd known, we'd have killed two birds with one stone,' said Brusca.

On the afternoon of 23 May 1992, Falcone and his wife Francesca were spotted by Mafia lookouts while driving down the autostrada that runs along the coast after leaving Punta Raisi airport. Their armour-plated car was one of a convoy of three travelling at high speed. Hiding in an outbuilding on the hillside nearby, Brusca flicked the switch on the remote control at the precise moment. There was a huge explosion that registered on the earthquake monitor on the other side of the island. The first car was blasted into an olive grove 60 yards away, killing the three bodyguards inside. Falcone's car teetered on the edge of a huge crater in the road. The judge, his wife and their driver were badly injured.

Falcone was heard to say: 'If I survive, this time I'll make them pay ...'

He and his wife died shortly after they arrived in hospital. Only the driver survived.

When Brusca arrived back in Palermo, the television news channels were still reporting that Falcone was fighting for his life. 'That cuckold, if he doesn't die he will make life hell for us,' said Brusca.

Then came the news flash: 'Falcone is dead.'

Brusca was paid handsomely and celebrated with champagne.

CRACKDOWN

The murder of Falcone – and, soon afterwards, of his colleague Paolo Borsellino – provoked an unprecedented outcry in Italy. It was immediately followed by a furious crackdown on the Mafia. In January 1993, Riina was arrested after 23 years as a fugitive. Undeterred, Brusca, Bagarella and Provenzano decided to continue the war against the state that Riina had begun. They discussed varous options, including poisoning children's snacks, planting HIV-infected syringes on the beaches of Rimini and toppling the Leaning Tower of Pisa. Instead they opted for a series of bomb attacks.

CHAPTER 5

The aftermath of the Falcone bombing, 24 May 1992

First, a bomb went off in Rome. The target was TV host Maurizio Costanzo, who had rejoiced at the arrest of Riina. Costanzo was unhurt, but 23 bystanders were injured. Two weeks later a bomb exploded outside the Uffizi Gallery in Florence, killing five, wounding 40 and damaging dozens of priceless works of art. The following month, there

was an attack on the Gallery of Modern Art in Milan, followed by another on Rome's Basilica of St John Lateran, killing another five people. Then a bomb was planted in the Olympic Stadium in Rome. It was timed to go off during a football match, but failed to detonate.

Mario Santo Di Matteo, one of Brusca's accomplices in the Falcone bombing, was arrested and became a *pentito*. Brusca sent six of his soldiers to kidnap Di Matteo's 11-year-old son Giuseppe. They were dressed as policemen and told the boy they were taking him to see his father. Giuseppe, whom Brusca knew personally, was held for 18 months and tortured. Grisly photographs were sent to his father in an attempt to make him recant. In the end, Brusca strangled the boy with his bare hands and threw his body into a vat of acid.

Following the murder of more relatives of Mafia informants – and direct attacks on the Church and Italy's vaunted artistic heritage – the race to capture Brusca was on. He began disguising himself, either sporting a beard or moustache or shaving his head. With his girlfriend Rosaria and their five-year-old son, Brusca frequently moved hideouts and sent coded messages to avoid using the phone. In January 1996, police swooped on a villa near Palermo to find Brusca gone, but his dinner still warm on the table.

But Brusca grew careless. Having moved to Agrigento on the southern coast of Sicily, he was using a mobile phone to conclude a million-dollar drugs shipment when a plainclothes policeman rode through the neighbourhood on a scooter without a silencer. This enabled police phone tappers to pinpoint his hideout.

Two hundred black-hooded men from the anti-Mafia squad surrounded the house. They burst in to find Brusca eating a steak and, ironically, watching a TV movie about the Falcone killing. He also had a copy of Falcone's book on Cosa Nostra.

Brusca quickly turned state's evidence. The prosecutor supplied him with a list of unsolved murders and Brusca went through it, ticking those for which he was responsible. He was sentenced to life imprisonment, which was then reduced to 26 years as a reward for this collaboration.

Then, in 2004, a court ruled that he should be let out for a week every 45 days to visit his wife and son.

GIOVANNI FALCONE AND PAOLO BORSELLINO

Investigating magistrates Giovanni Falcone and Paolo Borsellino were both born in Palermo and joined the Antimafia Pool created there in the early 1980s by Judge Rocco Chinnici. Falcone worked in the bankruptcy section and became an expert in forensic accounting. His cases depended on financial records, so there were no witnesses who could be intimidated. He only prosecuted cases which could be heard before a tribunal of three judges, so there were no jurors who could be bought. Combing through five years of bank records, he managed to prove that the Spatola Construction Company was a front for drug smuggling, and obtained 74 convictions in all.

Borsellino concentrated on prosecuting the killers of Captain Emanuele Basile, an officer in the carabinieri who had issued 55 warrants on drug charges to members of the Bontade and Inzerillo families. But the judge declared a mistrial, allowing the suspects back on to the street. Fearing for his safety, Chinnici removed Borsellino from Mafia investigations. But when Chinnici was murdered, his successor Antonino Caponetto let Falcone and Borsellino work together and share information with other investigating magistrates. Then, in 1983, a new minister of justice in Rome provided them with computers to deal with the huge amounts of financial data they had to handle.

Together with information supplied by *pentiti*, evidence unearthed by Falcone and Borsellino was used in the Maxi-Trial, where 475 defendants faced trial in a specially built courtroom bunker near Ucciardone prison in Palermo. The trial ran from February 1986 to December 1987 and over a thousand witnesses were called. In all, 344 of the defendants were found guilty and

sentenced to a total of 2,665 years in jail, not counting the 19 life sentences that had been handed down to the most important bosses in Sicily, including – in absentia – Totò Riina and Bernardo Provenzano.

Riina ordered Brusca to kill Falcone. After a bomb was found in Falcone's beach house, he was transferred to Rome where he continued to fight organized crime. However, his weekly commute from Sicily to Rome took him along the coastal freeway, where his car was blown up on 23 May 1992.

Borsellino was at Falcone's bedside when he died. Afterwards he went to inspect the site of the explosion; he knew he was next. For Borsellino, investigating the Mafia was now a race against time. A *pentito* named Vincenzo Calcara told him: 'We were to shoot you with a rifle equipped with a telescopic sight – a real professional job. They had chosen me as the killer. They even gave me the weapon.'

On the afternoon of 19 July 1992, Borsellino called his mother to tell her that he was coming to visit her. As he parked outside the apartment block in which she lived in Palermo, a car bomb exploded, killing him and his five bodyguards and wounding 18 people. There was damage to the apartment block as high as the 11th floor and it took the police a week to remove human remains from the street.

Today, the two judges are commemorated across the city in which they were both born and died. Palermo International Airport has been renamed Falcone-Borsellino Airport in their honour, a monument to Falcone stands next to the autostrada at Capaci where the bomb that killed him, his wife and their bodyguards was exploded. Outside the apartment block where Falcone lived stands a magnolia tree that has become a shrine to the two of them. Known as the 'Albero Falcone' ('Falcone's Tree'), it is covered in photos, letters and messages of support from members of the public.

CHAPTER 18

MONTREAL, MIAMI AND OTHER DRUG CONNECTIONS

The main destination for the heroin produced by the laboratories of the French Connection was Canada, and the Mafia capital of Canada was Montreal. Close to the United States, Montreal had a large Italian immigrant population and, as part of the French-speaking province of Quebec, it was also a natural home-from-home for French and Corsican gangsters from Marseille. It had its own Mafia family led by Vincent Cotroni, which was allied to the Bonanno family in New York.

As a staging post for French Connection heroin, Montreal seems to have been organized soon after the Second World War by a man called Antoine d'Agostino, a French Corsican hood who may have been put in place by Lucky Luciano. He supplied the Genovese family and was one of the organizers of what came to be known – after another Luciano protégé – as 'Gino's European Tours'. This involved a steady flow of holidaying Italian families, travelling by liner to Montreal – along with a car that had been specially fitted out in either Italy or France. From there they'd travel on, naturally enough, to see the sights of New York, where the car would be relieved of its hidden burden.

D'Agostino was run out of Canada in 1954, and settled in Mexico, where he was to open a new highway for heroin into the United States.

The Canadian side of the business was at this point taken over by Vincent Cotroni's younger brother, Giuseppe 'Pep' Cotroni, and by Carmine Galante, representing the New York Bonanno family. By 1956, these two – together with a representative of the Genovese family – had control of some 60 per cent of the heroin then reaching the American continent. The contraband would be driven over the border in Cadillacs with secret compartments that could only be opened if a number of the cars' gadgets were turned on at the same time. At its height, this seemingly foolproof method was delivering 50 kilos of refined heroin a month – with a street value of at least $50 million – into the United States.

The ring was broken open, though, in 1961 by a joint undercover operation of the US Bureau of Narcotics and the Canadian Royal Mounted Police. Pep Cotroni, Carmine Galante and the Genovese man were sent to jail. So another point of entry was needed.

It was found in Miami, where Meyer Lansky was living in what seemed to be, on the surface at any rate, retirement. The boss of the city's Mafia was Santo Trafficante Jr., whose father had been a close associate of Lansky and Luciano. With the success of Fidel Castro's revolution in Cuba, there were now any number of emigré Cuban couriers and hitmen, not to mention potential heroin addicts, available in the city. Miami also had access to traffic coming in from anywhere in the Caribbean, Central or South America. And these were the next staging posts for refined heroin arriving from Marseille and Sicily – and elsewhere.

THE GOLDEN TRIANGLE COMES ON LINE

By now, both Turkey and the Lebanon were beginning to dry up as sources of morphine-base. But a new source was arriving on line – and once again through the good offices of America's cold-war warriors. As the French were forced to abandon their colonies in South-East Asia, the Americans arrived to take on communist insurgency in the region

and soon became involved in roping in as allies the hill tribes of Laos – who happened to rely for survival on their opium crop. The price of their involvement in the anti-communist struggle was the flying of their raw opium out into the market by the CIA's proprietary airline, Air America. Once there, it was fed into a pipeline organized by the French-speaking Corsicans from Marseille and their Sicilian allies, and processed into refined heroin both locally and in Europe. A good deal of the trade was financed by American-backed South Vietnamese generals and some of it by Santo Trafficante, who made a tour of the area in 1962. Its most significant victims, ironically, were American GIs, who became hooked on heroin in alarming numbers.

With the Corsicans and their allies in Marseille as major players, much of the new heroin was sent into the United States via a South American network set up in the late 1950s by a Marseille hood called Auguste Ricord. Basing himself in Buenos Aires and Asuncion, Paraguay (where protection from the unimaginably venal régime was simply a matter of money) Ricord had organized a group of pilots, couriers and strong-arms. They used various methods to run contraband into North America, via carrier 'mules' or by plane to Mexico, from where it would be either driven over the border or flown to Miami by light aircraft. In the ten years up to Ricord's arrest in 1971, his group, which was joined by fugitives from Marseille, is reckoned to have moved five tonnes of 90 per cent pure heroin worth at least $1 billion into North America.

A favourite point of entry for heroin arriving from Europe and the Far East was Buenos Aires, which had a large Italian population – as did São Paolo in Brazil, which was where many of the Sicilian Mafia, exiled as a result of the island's gang wars, had settled. Some of the heroin went directly to Mexico, where it was shifted, first by what was left of Antoine d'Agostino's Corsican network, and then by a group financed by a wealthy businessman, Jorge Asaf y Bala, known as 'the Al Capone of Mexico'.

Another favourite gateway remained Montreal, though the method of shifting the heroin over the border had necessarily changed. Now it

was carried over by illegal immigrants, most of them Sicilians, who went to work in the pizza restaurants controlled by the Mafia, particularly in New York City. Over time, these pizza joints became the main storage and distribution points for imported heroin – the so-called Pizza Connection. The Sicilians were used as expert and untraceable hitmen by the local families, particularly the Bonnano family, which was riven by internal fighting over the heroin spoils.

THE PROVIDENCE MOB

During his six decades as a career criminal, Luigi Manocchio worked his way up to being head of the Cosa Nostra in New England. Then, in the FBI's biggest ever one-day raid on organized crime, his empire came tumbling down.

Manocchio was first arrested in the 1940s, before he enlisted in the US Army in 1946. Being a soldier clearly did not suit him as he was discharged after just 14 months. Nevertheless, he still took advantage of medical care at the VA Medical Center in Providence and received a military pension of $985 a month.

In 1948, he was arrested for robbery and given a five-year suspended sentence. Four years later he was charged with two counts of assault and robbery, illegal possession of a firearm and driving a stolen car. His charge sheet already listed two of his nicknames – 'Baby Shacks' and 'The Old Man'. Everything but the weapons charge was dropped and he received another five-year suspended sentence. However, in 1955 he went to jail – for just 11 days.

In April 1968, bookmaker Rudolph 'Rudy' Marfeo was gunned down with his bodyguard Anthony Melei in Pannone's Market in Providence's Silver Lake district. Marfeo was found holding a .38 revolver, but he had been unable to loose off a single round. The hit had been on the orders of the gang boss at that time, Raymond L.S. Patriarca, who had told Marfeo to close down his rogue gambling operation.

Mafia Killings 56

Joe 'The Animal' Barboza, San Francisco, 11 February 1976

He was known as 'The Animal', but that name doesn't come anywhere near describing the knot of contradictions that was Joe Barboza. A hit man who was responsible for some 20 or 30 murders, he was also an intelligent self-taught individual who was a trained chef, wrote poetry and painted pictures.

Barboza became involved in organized crime after making some contacts in prison during the 1950s. He freelanced in the New England area, offering his services to the Winter Hill mob and Rhode Island's Cosa Nostra family, the Patriarcas. A hulking ex-heavyweight boxer, he made a very imposing impression with his barrel chest, huge forearms and massive head. Barboza both looked and behaved exactly like what he was – an ex-boxer and a mobster. He got his nickname after taking a bite out of some thug's ear during an altercation in a bar. But, paradoxically, Barboza possessed a keen intellect, was fluent in three languages and had an above average IQ. He was also said to love animals and children, and would sometimes take the neighbourhood kids to the zoo. All he lacked was a conscience.

In 1966 the Mafia had finally had enough of his unpredicatability and decided to withrdaw their support for the combustible Barboza. In October of that year, Joe was picked up on weapons charges, his bail set at a hefty one hundred thousand dollars. There was no way that Barboza's crew had that kind of money, so they set up a collection fund, hitting local hoods for contributions. Shortly after they'd managed to put together a big chunk of the money, Barboza's men were hit and the bail money was scooped up by members of the Patriarca family. When he heard what had happened, Barboza understood exactly what it meant – the mob had turned its back on him.

While awaiting trial for the weapons charge, Barboza was approached by Federal Agent H. Paul Rico, who hoped to convince him to testify against the Mafia. After much soul-searching, Barboza came to the conclusion that he would co-operate – it was time to do to the mob exactly what they had done to him.

It was while he was in prison that Barboza penned his poems outlining Mafia treachery. In such works as 'Boston's Gang Wars', 'The Mafia Double Crosses', and 'The Gang War Ends', The Animal's anguish found its voice.

Barboza found another voice as well when he implicated mobsters Raymond Patriarca, Henry Tameleo and other members of the Patriarca family in just about every crime that had occurred in the last few years. Barboza's agenda was to cause as much damage to the mob as he possibly could and he wasn't too choosy how he went about it. He even accused mob men of a murder that he himself had committed.

Agent Rico had promised all sorts of protection to Barboza for his testimony – he was one of the first to enter the Witness Protection Program – but after he got what he was after, Rico reneged and Barboza was left to fend for himself. There was clearly no way he could have much time left, and the end came on 11 February 1976, four months after he had left prison. As he was leaving a friend's apartment on 25th Avenue in the Sunset neighbourhood of San Francisco, Joe Barboza was shot four times at close range and died almost immediately.

As he fell, witnesses heard him shout, 'You f******!, you f******!'

Adding to that a few lines from his poem, 'Boston's Gang Wars' might help explain the paradox of a sadistic murderer and a man who treated children with care, whose men were loyal to him to the point of death, who found two women to love and marry him and whose daughter, Jackie, grew up without knowing what her father had done and whose heart was broken when she finally discovered the truth:

It is better to die on your feet,
Than to live on your knees,
And know that your concepts are sound.

Than to try to run, hide and scurry
Out of fear of the dirt, the earth and the ground.

An excerpt from 'Boston's Gang Wars', written by Joe Barboza in Folsom Prison

The gunman, John 'Red' Kelley, joined the Federal Witness Protection Program, while Patriarca and several of his men were given ten-year sentences for conspiracy to murder. Manocchio was also arrested as an accessory, but was let out on bail. He then disappeared, spending ten years on the run in Europe, largely in France and Italy. It is thought that he returned to the United States several times, using a fake passport and wearing a disguise, on one occasion dressing as a woman to escape arrest.

In July 1979, Manocchio returned to Rhode Island and gave himself up. He was convicted of being an accessory to murder and conspiracy, and was given two life sentences plus ten years. However, a key witness suffered from Alzheimer's disease and was found to have lied in a related case. Manocchio was released on bail. The ensuing legal battle went all the way to the Supreme Court. Manocchio then cut a deal. He pleaded no contest to conspiracy and was sentenced to the two-and-a-half years he had already served.

Manocchio had earned himself something of a reputation among the Patriarca family, who referred to him simply as 'that guy'. While the headquarters of the New England family had moved to Boston when Francis 'Cadillac Frank' Salemme became boss, Manocchio remained in Providence as *capo* of a crew of thieves, loan-sharks and bookmakers.

In January 1995, a major push against organized crime nailed Salemme, Stephen 'the Rifleman' Flemmi and the Irish-American hoodlum James 'Whitey' Bulger. The power then shifted back to Rhode Island and Manocchio became boss.

THE SIMPLE LIFE

Manocchio was the very antithesis of the ham-fisted, cigar-chomping godfather. A small man, he was said to be a health nut. Rising early, he would jog around Providence golf course, stopping at a tree to do a series of pull-ups. He was also an accomplished skier.

'People watch mob movies and see these guys smoking cigars and living the good life. Louie Manocchio stayed in tremendous shape,' said Rhode Island State Police Colonel Brendan Doherty. 'He watched what he ate and would even recommend to his other mob associates they go on a diet.'

He did not dress flashily and maintained a low profile, like the old-style Sicilian Mafia bosses. Until his arrest in 2011, he lived in a small apartment above a café in the Federal Hill section of central Providence and ran his crime family's operations from a laundromat on nearby Altwells Avenue. He remained unmarried, but is thought to have three adult children.

He was also thought to have had a financial interest in several restaurants, though his name did not appear on any official documents. But he had been seen chatting to customers – in Italian, to those who understood it – and recommending wines.

After his plea bargain in 1988, he tried to steer clear of the law. But the police would keep tabs on him and make random visits to the laundromat. 'He was always a gentleman to me and to law enforcement,' said Doherty. 'But he made his point known that we were on the other side of the fence, and "catch me if you can."' However, in 1996 Manocchio was arrested at his elderly mother's home in Mount Pleasant, where he was installing appliances stolen from a store in Connecticut. He entered a no-contest plea and was given three years' probation.

This was frustrating for Doherty, as the police and the FBI knew Manocchio was a crime boss. He took care to avoid being seen around other gangsters, but in 2006 was photographed having dinner with underboss Carmen 'the Big Cheese' DiNunzio, who later got six years for bribery.

EXTORTION WITHOUT THREATS

Manocchio eventually stepped down as boss of the Patriarca family, and the power shifted back to Boston under Peter 'Chief Crazy Horse' Limone. This may have been because 'The Old Man' was now over 80, or because federal investigators were getting too close for comfort.

In 2008, two FBI agents approached him in a restaurant on Federal Hill after he had been handed an envelope by an employee of a local strip club. It was found to contain cash – protection money from the strip club's boss. Manocchio was with Thomas Iafrate, who worked as a bookkeeper at the Cadillac Lounge strip club. Iafrate was arrested along with Manocchio during the 2011 round-up that took 127 Mafia suspects into custody.

Manocchio pleaded guilty to extorting between $800,000 and $1.5 million in protection money from strip clubs, including the Satin Doll and the Cadillac Lounge, but maintained that he did not threaten anyone. 'By virtue of my position, I inherited the deeds of my associates,' said Manocchio. 'I don't want my family or any of my friends to believe I personally threatened anyone.'

However, Assistant US Attorney William J. Ferland said that after a strip club owner reduced his payment to the mob, Manocchio visited him and informed the owner he needed to pay $4,000 a month. 'It's his personal appearance. It is who he is and what he represents that constitutes a threat,' Ferland said. 'He fails to recognize that because of his position, these businesses were willing to pay. They weren't making charitable donations to Cosa Nostra.'

Manocchio was sentenced to five-and-a-half years. The judge recommended that the 85-year-old serve his sentence in North Carolina

or Florida, where the climate would be better for his health. 'I think you are going to make it through this prison sentence and come out on the other end,' the judge said.

There are conflicting stories about how Manocchio acquired his nicknames. One told that he was called 'Baby Shacks' because he liked slim young women; another said the moniker was actually 'Baby Shanks' and instead referred to his short legs.

MAFIA TAKEDOWN

Many Mafiosi were caught in the January 2011 'Mafia Takedown' – the FBI's largest mob round-up in history, which netted 127 alleged mobsters on charges ranging from loan-sharking to murder. In addition to arresting the top men in the New England Patriarca family, nearly the entire leadership of the Colombo family was taken into custody, and the Genovese, Gambino, Lucchese and Bonanno families were all affected.

Prize captive was Gambino *capo* Bartolomeo 'Bobby Glasses' Vernace, who had eluded justice for three decades. He was found guilty of murdering Richard Godkin and John D'Agnese, the hard-working owners of a Queens bar, in 1981, after a drink was accidentally spilt on the dress of mobster Frank Riccardi's girlfriend. Philadelphia underboss Martin Angelina was sentenced to 57 months for a racketeering conspiracy. Family boss Joseph Ligambi and 12 other members of the Philadelphia Cosa Nostra were also arrested in the sweep.

Others cuffed included 73-year-old Benjamin 'the Claw' Castellazzo – aka 'the Fang' or just simply 'Benji' – who had been seen brandishing a gun to intimidate a target in East New York just weeks before his arrest. He was sentenced to 63 months for racketeering. There was also Vincenzo 'Vinny Carwash' Frogiero, described by the FBI as a Gambino soldier. He got his nickname after running car washes for the mob in his younger days. Then there was Anthony

'Tony Bagels' Cavezza, who had a penchant for the humble bagel.

Also caught in the round-up were the colourfully named Jack 'the Whack' Rizzocascio, Joseph 'Junior Lollipops' Carna, Frank 'Meatball' Bellantoni, Anthino 'Hootie' Russo and John 'Johnny Bandana' Brancaccio. Nicknames have been part of mob culture since Lupo 'the Wolf' and Al 'Scarface' Capone. A threatening moniker is part of a mobster's profile. A lot of gangsters have names that are difficult to pronounce, so soubriquets are convenient. They also give them a degree of anonymity. But Mafiosi are often sensitive souls, so it is best not to address them by their nicknames – unless, of course, you want to end up sleeping with the fishes.

THE PRICE OF RICHES

The American Mafia had since its inception been heavily involved in the traffic of *babania*, as heroin is known in Italian-American street slang. But as the United States and the rest of the Western world brought in tougher new laws in the early to mid-20th century, restricting the use of the drug, a unique and money spinning black market opportunity arose for criminals across the world, much like the prohibition of alcohol in the US had done in the 1920s.

There are those who claim that the Mafia was unwilling to get involved in heroin trafficking, and there is some evidence of gangs wanting to keep drugs out of Italian neighbourhoods in the 1930s. There was also the fact that some mob bosses were unwilling to expose their gangs to the increasingly long sentences – often ranging from 35 years to life – handed out by the courts during the 1950 and 1960s. But in reality the Mafia has always existed to make money and the spoils of the heroin trade were enormous. One small-time Sicilian boss, later turned *pentito*, said of them: 'We all became millionaires. Suddenly, within a couple of years. Thanks to drugs.' Money poured into the island. Between 1970 and 1980, the turnover of banks in Sicily increased fourfold – and the

number of banks, immune from inspection by the central authorities, multiplied hugely. The little town of Trapani, for example, with a population of 70,000, at one point had more banks than the whole city of Milan, Italy's financial hub.

The money made everything possible. More and more of the heroin-refining labs were moved to Sicily, as President Nixon's war on drugs finally persuaded the French authorities to move against the Marseille French Connection. But the money was also divisive. More than ever before, it allowed individual Mafiosi to become entrepreneurs in their own right, financing and profiting from the trade in all kinds of different ways. This was destabilizing to the old order. It cut across established ties, like those that bound Joe Bananas to his drug-running relatives in Castellammare and those that yoked Carlo Gambino's family to his cousins in Palermo, Salvatore Inzerillo and Rosario Spatola.

It also meant that the stakes, both to risk and to play for, had become very much higher. It was true that the judiciary and police had extremely limited powers of investigation. They were not allowed access, for example, to the records of individual bank accounts, which were private and privileged, however suspect. But there were other ways of coming close: tracing international bank transfers, for example, or tracking down the hidden laboratories. There was also by now a further added complication: one caused by the bank collapse of the Mafia's chief financier Michele Sindona.

THE MAFIA'S BANKER

Michele Sindona was born in Patti, on the north coast of Sicily. His father dealt in funerary wreaths, but son Michele – after an early meeting, it is said, with Vito Genovese – came to specialize in banks. By 1961, he was the majority partner in the Banca Privata Finanzaria in Milan, and it was almost certainly then, when the massive profits from heroin were on the horizon, that he became the Sicilian Mafia's bank manager.

He served several other major interests on his way to the top. He was, for example, the conduit for the CIA money that poured first into

Greece at the time of the colonels' coup of 1968, and then arrived, four years later – $11 million of it – in the campaign funds of anti-communist Italian politicians. He had extremely close ties to the Christian Democratic Party and in 1969, via his purchase of the Vatican's property development company, he became financial advisor to Pope Paul VI. By now he controlled five banks and well over 100 companies in 11 countries. Yet this same Sindona had been identified two years earlier, in a 1967 letter sent by the head of Interpol in Washington to the Italian police, as heavily involved in drug trafficking.

Nothing at all happened. By now Sindona was regarded by the world's financial press as the most successful businessman in Italy and in 1971 he aimed right for the pinnacle, for control over the two biggest holding companies in Italy. With the first, he was successful. He took over the board and installed his own people, among them an obscure banker who was later to become extremely famous, Roberto Calvi. But the second takeover was blocked by the Bank of Italy, which ordered an inspection of Sindona's bank holdings.

Massive illegalities were found, but the Bank of Italy did nothing. By this time Sindona had taken over the 18th largest bank in the United States, the Franklin National, and had moved to New York. There he secretly speculated against the lira, only to be called in by the Italian government to repair the damage he'd done. Little by little, it seemed that his touch was becoming less deft. He lost a vast amount of money on the markets, and by October 1974 the game was up. Within a few days of each other, his banks on both sides of the Atlantic collapsed. Days before the Franklin National caved in, the Federal Reserve Bank had lent Sindona $1.7 billion to save it.

It was the largest bank collapse in the history of both the United States and Italy. It cost Italy the modern equivalent of $5.5 billion. It also cost the Vatican a huge unknown amount, and the Sicilian Cosa Nostra a great deal more, perhaps several billion dollars of the drug money that was by now pouring in from the American market. Cosa Nostra also had two extra problems: Sindona himself (by then living at the Pierre Hotel in

New York on bail of \$3 million), and a particularly dogged and stubborn man who had been appointed as receiver to investigate Sindona's banks in Milan: Giorgio Ambrosoli.

Considerable efforts were made with senior figures in the Christian Democratic Party to get Sindona off the hook even then. Sindona knew where the bodies were buried, and exactly how high in the party Cosa Nostra's tentacles reached. But receiver Ambrosoli was not to be shaken off. He soon found Sindona's secret mother-company in Liechtenstein and a web of other companies within companies stretching away from it across the world. It was clear that Ambrosoli had to be silenced – and in early July 1979, he was shot down by an unknown assailant in front of his house in Milan.

That left Sindona – and three weeks after Ambrosoli's assassination, he simply disappeared from the Pierre Hotel in New York. His secretary received a message saying that he'd been taken by 'communist terrorist kidnappers'. But, in fact, under the wing of Carlo Gambino's son, he had been taken to Palermo for meetings with Cosa Nostra's high command. It was from here that there issued a number of messages from the 'kidnappers', threatening to extort from Sindona full details of Italy's capital exporters and their foreign bank accounts, the companies which had been used to bribe politicians, and so on. It was a threat to bring down the whole Italian economic and political establishment. A meeting in Vienna was set with those concerned 'to arrange for Sindona's release'.

In the end, a letter carrying instructions to Sindona's lawyer about the Vienna meeting was intercepted as the result of a telephone tap. It was being carried by a Mafia courier, the brother of Rosario Spatola. So the meeting in Vienna was called off, and Sindona was soon back in the Pierre Hotel once more, announcing that he'd been released by his 'kidnappers'.

In the end, after legal manoeuvrings on both sides of the Atlantic, Sindona received prison terms for fraud, and in 1986 a life sentence in Italy for the murder of Ambrosoli. He never gave up any of his extraordinary secrets. However, three days after the Ambrosoli judgment,

in the maximum-security prison at Vighera where he was supposed to be watched 24 hours a day, Sindona died – like Lucky Luciano – after drinking a cup of coffee.

CARMINE GALANTE

Carmine Galante's Mafia nickname was 'Lilo' – in honour of the little cigars he constantly smoked. He was short, fat, bald and immensely violent. When he came out of federal prison in 1978 he had two ambitions: to make money by taking back control of the lucrative New York heroin trade and to become the ultimate man of respect: the *capo di tutti capi*.

Galante had grown up in East Harlem, New York, the son of Sicilian immigrants. He was to remain a Sicilian, out of tune with the pliable Italian-American businessmen who gradually took over the Mafia. He was another Riina, a man of vendettas; he lived by the gun and the code of honour and, as such, became in the early days a highly trusted member of the Bonanno family.

In the mid-1950s, he organized the so-called Montreal Connection and in 1957 travelled as *consigliere* to Joe Bananas to the Palermo summit of Sicilian and American Mafia leaders organized by Lucky Luciano. In 1962, he was sentenced to 20 years for his part in the Montreal Connection and, by the time of his release on parole in 1974, had had plenty of time to consider his response to the new order he faced.

His timing was opportune. Carlo Gambino, whom he loathed for the inroads he'd made into Bonanno turf, was ill and soon died, and his family was taken over by his brother-in-law Paul 'Big Paulie' Castellano. Phil Rastelli was behind bars at the time – and he rapidly stood down as soon as Galante hit the streets. Galante had planned well, for he'd gathered around himself a large group of old-country Sicilian hitmen who had no allegiance to anyone but him – and to the Mafia code he believed in. They quickly muscled and killed their way back to control of the heroin business.

Galante then rapidly became a 'business problem' to the Commission, especially to 'Big Paulie'. But no one seems to have wanted a bullying throwback, a 'Moustache Pete' from the past, to rock the boat. So the Commission ordered Galante's assassination – and the job was handed, as per custom, to a member of his own family, underboss Salvatore Catalano.

On 12 July 1979, as Galante was enjoying an after-lunch cigar with two friends on the rear patio of Joe and Mary's Italian Restaurant in Brooklyn, three men wearing ski masks and carrying shotguns walked in through the back door. Th hit was carried out so quickly that Galante's cigar was still in his mouth as he hit the floor. The traditional .45 bullet was then fired into his left eye and his guests were finished off by his own trusted bodyguards, who then calmly walked out with his killers.

That same day, at a meeting in prison, Phil Rastelli was reconfirmed as head of the Bonanno family, and Mafia bosses met in a social club in New York's Little Italy to celebrate. But Galante later came back to haunt them. As the result of wiretaps installed during the investigation into the so-called Pizza Connection, Salvatore Catalano and the members of the New York Commission were eventually charged with plotting his murder, though Bonanno foot soldier Anthony 'Bruno' Indelicato was convicted of actually pulling the trigger.

THE ICE MAN

The Mafia has always employed strong-arms and hitmen to do its dirty work. Violence and murder are endemic to the culture, most often as a means of making money but also to establish the status of the various gangs or families involved in any particular area of criminality or territory. The ferocity of the violence has often risen and fallen depending on the perceived need to strengthen or weaken the reputation of the clans involved in a particular argument. In his book on the Camorra, writer Roberto Saviano explains that the corpses of the victims 'may become maps on which messages are inscribed'. But there are some killers whose

love of violence and the cruelty they exhibit while carrying out their contracts points inevitably to mental instability and psychopathy.

One such killer was Richard Kuklinski, a Mafia hit man who claimed to have killed over a hundred people. A professional assassin, he earned the soubriquet 'The Ice Man' because of his habit of refrigerating bodies to disguise the time of death.

Curiously for a Mafioso, he was not a Sicilian or an Italian. His father was Polish, his mother Irish and he was brought up in the Projects of Jersey City. His father was an alcoholic who beat his children savagely for no reason. Richard's elder brother died as a result of these beatings. Kuklinski later regretted not killing his father. He actually went to a bar where his father hung out to put a bullet in his head, but he wasn't there.

Kuklinski tried to defend his mother from one of his father's beatings. This earned him a punch that put him out for half the night. But his mother beat him too, hitting him around the head with pots and pans, shoes, brushes and broom handles.

He was sent to a Catholic school where he was beaten by the priests and the nuns. Angry, he vented his rage on cats and dogs, torturing them and burning or beating them to death while enjoying their screams. Once he tied the tails of two cats together, hung them over a washing line and watched them tear each other to pieces.

When his parents separated, Kuklinski remained living with his mother and supplemented the family's meagre income by stealing food. He also stole true crime magazines, which he studied obsessively. By the time he was 13, he had graduated to stealing cars. At 14, he committed his first murder. Bullied by a gang headed by Charley Lane, Kuklinski beat Lane to death with a thick wooden pole. He put his body in the boot of a stolen car and dumped it in a river. First of all, though, he smashed the corpse's teeth and cut off its fingertips to prevent identification. Back in the Jersey City Projects, Kuklinski tracked down the rest of Charley Lane's gang one by one and beat them up viciously.

Richard Kuklinski, aka the 'Ice Man'

After quitting school, he hung out in pool halls where he learned that you could win any fight if you struck first with full force, usually wielding a pool cue. Anyone who got the better of him was later knifed.

He formed a gang whose members were tattooed with the words 'Coming Up Roses' on their left hands – the idea being that anyone who crossed them would end up as plant food. They planned robberies and stick-ups and Kuklinski armed himself with a .38 revolver with a six-inch barrel. When his father visited to administer another beating to his mother, he put the gun to his head and pulled back the hammer. His father did not bother the family again.

Then an Irish policeman named Doyle called Kuklinski a 'dumb Polack' in a bar. When Doyle went out to his car, Kuklinski poured petrol over it and struck a match.

PRACTISING HIS ART

The Coming Up Roses gang quickly came to the attention of the DeCavalcante New Jersey crime family and Carmine Genovese invited them to his house. Over spaghetti and meatballs, he hired them for a hit. They immediately drove out to the mark's home. When another gang member funked it, Kuklinski walked up coolly to the target as he sat in his car and blew his brains out. The gang members got $500 each.

Genovese then employed them as hijackers, but when two of his gang held up a card game run by a made man in the DeCavalcante family, Kuklinski quickly dealt with the situation. He shot them in the head before they knew what was happening.

Now a lone wolf, he practised his art as an executioner by taking the ferry over to Manhattan and murdering down-and-outs and homosexuals on the run-down Lower West Side. He killed with a knife, a gun, a rope and an ice-pick, figuring out the most efficient way of inducing death. He reckoned that he had killed more than 50 men there over the years.

In February 1956 he was playing pool in a bar in Hoboken when a truck driver called him a Polack. Kuklinski smashed a pool cue around his head and knocked out another man with an eight ball. When he

left, three men went after him. The truck driver attacked him with a length of pipe but Kuklinski shot him in the head and then killed the other two. He dumped their bodies down a sinkhole in Bucks County, Pennsylvania, and pushed their car into the Hudson.

Kuklinski beat Linda, the woman he was living with, even when she was pregnant. But he never laid a finger on their children. Anyone who did was given a severe beating. Later Kuklinski killed a friend of his when he asked him to kill his wife and child, explaining: 'I don't kill women and I don't kill children. And anyone who does doesn't deserve to live.'

When Kuklinski discovered that Linda was having an affair, he broke down the door of the guilty couple's hotel bedroom, broke every bone in the man's body and then cut Linda's nipples off.

ON A SHORT FUSE

Carmine Genovese then commissioned Kuklinski for another hit. This time the mark was to suffer. Kuklinski tied the man to a tree and cut his fingers off one by one, then took a hatchet to his feet and legs. Finally, he cut his head off to take back to Genovese, to show him he had done the job.

His reputation was soon so formidable that other Mafiosi steered clear of him. He always carried a knife and two guns, favouring a .38 Derringer. It was easy to conceal and lethal at close range – and Kuklinski liked to do his killing up close. He often used two different guns so that the police would think there was more than one gunman.

Genovese sent Kuklinski to Chicago to pick up some money. The mark kept telling Kuklinski that the money was coming. When he did eventually hand it over, Kuklinski killed him anyway for wasting his time.

A crooked police officer paid him to collect a suitcase from Los Angeles. Later he discovered that it contained a kilo of heroin and he had risked a long prison term. He killed the cop and buried him out in the middle of nowhere. On another occasion, a man who aimed to welch on a $5,000 gambling debt had his brains splattered over the side of his car with a tyre lever. Another target was having sex with his girlfriend

on board a boat. Not wanting to hurt the girl, Kuklinski waited half the night, then went and killed the mark, forgoing any torture as he was feeling in a good mood.

By the age of 24, Kuklinski was drinking heavily and getting into bar fights. When someone asked him to settle a difference outside, Kuklinski stabbed his opponent under the chin so hard that the blade penetrated his brain. Then a bouncer who kicked him out for being loud had his head beaten in with a hammer the next day.

As well as working as a hitman, Kuklinski also had other jobs. One day, while working for Swiftline, a New Jersey trucking company, he met an 18-year-old secretary called Barbara Pedricki. Fresh out of school, she was a clever, popular girl with a sarcastic sense of humour. Her idea of living dangerously was taking a flask of rum out on a Saturday night so she and her friends could spike their Cokes before going for Chinese food and a movie. Barbara had wanted to go to art school, but when she accompanied a friend to an interview at Swiftline and ended up being offered a job herself, she took it. Kuklinski worked on the loading dock there. He was seven years older than Barbara, married with two young sons but, nevertheless, she agreed to go out with him on a double date.

'He was the perfect gentleman,' she said. 'We went to the movies and then we went for pizza, and he got up and played "Save the Last Dance for Me" on the jukebox.' The next morning, he turned up at her house with flowers and a gift, and she agreed to a second date. 'And that was it,' she said.

Barbara had never really had a boyfriend before, and she was flattered by the attention. When she left work in the evenings, she would find him waiting for her with flowers; he was charming and courteous, constantly at her elbow. And although he wasn't Italian, her family came to like him. Yet as the months passed, Barbara gradually realized she had become isolated from her friends, and rarely saw anyone but Richard. Sitting in his car one day after work, she gathered the courage to tell him how she felt: that she was only 19 and wanted the space to see other people. Richard responded by silently jabbing her from behind with a

hunting knife so sharp she didn't even feel the blade go in. 'I felt the blood running down my back,' she said. He told her that she belonged to him, and that if she tried to leave he would kill her entire family; when Barbara began screaming at him in anger, he throttled her into unconsciousness.

The following day, Richard was waiting for her again after work, with flowers and a teddy bear. He apologized, and told her he wanted to marry her. He would get a divorce from his wife. He had threatened her because he loved her so much it made him crazy. Young, inexperienced and credulous, Barbara believed him.

After his first apology, Richard continued to be as charming and attentive as before, but also flew into rages in which he struck her or grabbed her around the throat. Convinced she could never leave him, she agreed to get married. Their first child, a daughter named Merrick, was born two years later, in 1964.

After the wedding Kuklinski tried to go straight, but it did not last long. To keep Barbara in style he returned to crime, stealing a truckload of jeans direct from a depot. While on his way to the buyer, he inadvertently cut up two guys in a red Chevrolet. Following an altercation, they came at him with a baseball bat. He shot them both in the head. After Kuklinski had stolen a truck full of Casio watches, the buyer tried to renegotiate the price. He shot him in the head, along with the three men unloading the truck. Another hijacked truck disappeared from a farm where he had left it. He tortured the farmer until he finally admitted that a friend had taken it. Then Kuklinski shot both of them in the head.

Kuklinski then went to work at a film laboratory, where he also developed hardcore porn which he began to bootleg to the Gambino family. When a union official at the laboratory berated Kuklinski for hogging all the overtime, Kuklinski punched him. He went down, hitting his head, and another body disappeared into the Hudson.

Kuklinski was only arrested after he intervened when his brother Joe was being held hostage over a gambling debt. Loading his

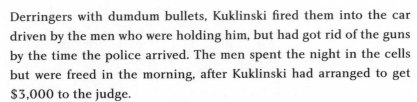

Derringers with dumdum bullets, Kuklinski fired them into the car driven by the men who were holding him, but had got rid of the guns by the time the police arrived. The men spent the night in the cells but were freed in the morning, after Kuklinski had arranged to get $3,000 to the judge.

The film laboratory where Kuklinski worked was just a block away from the famous Peppermint Lounge on West 45th Street in Manhattan. One evening Kuklinski had trouble with a bouncer there. Three days later he returned to the nightclub with a .22 revolver in a lunch sack, pulled out the gun, shot the bouncer in the head and walked away.

FULL-TIME CONTRACT KILLER

Through his porn industry connections, Kuklinski ran across Roy DeMeo, who put the squeeze on him. Ambushed by DeMeo's crew of seasoned killers, Kuklinski was savagely pistol-whipped by DeMeo. Later Kuklinksi and DeMeo agreed to go into the contract-killing business together. But first Kuklinski was put to the test. DeMeo gave him a .38 revolver and pointed out a man walking his dog. Kuklinski shot him in the back of the head.

For his first assignment, Kuklinski was given an address in Queens, a photograph of the mark and $20,000. He followed the mark, parked next to him and punctured his front tyre. When the man returned, Kuklinski offered to lend a hand, then pulled a gun and forced the man into the boot of his Cadillac. He drove him out to Pennsylvania, shot him in the head and dropped him down a sinkhole.

As he was not a made man, Kuklinski did not hang out with other mobsters and after a hit he would go home to his family. They moved into a middle-class neighbourhood in Dumont, New Jersey, where Kuklinski was known as a good neighbour who gave extravagant poolside barbecues. Indoors, he still had bouts of uncontrollable rage.

The next on the list was Paul Rothenberg, the lynch-pin of the porn business. Kuklinski shot him down in a busy street while DeMeo looked on. While making his getaway, a man in a red Mustang cut him up so

Kuklinski shot him dead at the next stop sign. DeMeo then sent Kuklinski after a man in Florida who had raped a fellow Mafioso's daughter. 'Make him suffer,' he said.

Kuklinski abducted the man, tore his testicles off with his bare hands, removed his penis, stripped him, carved away his flesh, poured salt in the wounds, disembowelled him and then put him in a life jacket and floated him out to sea for the sharks to finish off. On the way home through South Carolina, he was taunted by three rednecks. When they went for him with a club, he shot all three of them dead and drove off.

Back in Brooklyn, he handed DeMeo the victim's severed penis in a ziplock sandwich bag he had taken for the purpose. While the two men shared a plate of antipasti, DeMeo enjoyed Kuklinski's description of how the mark had met his end. By then Kuklinski had begun collecting torture ideas from movies, detailing them in a notebook. When a man in Los Angeles owed him $10,000, he went to his shop, handed him the pin from a grenade and dropped the grenade behind the counter. The blast threw people out of windows eight stories up.

A Sicilian Mafia boss did not like the man his daughter was seeing, so Kuklinski took the boyfriend out to the caves in Bucks County and wrapped him in wet rawhide with one strip around his testicles. He photographed his agony as the rawhide dried, then left him to be eaten – alive – by rats. Later he filmed these torture sessions and would watch them at night when everyone else had gone to bed. Even DeMeo could not bear to see them.

When a mark in LA proved elusive, Kuklinski rang his front doorbell, waited until he put his eye to the spyhole and then pulled the trigger. Contracted to kill a lieutenant in the Bonanno family, Kuklinski approached him in a disco with a syringe of cyanide. Everyone thought the victim had suffered a heart attack.

From then on, cyanide then became his favourite method of murder. He slipped it into drinks or sprinkled it on pizza or on a line of cocaine. He always used just enough to kill, but not enough to be detected. Ex-Special Forces man Robert Pronge taught Kuklinski to use cyanide in a

spray which was absorbed by the skin. He also taught him to keep the corpse in a freezer for a couple of months before dumping it, to confuse the police about when the victim had died.

HIGH-PROFILE COMMISSIONS

When it was decided that the notorious Carmine 'Lilo' or 'the Cigar' Galante, then head of the Bonanno family, had to go, DeMeo suggested Kuklinski for the job. On 12 July 1979, Kuklinski had lunch in Joe and Mary's Italian restaurant in the Bushwick section of Brooklyn, where Galante liked to eat. He ordered a sandwich, so he would not leave any fingerprints.The bodyguard who had fingered Galante got up from the table as two back-up gunmen came through the door. Kuklinski got to his feet, pulled out two guns and shot Galante and the other bodyguard. Then they walked to the car outside.

On the spur of the moment, Kuklinski shot a friend named George Malliband five times, then dumped the body in a back alley. It was known that Malliband had gone to meet Kuklinski that day.

After a meeting with John Gotti, 'Sammy the Bull' Gravano asked Kuklinski to kill a man named Paul Calabro, who cautiously took the back roads to his home in New Jersey. Kuklinski parked his van on the route in such a way that Calabro would have to slow down to get past him and then shot him with both barrels of a shotgun. The next day Kuklinski learned that his victim was a decorated NYPD detective.

According to Kuklinski, John Gotti also had a special job for him, so he went with John's brother, Gene Gotti, to abduct John Favara. Kuklinski said that he burnt Favara's genitals off with a flare and then stuffed them up his rectum, before Gotti cut him up. Kuklinski then killed small-time crook Louis Masgay for one of his few friends, a fence named Phil Solimene who ran 'the store' in Paterson, New Jersey.

POLICE HAD HIM TAPED

Things began to unravel when a small-time burglar named Percy House told the police that he had been part of a burglary gang run by 'Big

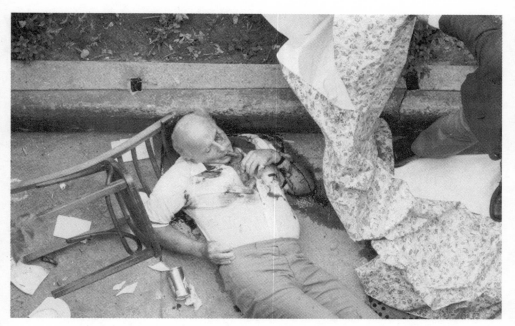

On 12 July 1979, at a Brooklyn restaurant, New York police detectives cover the body of Carmine Galante, shot to death as he ate lunch. Police officials and witnesses said that four men pulled up in a car and opened fire with automatic weapons and shotguns.

Rich'. The gang had dispersed after Kuklinski had poisoned a member named Gary Smith. Then when Kuklinski killed another gang member named Danny Deppner, Percy House began to talk.

Checking out Kuklinski, the New Jersey police found he had a reputation for punching a hole in the windshield of the car of any driver who offended him.

Meanwhile, Kuklinski killed Paul Hoffman, the chemist who supplied him with cyanide. As more bodies that had connections with Kuklinski were found, Pat Kane, a single-minded New Jersey detective, contacted the NYPD's organized crime unit, and discovered that Kuklinski was also linked to DeMeo.

Although the police were on to him, the killings continued. He murdered a hitchhiker who gave him the finger and he killed a man in a secluded street just to try out a new mini-crossbow he had bought.

Phil Solimene then came to the attention of the law and Kane persuaded him to let an undercover police officer named Dominick

Polifrone, aka Provanzano, hang around 'the store'. But Kuklinski was on money-laundering business in Zurich, where he killed rivals with a cyanide spray and a knife. Back in New Jersey, he killed the members of a ring of child abusers.

In 1985, Gotti and Gravano were planning to eliminate Paul Castellano. Kuklinski was called in to kill his bodyguard and driver Tommy Bilotti. When Castellano's car pulled up outside Sparks Steak House on East 46th Street, two men wearing trench coats and Russian fur caps approached the vehicle. Job done, Kuklinski and the other assassin then disappeared into the crowd.

With Kane on his trail, Kuklinski decided that the only way he could get rid of the nosy cop was with a cyanide spray and he asked Solimene if Provanzano could get him some of the poison. Polifrone telephoned Kuklinski and trapped him into admitting using cyanide in a spray, while the call was taped. They met at a service station where Kuklinski sold Polifrone a .22 revolver with a silencer. Polifrone then got Kuklinski to agree to a hit. He also talked of the murders of Smith, Deppner and Masgay. Everything was taped. When Polifrone delivered the cyanide, Kuklinski spotted that it was not the real thing and took off.

Just before Christmas 1986 the police stopped a car on Sunset Street in Dumont, New Jersey. Inside it were Richard Kuklinski and his wife Barbara. They were leaving the house where they lived with their three children, on their way to breakfast at the Seville in nearby Westwood. Kuklinski did not pull the .25 automatic from under the seat of his car for fear that Barbara might get hit. It took four men to wrestle him to the ground and handcuff him.

Kuklinski was formally charged with the murders of Deppner, Malliband, Masgay and Smith. When he discovered that Polifrone had been a plant, he knew he was sunk and mounted no defence. He was found guilty on all counts, but was spared the death sentence because there had been no eyewitnesses to his horrific crimes.

Already serving five life sentences, he pleaded guilty to the murder of Peter Calabro, earning himself another 30 years. Kuklinski was scheduled

to testify against Gravano, but died in the New Jersey Department of Correction in Trenton from 'undisclosed medical problems' on 5 March 2006, aged 70. He had served 25 years behind bars.

BARBARA KUKLINSKI

In 2008, a book called *The Ice Man: Confessions of a Mafia Contract Killer* was published. Written by Philip Carlo, the book tells the story of Richard Kuklinski, one of the most notorious professional assassins in the history of American gangland crime. A man who allegedly killed more than 200 people in one of the most sustained killing sprees ever recorded. The book was endorsed by his wife Barbara Kuklinski as she felt it captured the 'real' Kuklinski. On publication the story of the Ice Man shocked America because Kuklinski led an extraordinary double life, a sadistic killer and apparently a loving husband and doting father who hosted friendly neighbourhood barbecues in suburban New Jersey, ushering at his local Catholic church every Sunday. 'We were the perfect all-American family,' says Barbara, her voice laden with sarcasm. 'We were so perfect it would make you sick. The way we lived was surreal.'

Initially meeting him when she was 19, going on a double date as a favour to a friend, she quickly realized that he was not quite as charming and handsome as he seemed. But fear of his volatile moods and his determination to pursue her led further. Soon she became pregnant and, by 1961 unable to see a way out, she agreed to marry him after he threatened to kill her father.

When Kuklinski was finally arrested in 1986, Barbara was genuinely appalled by the charges laid against him. But gradually the reality of their marriage began to sink in. She came to realize that the psychotic rages into which he fell and the regular beatings he gave her were signs of an even darker side. 'There were two Richards,' she said, 'and I never knew who would be walking in the door – the good Richard or the bad Richard'. As for his work, which

brought the family a nice house and all the trappings of a good life, 'I rarely asked questions. He was a wholesale distributor, registered in Hackensack. He had an accountant. I didn't have a clue what his real business was. He was a good provider.'

'Richard was dangerous, cruel and charismatic,' explains author Philip Carlo who spent hundreds of hours interviewing the killer in Trenton State Prison, where he was serving multiple life sentences. Carlo was determined to 'shine light on the dark, violent phenomenon that was Richard Kuklinski's life.'

THE SIXTH FAMILY

Vincenzo 'the Egg' Cotroni was 14 years old when his family emigrated from Calabria to Canada. They lived in a shabby apartment at Saint-Timothée in Quebec. Cotroni did not attend school in his adopted country. Instead, he worked as an assistant to his father, a carpenter and then became a professional wrestler under the name Vic Vincent.

With his brothers Francesco – 'Frank' – and Giuseppe – 'Peppe' or 'Pep' – he became a petty criminal. By the time he was 20 he had built up a long rap sheet that included minor crimes such as theft, possessing counterfeit money, the illegal sale of alcohol, and assault and battery. He was also charged with the rape of Maria Bresciano, but she dropped the charge and became his wife. They had a daughter and stayed together until Maria's death, though Cotroni also had a son with his French-Canadian mistress, a teacher.

The three brothers moved into bootlegging, prostitution, gambling and drugs. By 1945, they had become powerful enough to use extortion to buy votes and intimidate officials at polling stations during elections. This brought them to the attention of Joseph 'Joe Bananas' Bonanno, who had taken over the Maranzano family in 1931 and made it the Bonanno family. He sent his underboss Carmine Galante to Montreal, which was to become the hub of the Bonanno family's narcotics importing business.

Galante soon found there were restaurants and nightclubs that had not been shaken down thoroughly enough and pimps, prostitutes, madams, back-alley abortionists, illegal gambling houses and after-hours lounges who were paying a mere pittance. So he imposed a 'street tax' on them. Cotroni and Galante grew close and Vic became godfather to one of Galante's children.

The drugs operation ran smoothly. Later a government witness, a little-known criminal named Edward Smith, described meetings with Galante and Vic, Pep and Frank Cotroni. In a Montreal apartment, Galante would open a suitcase on the coffee table. Smith's partner would count the bags of white powder inside and Smith would take the suitcase to Frank's Bar & Grill in Brooklyn, where the contents would be cut and distributed.

In 1956, the Canadian authorities began to crack down on American gangsters in their midst and Galante became a target because of his strong-arm tactics. Notorious for his cruelty, Galante would smash beer glasses on the floor in a restaurant he owned and make a busboy dance barefoot on the shards. Galante was deported to the United States. His associate Salvatore 'Little Sal' Giglio, who set up the drugs pipeline between Marseille and Montreal, was caught with 240 Cuban cigars and 800 American cigarettes he had failed to declare and similarly ousted.

THE GOOD LIFE

The Bonannos' Montreal interests were left in the hands of Vic Cotroni and the Sicilian Luigi 'Louie' Greco. According to Joe's son, Salvatore 'Bill' Bonanno: 'Cotroni was the head honcho. He was captain of the crew. Louie was his right-hand man. We had to have a couple of sit-downs to straighten that out, but we got it down. They trusted and listened to my dad ... Louie was big enough to respect that. Louie knew it was best for everyone ... If any of Louie's guys made trouble, Louie knew he had New York to answer to.'

In 1959, Pep Cotroni pleaded guilty to drug trafficking and was jailed for ten years. Galante was also arrested. His trial was repeatedly delayed;

one postponement occurred when one of the defendants absconded the day before the trial was scheduled.

Cotroni could neither read nor write, but in the 1960s he owned a limousine, along with a duplex in Rosemont and a house outside the city in Lavaltrie. This had marble floors, six bathrooms, a huge conference room, a walk-in refrigerator, crystal chandeliers and a cinema. He was also a pillar of the community, making large donations to Montreal churches and various charities.

After six months of what an appeal court judge would later call 'every conceivable type of obstruction and interruption', Galante's trial was halted on the eve of the summations to the jury. The foreman of the jury had broken his back. He seemed to have fallen down the stairs of an abandoned building in the middle of the night.

A retrial in 1962 began with one of the defendants, Salvatore Panico, shouting abuse before the jury had even been selected. Panico would later clamber into the jury area to rough up the front row while screaming abuse at them and the judge. Then Anthony Mirra, another Bonanno soldier – who was later whacked for introducing 'Donnie Brasco' Pistone to the family – picked up the witness chair and flung it at the prosecutor. This did not help their case and Galante was sentenced to 20 years.

By now Cotroni had learned to keep a low profile and when *Maclean's* news magazine referred to him as the 'godfather of Montreal', he sued for $1.25 million. The judge agreed that Cotroni's name had indeed been 'tainted' by the article, but awarded him only $2 for the English-language edition and $1 for the French-language edition.

In the 1970s, Cotroni turned over the day-to-day running of the family to the hot-headed Paolo Violi, another immigrant from Calabria. In 1955 Violi had pumped four bullets into fellow immigrant Natale Brigante in a car-park row about a woman in their home country. Brigante died, but not before he had stabbed Violi under the heart. Violi showed the stab wound in court, claiming he had acted in self-defence. The manslaughter charge against him was then dropped.

In the early 1960s, Violi hooked up with Vic's younger brother, Frank 'Le Gros' Cotroni. He ran an extortion racket in the Italian community of St Leonard and then went into counterfeiting and bootlegging. In 1965, he married the daughter of Giacomo Luppino, a member of the 'Ndrangheta from Calabria who had become boss of Hamilton, Ontario. Vic Cotroni and Ontario mobsters Paul Volpe and Johnny 'Pops' Papalia were godfathers to their children. When an underworld figure was forced to give testimony before a government commission about Violi's standing, he said: 'My Lord, his name, it's like a god … everyone is afraid of him. Violi, he's not one man – he's a thousand men.'

SHARED TELEPHONE LINE

In 1973, war erupted between the Cotronis and the French-Canadian Dubois gang. On a wiretap, Violi was heard saying they should go into the Dubois' club, 'clients or no clients, line everybody up against the wall and rat-a-tat-tat'. Cotroni had a cooler head and persuaded him to make peace.

The following year, Cotroni was called before the Quebec Police Commission's inquiry into organized crime and sentenced to a year in prison for giving testimony that was 'deliberately incomprehensible, rambling, vague, and nebulous'. His lawyers won a reversal, but not before he had spent several months in jail.

Cotroni and Violi were then caught on a further wiretap. They were threatening Johnny Papalia, who had used their names in a $300,000 extortion plot without notifying them or cutting them in. They demanded $150,000, but Papalia insisted that he had only netted $40,000. Cotroni was then heard to say: 'Let's hope so because, eh, we'll kill you.' The three men were sentenced to six years, but Cotroni and Violi had their convictions quashed on appeal.

After Luigi Greco was burnt to death in an accidental fire at his pizzeria, the Sicilian faction of the family under Nicolo Rizzuto made a bid for power. On 14 February 1976, Violi's *consigliere* Pietro Sciara was gunned down leaving a cinema with his wife. They had just seen

The Godfather. The following year, Violi's brother Francesco was on the telephone when he received a shotgun blast to the face. Then he was finished off with a couple of bullets from a handgun.

Violi was still in jail at the time. When he got out, Nick Rizzuto sought sanctuary in Venezuela. But on 22 January 1978, Violi was playing cards in a bar when two masked men walked in. One put a 12-bore shotgun to the back of his head and pulled the trigger.

At Violi's funeral, 31 black Cadillacs carried tributes from mobsters in North America and Italy. Three Sicilians were jailed for the slaying.

For weeks afterwards, Cotroni stayed inside his fortress in Lavaltrie while Rizzuto took over the family. It seems Cotroni had at least approved the hit on Violi.

Vincenzo Cotroni died of cancer in 1984. At his funeral, there were 23 cars carrying floral tributes; 17 brass bands turned out to mark the passing of Montreal's legendary 'man of respect'. By then, Galante was dead and the Bonanno family was in decline, their links with the Cotronis severed. The Montreal mob, led by Vito Rizzuto, was gearing up to become North America's 'sixth family'.

VITO RIZZUTO

The son of Nicolo Rizzuto, Vito was born in 1946 in the Sicilian province of Agrigento and migrated with his family to Canada in 1954.

At the age of 19, Rizzuto Jr. was fined $25 for disturbing the peace. Then in 1972 he was sent to prison for two years for conspiracy to commit arson with his brother-in-law, Paolo Renda. When war broke out between the Calabrian and Sicilian factions of the Montreal mob and his father fled to Venezuela, Vito stayed behind. The war was finally over in 1981, with more than 20 casualties in Canada and Italy, and Nick and Vito Rizzuto emerged as leaders of the Montreal Mafia. Vito became his father's enforcer.

Michel Pozza, a financial adviser who had worked exclusively for Cotroni before the split, now saw the Sicilians as his best bet. But it

was a bad move. A few days after he was seen talking to Rizzuto, Pozza was gunned down outside his home.

In 1987, the Royal Canadian Mounted Police seized 16 tons of hashish with an estimated street value of $350 million on an island off the coast of Newfoundland. Rizzuto was arrested and charged with trafficking, but the charges were dropped when a Supreme Court judge ruled that the evidence had been obtained unlawfully. However, four other men went to jail.

While out on bail, Rizzuto was charged with smuggling 32 tons of Lebanese hashish into the country. He was acquitted when a witness named Normand Dupuis refused to testify. Dupuis later claimed he had been offered $1 million not to take the stand, but had only made his decision after his family received death threats. Rizzuto walked free while Dupuis was given 32 months for obstruction of justice.

Vito Rizzuto took over the family in 1988 when his father went to jail in Venezuela for cocaine trafficking. Rizzuto Sr. was paroled in 1993 when Montreal mobster Domenic Tozzi delivered an $800,000 bribe to Venezuelan officials. Returning to Canada, he then became his son's business adviser.

In 2004, Vito Rizzuto was arrested again. After a 31-month battle he was extradited to the United States where he pleaded guilty to the 1981 killing of the rival Bonanno *capos*, alongside Big Joey Massino. This was part of a plea bargain and he was sentenced to just ten years.

He was released after only five years and deported back to Canada. By then his eldest son Nicolo had been gunned down; his father had been killed by a sniper who had shot him through his kitchen window; his brother-in-law and *consigliere* Paolo Renda had disappeared, and was believed dead; and his associate Agostino Cuntrera had been executed.

After Vito's release there were 14 hits in Montreal, thought to have been in retaliation. Until his death in 2103 from cancer, Rizzuto lived in a well-guarded apartment in downtown Montreal, driving around in a $100,000 armoured car.

THE DEMEO MOB

Born in Brooklyn in 1942, Roy DeMeo dropped out of school at 17, DeMeo involved himself in legitimate businesses while making the bulk of his money from loan-sharking, which he had learned from the sons of local Mafia boss Joe Profaci. DeMeo had no qualms about using violence on those who did not pay up on time. Gambino associate Anthony 'Nino' Gaggi got to hear about him and invited him to his home. DeMeo knew of the Gambinos through family associations with the Lucchese and set his heart on becoming a member.

Under Gaggi, DeMeo set up his own crew with his cousin Joseph 'Dracula' Guglielmo, marijuana dealer Harvey 'Chris' Rosenberg, Anthony Senter, Freddy DiNome, 'Dirty' Henry Borelli and Joey and Patrick Testa. They loan-sharked, sold stolen cars and laundered drugs money through the Boro of Brooklyn Credit Union, after DeMeo had talked his way on to the board. Gaggi and DeMeo also muscled their way into the X-rated movie business.

When their movie business was raided, Gaggi and DeMeo feared that one of their partners, Paul Rothenberg, might turn informer. DeMeo invited Rothenberg out to dinner in Long Island and then shot him in the head in an alleyway.

In late 1974, the crew got involved in a conflict with Andrei Katz, a body shop owner who was one of their partners in a stolen car ring. He had been arrested and as a result of the conflict was threatening to testify to a grand jury. DeMeo decided that he had to go. The crew abducted him.

Taking him to the meat department of a supermarket in Queens, they stabbed him in the heart, dismembered him and dumped the remains beneath some rotting vegetables in a rubbish bin. But the body parts were discovered by a homeless man searching for food. Borelli and Joey Testa were arrested and tried, but acquitted. These were the early days, before the gang had perfected the 'Gemini method' of dealing with its victims. From then on, the crew decided to be more careful.

THE GEMINI METHOD

As the mob's activities increased, DeMeo encouraged his crew to develop a system of dealing with its increasingly regular victims. The scheme was that victims would be lured to a charnel house called the Gemini Lounge in Flatlands, Brooklyn, where DeMeo and his gang of assassins hung out. Entering through a side door, they would be taken to an apartment at the back of the building. As soon as a victim walked in, he would be shot in the head using a gun with a silencer. A towel would quickly be wrapped around his head to catch the blood and someone would stab him in the heart to stop it pumping.

The body would then be dragged into the bathroom, put in the shower and drained of blood. Then the corpse would be laid out on a pool liner in the living room where DeMeo, who had been an apprentice butcher in his youth, had shown the crew how to take bodies apart bit by bit. The smaller the bits the better, because it hindered identification – the head would even be consigned to a rubbish compactor. The body parts would then be dumped at the huge Fountain Avenue landfill in Brooklyn, where it was unlikely that any trace of them would ever be discovered.

DeMeo enjoyed the business of dismembering his victims. Some, though, had to be left intact – as proof of death. Everyone knew that an invitation to the Gemini Lounge was likely to be a death warrant.

By the mid-1970s the DeMeo mob were working more or less directly for the Gambino family, through 'Nino' Gaggi. They carried out Mafia sanctioned hits and processed bodies using their perfected method.

In 1976, when Carlo Gambino died and Paul Castellano took over, DeMeo expected promotion, particularly as Gaggi was close to Castellano. Gaggi put in a good word for DeMeo, but Castellano did not trust him and refused to make him a made man. However, when DeMeo arranged a lucrative alliance with the Westies, an Irish-American gang from Hell's Kitchen, Castellano finally gave in and gave DeMeo his 'button'.

DeMeo continued dealing in drugs, despite the Gambino family's rule against it, but by then he had become too useful as a hitman. He even

used murder to discipline his own crew. Danny Grillo, a gambler who was heavily in debt to DeMeo, was disposed of in the Gemini Lounge.

Now a made man in the Gambino family, Roy DeMeo was well on the way to becoming one of the most feared hitmen in the mob. He killed over a hundred men and disposed of their bodies with assembly-line efficiency.

DEMEO KILLS DEMEO

Harvey Rosenberg, aka Chris Rosenberg, was an important member of the DeMeo crew. In fact, he was so tight with the crew's boss, Roy DeMeo, that he was practically a son to the mobster as well as his second-in-command and often called himself Chris DeMeo.

In the 1970s, cocaine, hashish and Quaaludes all flowed freely, and represented big money. Rosenberg was heavily into drug trafficking, and in 1979 had the opportunity to score a big haul from a loan shark in Florida – one Charles Padnick who, through a Cuban intermediate called William Serrano, had connections with drug merchant called 'El Negro'. As a general rule, Cuban drug lords are not the kind of people to mess with, but Rosenberg thought he'd pull a fast one and secured the funding through connections with the Gambinos.

Padnick, Serrano, and the cousin and girlfriend of the drug merchant met in New York to seal the deal. But as soon as the two groups met, Rosenberg and some others of the DeMeo crew plugged the opposition full of holes and had their bodies dismembered. They then took the drugs and the money.

When news of the double-cross reached the Cubans they demanded prompt restitution and they held the Gambino family responsible. In fact, they promised war unless Rosenberg was executed. The drug lords also demanded that the killing be sufficiently high profile that it would hit the headlines. That way they could be sure the job had actually been done.

The Gambinos agreed. After all, the stunt Rosenberg had pulled was bad for business, making it seem as if the Mafia could not be trusted.

No one wanted that. The order came down – Rosenberg had to go, and Roy DeMeo had to do it. This was bad news for DeMeo, who put off the killing and waited in the hope that maybe things would blow over.

They didn't, of course, and the Cubans became impatient. They sent over some enforcers and were ready to stir things up if Rosenberg wasn't executed soon. With the cartel's enforcers in town and under pressure to fulfil the contract, DeMeo became increasingly paranoid. One evening, in April 1979, when an 18-year-old student named Dominick A. Ragucci, who was selling vacuum cleaners door-to-door to pay for his education, turned up outside his house, DeMeo took him for a Cuban hitman. He and Guglielmo came out wielding guns. Seeing them, Ragucci slammed his car into gear and sped away. The two gunmen jumped into DeMeo's Cadillac and chased after him, firing as they went.

At an intersection, Ragucci crashed into another car. Despite two flat tyres, Ragucci made it another 500 feet before his disabled vehicle shuddered to a halt. DeMeo then jumped from his Cadillac and emptied his pistol into the unfortunate teenager.

Gaggi was furious with DeMeo when he heard about the incident and insisted that he kill Rosenberg before some other innocent civilian got hurt. Rosenberg was reportedly never informed about the Cuban situation and thus had no indication that his life was in danger. On 11 May 1979, he went to the regular nightly meeting with DeMeo and crew at the Gemini Lounge. As he sat with his associates, DeMeo pulled a pistol out of a brown bag on the table and shot Rosenberg in the head, wounding but not killing him. When Rosenberg got up off the floor and stumbled on to one knee, Anthony Senter stood and shot him four more times in the head.

Rosenberg's body was placed in his car, which was driven and left parked on a street near the Gateway National Recreation Area in New York City. Crew member Frederick DiNome then drove by the vehicle while Henry Borelli raked it with sub-machine gun fire, to ensure the murder was a blatant enough to guarantee a mention in the local newspaper. This gave the Cubans proof of the killing and defused the

situation. Witnesses claim that for years afterwards DeMeo expressed genuine regret at having to kill Rosenberg.

HITTING THE HITMAN

But there was more friction in the Gambino family in the form of James Eppolito and his son James Eppolito Jr., two made men. Eppolito Sr. told Paul Castellano that Gaggi and DeMeo were selling drugs. But Jimmy Jr. was out of favour with Castellano after he had appeared on TV's *60 Minutes* news programme with the First Lady, Rosalynn Carter, at a dinner for his crooked children's charity. If this was exposed, Castellano feared that President Jimmy Carter might react by sending a large contingent of FBI agents to New York to smash the Gambinos, so he gave Gaggi and DeMeo permission to whack the Eppolitos. They were duly invited to the Gemini Lounge for a sit-down. Gaggi, DeMeo and Brooklyn wiseguy Peter 'Petey 17' Piacenti went to collect them. On the way, Jimmy Sr. asked to stop so he could relieve himself. As he got out of the car on the service road of the Belt Parkway, Gaggi and DeMeo opened fire, killing both Eppolitos and putting a bullet through the windshield.

A witness alerted an off-duty police officer to the incident. As DeMeo made off, the officer approached Gaggi and Piacenti. Gaggi opened fire – and missed. The cop fired back, hitting Gaggi in the neck and Piacenti in the leg. They were arrested, but DeMeo had made his escape from the scene and was not implicated.

Nevertheless, he was experiencing difficulties from another direction. He had expanded his auto-theft operation and was shipping stolen cars to Kuwait and Puerto Rico. However, his partner in the operation, Vito Arena, had been picked up and agreed to turn state's evidence. This meant that DeMeo would have to appear before a grand jury. Castellano, who had never trusted DeMeo because of his thirst for murder and because he was attracting too much attention from the FBI, put out a hit on him. The problem was that DeMeo had such a fearsome reputation that Castellano was having trouble placing the hit; allegedly even John Gotti turned down the contract.

DeMeo, now paranoid, knew that the hit was coming soon. According to his son Albert, he considered faking his own death and leaving the country. Instead he left the house one day and never returned.

A few days later, on 20 January, his abandoned Cadillac was found outside the Varnas Boat Club in Sheepshead Bay, Brooklyn. The police who towed it away noticed dark stains on the seats. When they got it to the police garage they opened the boot and found the body hidden underneath a chandelier that DeMeo had been due to take for repairs. He had been shot multiple times in the head and had a bullet wound in his hand, assumed to have been the result of throwing his hand up to his face in a self-defense reflex when the shots were fired at him. Anthony Gaggi was suspected by law enforcement officials of being the one who had personally killed DeMeo, although it is likely that crew members Joseph Testa and Anthony Senter were the actual shooters. Other sources say that Gaggi put seven bullets in DeMeo's head in the Gemini Lounge and Richard 'Ice Man' Kuklinski also put in a claim. According to Philip Carlo's 2008 biography of Anthony Casso, DeMeo was killed at Patrick Testa's East Flatbush home by Joseph Testa and Anthony Senter following an agreement with Casso, who was given the contract by Gotti and DeCicco after they were unable to kill DeMeo in autumn 1982. The Casso biography notes that DeMeo was seated, about to receive coffee, when Testa and Senter opened fire. Anthony Gaggi was not present.

ANTHONY GAGGI

Anthony 'Nino' Gaggi's father was a barber from Palermo. Nino was born in 1925 on the Lower East Side of Manhattan, where his mother was a seamstress in a sweatshop. As soon as he was able, Nino was put to work sweeping up and polishing shoes to make a little extra money during the Depression.

Joining a local street gang, he learned to fight alongside Rocky Graziano and Jake 'Raging Bull' LaMotta, both of whom went on to become world middleweight champions. Snatching fruit from barrows

earned Gaggi a beating from the police which fuelled a festering contempt for the law that would last a lifetime.

Gaggi's mother had been a childhood friend of movie star George Raft. Frank Scalise, a founder member of the Gambino family, was his father's cousin. As a child, Gaggi had a clear ambition. 'I only want two things when I grow up,' he said. 'I want to be just like Frank Scalise and, when I die, I want to die on the street with a gun in my hand.'

At 14, Gaggi quit school and went to work in his father's barber's shop. He also delivered flowers. With a little money in his pocket, he quickly learned that gambling was not for him – he could not stand to lose. Instead, he began loan-sharking.

Much to his dismay, his parents bought a farm in New Jersey and moved the family out there. At the age of 17, he tried to escape by enlisting in the army, but even though there was a war on, he was rejected because of his poor eyesight. Again this fuelled his resentment of authority.

His parents found that, as city people, they were not well suited to the farming life, so they moved back to Brooklyn, buying a house in the Italian area of Bath Beach. Gaggi got a job on a truck dock, quickly rising to become supervisor. He hated it but, thanks to Scalise, it became a ghost job. On paper he was an employee and had a legitimate income to show the Internal Revenue Service, but his real income came from loan-sharking.

Gaggi was unequivocal in his praise of his hero. 'Frank Scalise was the finest man I ever met,' he said. 'He was there with Luciano at the beginning of all this. Him and his brother Joe, they were two of the shooters on the St Valentine's hits in Chicago.'

In 1954 Gaggi was charged with running an auto-theft ring but when the case came to trial, witnesses mysteriously forgot what they had seen and he was acquitted.

With the murders of Scalise and Anastasia in 1957, Gaggi's associate Carlo Gambino took over the family. Then Gaggi joined the

hit squad who killed Vincent Squillante, the man who was thought to have killed Frank Scalise and his brother Joe. 'We surprised him in the Bronx,' said Gaggi. 'We shot him in the head, then stuffed him in the trunk, drove to 10th Street, and threw him in a furnace.'

Having now killed, Gaggi became a made man. He brought DeMeo and his crew into the family. From then on, although most of DeMeo's hits were for the family, Gaggi also pursued personal vendettas. Vincent Governara was one of a bunch of teenagers who had subjected Gaggi's sister-in-law to catcalls. When he weighed into them with a hammer, Governara, a boxer, flattened him with a nose-breaking right hook. Afterwards, Governara sensibly moved away, but when he returned to Brooklyn 12 years later, Gaggi planted a concussion grenade in his car. Governara survived, but Gaggi and DeMeo then shot him down in the street in front of 20 bystanders.

On one occasion, Gaggi and his wife Rose were held at gunpoint while burglars ransacked their holiday home in Florida. Figuring that the thieves had been tipped off by electrical contractor George Byrum, who had done some work on the house, DeMeo lured Byrum to a hotel in Miami, shot him in the buttocks, then finished him off in front of Gaggi. They were cutting him up when they were interrupted by contractors fixing the hotel air-conditioning. The maid had to go into therapy after discovering the decapitated corpse.

After the Eppolito killings, Gaggi was shot in the neck by a police officer. As he collapsed, the gun flew from his hand. Despite being warned, Gaggi reached out for it anyway, but did not have the strength to lift it. The officer did not fire again, so Gaggi was denied his most cherished wish – to die in the street with a gun in his hand.

The officer who arrested him, and the witness who saw the killings, went into hiding and the jury was sequestered for the entire trial. However, one of the jurors was engaged to the son of one of Gaggi's loan-shark customers. Consequently, Gaggi was only found guilty of assault and sentenced to a term of 5–15 years. But the verdict was

overturned after Gaggi told the juror under his control to make a false complaint of sexual misconduct about a court official. Just to make sure, DeMeo killed the witness, thereby preventing a retrial. While Gaggi was in jail, his nephew Dominick Montiglio became a drug addict and was arrested for loan-sharking. He then turned state's evidence. Vito Arena also testified against Gaggi. With DeMeo dead, the crew began to fall apart.

Gaggi stood trial for automobile theft and murder alongside Castellano and others. When Castellano was murdered, Gaggi was lead defendant. He was convicted of conspiracy to steal cars. While awaiting a second trial on racketeering and murder charges, he died of a heart attack, aged 52.

CHAPTER 19

THE POLITICS OF THE MAFIA

One entered the world of post-war Italian politics at one's peril. It was a maze of constantly shifting alliances and power blocs, of continually changing governments and of treacherous new conformations, of favours granted and called in and traded. And the whole thing, the whole murky midden of Byzantine manoeuvrings, was fuelled by a compost of patronage and money.

Put at its simplest, politicians in the post-war period had more resources at their disposal than at any other time in the history of Italy and they were able to channel these resources in more or less any direction they wished. It made the best possible sense, then, for them to use this financial clout of theirs to help them remain in office: in other words, to build up a power base via those who now owed them for having been favoured.

Since this was very much the way in which the Sicilian Mafia itself worked, it was relatively easy for them to insert themselves into this system of distribution which, to put it very crudely, meant money in return for votes. So they organized many of the local offices of the Christian Democrats, attracted new members and delivered the votes. When it became clear that this was what was necessary, they moved

357

to take control of such local municipal governments that they didn't already own.

This was a crucial step, since controlling municipal government, particularly in Palermo, gave them the freedom to operate without any hindrance: to pollute and jerrybuild and to get building licences whenever and wherever they wanted them. This was triumphantly achieved during the time of the great construction boom at the end of the 1950s, when two of their own, Salvo Lima and Vito Ciancimino, became mayor and overseer of public works respectively in the same Palermo administration. Tomasso Buscetta later claimed that Lima's father was a made Mafia man, and Ciancimino was almost certainly inducted into the Corleonese family that came to be controlled by Totò Riina. Both were in constant contact with the Mafia, as were their friends Nino and Ignazio Salvo, who made their first fortunes in the lucrative business of tax-collecting.

Once this first step had been achieved (obtaining the freedom to act locally without hindrance or even much interest from its patrons in Rome, just so long as the votes were delivered), the tentacles of *la piovra*, the Mafia octopus, began inevitably to reach upwards. Salvo Lima, by the time he became a national MP in 1968, was both immensely powerful and extremely rich – and he chose the man to whom he now offered the rich plum of Sicily very carefully indeed.

SALVO LIMA, THE SALVOS AND THE 'APOTHEOSIS'

Giulio Andreotti – bat-eared, hunchbacked, bespectacled – had emerged after the war from the Vatican and various Catholic student organizations to become a minister in 1947, aged 28. He'd served in virtually every government thereafter, but he had never been prime

Giulio Andreotti always maintained strong links with Sicily

minister, for his group and influence in the Christian Democrats was too narrowly based. With Lima's help in Sicily, he was at last able to get what he wanted. And so, too, could Lima and his friends.

The Andreottani, as they became known in the island, soon achieved a reputation for unbridled corruption and though Andreotti himself always claimed to have no knowledge at all about what went on there, this notion flew in the face of his reputation as an endless and subtle collector of facts. He regularly visited the island for electoral campaigns and put time aside to discuss Sicilian matters. When the corrupt Ciancimino, having failed to build his own power-base in Sicily, came to visit him in November 1976 to make peace, he and Salvo Lima were graciously received in Andreotti's prime ministerial office. Lima described the meeting as 'aimed at establishing a general pacification of Palermo'.

In 1979, Andreotti flew to Palermo to address a huge rally on behalf of Salvo Lima's candidacy for the European Parliament. To the strains of the national anthem, he arrived on stage with Lima, to be surrounded there by all the major Sicilian players: Piersanti Mattarella, the regional president of the Christian Democrats (shot the following year), their secretary, Rosario Nicoletti (a suicide in 1984 after being accused of collusion with Cosa Nostra), Vito Ciancimino (arrested and convicted as a Mafioso five years later, the first Italian politician to be found guilty of Mafia membership), and Nino Salvo (arrested in the run-up to the Maxi-Trial but dead before sentencing – cousin Ignazio was shot in Palermo in 1992 after being convicted). The rally was followed by a banquet for 300 in the Salvos' Hotel Zagarella outside Palermo. The whole occasion, said a later witness, was 'like an apotheosis' – although Andreotti later claimed not to have known the Salvos at all.

ANDREOTTI MEETS THE COMMISSION

In 1980, Andreotti was back in Palermo again, via a private plane hired by the Salvos, for his first direct meeting with the Commission. He was

there to find out why Piersanto Mattarella had been killed. The venue was a Mafia-owned hunting lodge outside the city. Lima and the Salvos were there and one of the later *pentiti*, who'd been on guard outside the house, heard shouting. Stefano Bontate, the Cosa Nostra boss who was in charge of relations with the politicians and was assassinated by Riina a year later, later told him the message that had been given to Andreotti: 'In Sicily we give the orders. And if you don't want to wipe out the [Christian Democrats] completely, you do what we say. Otherwise we'll take away your vote. Not only in Sicily but … all over southern Italy. You'll only be able to count on the vote up north, and up there they all vote communist anyway. You can make do with that.'

Buscetta, who was a close friend of Bontate's, later described Andreotti's Christian Democrats as 'the political faction of the Cosa Nostra'. Another Mafioso *pentito*, who'd been a Palermo councillor, went further. He called the Christian Democrats a virtual Mafia family, one in which Andreotti was known to the Sicilians as 'Uncle Giulio', in exactly the same way as Riina was known as 'Uncle Totò'. Andreotti, Lima and Bontate almost certainly had a further connection – through freemasonry – in the shape of common membership of a secret masonic lodge called Propaganda Due (P2). And thereby hangs a very dark tale, as we shall see in the next part of the book.

PART SIX

THE 1980S AND 1990S: THE LAW FIGHTS BACK

The 1980s were a difficult time for the Mafia. First, there was the battle in Philadelphia caused by the assassination of not one but two Dons, Angelo Bruno and Philip Testa. Later on, there was the Scarfo/Riccobene conflict, which seemed to send Philadelphia back to the 1930s in terms of open warfare.

Big things were happening in New York, too. The Donnie Brasco affair led to the execution of Dominick Napolitano and the takeover of the Gambino family by the Teflon Don, John Gotti. All in all, it was no cakewalk to be a card-carrying member of the mob.

Cyber-crime, identify theft – organized crime is becoming ever more sophisticated. But have things really changed that much? In the end, it's still all about the money.

But it is possible that as far as the Mafia itself is concerned, there has been a change, a shift in power. The families in New York, Chicago, LA and other big US cities are still formidable, but things are certainly stirring north of the border. It's just possible that there's more going on in Montreal, Toronto and Hamilton than the general public knows about. Let's hope that twenty-first-century law enforcement is on top of the situation.

CHAPTER 20

THE SECOND SICILIAN MAFIA WAR

This, then, was the situation in Palermo in the summer of 1979: Michele Sindona was holed up in a villa belonging to Italian-American doctor and freemason Joseph Miceli Crimi. He was trying to blackmail, under Cosa Nostra direction, the Italian establishment, including Prime Minister Giulio Andreotti, to rescue his banks and reimburse the Mafia's money. The Commission was smarting under the loss of a huge pile of its profits and it was beginning to have a sense that, for the first time, it was not being properly protected by the Christian Democrats. The police and investigating magistrates were now getting too close; the old order was dying and Leggio and Riina were threatening to take over.

It was then that the killings began in earnest. Already Michele Reina, the provincial secretary of the Christian Democrats for Palermo, had been gunned down to get the attention of his political bosses in Rome. Then in late July, Boris Giuliano, the deputy police chief, was shot and killed in the city's Lux Bar – he'd had a suspiciously long meeting with the lawyer Giorgio Ambrosoli, appointed as liquidator in Sindona's banks, in Milan a few days before the receiver had been killed. Next was Cesare Terranova, a crusading judge who'd just taken over as chief examining magistrate in Palermo and had vowed to nail Luciano Leggio as Public Enemy Number One: he was gunned down just 100 yards from his apartment along with his police bodyguard Lenin Mancuso.

This was not the end of the list of what came to be known as 'the illustrious corpses'. On 6 January 1980, Piersanti Mattarella, the Christian Democrat president of the Sicilian region, was killed for standing in Cosa Nostra's way. And within a matter of months there were two more deaths. First was Emanuele Basile, the captain of the carabinieri who'd taken over the investigation of the Mafia's finances from Giuliano. He was shot repeatedly in the back while carrying his four-year-old daughter, who was miraculously unhurt. Then the chief prosecutor of Palermo, Gaetano Costa, was calmly assassinated while browsing at a bookstall near his home.

These killings, coming so quickly together, were unprecedented. They seem to have led to a final split in the Commission, which was by now packed with allies of Riina and Leggio. The last two independent chieftains on the Commission were increasingly isolated, and although an attempt at reconciliation was made by the respected Mafioso Tommaso Buscetta, it was unsuccessful. While on day release from prison, Buscetta fled to Brazil. It was just as well. In Palermo, on 23 April 1981, his friend Stefano Bontate was gunned down on his 42nd birthday while waiting at a traffic light in his Alfa Romeo. Salvatore Inzerillo soon followed him, murdered just as he was about to step into a new bullet-proof car after leaving his mistress's house. The same gun, an AK47, was used in both assassinations.

What followed was a massacre. In 1981 and 1982, there were at least 200 bodies on the streets of Palermo, besides 300 more disappearances – victims of the *lupara biancha*, the 'white shotgun'. One entire Mafia family was wiped out while attending lunches hosted by Riina and Michael 'The Pope' Greco on a single afternoon. The soldiers of Inzerillo and Bontate – even their relatives – were tracked down and killed. Inzerillo's 16-year-old son, who'd threatened to kill Riina, had his right arm – his shooting arm – cut off before he was murdered, his uncle disappeared from his house in New Jersey, and his brother was found in the trunk of a car in New York with his genitals cut off and with dollars stuffed into the mouth of his severed head. Gaetano Badalamenti's nephew – who'd taken over his family after his expulsion – was also assassinated. And not even the mediator Tommaso Buscetta was immune. His two sons, his son-in-law, his brother, his nephew – even the brother of his first wife – either disappeared or joined the list of those shot down.

There were also two more 'illustrious' corpses' in 1982 – and these were the most shocking of all. One was Pio La Torre, a communist member of parliament from Sicily who'd recently proposed a swingeing anti-Mafia law. It proposed making membership of Cosa Nostra a serious crime, permitting access to all banking records when such a crime was being investigated, and allowing the government to seize all assets suspected of amassment by crime. That was bad enough. But the second corpse had all of Italy bearing down on Sicily. He was a national hero: General Carlo Alberto Dalla Chiesa, the newly appointed Prefect for Palermo.

THE ASSASSINATION OF GENERAL ALBERTO DALLA CHIESA

General Dalla Chiesa knew Sicily well. Early in his career he had been stationed in Corleone during the days of Dr Navarra. Later, in the 1960s and early 1970s, he had done another tour of duty as commander of the carabinieri in Palermo. But he'd since achieved national fame by breaking the back of the well-organized terrorist Red Brigades which had paralyzed the country. Now he was expected to do the same for the Sicilian Mafia.

His first official duty was to attend the funeral of La Torre – where workers and young people gathered outside, chanting slogans like *'Lima! Ciancimino! Chi di voi è l'assassino?'* ('Which of you is the assassin?') and *'Governo DC, La Mafia sta lì!'* ('The Mafia is there, inside the Democratic Christian government!'). But he was outfoxed from the start. He demanded special powers from the government, but they never materialized. He

General Dalla Chiesa broke the back of the Red Brigades and was expected to do the same with the Mafia

became increasingly isolated. Using tax records, property deeds and rental records, he did begin to follow a thread of clues deep into the relationship between business, politics and the Mafia – and also into the alliance between the Corleonesi and the families of Catania on the other side of the island. But he didn't get far. On 3 September 1982, four months after his arrival in Sicily, he and his young wife were on their way to a restaurant with his bodyguard when their car was surrounded by gunmen on motorbikes, who forced them off the road and killed them. The assassins included Giuseppe Greco and 21-year-old Giuseppe

Lucchese. It was later said that there had been Mafia surveillance teams all over Palermo that evening, using two-way radios to monitor the Dalla Chiesas' whereabouts.

It seems likely then that his enemies knew that on the very last day of his life he'd paid a secret visit to the American consul in Palermo, asking him to urge the American government to put pressure on the Italians to give him the powers he needed and to pass the proposed La Torre law. He seemed to know that he was being deliberately denied these things. In a newspaper interview shortly before his death, Dalla Chiesa said: 'I have clear ideas about what needs to be done . . . [and] I have already illustrated these ideas to the competent authorities [some time ago]. I hope there will be some very rapid response. If not, we cannot hope for positive results.' He went on, in what sounds like weariness and resignation: 'I believe I have understood the new rules of the game: the powerful government servant gets killed when two conditions intertwine: he has both become too dangerous and at the same time he is isolated and therefore killable.'

Tommaso Buscetta, at the time in Brazil, later said of Dalla Chiesa's death: 'General Dalla Chiesa had to be killed because he was in possession of secrets.' Salvo Lima, the Mafia's representative in government, apparently agreed. He's reported as having said after the La Torre law was finally passed after Dalla Chiesa's death: 'For certain Romans he was more dangerous shoved aside with a pension than as Prefect with special powers.' Why?

THE MAFIA GOES INTO NATIONAL POLITICS

To answer this question, we have to go back to the aftermath of the Second World War and to the founding of the American- (and Pope-) backed Christian Democratic Party. Since 1947 the Christian Democrats had never been out of government – and were, in fact, to remain in power until 1992. Throughout this whole period Sicily – after the first election, at any rate – was a Christian Democratic stronghold; the votes – which represented 10 per cent of the whole Italian electorate – were regularly and reliably delivered by the Mafia. When the Mafia itself successfully got into politics, and took over the machinery of the local party, it was only natural that it should go looking for a patron at the highest level. Its choice fell on the wiliest Christian Democrat of them all, Giulio Andreotti.

When Lima, a former mayor of Palermo, became a member of parliament in 1968, he soon made approaches to Andreotti whose support, he believed, was too narrowly based in and around Rome. At the time Lima belonged to another faction of the Christian Democrats, but, as a close associate of Andreotti's later recalled: 'I met Lima . . . and he said to me: 'If I switch over to Andreotti, I'm not going to come alone, but with my lieutenants, colonels, infantry, fanfares and flags.' We talked for three days non-stop, and when the day arrived for the meeting in Andreotti's office ... Lima really did come as the head of an army.'

As a reward for his support, Lima was made under-secretary at the Ministry of Finance during Andreotti's second term as prime minister, and was made Minister of the Budget in 1974. However, a leading economist at the ministry resigned, having read about Lima's record as Mayor of Palermo, and 11 requests to impeach Lima soon reached parliament. Though none of them was acted on, Lima, in the end, had to be sidelined as a European MP.

THE DEATH AND DOCUMENTS OF ALDO MORO

By that time, as it later transpired, Andreotti had had meetings in Sicily, not only with the entire local Christian Democratic apparatus, but also with the Commission. He was, so to speak, a part of the family – and one very important man knew it: the President of the Christian Democratic party Aldo Moro.

Aldo Moro was the prime minister who commanded one-third of the vote and in the 1970s had forged a 'historic compromise' with the Italian Communist Party which was designed to change the face of Italian politics forever. On the morning of 16 March 1978, he was on his way to the swearing-in of the government of his successor as prime minister, Giulio Andreotti, who would govern for the first time with communist backing. He never arrived at his destination. His car was ambushed by members of the left-wing terrorist Red Brigades, his bodyguards and driver were killed and he was kidnapped. They would return him, they said, if the founder members of the Red Brigades, then in jail, were released.

In the meantime, Moro was 'interrogated' and 'tried' and – according to the communiqués issued by his captors – had written a series of letters to his friends among the Christian Democrats, begging them to negotiate his release. They'd refused. The government said it was not 'in the national interest' to negotiate with terrorists. Besides, it was clear that the letters – which grew increasingly bitter – were either 'written under duress' or actually 'dictated by' the terrorists. Why the government refused to negotiate wasn't clear to many people, since they'd negotiated over hostages with the Red Brigades before. But they remained obdurate – with the honorable exceptance of the socialists in parliament – and Moro was in effect condemned to death. A member of the Sicilian Commission, Pippo Calò, their representative in Rome at the time, explained why, according to a later *pentito*. 'You don't understand,' he'd said when Stefano Bontate had suggested that Cosa Nostra should mount a rescue mission, 'Leaders in his own party don't want him free.' Just under eight weeks after his abduction, Moro's dead body was found in the trunk of a car on the Via Caetani in the centre of Rome.

Less than five months later, anti-terrorist police under General Dalla Chiesa raided an apartment in Milan and arrested nine members of the Red Brigades who were busily typing out copies of letters and notes that Moro hadn't sent and a transcript of his long interrogation. The documents subsequently disappeared, and only an edited version was ever released – and this seemed to do nothing more than reheat old gossip about Andreotti. But it was soon clear that two people at least had seen the full version: first, Mino Pecorelli, the editor of a muck-raking journal, *Osservatore Politico*, and secondly General Dalla Chiesa – and the two of them seemed to have had regular meetings. Pecorelli was shot dead in the street in March 1979 before he could publish the documents. But by then, so it later transpired, Dalla Chiesa had given copies to Andreotti and asked for his comments.

What was in these documents, no one at the time knew. Andreotti later claimed never to have read them. But, in 1990, workmen renovating that very same Milan apartment found hidden behind a plaster panel what seemed to be another complete copy of the Red Brigades' Moro documents, and they were very damning indeed. They announced that a secret anti-communist military network had been set up at the end of the war with the help of the Americans, and was still in existence, that the Christian Democratic Party was funded by the CIA, and that the Italian state had been involved in fomenting right-wing terrorism in the 1970s. They also provided evidence of an extremely close relationship between Andreotti and Michele Sindona, and claimed to have proof that Andreotti had used a nationally owned bank to make loans to his cronies, some of them involving money from Mafia launderers run by the Commission's representative in Rome, Pippo Calò.

If they had been revealed at the time, they would have destroyed Andreotti's career. As it was, they were probably responsible for the death of General Dalla Chiesa. Palermo, after all, was a much more dangerous place than Rome – especially for an isolated man with little real power, and one already being whispered against.

'NDRANGHETA WARS

When he was arrested on 10 October 2012, Domenico Condello was at the top of Italy's 'most wanted' list. He had been on the run for 20 years, yet was found on the outskirts of Calabria's largest city, Reggio Calabria.

The day before he was arrested, the city council there had been dissolved because of its ties to the 'Ndrangheta, the crime organization that runs the 'toe' of Italy.

Formed in the late nineteenth century, the 'Ndrangheta considers itself an 'honoured society' like the Camorra in Naples and the Mafia in Sicily. It, too, is organized around blood ties, with towns and cities run by its 'ndrina (equivalent to a Mafia family), and it observes *omertà*. In the inverted world of organized crime, the name 'Ndrangheta comes from the Ancient Greek word for heroism or manly virtue.

While the 'Ndrangheta confined its activities to rural Calabria, no one took much notice of it, but then it went into the business of kidnapping. Between 1970 and 1991, there were 576 kidnappings in Italy. More than 200 of them were carried out by the 'Ndrangheta. In the province of Reggio Calabria, there is a town named Bovalino. One of its districts is called 'Paul Getty'. This is because, in 1973, John Paul Getty III, the 17-year-old grandson of the oil tycoon Jean Paul Getty, was kidnapped by the 'Ndrangheta. He was held in the hills surrounding the town for five months. The family only paid up after the teenager's ear was mailed to them. A month after he was found alive, the members of the kidnap gang, including a number of 'Ndrangheta bosses, were arrested. Two kidnappers went to jail, but the bosses walked free.

With the arrival of public works and, therefore, government funding in Calabria in the 1980s, skimming off money from the contracts became a huge source of revenue for the gangs. Arguments over how to divide up the spoils led to the first 'Ndrangheta war. Until then, the 'Ndrangheta had been dominated by three regional bosses – Antonio Macrì, Domenico Tripodo and Girolamo Piromalli. The head of the Condello clan – or *'ndrina*, which means 'one who will not bend' – was Pasquale 'Il Supremo' Condello. He is thought to have been one of the squad who killed Antonio Macrì in his home town of Siderno; Macri had tried to stamp out kidnapping and drug trafficking in 1975. His killing started a war that consumed at least 300 lives. One of the casualties was Domenico Tripodo, boss of Reggio Calabria. Opposed by his underbosses, the three De Stefano brothers, Tripodo made a pre-emptive strike, killing Giovanni De Stefano before he himself was stabbed to death in jail.

Pasquale Condello then allied himself with the De Stefanos. Paolo De Stefano was the best man at his wedding and Pasquale's cousins Domenico and Paolo Condello became the De Stefanos' underbosses. But then their sister Giuseppina married Antonio Imerti, the leader of the 'ndrina in Villa San Giovanni, which faces the Strait of Messina. There were plans to build a bridge across the Strait of Messina to Sicily. As the De Stefanos controlled much of the construction in the province, Paolo feared that this new alliance between the Condellos and the Imerti clan might rob him of some lucrative contracts.

A marriage between Paolo's younger brother Orazio De Stefano and Antonietta Benestare, niece of Giovanni Tegano, head of the 'ndrina of the Archi district, sealed an alliance between the De Stefanos and the Tegano clan. Paolo De Stefano then gave orders that Imerti was to be killed. A bomb attack killed three of his bodyguards, but failed to kill Imerti himself. Two days later, Paolo De Stefano was killed. Domenico and Paolo Condello were arrested for the murder.

Meanwhile, in 1985, the Second 'Ndrangheta War broke out with the Condello, Imerti, Serraino and Rosmini clans on one side, and the De Stefano, Tegano, Libri and Latella clans on the other. Over the next six years, more than 500 people were killed in the fighting.

A peace was eventually brokered by 'Ndrangheta bosses from Canada, including Antonio Imerti's cousin Joe from Ottawa and members of the Zito clan from Toronto, along with a delegation from the Cosa Nostra. To keep the peace, a board of control similar to the Sicilian Commission, named La Provincia, was set up.

Domenico Condello was sentenced to life for his part in the De Stefano murder, but he was released in 1990 because the statute of limitation ran out before his appeal was heard. Meanwhile, Pasquale Condello had jumped $100,000 bail after being let out of prison under Italy's leniency rules. Nine arrest warrants were issued for him.

While on the run, Pasquale was sentenced in absentia to four life terms, plus another 22 years for murder, Mafia association, extortion, money laundering and drug-related offences. He was also accused of ordering one of his hitmen to kill Ludovico Ligato, a former head of the Italian State Railways, in 1989.

In 1990 the fugitive Pasquale became a member of La Provincia. Meanwhile Domenico further secured the peace by having two children with Margherita Tegano, though he and his partner did not marry. This left her open to arrest when he went on the run in 1993 and found himself sentenced to life in absentia.

COKE MONOPOLY

After the end of the Second 'Ndrangheta War, the Calabrian clans began importing cocaine from Colombia through the container port at Gioia Tauro. By 2006, they were thought to hold a virtual monopoly on cocaine trafficking in Europe, with an annual turnover of some $50 billion.

In February 2008, 100 policemen surrounded the apartment of Pasquale Condello's 30-year-old son-in-law on the outskirts of Reggio Calabria. A crack five-man team from the carabinieri burst in. They found Pasquale Condello sitting there, with a bottle of champagne and a bottle of fine French brandy on the table. He put up no resistance and was quickly whisked away to northern Italy for interrogation after 18 years on the run. At his trial he was sentenced to four life sentences. Domenico immediately succeeded Pasquale as boss and took his place on the 'most wanted' list.

CUTTING THE TENTACLES

Maintaining close family ties, the 'Ndrangheta remains the most difficult Italian crime organization to crack. Justice authorities in Italy have rated the 'Ndrangheta as the most dangerous existing form of organized crime and believe that the super-secretive organization works with Turkish and Albanian mobs and, through the latter, with the Russian Mafia.

The tentacles of the 'Ndrangheta reached Milan. Wiretaps and secret recordings of members of the Condello clan revealed that they had business contacts with the brothers Giulio, Giuseppe and Francesco Lampada, who were originally from Reggio Calabria but had left to establish themselves in the north of Italy. As the noose tightened, Margherita Tegano, along with Condello's cousins Caterina and Giuseppa Condello and 15 others, were arrested for obstructing Condello's capture. Then, on 10 October 2012, Domenico Condello himself was finally brought to book.

SACRA CORONA UNITA

Along with the Mafia of Sicily, the Camorra of Naples and the 'Ndrangheta of Calabria, there is another crime organization in southern Italy – the Sacra Corona Unita (United Sacred Crown) of Puglia, the 'heel' of the Italian peninsula.

The so-called 'fourth Mafia' was set up in the 1970s when Camorrista Raffaele Cutolo decided to expand his operations into Puglia to make use of the Adriatic ports. He began collaborating with local gangs. By the end of the decade he had formed the Nuova Grande Camorra Pugliese.

However, back in Naples, Cutolo's Nuova Camorra Organizzata was losing ground to the rival Nuova Famiglia. It lost hundreds of soldiers in the 1980–83 Camorra War and in 1983 Cutolo and 1,000 members of the NCO were rounded up by the police.

With Cutolo out of the way, the mobsters in Puglia were formed into the Sacra Corona Unita by Umberto Bellocco of the 'Ndrangheta, who wanted to oppose Camorra influence in Puglia. They offered local crooks a better deal as they did not demand a share of their illicit profits. When Bellocco was also jailed, Giuseppe

Rogoli took over the SCU as an autonomous organization, even though he was in Bari prison at the time.

Using the Mafia as his model, Rogoli moved in on wine and olive oil interests. The SCU then committed a series of frauds, swindles and extortions before engaging in cigarette smuggling and arms and drug trafficking. Soon the SCU developed alliances with its counterparts in Albania, Romania and Russia and received pay-offs from other crime outfits for landing rights on the southeast coast.

The SCU is composed of three società or groupings: the Società Minore, the Società Maggiore and the Società Segreta – Minor, Major and Secret. Candidates must have no police connections. After a period of probation, they are required to swear the oath: 'I swear on the point of this fist, to be faithful to this formal societal body, to reject father, mother, brothers and sisters, up to the seventh generation; I swear to divide hundredth per hundredth and thousandth per thousandth until the last droplet of blood, with one foot in the grave and the other chained in order to give a strong embrace to prison.'

Recruits to the Società Minore must renounce all other affiliations and owe their only allegiance to the SCU. The *picciotto* or apprentice is then formally inducted into the organization as a *manovalanza* or worker.

The Società Maggiore has two ranks: *Lo Sgarro* and *La Santa*. To become a *Sgarro*, you must have committed at least three killings ordered by the SCU. The *Sgarro* are identified by a rose tattoo and can only leave the organization on pain of death. A *Sgarro* occupies a designated territory and can form a *filiale*, a branch or clan of *picciotti*, who report to him.

Sgarri who do well graduate to become *Sante* in a rite performed at midnight. During this ceremony they are given a cyanide pill, a rifle or a pistol, a lemon, a wad of cotton wool, a needle, three white silk handkerchiefs and the so-called *spartenza*, which means 'a division of spoils'. The cyanide allows the *Santa* to choose death rather than collaborate with the authorities and the firearm is for the same purpose, to be used on the *Santa* if he fails to live up to the expectations of the SCU. The lemon is to tend the wounds of comrades; the cotton wool represents Mont Blanc – or Monte Bianco – which is considered sacred; the needle is to puncture the index finger of the right hand; the lemon juice is mixed with the blood as another sign of fidelity; the handkerchiefs represent purity of spirit; and the *spartenza* usually consists of a gift of cigarettes.

Within the Società Segreta, there is a General Council, which makes the decisions. Those who reach those heights have to swear: 'I would rather rip out my heart and hand it to my padrino, have it sliced and distributed to the General Council than betray my sacred brotherhood. I swear, moreover, solemnly, in both good and bad, in calm and tempest, my padrino is inviolable, my brother of blood, and not even a universal flood can put an end to this union, sealed with our blood.'

The SCU consists of some 50 clans with around 2,000 members. Vendettas are particularly brutal. According to one report: 'Often the victim's body is brutally tortured in a procedure of death and revenge. Gouged eyes, severed tongues or genitals, each method of killing corresponds to a sort of Dantesque passage that reveals the 'sin' that irreparably stained the sinner.'

To date, the Sacra Corona Unita has made little headway in North America.

DIABOLIK

Matteo Messina Denaro is a new type of Mafia don, not least because he has slipped the old Mafia's moral straitjacket and emerged as a ladies' man – in defiance of the old Sicilian proverb that giving orders is better than sex.

Some Mafiosi worship Messina Denaro as a saint. Others see him as James Bond – he is said to have an Alfa Romeo 164 armed with machine guns that can be activated at the push of a button. He boasts that he has filled a cemetery all by himself. It is said he is the guardian of Totò Riina's treasure which includes not only a fabulous collection of jewellery, but also the Mafia archive. This is purportedly held in a secret vault under a jeweller's shop in Castelvetrano, which can only be entered using an elevator built into the strongroom. However, Denaro's police files give his profession as 'farmer'.

His father, Francesco Messina Denaro, aka Don Ciccio, was a member of the Cupola, or Mafia Commission, and an ally of the Corleone faction led by Totò Riina and Bernardo Provenzano. He and his two sons, Matteo and Salvatore, were on the payroll of one of the richest families in Trapani. Among its number is Senator Antonio D'Ali, who claimed he had no idea that the Messina Denaros were involved in the Mafia. Francesco and Matteo were employed as estate managers – a traditional job for Mafiosi – while Salvatore was a clerk in the senator's family bank.

Matteo's brother-in-law, Giuseppe Guttadauro, was also a Mafia boss, even though he practised as a doctor. He received patients in his surgery each evening between 5 p.m. and 7 p.m., after it had been open to the *picciotti* who had been collecting protection money.

Taught to shoot at 14, Matteo killed for the first time at 18. His father found him a job as an armed guard to the D'Ali family. During the Mafia wars, he worked for Totò Riina. When Riina ordered the execution of Vincenzo Milazzo, Denaro killed him and strangled his pregnant girlfriend for good measure.

He served as Riina's chief intelligence officer and spied on anti-Mafia judge Giovanni Falcone and former justice minister Claudio Martelli while both were living in Rome in the early 1990s. He also plotted the attack on the TV host Maurizio Costanzo.

In 1993, on Riina's orders, Denaro carried out car bomb attacks on the Uffizi Gallery in Florence and the Basilica of St John Lateran in Rome, which killed ten people and injured 93 others. Law enforcement officials also hold Denaro directly responsible for the murder of another six people, though he claimed to have killed more than 50.

After the bombing campaign, he went underground, using the pseudonym 'Alessio' in his clandestine correspondence with Bernardo Provenzano. It is thought that he attended a clinic in Barcelona, Spain, to treat his myopia (extreme short-sightedness).

However, while being on the list of the world's ten most wanted fugitives, he remained curiously well known. Addicted to video games, he rejoices in the soubriquet of 'Diabolik', after an Italian comic strip character.

THE PLAYBOY DON

According to the press, Messina Denaro is a notorious womanizer who revels in the high life, with an extensive collection of Porsches, designer watches and sharp suits. A detective at Trapani police headquarters said: 'Messina Denaro is generous, he's an effortless conversationalist and he can judge the perlage of a fine champagne.'

He can afford to. He is worth an estimated $3.7 billion.

Time magazine called him the 'playboy don'.

Giacomo Di Girolamo, author of *The Invisible*, a book on the mobster, says: 'Denaro is a modern Mafia boss, the opposite of the traditional image of the 'Godfather'. He has numerous lovers and a child out of wedlock. He knows which businesses to get involved in – and this is primarily drugs.'

His daughter lives with her grandmother in Castelvetrano, along with her mother – who dare not look another man in the eye because she needs to preserve the reputation of her errant lover and her own life.

In 2001 the Italian news magazine *L'Espresso* put him on their cover with the caption: 'Here is the new boss of the Mafia.' The magazine also reported that Denaro had killed a Sicilian hotel owner who had accused him of bedding young girls.

But it was only with the arrest of Provenzano in 2006 that Denaro became 'don of dons'. He did so only then as the result of a vicious

Matteo Messina, aka 'Diabolik'

Mafia war. According to Di Girolamo: 'Denaro is without doubt a very powerful and ruthless man who will stop at nothing to ensure he has utmost control of his territory.'

The FBI say Denaro is the Mafia's principal connection with the South American drug cartels and masterminds the importation of heroin and cocaine into Europe. As well as loan-sharking and extortion, Denaro has moved the Mafia into a new area of moneymaking – renewable energy. Land is bought at a fraction of its true value and sold at a huge profit to developers who want to build solar and wind farms. Then the European Union hands out millions of euros for their construction. Sicily is now dotted with these giant windmills and solar panels, but they have never been connected to the grid. Instead, investments are used to launder Mafia money.

The scale of the operation was revealed when police seized assets worth $1.8 billion from Sicilian businessman Vito Nicastri, who is nicknamed the 'God of the Wind' and is said to be a frontman for Denaro. They included more than 40 companies, nearly 100 properties, seven sports cars and luxury yachts. It was said to be the 'biggest ever seizure of assets linked to Denaro'.

Despite his fame and his continuing criminal activities, Denaro has been on the run since 1993. All the police have to go on are snapshots of him taken 20 years ago. In a bid to track him down they have used a special computer programme to age his image, but they admit that this may be of very little use as he is believed to have undergone extensive plastic surgery in the intervening years.

FOLK HERO

The other strategy open to them is to strip him of his assets. Building firms, cement companies, houses and shops worth around £455 million have been confiscated, along with supermarkets, which are one of the Mafia's main outlets for money laundering. But the forced closure of many branches has angered locals, who see Denaro as their benefactor. He provides jobs for them in the supermarkets and distribution centres that the Mafia has built for money laundering. 'The problem is many people in Sicily feel they have been abandoned by the Italian state,' said Di Girolamo, 'and see Denaro as a heavenly provider. He has given them jobs and money where the state has given them nothing so that's why many are attracted to the Mafia.'

Denaro's name has also been linked to a money-laundering account in the Vatican bank. In all, the state has seized $3.8 billion from him since 2009.

Di Girolamo is convinced Denaro has politicians and police officers on his payroll. He says: 'How else do you explain the fact that Denaro has been on the run for almost 20 years? He has a network of allies and is always on the move – I doubt he is abroad. If he left his home territory, then it would be a sign of weakness and he could lose his grip. I am certain that senior figures within Italian politics and the police are doing their utmost to keep him in hiding.'

Denaro was in the news again in May 2013, when a trial opened in Palermo. It involved senior politicians, who were accused of entering into secret talks with Cosa Nostra during Denaro's bombing campaign in the 1990s.

The elusive Denaro remains a folk hero. People reminisce about giving him a lift or having smoked with him and he is said to have the same appeal as the charismatic Mexican revolutionary Emiliano Zapata. One local mobster, caught on a wiretap planning to abandon his wife and daughter to join his idol on the run, said: 'Better one day as a lion than a hundred as a sheep.'

BIG BUSINESS

According to the Italian trade association, Confesercenti, the Mafia is Italy's richest company with a turnover of more than $172 billion in 2012. It makes a profit of $124 billion, which is equivalent to 7 per cent of the country's gross domestic product.

Confesercenti says that the Mafia is also the biggest bank in Italy with liquid assets of $80 billion. Thanks to extortion and intimidation, millions are handed over in protection money by shopkeepers, restaurant owners, cinemas, construction firms and thousands of other businesses. However, its loan-sharking and extortion practices had led to the closure of more than 190,000 businesses in the previous three years.

The 'Ndrangheta alone turned over $56 billion in 2008 from cocaine, gun-running, human trafficking and extortion rackets. The proceeds are laundered through 'legitimate' businesses such as bars, hotels, pizzerias and factories across Europe, often contracting out operations through alliances with foreign criminal organizations, particularly from China.

According to *pentito* Giuseppe Di Bella, the breakthrough came in 1992, when 'Ndrangheta bosses met their Chinese counterparts in a basement storeroom near Milan to discuss sharing out markets in textiles, clothing, restaurants and other outlets. 'It wasn't just a local agreement; it was a big deal; they were carving up the whole of Italy,' he said.

Drug dealing was outsourced to Africans; Albanians were first given a remit for prostitution and later for arms; the Slavs specialized in trafficking women and were used as hitmen 'when accounts needed settling'.

The recession plays into Mafia hands too: 'their supermarket trolley piled high with bankrupt businesses, answerable to no one', said Di Bella. Bound tightly by almost impenetrable family ties, the 'Ndrangheta has corrupted its way into the political world, organs of government, trade unions, courts and the police. Local elections are rigged and politicians reward their sponsors, often with construction contracts.

The 'Ndrangheta is believed to dominate the earth-moving equipment sector in northern Italy, and the billion-dollar cake of Expo 2015 – the universal exposition to be hosted by Milan – has already been sliced up.

Di Bella gives a chilling picture of the 'Ndrangheta's business methods. A wealthy accountant, who had already been beaten up by his abductors, had a rope tied around his ankles and was lowered slowly from a railway bridge into the moonlit river Adda, some 60 feet below.

'We put his head underwater for about a minute and then pulled him up to let him breathe for another three minutes,' said Di Bella. 'He started screaming, louder and louder. We repeated the process about ten times, until he gave in. By then his voice was so shrill it sounded like a woman's. He promised to do anything we asked him to do. Of course, we wanted his buildings.'

This did not happen in Calabria, or in the Mafia heartland of Sicily or southern Italy, but near the picturesque lakeside town of Lecco, 50 kilometres north of Milan, close to the Swiss border.

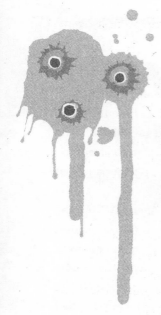

CHAPTER 21

THE PIZZA CONNECTION

The Pizza Connection, as far as American law enforcement was concerned, began in 1971 when US customs agents at New York's docks discovered 82 kilos of 90-per cent pure heroin hidden in a car brought in by an Italian cruise liner. They arrested the Gambino man who eventually took delivery – and he turned out to run a pizza joint. In fact, all the evidence thrown up by the case seemed to have some connection with pizzas and with a pizzeria operator called Michael Piancone. The arrested man ran a Piancone Pizza Palace and two brothers, Salvatore and Matteo Sollena, who were suspected of some involvement, ran several others.

At the time, the investigation didn't get very far. But in 1978 it came alive again. Salvatore Sollena's girlfriend was picked up by New Jersey police for carrying counterfeit money. She was found to be in possession of some real money as well: $51,000 in cash and $25,000 in cashier's cheques. It transpired that she and the Sollena brothers had bought a further $330,000-worth of cashier's cheques, all in values of less than $10,000, which meant that the transaction didn't have to be reported by the bank. These had then been transferred to an account in Palermo.

A year later, US customs found out that a further $4 million had been shipped over the past two years from New Jersey to Palermo, $1 million of it by a small-time pizza operator in New York. And in June that year, Boris Giuliano, the Palermo police chief who would be killed shortly afterwards, found $497,000 in cash in a suitcase at Palermo airport. It had been wrapped in pizza aprons that were traced to a pizzeria owned by Salvatore Sollena in New Jersey.

At the beginning of 1980, the Drug Enforcement Agency (DEA), the FBI and the US customs service decided to come together in a joint operation, and they soon discovered that most of their targets were Sicilians working under the aegis of the two families with the closest connections to Sicily, the Bonannos and Gambinos. The man in charge seemed to be another Sicilian immigrant, Salvatore Catalano. He had organized the killing of Carmine Galante and he owned a bakery and a half-interest in a pizzeria in Queens.

In the autumn of that year, a fancy Mafia wedding was held at the affluent Hotel Pierre in New York, and both Salvatore Catalano and his partner in pizza, Giuseppe Ganci, were guests. Other party-goers included major figures in the Sicilian, Canadian and American Mafias, among them relatives of the late Carlo Gambino, Salvatore Inzerillo from the Sicilian Commission, and money launderers and financial advisers from Montreal, Sicily and Milan. The watching joint task force made a record of the numbers they called during the reception, and the owners of these numbers were then traced and watched. With the net spreading, the task force finally applied for permission to use wiretaps.

It was a slow process. But then, in 1983, the task force had a lucky break. In two separate sting operations in Philadelphia, undercover DEA agents made offers to buy heroin from two suspected dealers, one a pizzeria owner. Both dealers immediately called Ganci's Al Dente pizzeria in Queens, the one he owned with Catalano. The dealers were then watched as they made the buys (for over $350,000). By following Ganci's movements, as well as his telephone calls, the team were able to start making a list of his associates, who were also then tapped.

Illegal immigrants went to work in New York's pizza parlours, bringing smuggled drugs with them – this became known as the Pizza Connection

It was time-consuming and difficult work. Not only did the members of the Pizza Connection talk in Sicilian dialect, they also used public pay phones rather than the phones at their restaurants and homes – and they changed phones and talked all the time. As a result, the problems of wiretapping and transcription of conversations rapidly mushroomed. Help, though, was soon at hand. For in another part of the investigation, the team was following the trail of the heroin money, and that soon came up trumps.

Mafia Killings 57

Cesare 'The Tall Guy' Bonventre, Garfield, New Jersey, 16 April 1984

Cesare Bonventre was a 'Zip', a nickname given to native Sicilians brought over to America by Carmine 'Lilo' Galante. He was one of the bodyguards who'd been sitting with Galante on that hot day in June when his boss was splattered all over the sticky back patio of Joe and Mary's restaurant in Brooklyn. Bonventre, along with Baldassare Amato, should have been looking out for Galante, even taking a bullet for the mob boss. Galante trusted his Zips when he wouldn't trust anybody else. But there's ample evidence to suggest that both Amato and Bonventre were in on the hit. Galante should have known – in the Mafia, there can be no trust.

The Zips probably got their name because of the fast way they spoke the Sicilian dialect, so fast that the American Mafioso could hardly understand them – the words just zipped by. The term was not meant as a compliment. The North American mob did not like the Zips; they were too violent, too secretive and not trustworthy. The antipathy was mutual.

Cesare Bonventre was a high earner in the drug trade. No doubt learning a lot from Galante, he was heavily involved in heroin trafficking. A scheme called the Pizza Connection smuggled drugs into North America on a billion dollar, international scale. Once the narcotics reached the United States, they would be passed through various pizza parlours, where the stuff could be distributed and money could be laundered – hence the name Pizza Connection.

By early 1984, the FBI had begun to catch on to the Pizza Connection and were issuing indictments like Halloween candy. By this time, Bonventre also had other problems. He had drawn the ire of Bonanno family acting boss Joseph Massino, who viewed him as a threat. With two strikes against him – a possible pending trial and Massino – Bonventre could not be long for this world.

It happened on 16 April 1984. Bonventre had been picked up by Salvatore Vitale and Louis Attanasio for a meeting that was to take place at a glue factory in Wallington, New Jersey. Once the group had driven into the factory, Attanasio unloaded two bullets into Bonventre's head. It's said that Bonventre, whose nickname 'The Tall Guy' was because of his height (6 feet 9 inches, though this may be an exaggeration) shrugged off his wounds and grabbed the steering wheel in an attempt to crash the car. When the car careened to a stop, Bonventre tried to drag himself across the factory floor in a bid for safety. But the game was up, of course. Attanasio stood coolly over Bonventre's struggling form and finished him off with two more shots to the head. Bonventre's body was hacked to pieces and dumped in three 55-gallon glue drums.

WHERE THE MONEY GOES

Phones were a problem for the Pizza Connection, but so was the money: huge amounts of it, mostly in small bills paid over by street-corner addicts. At first this had not been too much of a problem – the money would simply be picked up in suitcases and flown to Switzerland. But then the Connection had to start using a special – and highly athletic – money-changer, whose job it was to pick up the cash each week and run it from bank to bank in New York, turning it along the way into cashier's cheques, all of them for under $10,000. Soon even that wasn't enough. So the money-changer took to hiring private planes and freighting the money, millions of dollars at a time, to a discreet private bank in the off-shore tax haven of Bermuda. From there, it could be passed on to Switzerland.

This worked well for a while, but then the volume of money increased even more and special squads of Swiss couriers had to be brought in – their job simply to pick up as much money as they could and fly it straight back to Switzerland. The problem now was that with so many people involved there were inevitably thefts. So, in the end, the Connection took the path the Mafia was to follow from then on: they turned to the major financial institutions.

Over a period of less than six months in 1982, a Swiss financier called Franco Della Torre deposited at least $20 million in accounts at Merrill Lynch and E. F. Hutton in New York's financial district. The money was then passed through finance companies he'd set up in and around Lugano and it was laundered by being moved through yet more accounts till it reached its destination: either in a Swiss bank or in the account of a Mafia-fronted enterprise in Italy. Investigators believe that during the six years the part of the Pizza Connection they were watching operated, $1.6 billion of profit was cleaned in this and other ways.

The main heroin suppliers to the Connection were Peppino Soresi in Sicily, known as 'the doctor from far away', and Gaetano Badalamenti: the same Gaetano Badalamenti who'd been expelled from both the Commission and the Mafia in Sicily and whose nephew had later been killed by Riina. Badalamenti was operating from Brazil, and he was in regular contact with the Connection, either through a nephew who lived in Illinois or directly via the pay-phones. In October 1983, the surveillance team learned via the pay-phones that the Connection was in need of large deliveries from one or both of their suppliers. The deliveries were expected at the start of 1984. But there were delays, prevarications and arguments about terms of payment and delivery. Soon tempers in New York, Brazil and Sicily were getting frayed. Finally, Badalamenti demanded a crash meeting with his nephew in Madrid: FBI and DEA agents, deciding this was much too good an opportunity to miss, went along.

Badalamenti was arrested in Madrid on 8 April 1984. The next morning, with coordinated arrests in Italy, Switzerland and the United States, the Pizza Connection was closed down.

CHAPTER 22

THE DON OF TWO WORLDS

On the day of Gaetano Badalamenti's arrest, Tommaso Buscetta was in jail in Brazil, facing extradition to Italy and a meeting with Palermo prosecuting magistrate Giovanni Falcone. He wasn't to know it at the time, but in a sense he and Falcone were two of a kind. Falcone was a native Palermitan, one of the most knowledgeable men on earth about the workings of the Sicilian Mafia. From almost the first days of his appointment he'd been drawn into the Mafia's webs, because that was where all his cases seemed to lead him. And he'd been encouraged in this by his boss and close friend, Rocco Chinnici, the successor as chief prosecutor of the murdered Cesare Terranova.

When 233 kilos of refined heroin was found on a ship in the Suez Canal, Falcone had looked into the heroin traffic between Southeast Asia and Sicily. He'd even taken on the tax-collector millionaires, Nino and Ignazio Salvo. He'd had the financial police search their Palermo offices and homes and remove 30 cartons of documents, and had found out some interesting things: that 97 per cent of the money the cousins had spent on their opulent Zagarella Hotel in Palermo, for example, was paid for by the Italian government and that the hotel was a favourite for Mafia celebrations and for those of the ruling Christian Democrats.

A wedding party given by a Sicilian parliamentarian for 1,800 guests hadn't cost him a single lira.

With Chinnici, Falcone had also signed the warrant for the arrest of Totò Riina and the members of the Palermo Cupola for the murder of General Dalla Chiesa. And then, three weeks later, in July 1983, he'd had to attend the funeral of what was left of his friend Chinnici, killed by a car bomb along with his driver, two bodyguards and the doorman of his apartment building. Michele Greco was later sentenced to life imprisonment for Chinnici's assassination.

Falcone was a serious man; so was Buscetta. When they finally met in the Rebibia prison in Rome they must have both recognized as much. Buscetta began talking, and went on talking for almost two months – and what he said was to shake the Mafia on both sides of the Atlantic to its very foundations.

'REVIVING THE MAFIA'S HONOUR'

Tommaso Buscetta was born in Palermo in July 1928, the son of a glass-maker. He left school at 14, and a year later came to the attention of the Mafia – or Cosa Nostra, as he called it, identifying its real name for the very first time – when he killed a number of German soldiers. This was enough to qualify him for entry into 'the Honoured Society'. He was inducted into the Porta Nuova family by its boss, Gaetano Filippone, at the age of 18.

For a while he worked in the family glass-making business. He married his pregnant girlfriend but couldn't seem to settle down. He worked for a time in Turin and even briefly became a trade union activist back in Palermo. Finally, in 1948, he emigrated to Argentina with his wife and two children. He set up glass factories, first in Buenos Aires and then in São Paolo, Brazil. But his wife couldn't settle. So in 1951 – reluctantly – he returned to Sicily with his family.

Buscetta spoke wistfully to Falcone about the old traditions of Cosa Nostra and the 'men of respect' he encountered when he arrived back in

Sicily. He clearly regarded the new breed of Mafiosi – those who'd killed seven members of his family, including two of his sons – as betrayers of a long and honorable tradition. And he began to tell Falcone the long story of his life, beginning with his first meetings with Lucky Luciano in the early 1950s, the Palermo summit with Joe Bananas in 1957 and Leggio's killing of Dr Navarra the following year, which he said was the beginning of the end of the old traditions. He talked about the setting up of the Commission, in which he'd played a major role and about the first Mafia Wars of the 1960s, which he'd fled, first for Mexico and then the United States.

About his own cime connections, Buscetta was uncharacteristically reticent. But it was clear to Falcone as Buscetta told his story – the structures of Cosa Nostra, the make-up of the Commissions, the names of those involved in the drugs trade – that he'd been a man of great influence. He'd probably been involved in the early stages of the Pizza Connection; he'd almost certainly had a hand in the takeover by the Sicilians of the Corsican networks in Latin America; and he may even have been responsible, along with Michele Zaza of Naples' so-called 'New' Family, for the coordination of cocaine exports to Europe and the United States. But Falcone didn't care in the end. Buscetta was known as the 'Don of Two Worlds', the most important Mafia witness ever to confess voluntarily – and what he was saying was gold dust.

About halfway through their sessions, Falcone called in his American counterpart, who had become close to Buscetta's third wife. Together they began to talk about the possibility of Buscetta giving evidence on both sides of the Atlantic. Buscetta quietly agreed. He didn't want any special consideration for himself, he said, but he would be glad if help could be given to his family. He quite clearly believed that what he was doing was for the compromised honour of the old days and ways, the old Cosa Nostra.

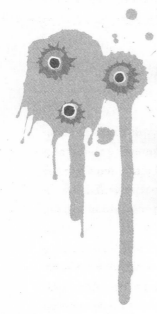

CHAPTER 23

OPERATION SAN MICHELE

O n the basis of Buscetta's testimony and what Falcone and his fellow members of the Sicilian Anti-Mafia Pool already knew, Operation San Michele was launched in the early morning of 29 September 1984. Armed with more than 350 warrants, police closed off the streets of Palermo and began their arrests, pulling Mafia leaders and soldiers alike out of bed. A month later they repeated the process and brought in more. In all, there were over 500 warrants issued. Though the Grecos and Totò Riina remained underground, the operation was a brilliant success. Three of the warrants were for the ex-land assessor and mayor of Palermo, Vito Ciancimino, and the fabulously rich cousins, Nino and Ignazio Salvo. The way to what was known as 'the Third Level' of the Mafia had been opened up.

Three months after the arrests of the Salvos – again on the evidence of Buscetta and what the American agencies had already found out via their wiretaps and hidden microphones (including one in a Mafia boss's car) – the entire New York Commission was arrested: Paul 'Big Paulie' Castellano of the Gambino family, Phil 'Rusty' Rastelli of the Bonannos, Anthony 'Fat Tony' Salerno of the Genoveses, Tony 'Tony Ducks' Corallo of the Luccheses and Gennaro 'Gerry Lang' Langella,

acting head of the Colombo family. Their average age was 70 years old. Their average bail was over $2 million each. They raised it in a matter of minutes.

After juridical moves, which involved some separate trials and the addition of other defendants, such as the head of the Colombos, Carmine Persico, as well as one of the hitmen who'd killed Carmine Galante, Anthony 'Bruno' Indelicato, the trial opened on 8 September 1986. Buscetta was the first and most important witness for the prosecution.

But there were others, including an assassin who had turned state's evidence because he couldn't bear to be separated from his boyfriend. There were also hours and hours of incriminating tapes. After four months listening to them all, the judge sentenced all those accused of belonging to 'an ongoing criminal enterprise' to 100 years each in prison, except for Indelicato, who got 45 years for the murder of Galante. The judge said of one of the defendants, but it could have been applied to them all: 'You have essentially spent a lifetime terrorizing this community to your financial advantage.'

One defendant, though, was missing from the sentencing: Paul Castellano, who had been generally reckoned to be losing his grip, judging by the evidence of the tapes to which the American agencies, and now the defence lawyers, had been listening. He had issued an edict against heroin several years previously which had seriously destabilized his family.

Now his house had been bugged, he couldn't control the union locals who had previously been in his pocket, and he was intending to appoint as his underboss a man who was no more than a chauffeur but with whom he discussed Commission business. A few days before Christmas 1985, both he and the aspirant chauffeur were gunned down in Manhattan by three men in trenchcoats and fedoras. The murder was almost certainly ordered by John Gotti, an ambitious *capo* in Castellano's Gambino family, but he must have had permission from the Commission.

JOHN GOTTI

Born to a family of Italian immigrants, Gotti was one of 13 children, five of whom became made men in the Gambino family. When he was ten, Gotti's family moved to Sheepshead Bay, Brooklyn. From an early age, his ambition was to become one of the wiseguys he saw on the streets. By 12, he was running with a local street gang. At 14, while trying to steal a cement mixer, he crushed his toes, an accident which left him with a permanent limp.

A perpetual truant, Gotti dropped out of school for good at 16. Between 1957 and 1961, as a member of the Fulton-Rockaway Boys, he was arrested five times, but the charges were dismissed or reduced, so he only served probation.

Married in 1962, he took legitimate jobs as a presser in a coat factory and a truck driver's assistant. The following year, he was jailed for 20 days for auto theft. Charges of petty larceny, unlawful entry and possession of bookmaking records followed. In 1966, he returned to jail for attempted theft.

That year he became an associate of a Mafia crew working out of the Bergin Hunt and Fish Club in Ozone Park, Queens, who targeted JFK Airport by carrying out truck hijackings.

In 1967, Gotti was arrested after driving out of United Airlines' cargo area with $30,000-worth of women's clothing. While out on bail he was arrested again for hijacking a truck carrying cigarettes worth $500,000 on the New Jersey Turnpike.

He served fewer than three years in the federal penitentiary in Lewisburg, Pennsylania.

On his release, he went to work for his father-in-law's construction company and returned to the Bergin crew where he became acting *capo* at the age of 31.

He reported to Gambino underboss Aniello Dellacroce at the Ravenite Social Club in Manhattan's Little Italy. When Dellacroce was jailed for tax evasion, Gotti moved up, taking orders directly from family boss Carlo Gambino.

Mafia Killings 58

John Favara, New York City, 28 July 1980

Furniture warehouse manager John Favara lived on the next block to John Gotti in the Howard Beach area of Queens, New York. His adopted son Scott was a friend of Gotti's children and Favara had a close friend who had joined the mob.

On 18 March 1980, 12-year-old Frank Gotti was killed when he darted out from behind a dumpster on a motorized minibike and was hit by Favara's car. Favara told the police he had been momentarily blinded by the sun. Investigators accepted that the crash was an accident and no charges were brought.

When Favara went to apologize to Frank's mother, Victoria Gotti, she attacked him with a baseball bat. For months he was subjected to harassment and death threats, and the word 'murderer' was spray-painted on his car. Not surprisingly, the family decided to move away.

On 28 July, three days before he was due to move from Howard Beach, Favara was grabbed while he was leaving work on Long Island and thrown into a van. Neither Favara nor his car were ever seen again. The police were told that Gotti had cut Favara up with a chainsaw while he was still alive. The dead man's remains were stuffed in a barrel of concrete and thrown off a pier in Sheepshead Bay. When questioned, Gotti said: 'I'm not sorry the guy's missing. I wouldn't be sorry if the guy turned up dead.'

It is now believed that John Favara was shot dead by hitman Charles Carneglia and parts of his body were dissolved in acid.

In March 1970, flanked by FBI agents, Carlo Gambino, 67, reputed to be the Mafia's 'Boss of all Bosses', was led from FBI headquarters following his arrest for plotting to rob the crew of an armoured car containing $6 million.

When Carlo's nephew Manny Gambino was kidnapped and killed, Gotti was part of the hit team that took out Jimmy McBratney, thought to be responsible. After a plea bargain, Gotti was sentenced to four years for attempted manslaughter. Released after two, he became a made man of the Gambino family, now under the leadership of Paul Castellano.

In 1984, Gotti was charged with assault and robbery after an altercation with refrigerator mechanic Romual Piekcyk. The following year, he was indicted for racketeering. One of his co-defendants, 'Willie Boy' Johnson, turned out to be an FBI informant.

Mafia Killings 59

Wilfred 'Willie Boy' Johnson, New York City, 29 August 1988

For a very long time, Wilfred Johnson played both sides of the fence. It must have been for 16 years or so that he fed the FBI information while working for the Gambino family in John Gotti's crew. It's a considerable time to keep a secret like that under wraps. Maybe Johnson felt that the mob owed him something, and he was going to make darn sure that they paid.

A pal of John Gotti's from a long way back, Johnson began to feed information to the FBI in around 1966. It was at that time that he went to prison on a robbery charge. During his stay in jail, Johnson believed – had been assured, apparently – that *caporegime* Carmine Fatico would provide for his wife and children while he was away, making sure that the family could pay their bills and wanted for nothing. That was the mob way, as Johnson understood it – a perk of being an associate. Fatico did no such thing and Johnson's wife was forced to go on welfare to make ends meet.

Once Johnson realized that Fatico had let him down, he started to look around a little bit, to see the world in a new light. His gaze fell on John Gotti. Though Johnson and Gotti were supposedly pals, Johnson began to feel that he had always been given second-hand jobs, the ones that nobody else wanted, and that he was being treated as little more than a gofer. Johnson also started to notice Gotti's slurs on his background. He was half Italian on his mother's side; his father was of Native American descent, either Mohawk or Cherokee (sources differ on this). Maybe Gotti was just trying to be funny, but every so often he would refer to Johnson in less than savoury terms, all the while professing to be the man's friend. Johnson found it harder and harder to let these comments slide.

Yet despite this, and despite the fact that Johnson was basically ratting out the mob, he refused to testify against the Gambinos – that he just wouldn't do. For one thing, if he ever did testify against them, he knew his life would be over.

This situation continued for quite a while until 1985, when John and Gene Gotti, Johnson and others were indicted on RICO charges. The authorities had been trying to build a case against Gotti for some time, and one prosecutor – Diane Giacalone – decided she wanted to use Johnson to bring the Don down. Giacalone's plan was to out Johnson as an informant. That way he would be forced to turn state's evidence in order to save his life. Afterward, he would be allowed into the Witness Protection Program. And Giacalone did just that. When she outed Johnson, he vehemently denied the accusations, but the cat was now out of the bag. Yet true to his promise to himself, Johnson refused to testify against Gotti.

Johnson was on his own then, with no WPP to guard him. On the morning of 29 August 1988, he headed for his car, which was parked outside his Brooklyn home, to go to work. Hearing the shots, Johnson's wife ran from the house, but it was too late – he was dead. And after all of this, after Johnson's cover was blown and his life forfeited, the prosecution's case against Gotti fell through. The Teflon Don was acquitted.

When Castellano was indicted for racketeering and other charges, he appointed Gotti acting boss, alongside Thomas Bilotti. Then Castellano discovered that Gotti was involved in narcotics, against Gambino policy. When Dellacroce died, Bilotti became underboss. This was considered a slight by Gotti and the Dellacroce family.

On 16 December 1985, Castellano was shot dead outside Sparks Steak House in Manhattan while Gotti and Salvatore 'Sammy the Bull' Gravano watched from their car. In front of a street full of Christmas shoppers, hitman Tony 'Roach' Rampino also pumped six shots into Bilotti, who was chauffeuring Castellano. Following the hit, Gotti took over as head of the Gambino family with Gravano as underboss.

Mafia Killings 60

Paul 'Big Paulie' Castellano, New York City, 16 December 1985
Paul Castellano was not the most popular Mafia Don ever to come down the pike. He was somewhat standoffish, aloof. In fact, there was a large chasm that existed between Castellano and the average soldier. The regular street thug felt it. What's more, some made men in the Gambino family felt that Castellano should never have become boss at all. One of those Mafiosi was John Gotti.

In the late 1970s through the early 1980s, the Gambino family was split into two factions – not a good thing at any time. One faction was loyal to Castellano, while the other felt more loyalty to Aniello Dellacroce. The latter had been in the Mafia for years, had been Carlo Gambino's underboss, and should have become the boss when Gambino died; at least that's what the Dellacroce faction felt. But Gambino wanted the leadership to stay in the family, so he bequeathed the top spot of the Gambinos to his brother-in-law, Castellano. Dellacroce was fine with this, at least outwardly. He was an old hardliner, and if the big boss wanted Castellano, then Castellano it would be.

Castellano was another one of those bosses who banned dealing in narcotics yet lined their own pockets with drug money. Gotti was a member of the Dellacroce faction, and he was dealing in drugs – hard dealing, hard drugs. And the ambitious Gotti thought he'd make a much better successor to Gambino than Castellano.

Things simmered for a while, with neither Castellano nor Gotti really doing anything while Dellacroce was still alive. The old mobster seemed to be keeping a lid on things. But on 2 December 1985 Dellacroce passed away from cancer, and the situation came to a head pretty fast. With Dellacroce gone, there was nothing to stop Castellano from using Gotti's defiance of the narcotics ban to whack Gotti and his whole crew. The only thing was, Gotti saw it coming and got there first.

On the evening of 16 December 1985, Big Paulie Castellano arrived at the famous and pricey Sparks Steak House on East 46th Street in Manhattan. He was there to attend one of those supper meetings that mobsters favour. As he was exiting his Lincoln – along with his chauffer and underboss, Thomas Bilotti – three men dressed in white trenchcoats and wearing black Russian hats stepped out of the milling crowd. Pulling out revolvers, the men shot Paulie six times, then plugged Bilotti full of lead.

It was a smooth hit; afterward, Gotti and Sammy 'The Bull' Gravano drove by the bodies to make sure the job had been done. Gotti must have been pleased with what he saw – there was nothing now to stop him from becoming boss of the Gambinos.

'I FORGOTTI'

Unlike other gangsters, Gotti did not shy away from the public eye. The 'Dapper Don' was always immaculately turned out. A celebrity gangster, he appeared to be above the law. At Gotti's trial for felony and assault in March 1986, the complainant Romual Piekcyk said that he could not see his attackers in the courtroom. When asked to describe the men who had assaulted him, he said: 'To be perfectly honest, it is so long ago I don't remember' – prompting the famous *New York Daily News* headline: 'I FORGOTTI'.

Piekcyk was declared a hostile witness and the charges against Gotti were dismissed.

Two weeks later, after a vacation in Florida, Gotti was back in court on racketeering charges. Standing trial alongside him were his younger brother Gene and five other members of the Gambino family. Not present was Aniello Dellacroce's son, Armond, who had also been indicted in the federal investigation into the Mafia Commission. Four days after his father's death, Armond pleaded guilty to racketeering and conspiracy charges, contravening Gotti's instructions that no member should admit that the Gambino family even existed. Frightened for his life, Armond disappeared before sentencing. Two years later, in 1988, his body was found in a house in the Pocono Mountains of Pennsylvania where he had been hiding out. The police reported that they had discovered he had been hiding in the vicinity and they were close to finding his hideout. A post-mortem concluded that he had died of a cerebral haemorrhage brought on by alcohol poisoning.

'THE TEFLON' DON'

With Aniello Dellacroce dead, Gotti was the chief defendant. He was charged with seven 'predicate acts' – that is, crimes committed to further an illegal enterprise. Three of these were crimes for which he had already served time: two hijackings and the killing of James McBratney. Under the RICO laws, the McBratney manslaughter was elevated to murder.

Bringing the charges, the assistant US Attorney Diana Giacalone took seven months to present the evidence, which included the testimony of almost a hundred witnesses and 30 hours of taped conversations. But Gotti's defence attorney, Bruce Cutler – himself a former assistant DA – claimed that the taped conversations were innocent and some of the witnesses were confessed criminals, murderers and kidnappers who had benefited by getting lighter sentences for giving testimony. They were hardly credible, he argued. Besides, wasn't it double jeopardy to punish someone again for crimes for which he had already done time? Gotti was acquitted. He returned to his home in Ozone Park, in Queens, where yellow ribbons had been tied around the trees. The press were now calling him 'the Teflon Don' because nothing seemed to stick. Indeed, an indictment for shooting union official John O'Connor failed to stick, too. Instead, as boss of the United Brotherhood of Carpenters and Joiners of America, O'Connor was convicted of racketeering.

While Gotti was immune to the law, he also seemed above retribution from the mob itself. When Vincent 'the Chin' Gigante, head of the Genovese family, ordered a hit on him, the FBI warned Gotti. He was therefore on his guard and the killers only managed to assassinate Gotti's underboss, Frank DeCicco.

With others in jail on RICO charges, Gotti promoted Gravano to underboss. He was also kicking back around $100,000 a month from the construction industry. Although younger Mafiosi were attracted to Gotti's flashy suits, his high profile was also attracting the attention of the FBI. They prepared a new RICO case, based around the murder of Castellano. When FBI agents managed to plant a bug in the apartment above the Ravenite Social Club – Gotti's new headquarters on Mulberry Street in Manhattan's Little Italy – Gotti was caught on tape discussing murder and other crimes. One soldier, they heard, had been 'whacked' because he did not come quickly enough when he was called. Another had been killed because Gravano said he had talked about Gotti behind his back. Gotti trusted Gravano to the point that he designated him acting boss if Gotti was taken off the streets. Meanwhile, Frank LoCascio took over as acting *consigliere*.

In December 1990, Gotti, Gravano and LoCascio were indicted for criminal enterprise, obstruction of justice, income tax evasion, loan-sharking, illegal gambling and four counts of murder. They were denied bail, so Gotti's son, John Gotti Jr., took over the day-to-day running of the organization.

Although Gravano had been a mobster since his twenties – first indicted for murder in 1974 – he had never served time before. Prisons used to be run by mobsters, almost as retirement homes. But by 1990 African-Americans made up the majority of prisoners, and Italian-Americans were definitely second-class citizens.

Gravano heard that Gotti was saying he had played the peaceful boss who spent his time restraining Gravano, who was a 'mad dog' killer. Eventually Gravano turned state's evidence in return for a reduced sentence. He admitted to having been involved in 19 murders, ten of which Gotti had ordered. These included the murders of Castellano and Bilotti. Nevertheless, Gotti still thought he would walk. But the jury returned 13 guilty verdicts. Gotti was sentenced to five life terms – four without parole – plus 65 years and a fine of $250,000.

He was incarcerated in the federal penitentiary at Marion, Illinois – reputed to be one of the toughest prisons in the United States. After being beaten up by a fellow inmate, he effectively spent the rest of his life in solitary confinement, only leaving his cell for one hour a day. He died of throat cancer in 2002.

Gravano was sentenced to five years, but after the time he had already done was taken into consideration, he served only one. On his release, he moved to Phoenix, Arizona, where he was rearrested in 2000. The following year, he pleaded guilty to drug trafficking charges and was sentenced to another 20 years.

CARMINE PERSICO

Carmine Persico is the last of the old-time New York Mafia bosses. He rose through the ranks from street thug to the head of the Colombo family, a position he held for 40 years, although for much of that time he has been behind bars.

During the Depression, the Italian and Irish denizens of the Carroll Gardens and Red Hook neighbourhoods of Brooklyn, where Persico was brought up, scraped a living working on the nearby waterfront or in

American mobster Carmine Persico, age 17, after being arrested on charges of fatally beating another youth in Brooklyn, New York, 1951

factories. The Persico family was well off. His father was a stenographer for a prestigious Manhattan law firm and brought home a weekly pay packet even in the hardest times. The area was run by the Profaci crime family. The big bankrolls of the wiseguys drinking coffee and playing cards outside the local social or athletic clubs impressed the Persico brothers – Alphonse, Carmine and Theodore. At 16, Carmine dropped out of school and joined a street gang called the South Brooklyn Boys.

At 17, he was arrested for the fatal beating of another boy during a brawl in Prospect Park. This was his first felony, and the charges were dropped, but they brought him to the attention of Profaci *capo* 'Frankie Shots' Abbatemarco, who employed the skinny, 5-foot 8-inch teenager as an enforcer. Persico then worked his way up through bookmaking and loan-sharking rings to burglaries and hijacking. By his mid-20s, he was a made man.

During the 1950s, Persico stacked up over a dozen arrests. His rap sheet spanned the whole gamut of mob activity – running numbers, dice games, assault, harassing a police officer, burglary, loan-sharking, hijacking and possession of an unregistered firearm. But he never spent more than two weeks in jail. Profaci lawyers got felony charges reduced to misdemeanours, while plaintiffs and witnesses changed their minds or were out of town at the time of the trial. Fines were considered a business overhead.

LEAD-UP TO THE GALLO WARS

Persico was tight with the Gallo brothers – Larry, Albert and 'Crazy Joe'. When Albert Anastasia, the head of Murder Inc., was gunned down while having a shave in the barber's shop of the Park Sheraton Hotel, Joey Gallo claimed it was the work of his 'barbershop quintet'. One of them was thought to be Carmine Persico.

When Frankie Shots was murdered, Persico and the Gallo brothers expected to inherit a large part of his Brooklyn rackets as a reward for icing Anastasia. Instead, Profaci's cronies were rewarded. The Gallo faction responded by kidnapping Profaci's brother-in-law and underboss Joe Magliocco, along with Joe Colombo and four other *capos*. The hostages were released after Profaci lifted the higher tribute payments he had demanded from the Gallos. But Profaci quickly reneged on this deal and war broke out.

Recently retired mob boss Frank Costello convinced Persico that his loyalties lay with Profaci. On 20 August 1961, a police sergeant on a routine inspection of the Sahara Lounge, a bar in South Brooklyn, found Persico strangling Larry Gallo with a rope. Persico fled and Gallo refused to press charges. This perfidy earned Persico the soubriquet 'The Snake'.

The Gallos struck back, peppering Persico's car with bullets. He was hit in the hand and arm, but he, too, obeyed the rule of *omertà* and refused to name the shooters. While his supporters said he had been hit in the face and spat out the bullets, Persico referred to his wounds as paper cuts. But he never regained the full use of his left hand.

In the 'Gallo War' that ensued, nine combatants were killed and three more disappeared, presumed dead.

Mafia Killings 61

Joseph Gallo, New York City, 7 April 1972

He was called 'Crazy Joe', and with good reason. After being arrested in 1950 he was immediately diagnosed with schizophrenia. But Gallo didn't let that condition keep him back, and liked to view himself as a Renaissance man. During one lengthy prison stay, he availed himself of his extra leisure time to read the works of Kafka, Dumas and Machiavelli. If it hadn't been for the war that Gallo had started with mob boss Joseph Profaci, maybe he could really have made something of himself – he 'could have been a contender'.

But at the very least Gallo had created a persona for himself, one that gave him a veneer of legitimacy – something he could use to his advantage. He was even a hit with the in-crowd of Greenwich Village – Jerry Orbach and Bob Dylan were Gallo fans.

Joe Gallo and his two brothers Larry and Albert were enforcers in the Profaci family, but they also ran some rackets of their own. In the early 1960s, Joseph Profaci decided he wanted a higher cut from all his underlings' operations. Word was sent out and most of the family acquiesced – all, that is, except for Joe Gallo and his brothers. In fact, the Gallos decided to force the issue by kidnapping a number of high-ranking members of the Profaci family, and demanding $100,000 for return of the captives. Profaci agreed, but it was the beginning of a war.

Score one was to the Gallos, but the next two scores definitely went to Profaci. In May of 1961, Profaci had Gallo operative Joseph Gioelli killed and in August of that same year Larry Gallo was attacked and nearly murdered. After these two strikes the Gallos stepped back and regrouped. Holed up in President Street in Brooklyn, they kept a low profile, surrounding themselves with a stockpile of weapons. But pretty soon money was getting tight, so Joe took some men and ventured forth to dig up a little of the green stuff. Putting the muscle on local businessmen, Joe managed to scrounge up some dough, but one of the shopkeepers had the temerity to go to the cops about the shakedown. As a result, Joe was sentenced to prison for up to 14 years.

By 1971 Joe was back on the street, but a lot had changed while he was in prison. Both Larry Gallo and Joseph Profaci were dead and the Profaci family was now run by Joseph Colombo. Hearing that Joe was out of jail, Colombo extended an olive branch, offering him a thousand dollars by way of a conciliatory gift. Gallo refused this gesture and demanded a hundred thousand instead.

As far as the mob was concerned, that was Joe Gallo's last chance; but Joe got to Colombo first. On 28 June 1971, Joseph Colombo was gunned down by a seemingly random shooter while speaking at an Italian Unity Day rally. Joe Colombo would remain in a coma for the rest of his life, and though no one could prove it, the mob knew exactly where the hit had come from.

In contrast, the end for Joe Gallo came fast and furious. On 7 April 1972, he was shot several times while celebrating his 43rd birthday at Umberto's Clam House in Little Italy. Overturning a table, Gallo staggered out onto the street, where he crumpled to the ground. He died a short while later.

Whatever else Joe Gallo could have made of himself, admittedly it was pretty gutsy – and crazy – to start a mob war.

A RISING STAR

When Profaci died of cancer in 1962, Magliocco took over, but the other dons intervened, forcing Magliocco out and installing Colombo as boss of the Profaci crime family. Persico was promoted to *capo*. A rising star, he now wore well-tailored suits and his crew became one of the most profitable in the newly renamed Colombo family.

But a federal indictment for a 1959 hijacking was still hanging over him. A battery of expensive lawyers dragged the case out for 12 years.

After five separate trials, Persico was convicted, thanks to the testimony of Mafia 'rat' Joe Valachi, and sentenced to 14 years. However, he was cleared of running a multimillion-dollar loan-sharking business when a key witness vanished before the trial started and another 12 failed to identify him in court.

In 1971, Joe Colombo was shot and paralyzed at an Italian-American civil rights rally. Although he was in prison, Persico took over the family with Tommy DiBella as acting boss.

Paroled in 1979, Persico was charged with attempting to bribe an agent of the IRS. Federal marshals looking for his fugitive brother, Alphonse 'Allie Boy', crashed a meeting Persico was holding in Brooklyn. He was immediately charged with violating his parole by associating with other known criminals. In a plea bargain, he went away for another five years.

Released after just three years, he got wind that a RICO indictment was being prepared, alleging that he was the head of the Colombo family. He went into hiding in the house of Fred DeChristopher in Farmingdale, Long Island. DeChristopher's wife Katherine was the sister of Andy 'Fat Man' Russo, Persico's cousin and a *capo* in the Colombo family. Terrified of Russo – who once, at dinner, had held a fork to a man's eye and said 'Next time you f*** up, I'll push this fork right into your f*****g eye' – DeChristopher confessed all to the police. One morning some time after this, DeChristopher's phone rang. A voice said: 'Can I speak to Mr Persico?' DeChristopher handed over the phone.

Persico said: 'Who is this?'

The voice on the phone said: 'This is the FBI. We have the house surrounded. Come out with your hands up.'

Persico did as he was told.

At the ensuing 'Colombo trial', DeChristopher testified that, while preparing pasta with garlic and olive oil, Persico had boasted that he had run the Colombo family from jail and had stashed away enough money from his crimes to 'last ten lifetimes'. He also said 'I killed Anastasia' and bragged that he was a member of Joey Gallo's 'barbershop quintet'.

Persico went down for 39 years. His son Alphonse, 'Little Allie Boy', was sentenced to 12 years for being one of his father's lieutenants. In a separate trial, Persico was convicted of being a member of the Mafia Commission and was sentenced to another hundred years.

Mafia Killings 62

Joseph Colombo, Newburgh, New York, 22 May 1978

After he was shot, Joseph Colombo lay in a semi-coma for nearly seven years. As life passed by without him, all he could do was raise one or two of his fingers in a feeble attempt at communication. It's said that he could recognize faces, but nothing more.

But before that, Colombo had been a godfather and the boss of the family that still bears his name. In charge for nearly ten years, Colombo was one of the youngest bosses leading a mob at that time. Today some people still praise him for being forward thinking, for trying to bring the Mafia into more legitimate enterprises, and as an Italian-American civil rights activist.

Italian-American unity was Colombo's passion. He wanted to remove the Italian stereotypes of violence and the mob that led, he believed, to targeting by the FBI and the police. To that end he created the Italian-American Civil Rights League, an organization he hoped would foster a feeling of unity within the country. Despite his position as mob boss, Colombo made real efforts with the IACRL, allying the organization with the Jewish Defence League in a quest for tolerance.

But despite Colombo's denial of the existence of Cosa Nostra (and they all denied it back then) and his activism, he had been in the mob for years and as a Don himself oversaw money-making operations that included smuggling, counterfeiting and extortion, to name just a few. Still, at least Colombo put some of his ill-gotten gains to good use.

Even after Colombo took over the family, there was still that lingering war that had begun in the early 1960s with the old boss and Crazy Joe Gallo and his crew. And Gallo wasn't one to let things go. When he got out of prison in 1971, he was still looking to settle the score with the Colombo family and, as usual, took his grievance straight to the top.

It happened at an IACRL rally at Columbus Circle in New York City in June 1971. The scene was festive, music was in the air and Colombo was just about to climb the podium to give a speech. That's when Jerome Johnson made his way to the front of the crowd, masquerading as a member of the press. With a clear view of Colombo, apparently in order to take pictures, Johnson whipped out a pistol and shot him in the head and neck. The Don fell, the scene erupted into pandemonium and in all the confusion someone shot and killed Johnson. Colombo was rushed to the hospital, but the damage had been done; he remained in a semi-comatose state for the rest of his life.

No one was ever arrested for ordering the shooting of Colombo or Johnson, but the authorities had a pretty good idea who arranged the hit. So did the mob, and ten months later Joe Gallo was shot at Umberto's Clam House. He died within minutes – an ending very much faster than that of Joseph Colombo.

THIRD COLOMBO WAR

From jail, Persico put out contracts on US Attorney Rudolph Giuliani, later mayor of New York, and other federal prosecutors. He also bribed prison guards for favours and arranged to have sex with a female attorney who visited him.

Despite being behind bars, Persico installed Victor 'Little Vic' Orena as acting boss until Little Allie Boy got out of jail. But Little Vic had ambitions of his own. After two years, he asked his *consigliere* Carmine

Sessa to poll the *capos* to see who favoured him taking over permanently. Instead, Sessa informed Persico. On the evening of 20 June 1991, Orena returned to his home in Cedarhurst, Long Island, to find a five-man hit squad waiting outside. He sped away.

For three months, Orena's and Persico's factions negotiated. Then bullets began to fly in the third Colombo war. Orena was backed by Joe Profaci's son, Salvatore, aka 'Sally Pro' or 'Jersey Sal', as he ran the family's interests in New Jersey. He said that The Snake had gone crazy.

Persico's faction was led by Gregory 'the Grim Reaper' Scarpa, who was also an FBI informant. In 1964, when three civil rights workers disappeared in Mississippi, the Bureau employed Scarpa to find out what had happened to them. Scarpa kidnapped a Ku Klux Klan member, beat him up, shoved a gun barrel down his throat, and said: 'I'm going to blow your head off.' Realizing that Scarpa was serious, the klansman revealed that the bodies had been buried under an earth dam.

That December, five Colombo mobsters were gunned down – one while hanging a Christmas wreath on his front door. Eighteen-year-old Matteo Speranza was murdered in the bagel shop where he worked by an Orena gunman who mistakenly thought he was a Persico supporter. Innocent civilians also died in the gunfire.

In an attempt to halt the war, Brooklyn District Attorney Charles J. Hymes subpoenaed 41 suspected Colombo family members before a grand jury. Only 28 showed up and none of them would talk.

As the body count climbed, Scarpa contracted AIDS through a blood transfusion and lost an eye in an unrelated dispute over narcotics. The Persico faction then had to apologize to the Genovese family for accidentally killing 78-year-old Gaetano 'Tommy Scars' Amato, a retired soldier who had mistakenly been at an Orena social club when Persico's gunmen paid a visit.

The FBI then subpoenaed Kenneth Geller, an accountant who worked for the Colombos. He had borrowed $1 million from their loan-sharking operation for a business deal that went sour; he sought to escape his debt via the Federal Witness Protection Program. Geller delivered Orena, who was arrested at his mistress's home where agents found four loaded shotguns, two assault rifles and six handguns.

Orena was handed life imprisonment without the possibility of parole on the RICO charges of murder, conspiracy to murder and heavyweight loan-sharking. Sixty-eight *capos*, soldiers and Colombo associates also went down, including Orena's two sons.

Andy Russo, Persico's younger brother Theodore and enforcer Hugh McIntosh were also sentenced to long prison terms. Persico's elder brother Alphonse, 'Little Allie', who was already serving 25 years for extortion, died in jail. Finally, Gregory Scarpa was arrested. His work for the FBI did not save him from a ten-year sentence for three murders and conspiracy to murder. He, too, died in jail. Nevertheless, the arrests ended the war and left Persico in charge.

In 2001, Little Allie Boy Persico went down for 13 years for loan-sharking. A life sentence for murder followed in 2007. Even so, Carmine Persico continued to run the Colombo family from the Federal Correctional Complex in Butner, North Carolina. The war he waged to maintain control cost 12 lives and led to some 70 wiseguys and their associates landing in jail.

STOOL PIGEON

As a child, Joseph Valachi was known for his ability to build makeshift scooters out of wooden crates. This earned him the nickname 'Joe Cargo'. When Valachi made the mistake of joining an Irish gang rather than an Italian one, he so displeased the Italian underworld that he was punished in a knife attack while he was serving a prison sentence for theft. The wound ran under his heart and around to his back, requiring 38 stitches.

He got the message. After his release, he joined the Mafia, starting as a driver. With the outbreak of the Castellammarese War, which pitted old-time Sicilian Mafia Don 'Joe the Boss' Masseria against

Salvatore Maranzano in 1930, Valachi got the chance to advance his criminal career. He rented an apartment in Pelham Parkway, overlooking that of Steven Ferrigno, one of Masseria's lieutenants. It was from there that a team led by an assassin known as 'Buster from Chicago' shot and killed Ferrigno and Al Mineo, another of Masseria's lieutenants.

Although Joe the Boss escaped unscathed, Valachi became a made man for his participation in these killings. He ran a numbers racket, an illegal 'horse room', slot machines and a loan-sharking operation.

During the Second World War, he made $200,000 from selling gasoline on the black market. In 1960, he was convicted for selling drugs and shared a cell in Atlanta Federal Penitentiary with Vito Genovese. Convinced that Genovese was going to have him killed, he beat another prisoner to death with a length of iron pipe after mistaking him for an assassin.

The following year, 1963, Valachi testified before Senator McClellan's committee, which was investigating organized crime. His testimony on the organization and activities of the Mafia was so detailed that the McClellan hearings became known as the Valachi hearings. In doing so, Valachi broke the *omertà*, becoming the first man to admit membership of Cosa Nostra.

Although the US Department of Justice banned the publication of Valachi's memoirs, they were used by journalist Peter Maas in his 1968 book *The Valachi Papers*. A movie based on the book, starring Charles Bronson, was made in 1972. After surviving a suicide attempt in 1966, Valachi died of a heart attack five years later at La Tuna Federal Correctional Institution in Texas.

REVENGE FOR THE DON

Big Paulie Castellano had been murdered right in front of Sparks Steak House in Manhattan. His body lay partially outside his Lincoln, his feet stretching out onto the frigid New York sidewalk, while his head rested just inside the car. John Gotti was now the boss of the Gambino family, possibly the most powerful of the Five Families, while the position of underboss went to Frank DeCicco, a mastermind of the Castellano murder. The Don was dead, long live the Don.

DeCicco was intelligent and capable, a solid guy who could be trusted. Gotti relied on him and gave him control of the so-called White Collar crimes, the rackets that Castellano had preferred over the street jobs such as robbery and narcotics.

However, the positions of Gotti and DeCicco were far from secure. Although Castellano was dead, Gotti had not received permission from the Commission for the job, and in the Mafia, that's a problem. Antonio Caponigro discovered as much when he killed Don Angelo Bruno in New Jersey – only the Commission can authorize a hit on a boss. The Commission was not pleased with what just went down in New York.

Genovese boss Vincent Gigante (aka 'The Oddfather') was enraged. He practically controlled the Commission at the time, and did not like Gotti's breach of Mafia protocol. Besides, he had been a tried and true buddy of Castellano's, making a lot of money with the Gambino Don. Gigante went to Lucchese boss Victor Amuso for support, and the two of them decreed that both Gotti and DeCicco had to go. The plan was to use explosives to make the hit look like the work of the Zips.

Amuso outsourced the job and hired Westies member Herbert Pate to do the deed. The set-up came on 13 April 1986, when both Gotti and DeCicco were attending a meeting at the Veterans & Friends Social Club in Dyker Heights, Brooklyn. As Pate strolled through the parking lot of the establishment, with two bags of groceries in hand, he pretended to drop one of the bags. When Pate knelt down to pick up the groceries, he affixed an explosive device underneath DeCicco's car. Then he went off to wait.

Some time later, DeCicco exited the club and headed to his car. He was accompanied by Lucchese soldier Frank Bellino, who coincidentally resembled Gotti to a certain extent. Pate, of course, mistook Bellino for Gotti, and detonated the device. The parking lot exploded. Bellino only lost a couple of toes, but DeCicco was blown to bits. When Sammy 'The Bull' Gravano came racing out of the club to see what had happened, he found that DeCicco was literally in pieces and beyond help.

The kicker was that Gotti hadn't even been at the meeting that day. He had planned to attend, but then had to cancel. Gigante and Amuso would have to be satisfied with the death of DeCicco for the time being – Gotti had been spared. But the violence between the three Families was not yet over.

Mafia Killings 63

Vladimir Reznikov, New York City, 13 June 1986

In the early to mid-1980s, the Russian Mafia – or Mafiya – was just beginning to get a foothold in the United States. One place that was rich in Soviet emigrés was Brighton Beach in Brooklyn. That's where Russian mob boss Marat Balagula set up shop and ran such rackets as credit card scams and gasoline bootlegging. He was making a sizeable profit for himself and his crew, and owned a beautiful mansion as well as the Odessa restaurant on Brighton Beach Avenue. But all that money flowing into Balagula's coffers was a red flag (or gold flag) to the Colombo family, and before long the Colombos began to shake down members of Balagula's gang.

There was only one thing he could do, Balagula concluded – in the end it would be best to try to swim with the Mafia sharks rather than against them. So he put out feelers and asked for assistance from Christopher Furnari, *consigliere* of the Lucchese family.

Furnari agreed to provide protection to Balagula – for a small fee, of course. As long as the Russian allied himself with the Lucchese family, they would make sure that nothing happened to him and his rackets. The price for this service would be insignificant – just a tax of two cents per gallon of gas sold. These profits could then be divided between the Five Families and everyone would be happy. It was a stroke of genius and the gas racket became a goldmine for the Mafia.

This is where Vladimir Reznikov comes in. Reznikov heard about Balagula's deal with the Italians and decided he wanted in on the gasoline pie too. Driving past Balagula's office one day, Reznikov pulled out a rifle and shot the place up. And that was just his opening salvo.

Now that he'd gained Balagula's attention, Reznikov became more brazen and stormed into the Odessa restaurant. Waving a Beretta in Balagula's face, Reznikov demanded the payment of $600,000. If Balagula refused to pay, Reznikov would make short and brutal work of him. Balagula agreed, and promised to get the cash; but then as Reznikov left the restaurant, Balagula collapsed to the floor, struck down by a heart attack.

Resting at his home, Balagula called in his mob contacts. Now was the time for the Mafia to earn its keep. As requested, Balagula handed over a picture of Reznikov as well as a description of his car.

On 13 June 1986, Reznikov returned to the Odessa with his hand out. When he found out Balagula wasn't there, he stormed out of the restaurant, got into his car and drove off. He didn't get very far before a gunman stepped up to his vehicle and fired through the window. Reznikov attempted to get out through the passenger side and pulled out a revolver, but one final bullet put a swift end to him.

Word went out on the street pretty fast after that – mess with Balagula, and you're dead.

Mafia Killings 64

Michael 'The Bat' DeBatt, New York City, 2 November 1987

So many hits over the years, so many goodfellas who have paid the price. Perhaps some Mafiosi are not at all happy with the way they shuffled off this mortal coil and are still hanging around, trying to come to grips with what happened to them. Take the case of Michael DeBatt, who was a mob casualty, one of many over the years. This is not to say DeBatt was completely innocent himself, but it's highly probable that he got in way over his head.

DeBatt was a friend of Sammy 'The Bull' Gravano and a member of Gravano's Gambino family crew. Gravano had at one time been very good to DeBatt, helping his family deal with loan-shark debts after the death of his father and more or less taking the young lad under his wing. According to Gravano, who later famously became one of the biggest mob informers in history, DeBatt took part in the murder of Frank Fiala. But that's just Gravano's testimony. No murder charges were ever laid against DeBatt.

DeBatt was doing OK for a while. He had a wife and child, a nice home and a restaurant in Bensonhurst in Brooklyn – Tali's – that was helping to pay off some of his father's debt, as well as giving DeBatt a new start. So what went wrong?

Unfortunately for DeBatt, it was drugs – cocaine and crack. Gravano's crew used to deal the stuff, but Gravano really didn't like his boys partaking in it, at least not heavily. DeBatt got hooked pretty badly and the drugs started to have an effect on his personality, causing bizarre behaviour. He developed paranoia and took to holing up in his house and keeping watch at the front window, waiting with loaded gun for an imaginary hit. In DeBatt's unsound mind, no one was going to get him without a fight.

DeBatt was becoming a liability and, as a rule, the mob doesn't put up with that kind of thing for long.

Allegedly, it was Gravano himself who arranged the hit. The old friendship that had supposedly existed between him and DeBatt was now irrelevant – DeBatt had to go. On 2 November 1987, after attending a wedding, DeBatt returned to his restaurant. There he was murdered in front of the bar, his body left to cool in the orange electric light of the jukebox.

And that should have been the end of the story, but it's not. It's said that the spirit of Michael DeBatt still haunts the restaurant where he was gunned down. From time to time, a ghostly voice can be heard whispering the name 'Mike', while phantom faces can be seen peering out of mirrors. Those who work there feel as though they are constantly being watched, as shadowy figures disappear down the basement stairs.

Who knows? Maybe it is DeBatt, trying to find a little peace and a little justice.

TOO MANY RATS IN PHILLY

Joseph 'Skinny Joey' Merlino was born to the mob. His father Salvatore 'Chucky' Merlino rose to be underboss to Nicodemo 'Little Nicky' Scarfo, boss of the Philly mob following the death of Angelo Bruno. Scarfo used Merlino Sr.'s bar to plan his takeover. Skinny Joey was also the nephew of Lawrence 'Yogi' Merlino, a Scarfo *capo* jailed for racketeering and murder. His sister was engaged to Scarfo hitman Salvatore 'Salvie' Testa. And he was at school with Michael 'Mikey Chang' and Joseph 'Joey Chang' Ciancaglini, who both became made men under Scarfo.

Joey Merlino used to hang out on the streets with Mikey Ciancaglini, Georgie Borgesi and Gaetano 'Tommy Horsehead' Scafidi. The latter was younger and witnessed the actions of the older boys. 'They used to beat up girls, they used to rob people,' said Horsehead. 'They used to go into clubs and start fights.'

In August 1982, Joey Merlino and Horsehead's older brother, Salvatore 'Tori' Scafidi, stabbed two men at the Lido restaurant in Atlantic City. Merlino was convicted of two counts of aggravated assault and one count of possessing a weapon for an unlawful purpose.

According to another friend: 'Joey Merlino was mob royalty and no way he wasn't going into the life ... Joey was born to follow in his father's footsteps. How could he not? He was the son of an underboss. People on the street respected and feared him. Girls went crazy over him. There

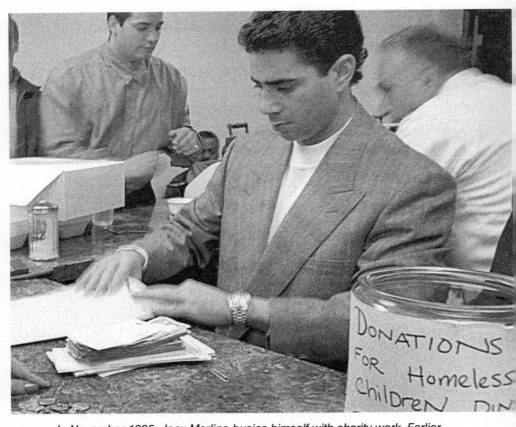

In November 1995, Joey Merlino busies himself with charity work. Earlier that day, Merlino's rival, John Stanfa, had been convicted of murder, extortion, kidnapping and racketeering charges.

was always plenty of money and the best tables in expensive restaurants and no waiting on line at the nightclubs. Big time sports celebrities and movie stars wanted to hang with him.'

In 1984, Joey and his father were barred from New Jersey casinos, and when Salvatore Merlino was stopped for drink driving he attempted to bribe the police officer who pulled him over. Scarfo decided that the family did not need this heat and demoted Merlino Sr. for his drinking. This started a feud and Joey broke off his friendship with Nicky Jr., Scarfo's son. Then, in 1987, Scarfo Sr. was convicted of conspiracy to commit extortion. RICO convictions the following year put him away for 45 years.

On Halloween night in 1989, Nicky Scarfo Jr. was shot eight times by a masked gunman inside a South Philadelphia restaurant. He was badly wounded but did not die. For years, police sources claimed that Joey Merlino was the masked gunman, but Merlino and his attorneys have always denied his involvement and no one has ever been charged with the attempted hit. Scarfo Jr. went to live in North Jersey and law enforcement sources claimed his father arranged for the Lucchese crime family to safeguard the younger Scarfo from further attempts on his life.

Convicted of robbing an armoured car in 1989, Merlino spent his time in jail plotting with Ralph Natale, a former friend of Angelo Bruno, to take over the Philadelphia crime family, which was then headed by John Stanfa in Scarfo Sr.'s absence. According to Natale, Merlino admitted in prison that he had been the shooter in the 1989 Halloween night attempt on Nicky Jr.'s life.

Natale said he authorized and helped Merlino plan the gangland murders of Louis 'Louie Irish' DeLuca in 1990 and Felix Bocchino and James 'Jimmy Brooms' DiAddorio in 1992. He also said that other members of Merlino's organization, including defendants Steven Mazzone, George Borgesi and Martin Angelina, visited him at different times in prison to discuss those plans.

Mafia Killings 65

Mario Riccobene, New Jersey, 28 January 1993

Once an informer is safely ensconced in the Witness Protection Program, it isn't often that they exit it again. It's hard to know why someone would leave the safety of a fresh start, the security of a new home and a new job, just to make himself a target for the mob once more. Maybe certain people get bored if they don't have a certain amount of mob work to occupy their time, or perhaps they simply can't leave the old life behind. Mario Riccobene, it seems, was one of those people.

In Philadelphia in 1984, the Scarfo/Riccobene war was over, and in a way both sides had lost. The Riccobenes were either dead (Robert), in prison (Harry) or dispersed. The supposed winners of the war, the Scarfos, were in disarray and mob boss Nicodemo Scarfo had received a hefty prison sentence that terminates in 2033, which means he will die behind bars.

It was around this period that Mario Riccobene became an informant. He had suffered some heavy losses in the Philadelphia conflict – his brother, of course, but also his son Enrico, who wasn't even a member of the mob at all but had been so disturbed by what was going on that he killed himself. Mario did some heavy soul-searching and decided it was time to get out of the family business. And for Mario, that meant not only testifying against the Scarfos – an act that he'd undoubtedly enjoy – but against his half-brother too. Brother against brother. Mario's testimony helped put Harry away for good. However, maybe that was a blessing in disguise for Harry, as he had spent so much time in jail he never really felt secure on the outside.

So Mario did the deed then entered the WPP. After that, he quietly slipped away somewhere and that should have been the end of the story. Except Mario Riccobene just couldn't say goodbye.

Riccobene hadn't lasted very long in the WPP. He'd been expelled from it in 1989 after twice contacting people from his old life – a violation of the Program's rules. Maybe he missed the excitement of his old life, or maybe he was just lonely. In any case, by 1992 Riccobene was in Philadelphia again, trying to get back into the swing of things – but everyone understood that he was really a walking corpse who just didn't know when it was time to call it a day.

On 28 January 1993, as Riccobene was sitting in his Ford Taurus in a parking lot outside a diner in New Jersey, a hitman quietly sauntered up to his car and blew him away. Riccobene died just as he'd lived the last few years of his life – alone, and no doubt waiting to get in touch with an old friend. Because that's how the mob does it – nothing is as effective as getting friends and brothers to stab each other in the back.

TAKING OVER THE FAMILY

At the time, neither Natale nor Merlino had been formally initiated into the mob, so they decided to initiate themselves. 'We'll make ourselves,' Merlino said. 'What's the difference if we have the button or not? We'll take over Philadelphia and kill John Stanfa.'

Merlino was formally initiated into the mob by Stanfa in 1992, while Natale was formally initiated by Merlino after being released from prison in 1994.

In 1993, war broke out between Stanfa and the Merlino faction. Merlino was injured in a drive-by shooting with a bullet in the buttocks, while Mikey Chang, who was with him, was killed. Stanfa's son Joseph was shot in the face in another drive-by shooting, this time in the rush hour on the Schuylkill Expressway.

Merlino went back to jail briefly for parole violation. Then Stanfa was convicted of labour racketeering, extortion, loan-sharking, murder and conspiracy to commit murder and was sentenced to five consecutive life sentences. When Merlino got out of jail he took over the Philadelphia family, with Natale as titular boss because he had connections with the Genovese family in New York. But when Natale went back to jail for parole violation in 1998, Merlino took his place.

Merlino's men gave drug dealer Louis Turra a severe beating when he refused to pay the mob's 'street tax'. Louis was then found dead in a prison cell, having apparently hanged himself. In retaliation for the beating, his father Anthony Turra suggested throwing grenades into Merlino's house to kill him and his 'scumbag' girlfriend. But Turra then went on trial for racketeering and drug offences. At 61, he was confined to a wheelchair. On the way to the court, he was shot dead outside his home by a gunman wearing a black ski mask.

Merlino himself survived at least ten assassination attempts – two of which were thwarted by the FBI – and there was a $500,000 contract out on him. 'I honestly don't know why so many people are seeking his demise,' said his lawyer, Joseph C. Santaguida of Philadelphia. 'He's really a likeable guy.'

Despite his violent reputation, Merlino was also known for his charitable work.

'I thought he was a gentleman, always been a gentleman with me, and I understand he's done a lot of nice things for underprivileged children and, for that, I commend him,' said South Philadelphia resident Pat Bombito.

In 1999, Natale was facing fresh drug charges that would have put him away for life, so he decided to turn state's evidence. He admitted ordering three killings in a gang war for control of the Philly Mafia's multimillion-dollar gambling and loan-sharking empire, a business enterprise that stretched from Philadelphia to Atlantic City.

Two years later, Merlino faced Natale in court while standing trial on 36 counts including racketeering, murder, attempted murder, extortion, illegal gambling and trafficking in stolen property. Merlino also faced a drug-trafficking charge. He was acquitted of three counts of murder, two counts of attempted murder and the drug-dealing charges. Nevertheless, he was still sentenced to 14 years for racketeering. 'Ain't bad,' he said. 'Better than the death penalty.'

NEIGHBOUR FROM HELL

After 12 years in jail, Merlino was released. He was no longer skinny, having spent much of his prison time in the gym bulking up. Although he went to live in a cul-de-sac in an upper-class area of Boca Raton, Florida, he showed little intention of settling down. 'We've had the police come several times,' said one neighbour. 'It's been very stressful living near them. There is always screaming and fighting.'

The neighbours said that what they found most disturbing were the banging noises in the middle of the night, as if furniture or equipment was being moved about. 'I'm not easily frightened,' another neighbour said, when told a convicted mobster lived a few doors away. 'I don't know who he is, but he does have a lot of visitors.'

Merlino appeared to work out of his home and named his wi-fi connection 'Pine Barrens'. This is a reference to the heavily forested area near Atlantic City, where Richard Kuklinski often disposed of bodies. It was the scene of one of the most famous episodes of *The Sopranos*.

'I can tell you that I would not want to live next door to Joey Merlino,' said Stephen LaPenta, a retired Philadelphia police lieutenant who had worked undercover as a mob informant, and had infiltrated Merlino's inner circle. LaPenta, who was spending his retirement in Florida, still kept tabs on the flamboyant mobster. 'The Joey I know was a hard-drinking, womanizing, gambling drug user who would strangle you,' he said. 'If Joey sneezed, 20 people would hand him a handkerchief.'

Merlino was no stranger to Florida, having spent time there when working for Nicky Scarfo, who had a house in Fort Lauderdale. There was speculation that Merlino was still living 'the life'. Although he was prohibited from associating with known felons, communication was easy enough in the digital age. He had been replaced as head of the Philly mob by Joseph 'Uncle Joe' Ligambi, though the law enforcement authorities speculated he was just a front for Merlino.

But Merlino insisted he was happy in Florida.

'It's beautiful down here,' he said. 'Great weather. No stress. People come here, they live to be a hundred.'

And he said he had no intention of returning to a life of crime.

'Too many rats,' he said. 'I want no part of that.'

BRENDA COLLETTI

In 1988, Brenda was a nude go-go dancer, supporting an unemployed husband. Then she met Philadelphia hitman Philip Colletti in the Dunkin' Donuts outlet she used on the way home from work. She had had a row with her husband and Colletti offered to take her for breakfast at Denny's.

But her husband walked in on them. Inflamed, he made a move to hit Brenda. Colletti put himself between them and said to him: 'If you touch her, I will kill you.' Then he turned to Brenda and said: 'If you want to go with this piece of shit, then go. But if you're afraid of him, stay put, and I'll take care of you.'

Brenda said she was staying.

Colletti revealed that he was a small-time associate of the mob, who threatened gamblers owing money to loan-sharks. Brenda married Colletti in 1990 and they had a son.

By then, Colletti was working as a plumber, but he was laid off and began going out at night to meet acquaintances from his old neighbourhood. Brenda learned not to ask where he was going or what he was doing.

On his birthday he took her to a Bucks County restaurant where he introduced her to an older man with grey hair. 'Honey,' he said. 'This is John Stanfa.'

Later her husband explained that Stanfa was boss of the Philly mob. What he did not tell her was that Stanfa was at war with Skinny Joey Merlino at the time. Because of his association with Stanfa, Colletti's life was in danger. He joined one of Stanfa's teams and roamed Philadelphia at night looking for Merlino's men. The crew would fetch up at Colletti's house and Brenda would feed them. Then they would start talking strategy.

'Here they were in my little house in the suburbs, trying to plan murder!' she said. 'They just wanted to find the other guys, pull out their guns, and start blasting.'

One night Colletti's friend Sal Brunetti suggested that they could hide under the front steps of a target's apartment building and then start shooting the second the front door opened. Brenda could not keep her mouth shut. 'What if the door opens and it's not him?' she said. 'You're gonna peg off an innocent person?'

She was told to 'shut the f*** up'.

One afternoon, Brenda got a call from Colletti, telling her to 'clean the house'. That meant hide all the arms and ammunition under a nearby woodpile. Then she heard on the radio that there had been a Mafia hit. Colletti and John-John Veasey had been driving by Merlino's clubhouse when they spotted Michael Ciancaglini and opened fire. Colletti's bullet had killed Ciancaglini, while Veasey's had wounded Merlino in the buttocks – making Colletti an instant hero among Stanfa's faction.

Fearing retribution, the Collettis began to sleep with guns under their mattress. They knew they would never be safe until Merlino was dead. Brenda volunteered to get dolled up, go to Merlino's favourite club and put cyanide in his drink.

Colletti was against this idea. Then there was a botched hit on Veasey and he contacted the US Attorney's office. 'He turned rat,' said Brenda. 'When that happened, Philip knew it was time for him to turn rat, too, or die. So he did, and we all went into hiding – even Philip's mom and dad.'

Once Stanfa's indictment was prepared, Colletti pleaded guilty to Ciancaglini's murder and other crimes. He got 12 years. Brenda was given three months' probation. Eventually she divorced Colletti and settled in Nashville.

THE MAXI-TRIAL IN SICILY

In February 1986, what became known as the 'Maxi-Trial' of the Sicilian Mafia began in a specially-built high-security bunker connected to the Ucciardone prison in Palermo. There were 456 defendants facing a wide variety of charges.

One of the Salvo cousins could not be present – he had died of cancer in a Swiss clinic; and Totò Riina was still underground. But Luciano Liggio was there, and so was Pippo Calò, the head of Buscetta's Porta Nuova family who'd become Cosa Nostra's emissary in Rome, where he owned 11 apartments. In one of them, police had found 11 kilos of pure heroin, and in another a vast quantity of T4 explosive which was linked to a murderous 1984 bomb attack on a Naples-to-Milan express train, which until then was thought to have been the work of right-wing terrorists. The idea was to divert public attention from the testimony given by Buscetta and other informants. One late arrival was Michele 'The Pope' Greco, who was arrested after a dawn raid on a farmhouse 25 miles east of Palermo shortly after the trial began. Until then he had been tried in absentia.

The indictment – an extraordinary piece of work by Falcone and his team – ran to over 8,000 pages and included the testimony of a number of *pentiti*, among them a close ally and friend of Tommaso Buscetta. But it had been gathered together at a cost. In April 1985, a bomb attack had been made on an investigating magistrate in Trapani and though he'd escaped, a passer-by and her two children had been killed. Then, in July and August 1986, within nine days of each other, the Palermo police chief, Giuseppe Montana, and the deputy head of his Flying Squad, Antonio Cassara, had been cut down. Half of Cassara's men had then successfully applied to be posted out of Sicily.

There were, however, signs of hope as the trial went on. Leoluca Orlando, a young radical politician, had been elected mayor of Palermo in July 1985, and he'd made the city an *ex-parte* participant in the proceedings. He talked openly about the Mafia wherever he went and attended the Maxi-Trial, making a point of sitting with the families of Mafia victims. The city took heart and what became known as 'the Palermo Spring' was born. There were demonstrations of support from university students and local Jesuits mounted a campaign to persuade the Church, at last, to speak out against Cosa Nostra.

The trial dragged on for almost two years, but in the end 344 of the defendants were found guilty. Nineteen life sentences were handed down to the bosses, among them Leggio, Pippo Calò and 'The Pope'. But the trial had failed to reach anyone higher than the foothills of what was called 'the Third Level' of the Mafia, the politicians who had backed and sustained it. It became clear that this network was still very active. During the investigation process, Falcone had told anyone who would listen that 'for months and months we've asked for men and means ... but little has been done.' Now, after the trial, he was simply shunted aside. Another man was chosen to fill the post of the island's chief prosecutor – a man whose last case as a criminal prosecutor had been in northern Italy in 1949 – and Falcone was forced to take up a job at the Ministry of Justice in Rome. Few new investigations were opened and there was a general fear that those convicted would soon have their sentences overturned in the appeals court – as had happened repeatedly in the past. In the absence of any encouragement from the national government, the flowers of 'the Palermo Spring' began to wither away.

Just how far they'd withered away by 1991 became clear when a Palermo small businessman called Libero Grassi made public the fact that he was refusing to pay protection to the Mafia. He appeared on national television to denounce Mafia racketeering and was casually shot down outside his house soon afterward. For all 'the Palermo Spring', virtually no one outside his immediate family attended his funeral. It was the same old story, one that had effectively undermined so many trials in the past: no one saw, no one noticed, no one could possibly say.

However, 15 years later, in October 2006, Mafiosi brothers Francesco and Salvino Madinia were convicted of Grassi's murder.

GIOVANNI FALCONE WORKS BACKSTAGE

And yet, something was happening behind the scenes: something that is even now very difficult to read. The prime minister between 1989 and 1992 had been Giulio Andreotti – and this period would in the end turn out to be crucial. Although Andreotti soon appointed as his Minister of the Interior a man who was later revealed to be a close associate of the Neapolitan Camorra, and although he campaigned vigorously for at least one blatantly Mafia candidate for parliament in Sicily, the fight against Cosa Nostra somehow went on.

With Falcone's help inside the Ministry of Justice, new legislation was introduced to set up a nationwide anti-Mafia police unit and an anti-Mafia prosecutor's office, among other things. In the meantime and under pressure, it is true, from lawyers and public opinion in the aftermath of businessman Libero Grassi's death, Guilio Andreotti, refused to allow the release of those convicted in the Maxi-Trial pending their appeal.

There had already been one appeal in Palermo and the Mafia had won. The court had rejected what was called 'the Buscetta theorem', the idea that membership of the Commission during a particular period also meant responsibility for murders which had occurred during that time. But summer 1991 was to see the final hearing of the case in the Supreme Court of Appeals in Rome, where it was generally expected that the sentences would be overturned. It was assumed that the case would come up before Judge Corrado Carnevale, who was known in legal circles as 'Amazzasentenze' or 'sentence-killer'. He'd already quashed the sentences of over 400 members of Cosa Nostra. According to later *pentiti*, the leaders of Cosa Nostra took it virtually for granted that their case would go the same way.

But it didn't. Under huge pressure from members of parliament, the judiciary and from the Ministry of Justice, the president of the Court, who had the final word, appointed, instead of Carnevale, another judge with a reputation for complete honesty. In January 1992, the sentences were upheld.

COSA NOSTRA MAKES WAR ON THE STATE

Within two months after the decision to uphold the sentences, the Mafia declared war on the state. Their fixer in Rome, Salvo Lima, who was supposed to have made sure that things went Cosa Nostra's way, was gunned down by motorcycle-riding assassins in the seaside resort of Mondello on 12 March. Lima was thought to be untouchable. He had been seven times mayor of Palermo and was a man of huge power, widely known, even in the European parliament in Strasbourg, as 'the viceroy of Sicily'. So his death – just as a new election campaign was beginning – was the clearest possible message to the centre: disobey us at your peril. Lima, as it happened, had been busily preparing for the arrival of Andreotti, due in a few days' time to support his Christian Democratic candidates. As it turned out, he had to come earlier, to attend Lima's funeral. He was, by all accounts, visibly shocked and shaken.

But Riina and the Commission didn't stop there. On 23 May, Giovanni Falcone and his wife flew from Rome to spend the weekend at their house in Palermo. They were on a secret flight in a government plane and were met at the airport by a cluster of bodyguards. But they also had another, secret, welcomer: a Mafia soldier who used a mobile phone to alert a group waiting at the turn-off of the airport road onto the autostrada at Capaci. The group was keeping watch over a drainage channel under the autostrada into which they'd stuffed 500 kilos of plastic explosive a few days earlier. As Falcone's motorcade approached, one of them pressed a detonator.

The bodyguards in the leading car were killed instantly, those in the car behind Falcone's only slightly injured. But Falcone, who'd been driving the second car, and his wife, also a magistrate, who'd been beside him, died that night, shortly after being taken to hospital.

Falcone's friend Paolo Borsellino, who'd taken over his old job in Palermo at the end of 1991, arrived in the emergency room in time to see him die. People said later that he seemed to make a pledge there. He began to work harder afterwards than he ever had: interviewing the new *pentiti* who'd appeared, following up and cross-referencing their stories.

His assistant prosecutor said: 'He was a man in a tremendous hurry . . . someone who knew that his hours were numbered . . . He felt that time was running out on him.'

On 19 July, as news from Milan was further exposing just how widespread Italian corruption really was, time did run out. After taking a rare Sunday off, Borsellino made a call to his mother in Palermo to say that he was coming to pay her a visit. The call, though, was picked up, and a primed car was hurriedly placed outside his mother's apartment building in Via D'Amelio. When Borsellino arrived, his six bodyguards spread out, holding their machine guns at the ready. But then the car-bomb went off, and all seven, one of them a woman, were blown to pieces. The apartments facing the road were destroyed all the way up to the fourth floor, though the road where the car had been was 30 feet away.

Between the deaths of Falcone and Borsellino, Judge Carrado Carnevale of the Supreme Court of Appeals delivered himself of a judgment in another Mafia case arising out of the Maxi-Trial organized by Falcone. He'd said that there was no such thing as a Commission or a Cupola, no such person as a Don and no such people as 'Men of Honour', in effect parroting the old Sicilian line of 'Mafia? Who?'. Carnevale was later transferred away from the court. Shortly afterwards, he would be investigated for the first time.

In 1993, Carnevale was suspended because of his ties with Giulio Andreotti who faced trial for his Mafia links. In 2001, Carnevale was sentenced to six years in jail for criminal conspiracy with the Mafia. In true Italian style, the verdict was reversed the following year and he was returned to the bench in 2007.

THE PUBLIC REACTS

The deaths of Falcone and Borsellino brought about a widespread change. Some 40,000 people attended the first funeral of Falcone and the other victims of 'the massacre at Capaci'. At the service the distraught young widow of one of the policemen ordered the assembled leaders of the country to their knees. After remembering and praising her husband, she said: 'The state, the state: why are Mafiosi still inside the state? I pardon you, but get down on your knees. But they don't change – too much blood. There's no love here, there's no love here, there's no love here. There's no love at all.'

Soon sheets inscribed with slogans appeared on balconies all over Palermo: 'Falcone, you continue to live in our hearts'; 'I know but I don't have the proof'; 'Palermo has understood, but has the state?' These soon spread to schools. There were demonstrations and work projects. Students even went to a village where there had recently been Mafia wars and symbolically took it over for a day.

After the second death, though, the mood changed to one of anger and despair. Borsellino's wife refused the offer of a state funeral. But when one was duly held in Palermo cathedral for the bodyguards who'd been killed, the national politicians and the chief of Palermo's police had to be protected from the fury of the crowds and from that of many of the police officers present. The scandal of Tangentopoli ('Bribesville') – the elaborate system of bribes and kickbacks at every level of the Italian state – was beginning to reach government figures at the highest level and the future looked horribly bleak. The UK newspaper the *Observer* wrote at the time: 'The country is in a state of chaos, a state of war. It has the highest murder rate in the European Community, the most rampant and blatant corruption, an ailing economy, a floundering government, and an anguished and embarrassed population.'

A NEW SONG

For the citizens of Palermo, however, there was a glimmer of hope. In the aftermath of Borsellino's death, 7,000 troops were sent to Sicily to boost their morale. Not long afterwards a senior Mafioso was captured, and so, finally, on 15 January 1993, was Totò Riina, after living 'underground' for 24 years. 'Who are you?' was the first question Riina asked as he was dragged out of a car and flung down on a Palermo sidewalk. He seemed to have expected some sort of coup attempt from inside Cosa Nostra –

anyone but undercover police – and appeared relieved by the answer. The man who'd led the police commando to him was a recent *pentito* called Baldassare Di Maggio who believed that Riina had condemned him to death. Once arrested by the police, he realized he had finally run out of options. 'I'm a dead man,' he'd said, 'but I am a man of honour. I can take you to Riina.'

With Riina taken, a number of *pentiti* who'd earlier agreed to give evidence on the grounds, in the words of one of them, that 'Cosa Nostra has undertaken an irreversible strategy of death', began to sing a new song. In their safe houses all over Italy and, in Buscetta's case, somewhere in the United States, they began to sing about Andreotti. And it was their and their country's great good luck that the man who listened to them was a man called Gian Carlo Caselli, Palermo's recently appointed new chief prosecutor and, in the words of historian Paul Ginsborg, 'quite the most courageous and dedicated public servant in the Europe of his time.' It was Caselli, after he'd heard them out, who in March 1993 formally informed Andreotti, the longest-serving politician of the Italian Republic and six times prime minister, that he was under investigation for collusion with Cosa Nostra.

CHAPTER 24

THE SCANDAL OF P2: THE VATICAN AND THE MAFIA

In March 1981, a finance police force, acting under the order of magistrates investigating Michele Sindona's bank collapse, raided a villa outside Florence owned by the financier Licio Gelli and found in his office a partial membership list of a hitherto secret lodge, P2. Gelli was its Worshipful Master. The list, which started at the number 1,600, included the names of all the heads of the secret services, 12 generals of the carabinieri, five of the finance police, 22 of the army, four of the air force and eight admirals. Fourteen judges were there, 44 members of parliament and ten bank presidents. So were the names of Michele Sindona, of the dead journalist Mino Pecorelli and of a businessman and future prime minister called Silvio Berlusconi.

The police also found in Gelli's house files of top-secret material which Gelli must have received from the secret service members of P2, and which were apparently intended to be used – or had already been used – for blackmail purposes. There was clear evidence, too, of a P2 plot to instigate a right-wing takeover of government – and a curious document relating to the deposit of $7 million into the Swiss bank account of the secretary of the Socialist Party, Bettino Craxi, by banker and P2 member Roberto Calvi.

Freemasonry in Italy had been banned under the dictator Benito Mussolini, but it was reborn under American influence after the Second World War as a secret bastion against communism. By 1971, though, it was clear that it had done little to counter the social upheavals of the previous decade. So the Grand Master of one of the Masons' most powerful groupings, the Grande Oriente d'Italia, asked the unrepentant fascist Gelli to reconsitute an old lodge called 'Propaganda' as P2.

Documents later found in a briefcase being smuggled out of the country by Gelli's daughter made clear who P2's enemies were: the communist party and the trade union movement. The aim, in the end, was 'overall control' of the government – to be achieved via a programme of extensive corruption. P2 had already bought Italy's leading newspaper, the *Corriere della Sera*, and its capital had been expanded with the help of an investment from the Vatican's own bank, the Institute of Religious Works, which was controlled by Chicago-born Archbishop Paul Marcinkus.

By the time the smuggled briefcase was found, Roberto Calvi – whose connections with the Vatican and Marcinkus had earned him the nickname 'God's Banker' – was dead, found hanged under Blackfriars Bridge in London. His bank, the Banco Ambrosiano, which had taken over the job of laundering the Mafia's drug money from Sindona, had recently collapsed with debts of $1.3 billion. The coroner's court in London pronounced Calvi's death a suicide, but a further enquiry in 1993 agreed that he had been murdered, possibly by the masons, as P2 members referred to themselves as 'frati neri' or 'black friars'. By that time, Italian *pentito* Francesco Marino Mannoia had named the man who killed Calvi: a convicted Mafia drugs trafficker called Franco Di Carlo, acting on the orders of Licio Gelli and Pippo Calò. The briefcase Calvi had been carrying with him in London reappeared – if only briefly. It and its contents had been bought by a Vatican bishop for over ten million American dollars and the cheques had been drawn on the Vatican bank controlled by Marcinkus.

Both Marcinkus and the bishop were exempt from prosecution in Italy as citizens of the sovereign state of the Vatican. Gelli was arrested in Switzerland and brought back, but made an escape from prison by helicopter and fled for his estates in Uruguay. And although he was subsequently extradited back to Italy, again from Switzerland, the terms of his extradition meant that he could only be tried on financial charges relating to the collapse of the Banco Ambrosiano, even though he had been formally charged with the murder of Roberto Calvi. He was later convicted of being the paymaster for a bomb attack in 1980 at Bologna Central Station which cost 85 lives, but he never served time. Only General Gianadelio Maletti of the secret services was ever given an unsuspended sentence in the matter of P2 – and by that time he'd fled to South Africa. Bettino Craxi, the Socialist ex-prime minister, later went the same way, taking up residence in his house in Tunis, and sentenced to 25 years for corruption in his absence.

Franco Di Carlo eventually turned *pentito*, but denied he had killed Roberto Calvi, though he had been asked to do so by Pippo Calò. Di Carlo said the killers were Sergio Vaccari and Vincenzo Casillo, who belonged to the Camorra in Naples and had since been killed. In July 2003, however, Pippo Calò, Flavio Carboni, Manuela Kleinszig, Ernesto Diotallevi, and Calvi's ex-driver and bodyguard Silvano Vittor went on trial for the murder in a specially fortified courtroom in Rome's Rebibia prison. In June 2007, all five were acquitted as there was 'insufficient proof' to convict them of murder. The acquittal was upheld by the Court of Cassation in November 2011.

THE MAFIA AND THE MASONS

How far was the Mafia involved in P2? The answer is that no one really knows. But some senior members of Cosa Nostra were certainly involved alongside Lima, Calvi and Sindona. There may very well have been a network of provincial lodges allied to it, particularly in Sicily and Calabria. A high-ranking officer of the Grand Orient Lodge has given evidence of links between masonry and the Mafia and another Grand Master even went so far as to examine the records of his own lodge. Afterwards, he promptly resigned, saying 'I have seen a monster'. There is evidence, too, that in the late 1970s, Mafia members joined masonic lodges in significant numbers and Palermo mayor Leoluca Orlando has always insisted that Cosa Nostra and masonry are now crucially interlinked.

Evidence of this interlinkage surfaced as the result of work done by a magistrate in Calabria who was investigating a European Economic Community (EEC) fraud. He uncovered letters between Gelli and a local Calabrian masonic lodge and was later able to name Gelli, along with 128 others, as deeply implicated in an arms, drugs and precious metals trafficking network he had uncovered. The investigation, though, got no further. The magistrate's staff was immediately cut and promotion denied him. He later claimed that corrupt police officers in criminal-dominated lodges were impeding his work and he provided the Council of the Judiciary with a list of magistrate masons who were helping organized crime. He even told the anti-Mafia commission in Rome that one of its own members was a hitherto unknown member of P2.

In the end, the whole P2 affair more or less disappeared, even though the first news of it had brought down the government of the day. The judicial inquiry was taken out of the hands of the magistrates and transferred to the prosecutor's office in Rome, where a judge in 1994 ultimately pronounced that P2 was a 'normal' masonic lodge, and secret only to 'the deaf and illiterate'. The Supreme Court's judgment was more balanced, but it basically agreed that P2 was not a conspiracy but 'a business committee'!

And was the Grand Master of this 'business committee' really Giulio Andreotti – as Roberto Calvi's widow said? Most Italians believed he was, since the master manipulator seemed to have a finger in every pie. But there has never been any evidence one way or the other. Andreotti did agree that he'd once bumped into Gelli at the official Buenos Aires residence of the Argentinian dictator Juan Peròn, but had only known him before that as the head of a company making mattresses. He said on a chat show: 'I thought, "There's someone who looks just like the managing director of the Permaflex mattress factory in Frosinone."'

THE KISS

Andreotti did, however, know Totò Riina – or so said the *pentito* Baldassare Di Maggio who had been Riina's driver and had fingered him to the Palermo police. In 1993, once Riina was safely behind bars, Di Maggio spoke to investigators of a day during the Chistian Democrats' annual Friendship Festival in September 1987, when he'd been asked to pick up 'Uncle Totò' for an important meeting.

Andreotti had been in Palermo that day, to stay at the Villa Igiea hotel and to give two talks: the first in the morning and the second at six o' clock in the evening. He had some time off in the middle of the day, so he dismissed his guards and agreed to rendezvous with them later in the day. He didn't take lunch with the others in the hotel restaurant. He, in effect, disappeared.

Meanwhile, Baldassare Di Maggio went to pick up Totò Riina, as agreed, and took him to the house where Ignazio Salvo was living, under house arrest while awaiting sentence from the Maxi-Trial. Di Maggio later described the layout of the house in great detail, as well as the furnishings of the sitting-room suite into which the two men were led by Salvo's Mafia driver/assistant. Three men were sitting there, he said: Ignazio Salvo, Salvo Lima and Giulio Andreotti, 'whom I recognized without a shadow of a doubt.' Di Maggio added that he kissed Ignazio Salvo and shook hands with the others before retiring to another room, but 'Riina, on the other hand, kissed all three persons, Andreotti, Lima and Salvo.'

In the Mafia, a kiss sometime signifies a sentence of death. But it is also the ultimate sign of respect. It symbolized on this occasion that it was a meeting between equals, a summit meeting between heads of state. 'Uncle Totò' and 'Uncle Giulio' were meeting to discuss matters of life importance – and perhaps of death too.

Whatever was said, Di Maggio claimed the meeting lasted three or three-and-a-half hours. He took it for granted that its subject was the Maxi-Trial, which had been going on for a year-and-a-half by then and still had another three months to run. Cosa Nostra had tried everything to wreck it. They'd tried to have the judge removed for bias and misconduct – and had failed. They'd also demanded that all the documents in the case – over 8,000 pages of them – should be read aloud in court, so that the trial would carry on over the time legally allowed for defendants to remain in custody – but the Italian parliament had passed a new law specifically to prevent this. What Riina must have wanted to know was why on earth the Christian Democrats hadn't done more to stop this new law. He must also have demanded some guarantees from Andreotti for the future.

After the meeting, Riina kept quiet. Di Maggio simply drove him back home. As for Andreotti, he reappeared at his hotel, met up with his bodyguards, and arrived just in time for his second talk of the day.

ANDREOTTI ON TRIAL

By the time this partial eyewitness account became public knowledge, Andreotti had been passed over for President of the Republic because of the clouds gathering around his name. Instead, he'd been made Senator for Life as a sort of consolation prize. But this meant that he had lifelong immunity from prosecution, an immunity which now had to be removed if he was ever to be tried. By this time, however, Buscetta had given testimony to the senate, claiming that Andreotti headed in effect the political wing of the Mafia. Another of the *pentiti* had said bluntly: 'The most powerful political reference point for Cosa Nostra was Senator Andreotti.' The Palermo magistrates also brought in as evidence a private diary that had been kept by the murdered General Dalla Chiesa. In this diary – of which the magistrates said: 'It can be ruled out that the general would have written falsehoods in a completely personal document' – Dalla Chiesa had recorded a number of meetings with Andreotti, then the prime minister. In one meeting he had complained of not getting enough backing from the Christian Democrats – and

Andreotti was brought to trial twice during the 1990s

Andreotti had replied obliquely. He'd told the story of Pietro Inzerillo, whose dead body had been shipped back to Sicily with dollars stuffed in his mouth. Andreotti was definitely implying, said the magistrates, that the General should think before he went too far.

At another meeting, Dalla Chiesa told Andreotti that he was not going to favour any Christian Democratic politicians who might be involved in corruption. Andreotti was recorded as having 'gone white' at this news.

With his immunity lifted, Andreotti was first questioned in December 1993. He had, of course, a completely different memory of his meetings with Dalla Chiesa. He also said he had never known either of the Salvos (both of whom were by now dead, as was Salvo Lima). Even when confronted with Baldassare Di Maggio, he remained completely calm.

Nevertheless, he came to trial in Palermo in 1995 for association and collusion with Cosa Nostra and was further arraigned in Perugia for the murder of Mino Pecorelli. Between the staggered starts of the two trials, in the words of author Peter Robb in *Midnight in Sicily*: 'His Holiness Pope John Paul II found time in the Vatican to clasp Andreotti's hands fervently between his own in a photo opportunity the media described as "almost an embrace". The former prime minister seemed heartened by the Holy Father's attention; but a student challenged the Pope from the pulpit of St Peter's over this; and it was the first time a pope had been challenged in his own church in seven hundred years.'

PART SEVEN

THE MODERN MAFIA

Although perhaps a shadow of its former self, the Mafia has not gone away. Today it is no longer the sole criminal enterprise in operation and has to share the headlines with many others, like the Mexican drug cartels, the Russian mobs, the Yakuza groups and the Triads. Despite being pushed out of politics and the unions, the mob is very resilient and is still operative on a global scale, powerful and profitable. Killings are now few and far between, but there are still the old-style scams, like drug smuggling, loan-sharking, racketeering, casino gambling; along with some original thinking such as the Coffee Boy Scandal, or the 'phantom jobs' at Ground Zero in Manhattan, which saw hundreds of tons of equipment removed from the site and sold as scrap metal, along with newer schemes in sports betting and health care and credit card fraud.

But the real truth is that the face of organized crime has moved on. The new face, one that does not always include the Mafia, is high-tech fraud that exploits vulnerabilities in the financial services and retail industries. Organized crime syndicates are recognizing that there is big money in identity theft, credit card fraud, mortgage fraud, internet-based scams, organized retail theft and related money laundering.

CHAPTER 25

A CHANGE OF ALLEGIANCE

At the start of the twenty-first century, the political dispensations that had ruled Italy since the Second World War were more or less in a state of complete disintegration. The reason for this was the welter of charges that had been brought against politicians and bureaucrats all over the country in what had become known as Tangentopoli. Besides, with the fall of the Berlin Wall and the threat from Russia neutered (for the time being), America felt much less inclined to prop up an administration which, with its help and encouragement, had become terminally corrupt.

Cosa Nostra agreed. In the 1994 elections, ex-P2-member Silvio Berlusconi and his recently-founded Forza Italia party swept to power in Italy – and, notably, in Sicily. It was said that the new Cosa Nostra boss on the ground, Giovanni Brusca, had decided to punish the Christian Democrats where it most hurt. Brusca was the man who'd thrown the detonator switch which had blown up Giovanni Falcone. He'd also had the 12-year-old son of one of the *pentiti* held for two years, then finally strangled and dissolved in acid. Although Forza Italia lost the next national election in 1996, it still held on to Sicily – thanks in part to Giovanni Brusca, who had made it his business in the interim to kill as many of the *pentiti's* relatives as he could find.

THE MAFIA PICKS UP THE PIECES

There were some successes as the Andreotti trial dragged on. Brusca was finally picked up in 1996, and not long afterwards so was another important lieutenant of Riina's, Leoluca Bagarella. Gian Carlo Caselli also successfully prosecuted Bruno Contrada, who'd been head of the investigative police force in Palermo before rising to third in command of the Italian secret services. It was Contrada, said the *pentiti* – who by now numbered over 500 – who had been responsible for Totò Riina's 23-year-long avoidance of capture.

The trial of Giulio Andreotti on Mafia charges in Palermo dragged on for more than three years, ending in 1999 with his acquittal. However, in 2002 he was sentenced to 24 years in jail for the murder of the journalist Mino Pecorelli, who had published allegations that Andreotti had ties to the Mafia. But the 83-year-old Andreotti was immediately released pending appeal and in 2003 his conviction was overturned by Italy's highest court. Prime Minister Silvio Berlusconi condemned the acquittal, and the judge in Perugia who had originally found him guilty was given police protection after receiving a death threat. Palermo justice remained unreliable, to say the very least. One Mafia boss, Vito Vitale – who'd been captured to enormous fanfare – was also released without having to go through the charade of an appeal; and Totò Riina was actually found innocent, for the first time in his life, of the murder of a judge – though he remained in jail convicted of over a hundred other murders.

It was a measure of the continuing power of Cosa Nostra that in 1998 a high-level meeting of the Sicilian *capi* was actually held behind the walls of Ucciardone prison, with guests from outside staying overnight before being sent on their way. This event, widely reported in Sicilian newspapers, was described as consisting of 'constructive discussions'. Giovanni Brusca, behind bars for the kidnapping and strangulation of the *pentito's* young son, was said to have made a moving speech about the importance of human values. He was, in the words of Norman Lewis in his book *In Sicily*, 'assured by those present that this was the common aim'.

Perhaps, in a sense, it now is. Certainly the yearly murder rate in Sicily has dropped from several hundreds to double figures. With Brusca behind bars, the only major known Mafia figure still at large was Riina's lieutenant Bernardo Provenzano, who turned against the bombing campaign that had brought the Mafia such bad publicity. He also tried to stem the flow of *pentiti*, not by targeting their families, but by trying to re-establish the old Mafia rules undermined by Riina and Leggio, and using violence only when absolutely necessary. He communicated only by courier via typewritten notes – *pizzini* – which characteristically started: 'Dearest, in the hope that this finds you in the best of health' and ended: 'May the Lord bless and protect you.' Although Provenzano was known in his youth as 'U Tratturi' – 'The Tractor' – because, as one *pentiti* put it, 'he mows people down', he later became known as 'The Accountant' for his gentler style of leadership and his systematic infiltration of public finances.

In 2006, Provenzano, then 73, was arrested in a small farmhouse outside his home town of Corleone after police had followed fresh laundry sent by his wife. He had been on the run for 43 years. He had been convicted in absentia of more than 12 murders, including those of Giovanni Falcone and Paolo Borsellino. Ten more arrest warrants were outstanding. Fifty-seven other Mafiosi were jailed for a total of 300 years for protecting him while he was in hiding.

Provenzano's first court appearance was by video link from the high-security jail in Terni, central Italy. He appeared on screen alongside Totò Riina, another inmate, who Giovanni Brusca claims had been 'sold' to the carabinieri by Provenzano in exchange for an archive of compromising material that Riina held.

Both men were handed multiple life sentences, which they are currently serving in solitary confinement, communicating only with their lawyers. Both unsuccessfully appealed for release on health grounds in 2011. On 17 December 2017, Totò Riina died in prison after failing to regain his freedom.

CHAPTER 26

THE GODFATHER AND THE GOODFELLAS

The Mafia is not what it was. In America it became something of a laughing stock. After the murder of Paul Castellano, John Gotti took over the Gambino family. Instead of keeping a low profile, Gotti appeared in public wearing $10,000 hand-made suits and quickly became known as 'The Dapper Don'. In his neighbourhood in Queens, he organized lavish street parties and festivals, and was praised by local people for keeping crime out of the area. In Little Italy, he would shake hands and pose for pictures with tourists outside the Ravenite Social Club, where he conducted business, and he basked in the media spotlight.

Mafia Killings 66

Frank 'Bomp' Bompensiero, San Diego, 10 February 1977

Was Bompensiero a slick mobster or an inept fall guy? Certainly he was around for a long time, which is impressive for a Mafioso. Also, when Frank Dragna ran the Los Angeles mob, he believed Bompensiero capable enough to be the boss of the San Diego crew.

But, significantly, Bompensiero was demoted to the rank of mere soldier after Dragna's death in 1956, when Frank DeSimone took over the mob. DeSimone and Bompensiero just didn't see eye to eye. Bompensiero had been a prolific hitman for years, specializing in something called the Italian rope trick. In this, the victim is greeted with a hug by someone he considers a friend. While he is occupied, two other mobsters come up on either side of him and wrap a rope around his neck. Bompensiero wasn't trusted, or even liked, by many people. He did have one pal, though – Jimmy Fratianno. The two had met in prison, and Fratianno relied on him for many years.

Naturally, after Bompensiero was demoted he became dissatisfied with his position in the LA mob, and asked for a transfer to Chicago. Unfortunately, his request was denied, so it was understandable that he began to chafe a bit in his new, diminished role. An unhappy mobster is a dangerous mobster, and by 1967 Bompensiero had become an informant for the FBI.

His arrangement with the agency went on for a number of years, and for a while Bompensiero was able to get his own back on the sly. But a deal like that couldn't last forever, and some time in the early 1970s Dominic Brooklier, the new boss of the LA mob, began to grow suspicious.

Pretty soon a contract was put out, but the wily Bompensiero was very hard to pin down. He knew every trick in the book, having used most of them himself. Around the same time though, his usefulness to the FBI had begun to run dry. The fickle agency had now set its sights on Bompensiero's old friend, Jimmy Fratianno. Mob boss Brooklier had just been sent to prison and in his absence Fratianno had become a very important man – acting boss of the LA mob.

So the FBI decided it was time to sell Bompensiero down the river in a trade-off that would net them Fratianno. In 1977 Bompensiero came into possession of information regarding a couple of small-time pornographers who were ripe for a shakedown. He passed the information on to Fratianno, who sent over some enforcers to pay the guys a visit. The film distributors were actually undercover FBI agents who proceeded to lower the boom on the hired muscle. After Fratianno questioned Bompensiero, and didn't like what he heard, the penny dropped – he realized that Bompensiero was an informer.

On 10 February 1977 Frank Bompensiero was shot down as he made a few calls in a telephone booth in San Diego's Pacific Beach. There's plenty of irony in this story, though, at least as far as Fratianno is concerned. Some time before Bompensiero's death, Brooklier was released from prison and took up his old role of LA mob boss. Fratianno, in his turn, was demoted – and he became the next FBI informant, one of the highest ranking in the history of the mob. So much for *omertà*.

Gotti had served time in both state and federal prison, and had even been jailed for manslaughter. He had shot an Irish-American gangster named James McBratney in front of witnesses in a tavern on Staten Island in 1973, after McBratney had kidnapped and murdered Carlo Gambino's son. Nevertheless, as head of the Gambino family, Gotti quickly became known to the media as the 'Teflon Don' when he beat two seemingly watertight cases for racketeering and assault by bribing or threatening jurors. Nothing seemed to stick.

With informants inside the police department, Gotti kept one step ahead of the NYPD. However, he had come to the attention of the FBI, who bugged his phones, his club and other places of business. To get round this, he used public phones, held meetings walking down the street and played loud tapes of white noise. But eventually the FBI taped him in an apartment above the club discussing a number of murders and other criminal activities – and, crucially, they caught Gotti on tape denigrating his underboss Salvatore 'Sammy The Bull' Gravano. On 11 December 1990, FBI agents and New York City detectives raided the Ravenite Social Club and arrested Gotti, Gravano, Frank Locascio and

Thomas Gambino. Gotti was charged with loansharking, racketeering, obstruction of justice, illegal gambling, tax evasion, conspiracy and 13 counts of murder. Among the alleged victims were Paul Castellano and Thomas Bilotti, Castellano's driver.

The case against Gotti was overwhelming. Not only did the FBI have Gotti on tape, they had several witnesses. Philip Leonetti, former underboss of the Philadelphia crime family, testified that Gotti had bragged that he had ordered the hit on Castellano. Armed with the tapes, federal prosecutors persuaded Sammy 'The Bull' Gravano, who was with Gotti when Castellano was killed, to testify against his boss on the promise of a reduced sentence and safekeeping under the Witness Protection Program. The trial became a media circus, with movie actor Mickey Rourke and other celebrities jostling for seats.

On 2 April 1992, Gotti was found guilty on all charges and sentenced to 100 years in prison. He was sent to the United States Penitentiary at Marion, Illinois, where he was kept in an underground cell, measuring just eight feet by seven, for 23 hours a day with only a radio and a small black-and-white TV set for company. His meals were shoved through a slot in the door and he was allowed two showers a week. The one-hour a day he was allowed out of the cell, he spent alone in an exercise yard surrounded by a concrete wall. To all intents and purposes, he was held in solitary confinement, but at least the federal authorities could be sure that he was not continuing to run the family business from jail.

Gotti died of throat cancer in jail on 10 June 2002. The Roman Catholic Diocese of Brooklyn refused a Mass for his burial. By then the Gambino family had been taken over by his son John Gotti Jr., who pleaded guilty to racketeering, bribery, extortion and threatening violence in 1999. More charges followed. However, he claimed to have given up his life of crime, though he refused to testify against others.

While the Gottis attracted the media attention, other New York crime families could go about their business in the shadows. Meantime, the media gave the Mafia a makeover. *The Godfather* movies, based on the

1969 book by Mario Puzo, made people nostalgic for a time when 'men of honour' put their family first. Black humour was added to the mix in *Goodfellas* and, in 1999, the Mafia entered people's living rooms with the long-running series *The Sopranos*.

Mafia Killings 67

Thomas 'Two-Gun Tommy' DeSimone, New York City, December 1978/January 1979

In the movie *Goodfellas*, the character Tommy DeVito is based on that of Thomas DeSimone. Actor Joe Pesci won an Academy Award for the role. Mobster Henry Hill has been quoted as saying that the actor's performance was dead on, and he would know.

DeSimone was a pal of gangster James 'Gentleman Jim' Burke and a member of the Lucchese family. Described as a psychopath even by those who knew and admired him, DeSimone once killed a man in the street – an innocent stranger – just to prove how tough he was.

Tommy DeSimone's brother Anthony had been executed for being an informant and DeSimone expended a lot of energy trying to live this dishonour down. Anyway, he loved violence for its own sake. He used to take great pleasure in breaking noses and teeth, or shooting off kneecaps with the guns that he used to carry around in paper bags.

Nobody ever knew what was going to set DeSimone off next. Things got so bad that he once killed a made man – William 'Billy Batts' Bentvena – for making an offhand remark about DeSimone once having been a shoeshine boy. Killing a made man without permission was not done in Mafia circles. DeSimone tried to dispose of the body, stuffing it in a trunk and hauling it off somewhere for burial. But Bentvena was not quite dead yet, and began pounding on the trunk for release. This didn't deter DeSimone, who stopped the car, and together with Jimmy the Gent, proceeded to finish the job.

DeSimone's biggest claim to fame, though, was his involvement in the Lufthansa heist of 1978, a robbery that netted Burke's crew around six million dollars in cash and jewellery. It was a spectacular job, beautifully planned and beautifully executed. And the loot has never been recovered.

One thing went wrong with the heist, however. Immediately following the job, driver Parnell Edwards decided to get high and flop at his girlfriend's pad instead of disposing of the getaway van like he was supposed to. The van was found in a no-parking zone and the FBI immediately tried to tie the case to the Burke crew. Edwards had to be removed from the picture.

It was up to DeSimone to deal with Edwards, a job that he carried out several days after the heist. In fact, Edwards was only the first to die because of his involvement in the Lufthansa robbery. Burke managed to dispose of a total of ten people associated with that robbery, which, of course, meant more money for him.

With his latest murder under his belt, DeSimone was feeling pretty good. He'd been promised that with this job he'd become a made man. So some time in December of 1978 or January of 1979, DeSimone was brought to an unknown location where the induction ceremony was supposedly to take place. Of course, there was no ceremony, and Tommy 'Two-Gun' DeSimone disappeared without a trace. No one really knows who killed DeSimone, but the prevailing theory is that the Gambino family was responsible because of that Billy Batts Bentvena incident all those years ago.

Mafia Killings 68

Adolfo Bruno, Springfield, Massachusetts, 23 November 2003

When you're a Mafia boss, a *caporegime* or a crew leader, you're always looking to see who's coming up behind you. It's a hard fact, but when you're at the top, there's invariably someone waiting to take your place, and willing to do anything to get there. The bottom line is that you can't trust anyone, especially the members of your own crew. Sometimes that's a lesson that's only learned in the last few moments of life, when it's too late.

That's the way it was for Adolfo Bruno, leader of the Genovese family's Springfield, Massachusetts crew. The bullets that took 'Big Al' down had been bought and paid for by a man who had not only been a childhood friend of Bruno's son, but had been a protégé of Bruno's. Betrayals don't come more bitter than that.

The killer was Springfield crew member Anthony Arillotta, hungry for control of the crew. It was the usual Mafioso social Darwinism – kill or be killed. Arillotta must have been waiting for quite a while to see off Bruno and his chance came when he stumbled upon an unsubstantiated report incriminating Bruno as an FBI informant. With this golden nugget of information, Arillotta went straight to Genovese acting boss Arthur Nigro. The evidence, such as it was, really wouldn't have stood up in a court of law, but then it didn't have to. The story only had to be good enough for Nigro.

Arillotta got the go-ahead. On 23 November 2003, Bruno spent a pleasant enough evening playing cards at the Our Lady of Mount Carmel social club. It was the last evening Bruno would ever spend, pleasant or otherwise, for as the *capo* exited the club, a man stepped out of the bushes and shot him six times. Bruno fell dead in the parking lot and Arillotta became the boss of the Springfield crew.

Now here's the kicker, and it is pretty rich. In 2010, Arillotta was arrested for Bruno's murder and in order to avoid grievous punishment, he immediately flipped – became an informant. Almost everyone who had anything to do with the killing of Bruno, from the actual triggerman to the guys who set up the hit and the top banana himself – Arthur Nigro – were brought down, the bulk of them getting life.

Arillotta was praised for being one of the 'best' informants ever. Instead of lengthy imprisonment, he received a scant 99 months (with time already served counting toward the total sentence) and a fine of $2 million for planning Bruno's murder. Ninety-nine months and $2 million – that's how much Adolfo Bruno's life amounted to in the end. Sometimes the bad guys win; but hey, it's the mob. They're all bad guys.

Things were also changing in Sicily. With Bernardo Provenzano in jail, Mafiosi began a power struggle over who would be the next *capo di tutti capi*. 'We should not make the mistake of thinking that the arrest of Bernardo Provenzano will mean the beginning of the end of the Mafia,' said Sicily's leading anti-Mafia magistrate Antonio Ingroia. 'There is a generation of fifty-somethings ready to carry on.'

He named at least two people qualified to take Provenzano's place: Salvatore Lo Piccolo and Matteo Messina Denaro. A gang boss from the Resuttana district of Palermo, 63-year-old Lo Piccolo was the closest to Provenzano and considered 'old school'. Denaro was just 46. From the impoverished western Sicilian provincial city of Castelvetrano, he was known as the 'playboy boss' because of his passion for gold watches, fast cars and beautiful women. Like Riina and Provenzano, both men had been on the run for some time – Lo Piccolo since 1983, Denaro since 1993. Other key players in the power struggle were Totò Riina's physician Antonio Cinà, builder Francesco Bonura, pioneer of the heroin refineries Gerlando Alberti and Nino Rotolo, a henchman of Luciano Liggio and convicted gangster who was kept under house arrest due to a medical condition.

When it was clear that the 'Pax Mafiosa' – which had held since Provenzano took over in 1993 – was falling apart, the police swooped on 52 bosses and 45 '*capimandamento*' (district bosses) and acting bosses – among them Cinà, Bonura, Alberti and Rotolo, though seven suspects avoided capture. The code Provenzano used in his *pizzini* had been broken, providing the evidence needed for the arrests. Piles of these notes to his lieutenants were found in the farmhouse where Provenzano was captured.

Further evidence came from a bug in the Palermo flat that Francesco Bonura used as an office, and from the surveillance of a builders' hut next to the swimming pool of Nino Rotolo's villa, on the outskirts of the city. The police had secretly videoed the supposedly sick man vault the fence between the villa and the pool. It seems that Rotolo's doctor had given him pills to raise his blood pressure enough to get him out of jail.

In the steel-lined cabin, there were no phones or electronic equipment, just a table, eight plastic chairs and anti-bugging devices which Rotolo thought would make it impossible for police to listen in. He was wrong. Unaware that his security had been breached, Rotolo regularly hosted meetings with other mobsters in the hut with a football being placed outside the door as a signal to the sentries that a confidential session had begun.

From the evidence gathered, it became clear to the police that Rotolo – number 25 in Provenzano's numbered code – was planning a coup, along with his lieutenants Cinà and Bonura. Even while Provenzano was at large, Rotolo had assumed the authority to pass death sentences on other Mafia bosses. Transcripts of conversations in the cabin show him inveighing against a jailed clan chief, describing him as a 'pederast' because of a relationship he had had with an under-age girl. 'Even if he comes out aged a hundred, one of my lads will be there waiting for him,' Rotolo was recorded saying.

It seems Rotolo had passed a death sentence on Lo Piccolo and his son, Sandro. In September 2005, he was heard saying he was looking for barrels of sulphuric acid to dispose of their bodies. The two families had clashed over the remnants of the Inzerillo family, who had been exiled in the US since the Mafia war of the 1980s where they had become involved with the Gambinos. Now they wanted to return to Sicily. Lo Piccolo was for their return, Rotolo against it. 'If they start shooting, I'll be the first to get it and then it will be your turn,' he told Bonura.

Killing the Lo Piccolos would have propelled Sicily into another Mafia war. Swift action on the part of the police and prosecutors had prevented it. However, it also revealed that the Mafia's political influence was undiminished. On 11 July 2006, Giovanni Mercadante, the regional deputy for Forza Italia, was arrested on suspicion of having Mafia connections. A hospital physician, he was thought to have been Bernardo Provenzano's doctor, while he was in hiding, in return for electoral favours.

He was found guilty and sentenced to 10 years and eight months in 2009, but released in February 2011 by the Palermo Court of Appeal.

Mafia Killings 69

Nicolo Rizzuto, Montreal, 10 November 2010

When Nicolo Rizzuto was assassinated in his Montreal home, he was 86 years old. The mob don't generally kill people in that age group; by and large they leave the 'vulnerables' alone. Mothers, children, the aged – they're usually off limits. But the murder of Nicolo Rizzuto was a cut above the usual mob slaying; it was part of an overall assault on the Montreal family. As such, his death was meant to drive home the following message to Vito Rizzuto: 'It's open season on the Rizzutos. No one is safe.'

Two things precipitated this bloody power play. First, the position of Vito Rizzuto, Montreal's formidable mob boss, was compromised when he was extradited and sent to prison in the United States in 2007. He had been convicted for his role in the 1981 murder of the 'Three Capos' – Philip Giaccone, Dominick Trinchera and Alphonse Indelicato.

The second factor was the deportation of the reputed acting head of the Bonanno family, Salvatore Montagna, from the United States into Canada. So Vito was sent to the United States, while

Salvatore was shipped back to Canada. That meant that an out-of-work mob boss from New York was residing in Montreal, where there was a power vacuum in the cities major Mafia family. The results were inevitable and devastating, especially for Vito.

It's alleged that once he arrived in Montreal Montagna got right down to business. The first to go was Vito's son, Nick Junior, who was murdered in December of 2009, just eight months after Montagna had set foot in Canada. After that, bodies began to drop at an alarming rate, including Rizzuto's brother-in-law and culminating in the murder of Vito's father, Nicolo.

Nicolo was no frail octogenarian; he was an active member of the family, a ruthless Mafioso in his own right. Nicolo played the game like it was still the 1930s. That's what made his assassination all the more brazen. On 10 November 2010, Nicolo was at home with his wife and daughter in their residence in the Cartierville borough of Montreal. He was killed when a single bullet from a sniper's rifle punched through two layers of toughened glass in the rear patio doors.

In the Mafia, it doesn't get any worse than this. The murder of Nicolo Rizzuto was a flagrant affront; a declaration of war.

Vito had suffered much. In less than a year, he had lost both his son and his father. Though he would not be released from prison until 2012, he would not wait to exact his revenge. Very soon Montreal's underworld understood the nature of his vendetta.

It seems the battle is far from over. It also seems that life is not too hard on ex-Mafiosi. In Fortezza Medicea jail near Pisa, convicted mobsters have been allowed to open a restaurant, where a clientele vetted by the Ministry of Justice are served by multiple murderers. It has proved so popular that Italy's prison department are thinking of opening restaurants in other jails. Mafiosi, like other Italians it seems, take their food very seriously.

Mafia Killings 70

Salvatore Montagna, Charlemagne, Quebec, 24 November 2011

What a story – murder mob-style, betrayal, more murder. And the ending? Well, for Salvatore Montagna, the end came when he was face down in the icy waters of L'Assomption River. Moments before, Montagna had been very much alive, running for his life through the trees of a northern Montreal suburb. His plan, born of desperation, had been to fling himself into the river and swim across to the opposite shore. But a single bullet put paid to that idea, and he only made it as far as the shoals. That was it for Montagna.

In the violent realm of the Montreal underworld, a bloody battle had been raging for several years. Mob boss Vito Rizzuto, godfather of the Montreal family, was in prison in the United States, and had left a vacant chair. Vito's brother-in-law, son and father had been killed and the foundations of the Rizzuto family had been shaken from forces both within and without. And it was allegedly Montagna who had been the cause of most of this.

Montagna had been termed the acting boss of the Bonanno family, and was one of the youngest bosses ever. At just 36, he was referred to by the press as the Bambino Boss, and he had a seat on the Commission. But in 2009, Montagna refused to become an informant and as a Canadian citizen, he found himself deported back to Montreal. And that's when all the trouble started in Quebec. Apparently Montagna was not alone in all this excitement; allegedly he also had Montreal native Raynald Desjardins to help him.

Desjardins was a tough customer. He'd been a friend of Vito Rizzuto – a very close friend at one time. He and Rizzuto had lived on the same street together, and Desjardins had supposedly worked as the Rizzuto liaison to the Hell's Angels.

And this is where the betrayal comes in. It appears that Desjardins decided to take advantage of the weakened condition of his old friend Vito and to strike while the iron was hot. With the backing of Montagna, and the latter's connections to New York, the timing could not have been better. So in short order, Montagna and Desjardins apparently worked on reducing the numbers of the powerful Rizzutos, who had an empire worth billions and mob connections all over the world.

But something went terribly wrong. In the murky world of the Mafia nothing is ever written down, so just what happened is anybody's guess. In any case, in September of 2011 Desjardins found himself the target of an unsuccessful assassination attempt. Evidently Montagna and Desjardins were no longer the best of pals.

It's dog eat dog in the mob, so retaliation has to be swift. With Vito Rizzuto sitting in jail in Colorado and ordering the elimination of everyone who had been involved in the death of his loved ones, Desjardins decided he'd do his bit and get his own back on his friend from New York.

And that's how Salvatore Montagna ended up face down in the icy waters of L'Assomption. At the time of writing, though Desjardins has pleaded guilty to conspiracy in the murder of Montagna, he has yet to be sentenced. Very few charges have actually been laid, and all of the above is only alleged. It remains to be seen what the courts have to say with regard to Desjardin's role in this. Hold on to your hats though – the battle for Montreal is ongoing.

INDEX

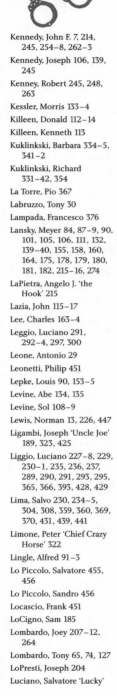